SIXTEEN TO SIXTY

Memoirs of a Collector

LOUISINE W. HAVEMEYER

SIXTEEN TO SIXTY

Memoirs of a Collector

by Louisine W. Havemeyer

Edited by SUSAN ALYSON STEIN

Introduction by GARY TINTEROW

A Nancy Richardson Book

URSUS PRESS, NEW YORK

ISBN 1-883145-00-7 (cloth)
ISBN 1-883145-01-5 (paper)

CONTENTS

NOTE TO THE PRESENT EDITION

Mrs. Havemeyer's memoirs were published posthumously in 1930 and reprinted, with some changes, in 1961. This book is a facsimile of the 1961 edition, which included fourteen chapters. The final chapter, on Mary Cassatt, is here published for the first time. It was omitted from the earlier editions because it is clearly only a rough, unfinished draft. The text includes, however, a number of fascinating insights and anecdotes unavailable elsewhere. We have faithfully transcribed the typewritten manuscript for this chapter, preserved in the Archives of The Metropolitan Museum of Art, with the exception of corrections to spelling and punctuation. All other editorial interventions are signaled by brackets.

This edition is supplemented by a new introduction, a brief chronology and annotations. In preparing the supplementary material, we have relied on a number of sources. In particular, we should like to acknowledge the Metropolitan Museum's *Splendid Legacy: The Havemeyer Collection* (New York, 1993), and the researches and publications of Frances Weitzenhoffer, whose contribution to our knowledge of the Havemeyers and their collection was immense.

We would like to thank Alice Cooney Frelinghuysen, Linden Havemeyer Wise and Henry Waldron Havemeyer for their review of the present edition. This publication owes its realization to Nancy and Frank Richardson, to whom we are immensely grateful for support of the project, as we are to Peter Kraus, publisher. For the production and design of the book, we would like to thank Spencer Cholmar and Ron Gordon, and we extend our special thanks to Christopher Sweet, the editor.

GT

SAS

INTRODUCTION

I answer art, art, art. It is there appealing to you, as it appealed to us. You must feel it. You must hear the voice calling to you, you must respond to the vibrations...[1]

In 1915, when Louisine Havemeyer sat down at the age of sixty to write these memoirs, she was on the crest of a new wave of personal expression in public speaking and political activism. Having lived a privileged existence as the wife of the wealthy "sugar king," H.O. Havemeyer, she had survived his unexpected death, as well as that of her mother and her twin grandchildren, all within one month in 1907. She had endured a deep depression that included a suicide attempt, but she then rose to prominence in the National Women's Party, becoming one of the most accomplished campaigners for the vote, yet managing, nonetheless, to add to the art collections that she and her husband had established.

It is to Mrs. Havemeyer's activity as a suffragist that we owe these memoirs, because it was for women's rights that she learned to speak and write for a large public. "It was Mrs. Blatch [Harriot Stanton Blatch, daughter of Elizabeth Cady Stanton] who insisted that I could speak; that I must speak; and then saw to it that I did speak."[2] In her 1922 "Memories of a Militant," Mrs. Havemeyer explained how she managed to link her interest in art with the issue of women's rights by organizing benefit exhibitions at Knoedler's art gallery in 1912 and 1915. "It goes without saying that my art collection also had to take part in the suffrage campaign. The only time I ever allowed my pictures to be exhibited collectively was for the suffrage cause....Furthermore, the only time I ever spoke upon art matters was at one of these exhibitions....I spoke upon the art of Degas and Miss Mary Cassatt, whose work was for the first time creditably exhibited in America and formed about half of the exhibition, while the other half was made up of an unusually interesting collection of Old Masters...It was very easy to talk about the emancipation of women but art was a very different and difficult subject. I knew every art critic in America would be ready to challenge my remarks about Degas, and, as I had brought his first picture to America and had been his friend and champion for over a generation, they would be curious to hear what I would say about him."[3] She asked Royal Cortissoz, a writer at the *New York Tribune* and the dean of American critics, to review her remarks, and he pronounced them "sluicy"—a compliment. Emboldened by his encouragement, and by the remark of a friend "You made me understand Degas for the first time,"[4] she must have resolved to record her impressions of the artists whom she knew and the works that she had collected, for internal evidence suggests that she began these memoirs in the summer of 1915. [5]

Mrs. Havemeyer wrote that she came to the suffrage movement by right of heritage. "My mother and her associates were interested in it and were friends of the pioneers of the movement."[6] Born in 1855 to an affluent New York family with connections to the sugar business, Louisine Waldron Elder was well educated if not formally schooled. It appears that she was a lively and curious child, open to adventure, and when at age eighteen she was introduced in Paris to an experienced and highly opinionated thirty-year-old artist named Mary Cassatt, she was ready to live up to a new challenge. Only a little encouragement was necessary to induce her to spend her pin money on a pastel by Degas that Cassatt showed her, and she made plans to buy a Monet and a Pissarro. Thus by the time she was twenty-two, the *demoiselle américaine* was making ripples in the Paris art world, probably becoming the first American to own works by these three artists. She furthered her art education by visiting exhibitions of advanced art in America and abroad, lending her own pictures when requested, and making the acquaintance of celebrated artists like James McNeill Whistler.

Louisine Elder's activities were redirected when she married Henry Osborne Havemeyer in 1883. H.O. Havemeyer (1847–1907), known in the business world by his initials and by his family and friends as Harry, had been raised after the death of his mother by his oldest sister, Mary, who had married Louisine Elder's uncle. After the age of fifteen, he was looked after by Louisine's parents, and at twenty-three, he married Louisine's aunt, Mary Louise Elder (1847–1897). Their marriage was said to have been strained by Harry's drinking,[7] and they soon divorced. When he married his former wife's niece, Louisine, she reputedly stipulated that he was never again to touch a drop. He seems to have kept the vow, and all indications are that their marriage was hugely successful. Over the next ten years, they had three children—Adaline (1884–1963), Horace (1886–1956), and Electra (1888–1960) — they built a house at 1 East 66 Street as well as one on Palmer Hill in Greenwich, Connecticut, and they began buying Asian objects in bulk and several Old Master paintings of great quality, most notably Rembrandt's *Portrait of Herman Doomer,* which remains one of the glories of their collection. All of this was financed by the Sugar Trust that Mr. Havemeyer set up, a consolidation of seventeen sugar refining plants in the East and South, of which Havemeyers and Elder, the family's huge refinery in Brooklyn, was the largest. Modeled on the Rockefeller oil trust, the Sugar Trust, later known as the American Sugar Refining Company, posted profits of twenty-five million dollars in the first two and a half years. The success came with a price, however: H.O. Havemeyer's aggressive manner alienated some members of New York's business community, especially J.P. Morgan, who regarded Havemeyer as a rival. Mr. Havemeyer's divorce and second marriage gave additional ammunition to those who wished to scorn him. Thus despite the gift to The Metropolitan Museum of Art of a Gilbert Stuart portrait of *George Washington* in 1888, of Julius Schrader's *Portrait of Alexander von Humboldt* in 1889, of Samuel Colman's *Spanish Peaks, Southern Colorado* in 1893, of Tiffany glass and Japanese textiles in 1896, and of ten thousand dollars in 1892 to keep the museum open on Sundays, Mr. Havemeyer was never elected a trustee of the museum. Mrs. Havemeyer held no grudge. Her belief in civic duty and in the uplifting power of art led her to bequeath the cream of their collection to the Metropolitan as a memorial to her husband. The several thousand objects that now constitute the H.O. Havemeyer Collection at The Metropolitan Museum of Art comprise what is arguably the largest and most important collection ever given to the museum.

The core of the collection was formed between 1888, when H.O. Havemeyer began to buy expensive old masters, and 1907, when he died.

At the beginning of their marriage, they bought Barbizon paintings, Dutch and Flemish Old Masters, Chinese ceramics, and Japanese screens, woodblock prints, lacquerware, and ceramics.[8] Like most women collectors throughout the ages, from Isabella d'Este to Isabella Stewart Gardner, Mrs. Havemeyer was concerned with the display and arrangement of their collections, and much of her energy in the late 1880s and early 1890s was devoted to collaborating with Louis Comfort Tiffany and Samuel Colman on the design of the elaborate interiors of their houses. Mrs. Havemeyer's recollections of her work with Tiffany and her descriptions of the rich, multilayered decor that extended from flatware to picture frames, from dense carpets to ceilings decorated with thousands of antique Japanese textiles, give extraordinary insight into what may have been Tiffany's greatest interior, one that is now known only through dim black-and-white photographs and a few brilliant remnants.[9]

Once the house was completed in 1892, Mrs. Havemeyer returned to the passion she had cultivated before her marriage: modern French painting. With her husband's acquiescence, they began to buy important works by Courbet and Manet. H. O. Havemeyer was a quick convert, and in 1894 the Havemeyers became the most active collectors of Impressionist painting in the world. For the next ten years, they were often given first choice of virtually anything on the market by the dealers Durand-Ruel and Ambroise Vollard. They used this privilege to assemble exhaustively complete collections of works by Corot, Courbet, Manet, Degas, and Monet that numbered over thirty examples each. Mrs. Havemeyer's memoirs reveal the complexities of their relations with dealers. At times they trusted them to the point of financing their operations, and at other times they resented their presumptuous advice or resisted ever-higher prices. The memoirs also reveal how trips to Italy and Spain in the company of Mary Cassatt kindled new interests, especially a fascination with El Greco and Goya. In the search for fine works, the Havemeyers brought a taste for Spanish painting to America, and in the process acquired masterpieces such as the *Portrait of a Cardinal* and the *View of Toledo* by El Greco. Unfortunately, with Goya they did not fare so well. By letting their interest in Goya become widely known, they flushed many copies and some outright forgeries onto the market. Out of some seventeen Goyas bought by the Havemeyers, only four are today generally considered authentic.

The death of Mr. Havemeyer in 1907 hit Mrs. Havemeyer hard. Mrs. Havemeyer's acquisitions ground to a halt. It was only through her devotion to the cause of woman's suffrage that she emerged from depression, around 1910. "Slowly my interest in art returned. After a period of indifference and depression during which I missed several important paintings...a sense of self-protection awoke me to my present duty."[10] In the pages that follow Louisine Havemeyer recounts not only how she came to write her memoirs but also how she made, singlehandedly, some of the most important acquisitions of her life. She does so with wit and candor, opening new vistas into the lives and personalities of the great artists and remarkable men and women of her day.

GARY TINTEROW

NOTES

1. P. 239.

2. Louisine W. Havemeyer, "The Suffrage Torch: Memories of a Militant," *Scribner's*, May 1922, p. 528.

3. Ibid., p. 529.

4. Ibid., p. 530.

5. See Susan Alyson Stein's note on the dating of the memoirs in *Splendid Legacy: The Havemeyer Collection*, p. 269 (entry: July 28,1915).

6. Suffrage Torch, p.528.

7. According to J. Watson Webb, speaking in the film *Merchants and Masterpieces*.

8. See Gary Tinterow, "The Havemeyer Pictures," and Julia Meech, "The Other Havemeyer Passion: Collecting Asian Art," in *Splendid Legacy*, pp. 3-53, and pp. 129-50.

9. See Alice Cooney Frelinghuysen, "The Havemeyer House," in *Splendid Legacy*, pp. 173-98.

10. P. 8.

"Art [will] hold up her head and say: 'I am a first necessity; all else may be cheap, but I shall ever be in demand. My present owner's fortune may crumble, his title may vanish, his manhood deteriorate, but I shall survive and with proud prestige of fame, passion from generation to generation, from one great land to another, bearing regardless of race or time my message unto all mankind.'"

CHAPTER I

Sixteen to Sixty: Memoirs of a Collector

T H I S is not an absolutely correct title, for I began collecting before I was sixteen and I am now over sixty and I am still collecting; but it will serve.

Many years ago Mr. Dean Sage of Albany, a genuine bibliophile, presented me with a rare book. The title read: *Memorials of Christie's. A Record of Art Sales from 1766–1896*, by W. Roberts. The frontispiece was a portrait of " 'The Specious Orator,' i.e., James Christie I, from a print by R. Dighton." Mr. Sage had found the copy somewhere in England, perhaps through his friend Quaritch, and probably thought that the work with its many revelations about the famous pictures that had become obscure, and the obscure pictures that had become famous, would afford me much interesting data, as indeed it did. Mr. Havemeyer and I spent many happy evenings together reading its pages, and the current of its suggestings, like a live wire, fired my mind with the desire to write this present volume. Pictures were forever reappearing in those active auction rooms; some with incredible rapidity acquiring the reputation of masterpieces and commanding enormous sums, while others failed to maintain the standard, or some critic found a blot upon their escutcheon, and they fell as rapidly out of public favor and out of public sight. Queer annals were those of Christie's, and yet no doubt it was the repeti-

tion of our own experiences which I read in its pages and
the thought that I could cap its strange tales with others
still more curious, which led me to write these reminiscences.

To my husband I said : "Museums have histories of their
own, but how little is known of the making of private collections. Guidebooks tell you when the Hermitage was begun,
what Napoleon did for the Louvre, how the Spanish king
allowed Madrazo to gather paintings from palace and
monastery as a nucleus for the great Prado. Yet who knows
how those Englishmen, inspired by the cultivated Charles
with the art-loving tastes, found the masterpieces that adorn
their private galleries! how the Dorias, the Demidoffs, the
Liechtensteins and the Wallaces made their collections, or
how those Dutch burghers bought and loved their little
gems!"

"How about that Frenchman, Lacaze?" said Mr. Havemeyer laconically.

"Of course!" I admitted, "but you see he left his collection
to the Louvre, and it became historical too, and then he was
a painter himself, an enthusiast, and probably told much to
his friends who, in their turn, told it to others." It was, I
believe, one of his friends who related how Lacaze watched
unceasingly for three months before a dealer's door, fearing
someone might buy the "Susanna" by Rembrandt before he
could obtain the necessary three hundred francs to pay for it.
How he must have suffered, poor man! I am never easy
myself from the moment a painting is under consideration
until it hangs in our gallery.

Vasari's reputation rests, not upon his paintings, but upon
his *Lives of the Painters*, giving us with excellent reflections
a history of the lives of the masters of the Renaissance and a
record of their works, but a record far from complete as the
oft-repeated words "it is lost" testify. With such a warning
before us, it is unconceivable that today there is so little

known or written about the lives of many painters whose works hang in the great galleries and in our private collections.

However, it is easy to read between the lines that Italy's Renaissance gave us a revival of classic art in the great frescoes, the huge canvases of church and palace. For the popes had to have their *camere* done by the Raphaels and the Pinturicchios, and their tombs by the Minos and the Rossellinos; the great families made it their pride to have their Titians and their Veroneses; but the people—well, they could go to the little chapels in the hills and fold their hands before the Holy Families of Lippi and Botticelli and exclaim: *"Com' è bello!"* and be content with that. Christianity gave a lugubrious tendency to art in the decapitations and martyrdoms and the flowing robes of the heavily draped figures, which gave Diderot occasion to make his scathing criticism about the influence of Christianity upon the Renaissance. Sometimes a rebellious Mantegna in a great composition left those flowing draperies of saints and martyrs, and painted the human figure in all the beauty of the Greek tradition; or Giorgione dared to paint the nude in the formal gardens of Florence, and possibly shocked his contemporaries as Manet did his Parisians in our own day with his "Déjeuner à Bougival."

Art in Italy, great as Vasari represents it to us, was not so personal as it was in Flanders. Even in painting religious subjects, the Holy Family or the saints are usually surrounded with the portraits of the various donors and their families. Although Rubens and Van Dyck went to Italy and brought back the grand style of the Venetians, Rembrandt remained at home, and with his gifted nature he created an art for himself, which made him the supreme master of portraiture. His portraits of the simple burghers who lived within a few miles of his home, unknown by name or family,

became on Rembrandt's easel the superb masterpieces, the
likenesses of gilders and their families, of the burgomaster
and his wife looking at each other with genial affection—
pictures intended to hang upon the walls of a home, to keep
alive family affection, and what is better still to cultivate a
taste for art that lasted through generation and generation,
until today they adorn our galleries and delight our eyes.

Spain, too, had her art, and the great Velazquez, although
he was a votary of the Italian Renaissance and had to make
a voyage to Italy, soon shook off the Venetian influence and
true to his own perceptions gave us the "Spinners" as well
as the philosophers and the dwarfs.

But of all the countries, perhaps France is the one whose
art is most "of the people and for the people." The formal
Pourbus is supplemented by the noble Clouet. We need not
mention the portrait painting of the eighteenth century; it
represented the satin petticoats of the ladies and the lace
doublets of the courtiers of Versailles. Poussin had taught
the people, Claude Lorrain was teaching the people, David
and Ingres were soon to come to paint not only Napoleon
and the Pope, but to make the portraits of the *bourgeoisie*, of
M. and Mme Rivière and that great one of M. Bertin, that
hang in the gallery of the Louvre. Corot painted his "Femme
au Perle" that one day was to replace the stolen "Gioconda";
and even Courbet loved to paint the peasants and the people
of his native Ornans.

The French enjoy art as they do their châteaux and beautiful parks, their good dinners and the cool drinks on the
boulevards, as they do their humble homes, and their *pot-
au-feu*. It is in the race to love art, both rich and poor, and
that I believe is the reason it has flourished there like a
growth of the soil, since the days when Leonardo came up
to Amboise to pay a last visit to Francis I. In France today
you do not have to go to the great houses to see the best

pictures. I found, for instance, that when we wanted to see Corot's finest nude, we were taken to the home of a jeweler; a member of the grand opera owned some of the greatest pictures Manet ever painted; and to see Courbet's wonderful "Casseurs de Pierres" which today is in the Dresden museum, we were obliged to ask permission of a blacksmith.

And again, of the private collections, who knows of the character and lives of the men whose works we gaze upon with so much admiration? Who knows of Corot's great heart, and how he harbored Daumier in his house? I have a sketch of Corot working under the trees at Ville d'Avray made by the grateful Daumier, who afterward became so well known as the painter of the "Third Class Carriage," a picture which I own. Who knows of Courbet's radical views which obtained for him the credit of having helped pull down the Colonne Vendôme? Or who knows how he almost broke his heart in prison and was only saved through the kindly efforts of the doctor, who succeeded in getting him colors and brushes, and so Courbet painted some of the greatest fruit and flower pictures? Today they are treasured in many museums. Or who knows that he died an unhappy exile in Switzerland, dying day by day of an incurable disease and with sorrow and bitterness of heart? Who knows of Goya and his encounter with Wellington over the portrait of the latter, which I possess and of which I shall write later? This very day there lies upon my writing table a letter from Spain, begging me to send a photograph of the Duke's portrait to Señor Beruete of Madrid, in order that he may put it in the work he is now writing on Goya.

Periodically I expressed such opinions to Mr. Havemeyer and once I remember that he said to me laconically: "Do it." I resolved that I would, but many years passed before I settled down to my task. My friends importuned me to jot down the interesting stories I told them concerning the

purchase of this picture or that object, to relate the rare remarks of the celebrated painters I had met, to record the curious circumstances attending the purchase of some unusual work of art, to keep for the following generations— or perhaps for centuries as Vasari did—valuable information for art collectors. It was very flattering, but only when hard pressed did I half promise that when I grew old I would consider it, and perhaps write a Collector's Manual telling them all I knew. However, I did not think seriously of it for many years, and although frequently reminded of my promise, my life was far too busy, too rich in happiness, too full of action for me to do more than live it to the fullest. It was
17   only when sorrow came and I reeled beneath the blow, and listened in the silent hours of loneliness to the echoes of the past, that my thoughts sought consolation in these recollections and my memoirs were begun.

Patiently did I have to thresh my grain and blow away the chaff. Patiently did I have to arrange, resisting with determination the maze of suggestion each subject awakened. My memory with the mischievousness of little Puck put confusion in my eyes and in my thoughts, and played me so many tricks that I felt that I too should have to don the ass's head and have my ears tickled in the moonshine. In spite of all my difficulties, however, they were happy hours that I spent over my manuscript. Slowly my interest in art returned. After a period of indifference and depression during which I missed several important paintings, most of which are in museums today, and after some remarks about my lack of intelligence and a dealer's lack of—well, I shall leave it to my readers to say what he lacked when I tell them that
18   I sold him three of my best Cézannes, for which he paid me only three thousand dollars—a sense of self-protection awoke me to my present duty. I found myself upon the crest of the wave in Spain for Grecos and Goyas, in Europe

for Rubenses and Veroneses, and my opportunities put several more examples of these masters in our collection.

I have now written of the beginning. If you will read the following chapters you will see that I have tried faithfully to record both my failures and my successes.

CHAPTER II

The Music Room

T<small>HAT</small> is a lovely chandelier," I said one day as I stood in
the nearly completed music room with Mr. Tiffany, admiring the results of his effort. "I know a flower suggested it,
for you always go to them for inspiration, but dear me!
what flower was it?"

Mr. Tiffany threw a mischievous glance at me. "That is
severe," he said, "where is your imagination? You surely
are too familiar with flowers not to know this one, try again."

"Of course," I exclaimed as I looked again, this time
more carefully. "Queen Anne's lace—the wild carrot! How
well you have adapted it. Even the stems twine themselves
together and disappear into the ceiling as if you had but just
gathered them."

"It gave me an opportunity to make the chandelier as large
as I pleased," answered Mr. Tiffany, "and to diffuse the light
for the musicians' needs. I put but one light in those bays
over there, so those who listen will not be disturbed by any
glare."

Mr. Tiffany appeared well pleased with his part of the
work, for the music room was the only one he and Mr.
Colman decorated together, as usual with the object of
making it a background for some of Mr. Havemeyer's possessions. This time it was for the Stradivarius violins and
'cello, and for the "King Joseph" Guarnerius violin and the

10

viola. All of these were used at my musicales on Sunday afternoons and delighted my guests who divided themselves between this apartment and the adjoining library, with a distinct line drawn between the art of music and the art of painting. As I looked around I would find the painters grouped about the Rembrandts, while the music lovers came early and made themselves cosy and comfortable in the warm sunlight of the western windows and never stirred until the last note was sounded, the last bow was drawn.

The music room was designed for a collection of Japanese lacquer and some Chinese embroideries in beautiful tapestry colors. There was much gold in the decoration of the room, but it was of a subdued somber tone which harmonized with these embroideries and the other objects in the room. The furniture was always a subject of interest to my visitors. Over and over again I was obliged to show them the carved ivory inro in the large glass cabinet which covered the end of the room behind the musicians and by a curious chance, and without our intention, made a sounding board for the instruments. This ivory inro not only suggested the carving of the furniture, but served as a model for the carving and taught Mr. Colman how to produce the effect. After the carving had been done, a fine gold leaf was applied and then slightly rubbed off leaving the relief a little bare, which made it look old and as if it had been handled for many years like the model. Many coats of varnish were applied and each coat rubbed down until it had the transparency of enamel. When finished it did have the quality of the old ivory inro, for Mr. Colman, probably the first to appreciate Oriental art, had made a long study of Japanese productions and had found out most of these secrets.

My guests would examine the carved inro and then examine the carving of the furniture. Many would find the carving of the furniture more beautiful than that of the inro, others would disagree and a discussion on art was sure to follow. In feeling and execution, the inro and the furniture were as different as Western and Oriental art could be, but here applies a little phrase which explains the secret of many an art production. We say "under the influence of"! and accept with gratitude the new note, the new production done "under the influence of" some other gifted artist.

How often I have wished that those who are building new homes or decorating old ones would try and get away from the old moth-eaten Tudor embroidery or the heavy ornate gold of the French "red brocade period" and try to create something for themselves, or if that is not possible, have faith in someone who has artistic ability and give him a chance to add another paragraph to art's long and intricate history. Every great advance in art must be supported and will be, if it is worth being supported. If the convents of Spain had not given orders to Greco, we should be bereft today of one of the world's masterpieces, the "Burial of the Count of Orgaz"; if Veronese had never been appreciated we might have lost the modern French impressionist school. A clever young architect once said to me:

"My patrons all want Louis Fourteenth 'street' apartments."

I recall saying to Mr. Havemeyer one afternoon after paying a number of visits: "I felt dizzy and confused as I was ushered into one room after another, for they were all alike. The popular decorator of the day has done them all with impartial similarity." This making of homes was a hobby of mine and I offer no apology for the above digression.

But to finish the description of our music room, blue and gold Chinese rugs covered the floor and the large cabinet held the well-known *sang de bœuf* vase, Mr. Havemeyer's first purchase for our new home and I think the best-known

piece of *sang de bœuf* in America. The shelves of the cabinet
held many specimens of lacquer of the Korin school, examples
of Koyetsu and of Ritsuo. Several examples came from the   25
Gillot sale in Paris in 1904. Gillot was a Parisian and an
early patron of Oriental art, and had exquisite taste. When
after his death his collection was sold, every piece was disputed, disputed hotly as is sometimes the case at an auction,
and thereby hangs a tale—an interesting one about a pair   26
of screens, one of which belongs to me and the other, the
one from the Gillot sale, is in the Metropolitan Museum.
No more digressions however! I can tell you nothing about
it at present.

Now you know that my guests entered through the mosaic
hall, where the fountain was allowed to splash but a few
drops at a time, and were then ushered into the library
where we greeted them and where old friends sought their
favorite chairs, or showed strangers how to find desirable
ones for themselves. I can assure you the few minutes given
to assembling soon passed; the 3:30 on the invitations meant
precisely 3:35 to begin, and as the musicians entered carrying their instruments and the "A" was given upon the grand
piano, there was an instant hush; I drew the heavy curtain
and sat down by Mr. Havemeyer to enjoy the music with
our friends. If any came in after the music had begun, they
were courteous enough to seat themselves in the hall and
wait until the first movement of the quartet was finished. It
was not a long program, two quartets and a solo or two.
The music ended; the lights were turned on and our guests
could wander through the house and enjoy anything we possessed. Although the music was over by five o'clock and tea
was served at once, often I heard voices in the gallery above
and groups of friends would hurry toward me and apologize
for remaining so late; perhaps some question would be
asked me and then—oh! I blush to write it—I would be

caught in the whirlwind of discussion, or under flattering persuasion I would indulge in some reminiscence. Mr. Havemeyer having given his guests all he promised, good measure, pressed down, running over! would frankly show he was tired and would retire to "my library" and wait for me there. When I finally joined him, to anticipate a reproachful look I would say:

"How could you leave me alone with all those people?" and he would answer with a smile it gives me pleasure to recall to this day: "Oh! you were having such a good time!"

There I have given you an idea of my Sunday musicales! They acquired a reputation all their own, and we were justly proud of the musicale standard we kept up. I also gave musicales on a larger scale in the upper gallery, of which I will write in another chapter. I believe these musicales gave keen delight to numbers of my friends, and I do believe that Mr. Havemeyer made them feel we enjoyed our music more because they were with us, and that they could enjoy our art as much, if not more, than we could. When someone would exclaim:

"Oh! how lucky you are to own such a collection," I would quickly answer: "Yes, but these Rembrandts have been admired for over a hundred years, and others' turns will come after mine."

The musicales became so well known that they were acknowledged the best entertainment I could offer to my friends, and not only to my friends but to their friends, for any stranger that came to our city, if properly recommended, was sure of a welcome and an opportunity of seeing the pictures. In this way I met many distinguished strangers, some of whom I can still vividly recall. To me many are familiar through my personal recollections. To my readers they will be familiar through their association with the history, music or art of their time.

CHAPTER III

The Library

I HAVE purposely refrained from mentioning our library   27
until, with a new chapter, I felt I had both space and opportunity to do it justice, to give credit to the man who designed
it and who gave two years of his life to its completion. I
want to tell you of the paintings and art objects it contained
and to recall some of the distinguished people who visited
it from time to time.

Our library was equally well known as "the Rembrandt
room," for even in later years when we had added the gal-   28
lery—so called simply because it had a skylight—we were
earnestly besought by our friends not to transport the Rembrandt portraits there, but to leave them in the library,
where they had hung for many years and where they looked
their best.

"Think of it," said a friend to me, "eight Rembrandts   29
hanging in one room and in America; it is unique. If you
change them, they become only part of a collection, while
here they are 'the Rembrandts' and they give a special
interest to the room." Therefore the Rembrandts remained,
and they will remain as long as I live, hanging in the room
our friend made for them.

Our library was the special effort of Mr. Colman in our   30
behalf. He had long considered the scheme of a room for our
Rembrandts, and possibly had designed it before the house
was begun. It came about in this way. In 1876, Mr. Samuel

15

31 Colman with Mr. Havemeyer visited the Centennial Exhibition in Philadelphia. They became interested in the exhibits of China, and especially in those of Japan, with the result that my husband bought many beautiful objects of art and a collection of Japanese textiles, a wonderful lot of brocades of lustrous gold and silver, and rich blues, reds and greens. Never did more splendid fabrics come out of the East; some of them serve to this day as backgrounds to the glass cabinets which contain our Oriental potteries and porcelains.

"Some day I will make you a ceiling out of these beautiful silks," said Mr. Colman to my husband, and true to his words, in 1889, thirteen years later, Mr. Colman had all these remarkable stuffs sent to his home in Newport, where in his studio, with the help of many nimble fingers, he had them made into the design he wanted for the various panels of our library ceiling.

32 How shall I describe this ceiling? It glowed like the rich mosaic of the East, like Saint Sophia and the splendid tombs of Constantinople, like the Palatine Chapel of Palermo, the pride of Roger of Sicily. Like them our ceiling recalled the art of the East both in color and in design. The interwoven pattern of Byzantium prevailed, and when all was completed and fitted into the several panels, the design was outlined by a heavy braid and it held the colors which were so beautifully distributed throughout. Many and many a time have I been questioned about this ceiling which was so full of beauty and brilliancy, so rich and yet so subdued. These panels were framed by richly carved moldings of the same design, and their burnished gold has never tarnished, even after twenty years of exposure to a climate by the sea.

Naturally there were some visitors who could not understand nor feel the beauty of our ceiling, for the world will always have a quota of those to whom a yellow primrose is "a yellow primrose—nothing more." These were far more

interested in knowing how it was made than in appreciating
the effect it produced.

I remember once when Mr. Havemeyer and I were in
Boston, we dropped in at a shop in passing to see some
Oriental art objects. The dealer himself happened to wait
on us and, observing that we were interested in his wares,
he showed us his objects and chatted quite freely about his
customers and the collectors.

"Have you ever heard of Mr. Havemeyer of New York?"
he suddenly asked. Mr. Havemeyer, of course, answered
that he had.

"Have you ever seen his collection?" he asked again, and
again my husband answered in the affirmative.

"It is wonderful, isn't it?" he continued. "I have never
seen it, but I hope to see it some day, for I've heard so much
about it and about his library ceiling which is a marvel I
hear. Sir William van Horne tells me he has a whole ceiling
made of tea jar covers."

This was too much for Mr. Havemeyer; he laughed outright, and disclosed his identity. The dealer was quite
abashed, but Mr. Havemeyer put him at his ease, bought
some bronzes, and promised him a sight of the tea-jar-
covered ceiling. I must explain that the Japanese greatly
prize the tiny jars that contain the precious green powder,
which was always used in the tea ceremony, and these jars
were invariably kept in beautiful silk bags, sometimes in
two lacquer cases besides.

Mr. Colman made this library of ours a labor of love. He
mixed the stains for the walls, he guided the Italians in their
wood carving, he modeled the furniture to be reproduced
first in wax, and taught the painters how to apply coat after
coat of varnish, rubbing each one to a lovely amber transparency which gave it the value of a Chinese porcelain. From
our collection Mr. Colman selected a piece of bronze he had

long admired and a panel by the celebrated Japanese lacquer-worker, Ritsuo, as his inspiration. The softly rounded vase gave him suggestions for the woodwork and moldings, over which you could pass your hand without feeling an edge or an outline. The Ritsuo panel, rich in color and of olive tones, he kept always before him, for he colored the oak himself, using the acid stains which he invented, obtaining astonishing results both in beauty and transparency. I hope to speak further of these stains in another chapter, for I caught the infection from Mr. Colman for this fascinating work and it furnished me with diversion for several years.

A Celtic design was used freely as the motif for the decoration and the carving of the woodwork. The design for the furniture Mr. Colman found in the home of the Vikings, in some old Norwegian books, and modeled the chairs and the difficult parts himself in wax. He superintended the carving again and he also did the staining, and when the last of the many coats of varnish was finally rubbed to a soft finish you felt like caressing the arms of the chairs and the tops of the tables; they had the quality of a Chinese porcelain. The covering of the furniture was of an olive suede leather, soft enough to lend itself to being quilted with various colored silks, also in a Celtic design to correspond to the carving of the woodwork and chairs. A huge olive-green plush curtain covered the large window at the end of the room and upon the low bookshelves Mr. Colman placed our choicest bronzes, specimens of the Chinese Chou, Han, and T'ang periods, tripods rich in green and blue incrustation, the Han four-handled vase with the leaping tigers and the low covered sacrificial cup. The highly esteemed Chinese bronzes in the form of grotesque animals never appealed to Mr. Havemeyer; the reason is obvious.

The Ritsuo panel guided Mr. Colman in his color scheme for the decorations of our library walls. Upon a canvas covering he evolved a background for the Rembrandts so truly harmonious and sympathetic to the paintings, so truly a background and not an assertion of its own expensive importance, so modestly submissive to the pictures that hung upon it that it was the admiration of all the artists and amateurs who visited our home. Backgrounds were a hobby of mine and I was often requested to speak about them. I often used Mr. Colman's decorations to demonstrate the necessity as well as the value of a suitable background to a picture and deplored the murky red velvet which was in vogue with our dealers, and many amateurs also, who could not get away from the enticing "red satin brocade." So often have I been consulted upon the subject, that I should like to write a chapter on backgrounds alone. The subject was of keen interest to Mr. Colman and to Mr. Tiffany also, and one could not please them better than to notice their successful efforts, or, as someone aptly expressed it, by saying: "The whole house is a background for the objects it contains."

Over the broad chimney place hung Rembrandt's "Gilder" (1640), his portrait of an "Old Woman" (1640), and between them was De Hooch's "Interior, a Glass of Wine" that I bought in the Secrétan sale in Paris in 1889. Opposite the window at the entrance of the room hung upon one side Rembrandt's "Portrait of a Man in a Felt Hat," and upon the other side "The Treasurer," a Rembrandt from a collection in Vienna. On the wall opposite the chimney hung a pair of Rembrandt's portraits, "Nicholas and Volkera van Beresteijn" (1632). Then as we passed the door which united the library with the music room, I would say facetiously to my guests:

"Our Rembrandt is now marrying his Saskia, and with the independence fortune has given him, he has developed his theories on light and shadows, as you will see in the next

38   two portraits, those of a 'Dutch Admiral and his Wife.'"
Their names are not known as is often the case in Rem-
brandt's portraits, but they came from the collection of the
Princess of Sagan. On the left of the chimney place hung our
Bronzino, of which I shall write later. He had, one on each
side, our two small Frans Hals portraits of "Jan Scriverius
and his Wife"; these also come from the Secrétan sale in
Paris. On the other side of the fireplace hung Holbein's
"Jean de Carondelet" with a Lucas Cranach "Man with a
Rosary" on his left and an Antonello da Messina "Portrait
of a Man" on his right. That was all.

Everyone knows how difficult it is to light pictures, to
throw the diffused light over the whole picture and not to
concentrate it on any one spot. Our lighting was suggested
by a curious Japanese tobacco pouch. The electric bulbs
were concealed by several mosaics of Tiffany favrile glass,
which were suspended from the ceiling by a multitude of
tiny chains, and lighted the pictures on the wall. A central
light in the form of a disk, also of mosaic, hid the bulbs which
were needed to light the silk panels above, and those who
sat by the table were conscious only of the brilliant reflected
glow. I do not pretend it was perfect, but at least one could
sit in the room undisturbed by the unpleasant glare of gallery lighting and could admire the fixtures themselves which
were very beautiful. With the portrait by Holbein, painted
a century before those of Rembrandt (who was represented
from his earliest to his latest period), with a Cranach and
two Frans Halses, with an early Italian portrait and a
splendid example of the Tuscan school, it made an interesting collection of pictures and we did not wonder that our
friends requested us not to disturb them.

Below the central light upon the library table was a
39   bronze statue, about two feet high, a small "Venus of Milo"
which Mr. Havemeyer acquired during one of our visits to

Paris. My husband told me that M. Feuardent, an acknowl- 40
edged expert, had sent him a note to call as he had something
interesting to show him.

"When I reached there," said Mr. Havemeyer, "I found
the old gentleman very much excited over the refusal of the
directors of the Louvre to buy the bronze statue which he
had at last succeeded in bringing to Paris after much time
and trouble. He told me the directors of the Louvre pleaded
lack of funds, but that they should buy it at any cost for the
reason that the missing arm of the great marble statue was
here intact, for this was undoubtedly a small replica of the
Venus of Milo. It was a practice of the Greeks to make small
copies or variants of their renowned statues and sell them
for domestic purposes. This bronze Venus had been found
on the island of Milos, and Feuardent was enthusiastic over
the historic and artistic value. 'See,' he said, 'she was doing
her hair and about to look at herself in a mirror.'

"I didn't care what she was doing," continued Mr. Havemeyer, "I considered it very beautiful and I bought it. I
think you will approve of it and it will look well in our
library I am sure." It did, and it is there today.

I think Feuardent that morning must have been in an aggressive mood toward the Parisian amateurs, for he also
sold to Mr. Havemeyer a precious coin which a customer 41
had refused as "too dear," but which years after he begged
me to sell him "at any price." Alas, he had not learned Mr.
Havemeyer's axiom that great works of art can never supply
the demand and that they do not become cheaper, therefore
beware of allowing an opportunity to pass you by. I placed
beside our Venus two Greek helmets, one of 300 B.C. and 42
the other of 500 B.C. Often I noticed my husband passing his
hand over the rounded surface of the helmets and I knew
that he, at least, thoroughly appreciated the marvelous
workmanship.

I now think I have about completed the description of our library except to add that a heavy Axminster carpet muffled the footfalls and we could look at the pictures in silence, or listen to a Beethoven quartet without being disturbed.

LIBRARY VISITORS

As I think of my library, far too many forms and faces pass before my memory for me to attempt to write of them all. I had the privilege of meeting many distinguished men and women of my time, who offered me, in return for my hospitality, the benefit of their intelligence, the charm of their wit, and the pleasure of their appreciation. Often have I been asked why I did not keep a visitors' book. Why, I should not have dared even to suggest such a thing to Mr. Havemeyer who, whenever he was asked to sign his name in one, never failed to express his opinion of those who did. Mr. Havemeyer disliked notoriety more than anyone I ever knew, and believed that a man had a right to the quiet enjoyment of his own home. He therefore had no hesitation in answering *no* to a request, or in dropping a letter from a stranger into the wastebasket. While he was a delightful and most genial host, his strong character, rendered still more forcible by his business career, made others rather afraid to approach him, and I am afraid some thought him brusque. Nevertheless, no one who had the privilege of seeing our collection in company with Mr. Havemeyer failed to be impressed with his knowledge and love of art, and they constantly came to me to repeat some remark he had made and which had made a deep impression upon them. His wonderful insight into character was to be expected in so intelligent a man, but his quickness in detecting insincerity or pretension in his guests was quite remarkable. He had a deep respect for men like Saint-Gaudens and Charles

43

McKim, for pioneer collectors such as J. J. Hill and Oliver 44
H. Payne, through whose generosity the Metropolitan Mu- 45
seum is the possessor of a splendid fifteenth century tapestry,
but he had no taste for artists who came to paint extraordinary portraits — so extraordinary that today most of
them hang in some unused apartment or in a storeroom
with their backs to the wall—or who hawked about a
propaganda of the greatness of their own talent. With these
my husband indulged in a joke at their expense. I recall
that after a musicale Mr. Havemeyer said to me:

"Who was that painter who spoke to me and wished to
give the impression that he was English? He told me he
painted only marines and began telling me how few marine
painters knew how to paint water. I wanted to get free of
him and I told him he might find someone upstairs who
knew how to paint marines. I think Manet's marines taught
him something. He came down almost the last one and told
me he knew what I meant, and that Manet was a great
master and had taught him much. Do you know who he
was?"

Of course I knew who he was and Manet's painting of
water outweighed his by just the weight of the ocean itself.
He was a marine painter very popular at that time and I
believe very prosperous.

Zorn spent an afternoon with us. I saw him speak to Mr. 46
Havemeyer who was standing by a Rembrandt; his manner
was patronizing and I was just in time to hear his remark.

"Do you call that a Rembrandt?" he asked Mr. Havemeyer.

"No. I did not call it a Rembrandt, do you?" answered
my husband. Zorn for once was disconcerted.

Mr. Havemeyer was a generous and hospitable host and
could rebuke me if I failed in courtesy to any stranger that
requested permission to see our collection. I recall that upon

47 one occasion Mrs. "Jack" Gardner of Boston wrote me she
would like to visit my collection on a Saturday morning.
I grumbled about it.

"Does she not know Saturday morning is reserved for
cleaning?" I exclaimed to Mr. Havemeyer.

"It seems to me," he replied, "that if you intend to allow
strangers to see your pictures, you should permit them to
come at their own convenience; possibly she must return to
Boston this afternoon."

I allowed her to come and even spoke to her for a few
moments and listened to her pressing invitation to visit her
wonderful Fenway Castle; but when the time arrived she
ran true to Gardner form and gave some feeble excuse in
order that a competitor should not see her works of art. I
was very angry, but I have learned to know people better
since those days.

Mr. Havemeyer always played on his violin before going
to his office and only when the music ceased would I disturb
him by going in to say good morning to him. He never let
me leave him without making some remark about some-
48 thing in the room, either to give me something to do, to ask
me if I had ever noticed the shadow under the Gilder's hat,
or if I did not think we should give the Holbein to Horace
for his twenty-first birthday. Mr. Havemeyer's library was
indeed his castle; he never took his personal affairs to his
office nor brought his business into his home. I can scarcely
remember an occasion when a business associate was admitted to the library. But even with a desire to avoid
notoriety and lead a quiet life, with the come and go of a
great city which each year became more and more the
rendezvous of the strangers in our land, we met many distinguished people, men of all professions and nearly all the
brilliant women of my day.

If I kept no visitors' book, I nevertheless received many a

token of gratitude for the pleasure I had given them, either at my musicales or on my days at home, for I received every Tuesday during the winter months. I recall that I received a volume one evening as I was dressing to go out. I opened and found it was a volume of poems and the author had written a stanza "to Mrs. Havemeyer, composed while listening to the music the previous Sunday." I was delighted as may be imagined, and I hastily placed it upon my writing table to enjoy it later. When I returned, the volume had been taken and in its place was a note from my daughter Adaline saying: "Dear Mother, you don't want it and I do —so much, please! Adaline." She was then a college student at Bryn Mawr and she had a brilliant mind and a great fondness for poetry. Needless to say I gave Adaline the book and I hope the author, Edith Thomas, approved. It 49, 50 gave me an inspiration: I made Adaline custodian of all my letters, autographs, books, mementos, for I was ever seeking ways to interest my children, and Adaline to her infinite delight received many interesting things, which if these memoirs are ever published must appear upon their pages.

CHAPTER IV

Visitors I

MEMOIRS are valuable, it seems to me, only if they are a record of the writer's personal experiences, or when they relate incidents of individuals or state facts which in time may become matters of history. Writers should be careful in expressing their own opinions and confine their remarks to a simple and truthful statement of facts. Milton says: "True eloquence I take to be none other than a serious and hearty love of truth." Let me, then, try to be eloquent.

In or about the eighties a new form of industrial development attracted the eye of the business world and caused more excitement, I may truthfully say, than any long-tailed comet that ever appeared in the darkened skies. The so-called trusts! They were violently attacked but in one form or another they survive today and fill the financial columns of our journals, and their lists are longer than those of any securities dealt in on our stock exchange. I won't go into details. Every new development has to have its pioneers and its martyrs as well as the profiteers in politics and blackmail. It is the history of the world from the days of Galileo to our present time.

Cornelius Vanderbilt, the man who introduced railroads as a system in the United States, his patience exhausted with the pettifogging law-diggers who preyed upon him, threw up his hands and exclaimed: "My —— (too strong a word for me to write)! You don't think you can run a railroad ac-

51

cording to law, do you?" As we pass in the great march of civilization, the names of Vanderbilt and the other great pioneers of our railroad system will shine ever more and more brightly, and those of the little sycophants will, like barnacles in fresh water, fall off and perish.

The Rockefellers with the Standard Oil and Mr. Have- 52
meyer with the sugar trust started the ball rolling. Combination for cheaper production; stockholders instead of partners; employees sharing profits while presidents and directors were paid a salary. You see the new order turned things topsy-turvy for a while, for, like everything new, it had to be "talked up" or "cried down," sifted and digested by everyone from the government to the people. Needless to say, politics had to have its profits as well. Reduction in price to the consumer was the blessing of trusts, apprehension of a monopoly was its crime, but as all the dangers, difficulties and prejudices which the trusts presented have today been overcome, the trusts, form and substance, are facts and factors in the business world.

I will refrain from expressing any views on political economy and content myself with relating a few incidents connected with that exciting period. With the Rockefellers, Mr. Havemeyer was a pioneer of the trusts. The sugar trust was formed in 1887 under President Cleveland's administra- 53
tion. My husband was an admirer and warm friend of President Cleveland and I recall his frequently answering the telephone (then also an innovation) for a long-distance 54
talk with the President. He was a still closer friend of John G. Carlisle, then Secretary of State, one of the ablest members of the cabinet. I remember that one summer morning Mr. Carlisle saw Mr. Havemeyer in the Grand Central 55
Terminal; he approached my husband eagerly, threw his arm about his shoulder and exclaimed:

"Well done, Mr. Havemeyer, well done! That remark

56   about the tariff will last." Mr. Havemeyer had just written
an article upon the tariff, designating the customs tariff as
"the mother of trusts," which later became a free-trade
slogan.

The new development spread rapidly over the United
States, bringing to the front men of intelligence and great
business acumen. I truly enjoyed meeting them, and many
became old and dear friends. My husband would tease me
about my predilection for these clever, hard-working
citizens.

"Are you going to do all the trusts?" he would ask. "It
seems to me there are very few you have neglected."

This was quite true, for no matter what they were or
what they became, in the beginning they were truly demo-
cratic. Shoulder to shoulder was the byword and the ranks
often furnished the masterminds of our country. They were
for the people, the stock-owning, profit-sharing people.
Most of the evils of which they were accused were the result
of pre-existing methods or the questionable practices of
high finance.

I knew nearly all the Rockefellers, a family of varied and
strong characters. The two brothers were very different.
One impressed me as astute, impenetrable and reticent; the
other expansive and genial. Both were home-lovers, good
fathers, and both had devoted wives. I heard many stories
of their petty economies which were funny only in comparison with their great wealth; and who has not a pet economy
which permits him to indulge in many more rash extrav-
57, 58   agances? I knew Mr. and Mrs. William Rockefeller better
than I did Mr. and Mrs. John D. Rockefeller. I visited the
former in their home on the Hudson and I recollect that the
house impressed me as being huge, so huge that it was no
longer homelike. As we arrived, my husband and I, I looked

through the hall and saw Mr. and Mrs. Rockefeller rise and come forward to greet us. The distance was so great that they appeared to lose size and seemed smaller than they should be. Again, when we were shown to our apartments, I said to my husband:

"I cannot whistle, you can, please do or I shall never know where you are in this vast apartment."

Mr. Havemeyer tripped over a broad platform at one end of the room upon which rested a bed of royal dimensions.

"If that is a dais, it is damnable," exclaimed Mr. Havemeyer as he rubbed the injured spot.

"Never mind," I answered soothingly, "I will put the night light on that sector and we can establish a turnpike with some chairs."

It made us rejoice in our simpler Connecticut home and we agreed that it was better to keep your broad acres outside your four walls. Our friends in spite of their great wealth and estates share our views, for when they returned our visit, they not only admired our smaller home but they were found at breakfast time in the farm buildings, which they said they had been inspecting since six o'clock and had found delightfully homelike.

Mr. Rockefeller's nature was wonderfully kind and genial and he was very fond of a joke. I remember he entertained us after dinner with a story of a minister who, not knowing that all the Rockefeller family were ardent Baptists, had come to beg a contribution for the Methodist church. "After stating how much he hoped for as my contribution," said Mr. Rockefeller, "he told me that if I would only double that amount he thought he could drive that Baptist fellow out of town."

I saw less of Mr. and Mrs. John D. Rockefeller; both cared little for society and spent much of their time in Cleveland. His son became a prominent person of the next

generation and married a charming woman, the daughter
of one of my husband's close friends. One of Mr. John
60   Rockefeller's daughters rather interested me. She had inherited more of her father's disposition, and was obliged to
adapt it to the limitations of a woman's sphere still cramped
in its silk cocoon; it was not easy. To relieve her from the
loneliness of a great hotel, I asked her to luncheon one day,
telling her frankly I was obliged to go afterwards to the
"Box Corner," a philanthropic enterprise where boys were
taught to use tools and to make simple furniture out of old
packing boxes.

"I will go with you," she answered over the telephone.

"Very well," I replied, "I shall expect you at one o'clock,
but remember we must go into the slums and all I can
promise is that it will interest you." She appeared at one
o'clock dressed like the Queen of Sheba and after luncheon
we left together in my automobile.

"Why do you not dismiss your automobile?" I asked,
thinking her fine auto with two men following mine would
attract attention in the East Side where we were going.

"They always follow me," she answered positively, "they
have to sleep when I sleep and go out whenever I go out."

"Poor men," I thought. "What must they think of such a
foolish creature. I suppose a good wife and a happy home
reconcile them to such a ridiculous position." Still, when we
were among the bright happy boys, she caught the infection
of their interest, forgot she was ever bored with life, and her
keen intelligence kept the forewoman busy answering questions. She made a thorough examination of the entire
building, showing the kindliest interest in the busy boys.
"What a pity," I thought, "that such possibilities should
be lost to needing humanity."

Leaving the oil and sugar trusts, I should say a few words
about the steel trust and its controlling figure, for whatever

may be said of him he will always be associated with that industry. I knew Andrew Carnegie when I was a young girl, long before my marriage. He with a number of others en-joyed an early ride in the park, and many and many a morning found us riding together before the breakfast hour. After the spin, we would chat together and I recall Mr. Carnegie's answer when I asked him to what he attributed his success in life.

"Well I think," he answered with feeling, "it was seeing my mother work the loom in Scotland."

"I don't wonder, Mr. Carnegie," I replied. "I have seen one of those dreadful machines in a museum in New England. It took up nearly all the kitchen."

"Yes," he answered, "and it took nearly all my mother to work it. Father was a poet and she had to look after Tom and me."

Again, I asked him: "Did you meet success right from the start or were you often discouraged?"

"Oh, my!" he replied quickly. "I was often down and out."

"What did you do then?" I queried.

"Why, I up and hammered at it again," was the response.

How well I remember those words! They were characteristic of the man. He and his mother were of the same mold, not oversensitive and very shrewd. The leading trait in both was shrewdness, but Andrew was ambitious as well. He had to satisfy a love for business results with the notoriety attached, and I think he did the best he could. Finally he married a fine woman and his later years were influenced by her good judgment. I always had a deep admiration for Mr. Carnegie. A strange coincidence is that it was in my home that he made his first donation to a free library! It happened this way. During one of his Sunday visits my older sister, who was very fond of books, happened to say before him that two New York ladies were trying to form a free

library and she did hope they would succeed. The next time
Mr. Carnegie came to pay us a visit, he handed my sister a
check for one thousand dollars, saying:

"I believe in free libraries and should like to offer a contribution to aid those two ladies in their effort."

What Andrew Carnegie afterwards did to establish free
libraries is a matter of history, but so far as I know this was
his first attempt and was the result of conversations with
my sister.

64   Two of Mr. Carnegie's associates were also good friends
of mine, Mr. and Mrs. Phipps, so kindly and gentle and full
of good works, living with pleasure among friends and
children and apparently tormented by neither ambition nor
disappointments.

65   This was not the case with Mr. Frick, the hero of the
celebrated Homestead strike, one of the earliest and the
worst strikes in the history of our industrial development,
and one in which women finally took part, not to incite but
to sooth and placate. Mr. Frick was severely wounded but
survived to fill a leading role in the steel trust, and leaving
after a dispute with Carnegie he amassed a still greater
fortune by his own efforts and acquired a collection of pictures which for price and renown was unequaled in the
United States. He built a stately gallery on Fifth Avenue
for his treasures; he entertained lavishly and during the
many years I knew him I always found him most cordial
and friendly. He enjoyed coming to see my pictures and we
would spend many a pleasant hour together in the library
or in the gallery.

You see, dear reader, no matter where I start I always
end with art. While I could speak of many members of trusts,
I will mention only two: first another of the oil trust, a
veteran of the Civil War, and a collector of pictures, or to

put it more truthfully, the possessor of a fine lot of pictures which Mr. Havemeyer either bought for him or waived his rights to them in his favor. Oliver H. Payne was our dear friend and neighbor, and for a generation or more we lived side by side in the most cordial relations. Colonel Payne was one of the great men of our country, a gallant soldier in our Civil War, a pioneer in all our industries, a member of nearly all our trusts. A man who not only built a great medical school, but endowed it—and how few endow their gifts! He was also a generous benefactor to the children of his sisters. Is it a wonder that Mr. Havemeyer and I prized his friendship and valued him as a neighbor?

It was during the pleasant evenings we spent together in the early years of our acquaintance that I think the Colonel began to take an interest in pictures. Often Mr. Havemeyer would suggest a fine picture to him or even let him have one he had intended to buy, and I have frequently heard Colonel Payne say that he owed many of his finest canvases to Mr. Havemeyer's advice and generosity. The Colonel had a fine Degas which Mr. Havemeyer had fairly forced him to buy, a good Turner, and several splendid Corots.

He rarely referred to the Civil War and only on one occasion could I induce him to speak of it, and that was when Saint-Gaudens's statute of General Sherman was placed at the entrance of Central Park.

"I should like to put up a statue to my general," he said. "I thought him one of our very greatest men and he did wonderful work in Tennessee during the campaign of Missionary Ridge and the fighting about Chattanooga, and also when Sherman was on his march to the sea. He will stand out boldly in history some day."

"Who was he?" I asked.

"General Thomas," he replied, "and he was not afraid to fight, I can tell you."

"Were you ever wounded?" I again asked, hoping he would speak of himself.

"Yes," he said, "I was shot through the thigh."

"But you do not limp," I persisted.

"No, but if I had let the surgeons have their way I would be without a leg today. The surgeon insisted that only amputation could save my life. I told him I would take my chance as I did not want to live without my leg, and somehow I survived it although I was lame for a very long time."

That was all Colonel Payne would say about himself. But to keep on the subject I continued: "Well, if ever you put up a statue to your general, I should suggest placing it in the Morningside Park, by the Columbia College library. I cannot conceive of a more splendid site for a great equestrian statue like that of Colleoni in Venice."

The Colonel was much impressed with my suggestion, but the great opportunity was lost. He told me afterwards that he had made every effort to have General Thomas's statue placed there, but before he could accomplish his object Saint-Gaudens died, and he knew of no one else who could do the work. Anyone who sees the site today can judge for himself what might have been done if the Colonel had had his way.

"Fighting is pretty hard work, isn't it?" I ventured to say.

"Yes," he answered, "but my twenty years with the Standard Oil were far harder. Those were the hardest years of my life."

And indeed, as I write these lines, I wonder if succeeding generations will ever realize the energy and brains these giants of industry put into their work, the efforts they made, the responsibilities they assumed, what was behind the great commercial enterprises they launched; or what it meant to the United States when men like Sidney Dillon and James Blair, etc., drove in the golden nail and completed the first railway across our continent. How well I can recall Sidney Dillon who was my near neighbor in our summer home for many years. A stately, handsome, white-haired gentleman with a flash in his eyes, a resoluteness in his gait, a distinction in his presence which made you think of a diplomat in some foreign court. Blair too was a splendid-looking man. These and many others were the men who "builded better than they knew" in the United States in the nineteenth century, and they did not accomplish their task, I assure you, without being "workmen noble and true."

There was a garrulous man who aired his visions at the corner store of a town in the upper Northwest, with the result that another great railway system was thrown across our continent, and another great railway magnate was working for the good of his country. I refer to James J. Hill of St. Paul. We knew him intimately for many, many years and almost as I write I must mourn him as a friend, for within the month James J. Hill has been laid to his rest, while thousands of miles of traffic were stopped and thousands of men lifted their hats out of respect to the master builder of the Great Northern Railway. He had a striking personality; high cheekbones and a firm nose, all needed to support his ample forehead, rather rugged features I thought, but no one in the "far and wide" could touch him for a pair of the brightest eyes I ever saw. A strong chin he had and a pleasant mouth, and a soft low voice which he considered indispensable to everyone. His shoulders were as if made to carry a burden and to carry it easily; they made him appear taller than he really was and his swinging gait added to his height.

He had plenty of brains to spare for other things outside his work and I know he was an indefatigable collector of the very best books. One had only to walk into his library in his beautiful St. Paul home to see that. The large quiet room told you that at once; the walls were lined with low book-shelves and above them hung some of his loveliest pictures, splendid Corot figure-pieces that were so rare, and Gustave Courbet at his best. At that time he was, with Mr. Have-meyer, so far as I know the only amateur to collect Courbet's pictures, and our mutual admiration for them was as I recol-lect the means of our meeting each other. Mr. Hill was very companionable, fond of a good story, capable of talking for hours without losing interest or showing fatigue. You could almost hear the click of the current as one thought caught another and the sparks flew about in his active brain.

74   I happened to be whirling to Chicago one summer eve-ning on the Twentieth Century train. I thought myself quite alone and unknown, when the porter of the Pullman, a respectful old darky of the type of "long ago," approached me and said:

"Mrs. Havemeyer, Mr. Hill is on board."

I looked up, startled at the sound of my own name, but he was smiling down on me benevolently and added: "You's all alone and so is he, I thought you might like to see each other."

I grasped the situation and answered: "Why so I should, suppose you let him know I am here."

He was off in a second and in a few minutes Mr. Hill ap-peared, and I spent a most delightful evening. Literature, art and politics, the latter very amusing, for he entertained me discussing an ex-President he did not like, and as I heartily shared his views I wished our victim could have heard the conversation. Mr. Hill riddled his administration unmercifully, and laid his selfish motives bare. We both enjoyed the little orgy of cruelty. He also told me a funny story about the administration of his own roads—a joke upon himself as he said.

"I was very anxious that extreme precautions should be taken to protect the wooden bridges that were built in those early days, and my orders were that a man should stand at each end of the bridge with a bucket of water in his hand, and watch each train that went by and if the engine emitted any spark, he with the water in the bucket could put it out before it could do any damage." I was much interested and he continued: "I frequently went over the road to see the condition it was in, and of course those bridges were always an anxiety to me. One day, as I passed over one of them, I saw the man standing there as usual holding the bucket. I really don't know what induced me to stop the train, but I thought I would go back and speak to him. I noticed he seemed much embarrassed as I approached him, and looking down I saw the bucket he held had no bottom to it."

Perhaps I laughed too loudly at this, for our genial Sambo appeared at the door and in the same patronizing tones asked us if we knew "it was long after eleven o'clock."

Another recollection of James Hill was during one cold winter when we both had been to Jekyll Island. When we left, Mr. Hill joined Mr. Havemeyer and me, and we left together to pay a visit to Colonel Payne in Thomasville, Georgia. It was a disagreeable journey across two Southern states where the railroads seemed to have no idea of time-tables nor the benefit of proper connections. We had a wait of two hours in a little town that apparently had nothing of interest in it. We sat on a tree trunk by a bit of green no one could possibly call a park, and ate the luncheon that had been prepared for us at the club. We took as much time to do it as we possibly could, and fed a lot of sparrows after we had finished. Then we took a long walk over some railroad tracks and finally found a turpentine factory where they were making turpentine from old pine knots. The foreman showed us most obligingly through the factory and soon realized

his visitors were men who understood the business. He rose
to the occasion, found the "boss" and the result was an
exhaustive examination of the premises. All this tired Mr.
Hill and Mr. Havemeyer, and when the express came along
and they finally found themselves in the comfortable Pullman chairs they promptly went to sleep. Pretty soon the
conductor came along and I called him to me and asked him
not to disturb them as they were very tired.

"They have their tickets, have they?" he asked.

I assured him they had and would surrender them as soon
as we reached Thomasville. When we approached the station, there was Colonel Payne waiting for us, and of course
names were mentioned in the greetings. The conductor
naturally heard them and received a few gracious words
from his sleepy passengers. He looked at me in a funny
embarrassed way, and I smiled back at him but said nothing
about the incident until at dinner that night, and it led to a
conversation on the evil of passes, private cars, etc. It
developed that none of those gentlemen ever rode free, or
accepted a pass, except, of course, Mr. Hill on official
business.

And now I must speak of one of the biggest men our
country has produced; big of brain, big of body, big of heart
and big of soul. Only of late years have I known him, and I
doubt if Mr. Havemeyer ever met him, for he spent the
years of the storm-and-stress period in South America.
There he achieved a fortune which upon his return to the
United States he made use of, indifferent to more work and
desirous to spend his remaining years in his boyhood home
in one of the lovely New England states. Yet, when the
consensus of public opinion was that no one but Theodore
N. Vail could manage the stupendous and ever developing
telephone system, he consented to adjust again the harness
to the load and to assume its presidency.

It was then that I first met him. I like to recall him best as he sat in my library on a winter's evening in one of my easy chairs, which it seemed to me for the first time offered ample accommodation for the three hundred pounds he had to manage from morn to night. He was always immaculately dressed, and the firelight threw high lights upon the finely plaited shirt front, and again upon the mass of soft white hair that covered the massive head. His face was broad and round, but without a trace of the heaviness which usually accompanies such weight; on the contrary, although placid he was alert, the wide-set eyes looked calmly but directly at you, the features were well proportioned though large, and the clean-shaven face left a strong firm mouth distinctly in view. You knew it "could utter things" but in debate it would ever be in the control of the deliberate brain, ever guided by great mental poise.

Poise, yes, I think that his strong characteristic, I think that word describes him best; he had more poise than anyone I ever knew, except perhaps my husband. I always thought they resembled each other. They seemed to have the power to mount into the cells of their brains, as it were into a turret, in order to view a subject on all sides, and when a report was made or an opinion given it was not the work of a dashing brilliant mind that only blazed the way and left it to others to do the pathfinding, it was the work of a steam roller which smoothed everything out and left no other way possible. Among businessmen, Mr. Vail's annual statement of the telephone company was considered a masterpiece of clear comprehensive statement.

I think Mr. Havemeyer and Mr. Vail resembled each other in many other ways; their firmness and determination could relax and swing like a pendulum into a gentleness that was touching, I might say humble. They were both fond of the pleasant glow of home life, devoted to those they loved and charitable to their fellow men. I recall that as we sat chatting around the fire a gentleman spoke to Mr. Vail in a tone that nettled me and attracted my attention.

"Mr. Vail," he said, "are you not apprehensive about the present tendency toward socialism?"

Mr. Vail waited a minute and then replied quietly: "Well! that depends upon what you call socialism. You see, in a broad sense, I am a bit of a socialist myself," and he gave a sly look at me. I knew the socialism he referred to, it was permeated with the golden rule, so that he left the bulk of his fortune and his beautiful home in Vermont to others in order that they might profit by his labors.

I enjoyed having him by me at dinner and hearing him apologize for his appetite, telling me "eating was his besetting sin" while I assured him it was a duty he owed to his "make-up." He was very honest about his fads and fancies, and frankly said that he wanted a cucumber at every meal and it was a necessity for him to have fresh butter if he had butter at all. He often mentioned how much he enjoyed dining upon the terrace of my Connecticut home, eating a simple good dinner, refusing champagne to drink a bottle of good old russet cider that effervesced and beaded in his glass. Afterwards he would draw his chair to the edge of the terrace and smoke a cigar and look at the waving grain that was ripening on the southern slope. He would not leave until about eleven o'clock and then, with Mr. and Mrs. Kingsbury who were always with him, would start for a run to the city.

The rapid development of the telephone company touches upon the marvelous, but as that will be a matter of history, I will only mention a few incidents, which in view of further discoveries may some day appear both funny and fanciful to my readers. Just as there were but a few years between the first monoplane of the Wright brothers and the wonderfully useful aircraft of the Great War, so there was only a short space of time between the first telephone, which I distinctly remember, and the following incident.

In 1914, less than a month after Mr. Vail had first spoken across the continent, I was summoned to the telephone and told that I would be called up in New York City at 3 p.m. to speak to Mr. Kingsbury and to my daughter and her husband, all of whom were in San Francisco visiting the Panama Exhibition. I asked my "co-mother-in-law," Mrs. Webb, to be with me so she could speak to her son. She was almost totally deaf and she was fearful that she would not hear the voices. To my surprise as the bell rang, although she stood behind me without using the earpiece, she called out in delight as my daughter spoke to me:

"Oh! I can hear Electra! I can hear her voice"—and for many minutes we conversed with our children three thousand miles distant as easily, and heard them as distinctly, as if they were in the room with us.

Again, several months later Mr. and Mrs. Kingsbury were dining with me in my Connecticut home. After dinner, as I sat before a dainty little machine that made delicious coffee in three minutes, Mr. Kingsbury said suddenly:

"Where is Doris?" referring to my daughter-in-law.

"She is in Denver," I answered.

"Do you know her address?" he asked.

"Certainly," I replied, and gave it to him.

"Well, I think we should like to speak with her," he continued and he arose and went to the telephone. Before the last drop of coffee had percolated through my little machine, Doris was on the telephone and we chatted with her at a distance of two thousand miles as clearly as if she had been standing beside me. As we hung up the receiver Mr. Kingsbury said to me:

"Before long you will speak to Miss Cassatt in Paris, as

easily as you have just now spoken to Doris," and he went
on to explain to me how Mr. Vail, through buying up patents
82   and with the aid of a wonderful man by the name of Carty,
was about to develop the wireless telephone.

I suppose if these memoirs last long enough, my readers
will laugh over my enthusiasms and wonder what I would
say, if I went to a telephone and not only spoke to a person
three thousand miles away, but could circle the globe with
the sound of my voice and at the same time could distinctly
see the face of the person addressed and watch the changing
expression caused by the words I uttered.

I remember being in Mr. Vail's box in Carnegie Hall
83   when a special medal was presented to Dr. Graham Bell.
It was an inspiring sight to see all the great telephone men
upon the stage and a great delight to hear them tell of their
early efforts, discouragements and disappointments, and of
their ultimate success. Never shall I forget Dr. Bell as he
said: "And I listened and I heard the word 'Hello.'" When
Dr. Bell finished speaking, his old friend and running mate
told us more of the early days and looking at the fine form
of the inventor, who sat erect with his wonderful hair circling his head like a halo, he said: "I want to tell you that the
Doctor has a great deal more gray matter inside of his head
than he has on the outside of it." No one laughed more
heartily than the Doctor, and he looked hastily up at the
box where his deaf-mute wife sat following the lips of their
daughter, who interpreted each word to Mrs. Bell by the
lips as it was uttered upon the stage. It was the early romance of his life and his love for the beautiful woman who
became his wife that stimulated him to continue his work
upon the telephone.

I recall those days with keen pleasure, and am deeply
grateful for all the opportunities good fortune brought me
in the company of such friends.

CHAPTER V

Visitors II

BARON KAMURA

O<small>NE</small> of my Sunday visitors who made a deep impression upon me was the Baron Kamura, the Japanese envoy to the United States during the Russian-Japanese war; medium-sized, middle-aged, earnest and frail, an intense and thoughtful personality, and I was told a most skillful diplomat. The Russian envoy Witte speaks admiringly of him in his memoirs. When he was ushered into my library and presented to me, I thought of the Japanese music and feared even Beethoven would be unfamiliar to his ears, and I fairly quivered when they began a quartet by Brahms; yet what was my astonishment to see the Baron listening to it with apparent enjoyment. I found out later that he had spent several years in one of our colleges, and that also explained the perfect English he spoke. I always regretted I could not see more of Baron Kamura and know him better than I possibly could through the few short conversations we had together, although he gave me a glimpse of his inner self when he sent me a little volume exquisitely bound in white and gold. It was a beautiful pathetic story of old Japan, which I read with the greatest pleasure, and while I smiled over some of the quaint expressions of his English translation, I was deeply touched to see how much feeling he had put into the sad story of a woman's affection and the cruel

84

separation she endured. I know there were tears in my eyes
when I read how the poor little Japanese dressed herself in
white and plunged the sharp knife into her throat. I wrote
him how much I appreciated his story and he called and we
had a pleasant conversation together, and soon after he
returned to Japan and then came the news of his untimely
death.

LORD KITCHENER

85   Lord Kitchener was perhaps the most distinguished military man that ever visited me. I think he was returning from
China to England by the Canadian Pacific, but I remember
that he was to visit New York and the papers had much to
say of the hero of Khartoum. Several years before, I remember Mr. Havemeyer with the help of an agent had booked
us to Khartoum while seated in his comfortable library chair,
and that just thirteen days later we dined at Shepheard's in
86   Cairo, and it was considered a remarkably fast trip. Although we never saw Khartoum, due to a violent sandstorm
raging when we arrived at Wadi Halfa, I was much in-
87   terested in the avenger of General Gordon and the
destroyer of the Mahdi's tomb.

Well, one evening I was reading about the General's
expected visit, when I was called to the telephone and Mr.
88   Paul Dana asked me if I would receive Lord Kitchener the
following morning.

"He wants very much to see your collection," said Mr.
Dana, "but he is a very busy man as he is sailing the day
after tomorrow. How early could you receive him?"

"Well," I answered, "I breakfast at seven-thirty, I suppose he could come at eight o'clock." There was a pause,
which I enjoyed, and then Mr. Dana said:

"That is pretty early isn't it? But I think we could make it
by nine o'clock."

"Suit yourself," I said, "the morning is yours. When you reach here I will be ready." You see that receiving people, while it means a great amount of pleasure, also means a great amount of effort and much time. Again, there is the uncertainty as to which objects will interest your guests and the question of which pigeonhole of your brain you must look into for the information that may be required.

I was too busy then to consider what might interest Lord Kitchener, in fact I thought little about the visit until the following morning when I gave orders to admit two gentlemen who would arrive about nine o'clock. They arrived shortly after nine o'clock and I shook hands with a sturdy well-built man, who while very straight did not impress me as tall. As he stood before me, so little did his military bearing impress me that I did not picture him in uniform or even on horseback. I felt his strong personality and what impressed me most were his eyes. They were large, wide apart and very direct in their gaze. Yes! Lavater would have said "a stern disciplinarian," a man who could say: "We fight now, there will be plenty of time to mourn afterward." I irresistibly thought of Mr. Havemeyer and I silently wished the two men could have met. How I would have enjoyed seeing the two strong natures together and comparing them with each other. I had to remember my duties as hostess, however, and not indulge my fondness for sidelight observations. Besides, after a few moments, Mr. Dana said he was obliged to go and would leave Lord Kitchener to see my treasures, all after the trite formula of politeness as he tripped down the gallery steps.

After he had gone, I turned toward my guest. He stood in an attitude which plainly said: "Now let's get at it! What is there to see?"

I at once "saluted" so to speak, and said: "Lord Kitchener, you cannot see everything in one morning; if there is anything which especially interests you, tell me and I will show it to you with pleasure."

That appeared to please him and he replied, I thought rather timidly for a man who could blow up tons of brick and scatter a prophet's ashes to the winds: "If you don't mind, I should like to see your peachblow."

89   "Peachblow!" Luckily for me I was accustomed to the unexpected, but peachblow! the most delicate, I might say the most feminine of all the art objects I possessed. Strange to say, I felt a sensation of pleasure, of humor. I knew I should enjoy showing my dainty peachblow porcelains to him. It was so different from any other experience, and Lord Kitchener was so different from any other visitor!

I led the way to a glass cabinet where I had arranged some of our largest pieces, but not the choicest—those were kept in boxes tucked carefully away and only shown upon rare occasions. I saw Lord Kitchener was much interested and very appreciative and when I felt he had satisfied himself with that cabinet, I led him to my own sitting room. I offered Lord Kitchener an easy chair which I pushed up before some drawers under a large glass cabinet which extended across the room, and I asked him not to mind my sitting upon the floor, as I could work better and quicker from that position. Although the day was gloomy, the corner windows gave us plenty of light and the logs flickered cheerily in the fireplace. I opened one box after another and placed in his hands the lovely little vases, beautiful with the bloom of the peach and the soft green of the clinging moss. I went too fast even for his impulsive nature and I was soon holding one or two vases in my hand waiting for him to relinquish the one he already held. I was astonished to see such feeling, so much delight. Lord Kitchener put his palms tenderly together to receive the little vase I offered him and he gently turned it from side to side, while the military tension relaxed and he sank into an easy position and his eyes lost their fierce directness as they looked at the dainty object he held.

It had taken about ten minutes to convince me that the man had a shy, sensitive nature which he tried to conceal under a formal kind of dignity, which I thought made him somewhat self-conscious. I am sure he had analyzed his own character just as he would the plans of a campaign, that he knew better than anyone of his shyness and timidity and, knowing as he did that he represented His Majesty's Service, he guarded his military reputation with the utmost vigilance. He concealed these two flaws in his armor by a circumspect reserve which had earned for him the reputation of being harsh and brusque. I instinctively felt the armor he was constantly adjusting and I wanted to see through it and have a glimpse at the real man whom I knew to be worthwhile. It annoyed me to see him force himself to be so self-contained, waiting for me to make every move, every suggestion. I longed to touch a spring somewhere in his nature and see if he could be spontaneous, whether he could adjust himself to new impressions or whether he always had to think of India and Egypt to the exclusion of his own pleasure. I also knew how guarded I must be lest he suspect my thoughts, and yet I have never felt a greater longing to make anyone enjoy himself. I often wondered if I succeeded, for he was soon on the floor beside me helping me open the boxes, taking out the peachblow ink bottles, the tiny salve cups and the slender vases. Suddenly I saw his hand steal into his pocket and he drew out a pair of spectacles—huge ones, in tortoise shell, like those of the cardinal in my Greco portrait. Unconscious of vanity, he put them on and quietly continued his inspection. With the training of a collector I had reserved the best for the last and as I uncovered a beautiful coupe—my husband's favorite—Lord Kitchener uttered an exclamation of delight, took the coupe in both hands and went to the window to examine it more carefully. He was silent for some time, but as I watched him I knew he was going to talk, and he did. He looked at me sharply and said:

"Do you know what a wonderful piece this is? It is the best I have ever seen and the kind the Chinese value most highly. I understand this mossy green effect is greatly prized and as difficult to find as it is difficult to make, and until it leaves the kiln no one can tell how it will turn out. Sometimes the most beautiful results are accidental."

"Yes," I answered, "my husband felt as you do and he always sought just such pieces. The vase you hold in your hand is the second one he ever bought, and strange to say he could never find a better one, so he kept it in truly Oriental fashion, carefully put away, and showed it only on rare occasions. I see you are a true amateur," I added, hoping to lure him on to satisfy the interrogation point that had been tingling in my brain ever since he arrived. I did want to know what had led him to care for peachblow and my curiosity was soon to be satisfied. Lord Kitchener, not mentioning his services to his government, simply said:

"When I was in China I was told I could have any vases I wanted in the Palace. There were so many and all so beautiful I did not know which to choose and I became quite confused. Finally I told them to put a lot on a table each day and I went and examined them for hours and at last I selected two peachblow vases."

How natural! The dainty pink vases appealed to the sturdy soldier far more than the larger beakers with their gorgeous decoration of the Mings or the Ch'ien Lungs! Ah! dear Lavater! here is another sidelight upon character! The strong and the delicate, the fierce and the tender. Nature will swing her pendulum from one extreme to another and it is only the commonplace that are content to repose midway.

It was a long and memorable morning. Lord Kitchener was very frank about my paintings. He swept his arm around my library and said:

"I don't care for those, I know nothing about them."

"I am glad you have such a good reason," I answered.

My Persian pottery, on the contrary, greatly interested him, and he examined it carefully. "I should like to get some pieces of that kind," he said pointing to the sixteenth century luster bottles, "but what can a poor soldier like me do? I have no fortune."

"Fortune is not everything," I answered. "Judgment counts for much," and then I added just for mischief, "you are on the spot and can choose."

"True!" he answered, "I may get some yet!"

I have often wondered what he did upon his return to Egypt, whether its wonderful art attracted him. I fancy it did not; black diorite and gray granite resembled too nearly his own hard formulas to find sympathy with him. He needed the luster of the sixteenth century and the rainbow glow of the early Persian.

When he said good-bye, he shook my hand heartily and thanked me in a few words any boy might have used.

"Do you know your way about in our city?" I asked.

"I want to go to the Metropolitan Museum," he answered, "and I have not much time as I have an important engagement this afternoon."

I said: "You have not much time, you had better let me call a taxi for you." He accepted my offer and waited patiently until it arrived. He wore a well-used covert coat and a soft felt hat and as he left I reflected, there goes a great big-hearted boy who has honestly tried to make good in this world. I only wish he had had more pleasure in his life and less hard duty. No one could dream that the simply dressed, energetic figure that left my house was the man that subdued Egypt, ruled India and reorganized the Chinese army.

I read in the evening papers that "the important engagement" was a baseball game. Again the pendulum! The soldier and the boy! Somehow it leaked out that Lord Kitchener had been in my home. He had refused all other invitations and I was besieged with questions about him. I had forgotten what he wore, except the comfortable coat and the old hat, and I could not even tell if he had a medal on his breast. I humbly said that I believed he did not, that I did not think he even had a ribbon in his buttonhole. I knew that what had interested Lord Kitchener would not interest my questioners and that I could give them little satisfaction. I recall one beautiful leader of society, who said to me eagerly:

"I hear Lord Kitchener has been to your house. What did he say about Khartoum?"

"We did not mention it," I was obliged to answer.

"Did not mention it?" she exclaimed. "Why, what did you talk about?"

"Peachblow vases," I said simply. But I suddenly perceived that she thought I was joking with her, so I made my peace by giving a little account of the tortoise-shell spectacles, which seemed to satisfy her curiosity, and for a long time to come I was often called upon to tell the story of Lord Kitchener and his spectacles.

CHAPTER VI

Visitors III

M. COQUELIN

FOREIGN ambassadors, cabinet ministers, members of legations and directors of museums all found their way to our home. To some Mr. Havemeyer sent a card when it was impossible for me to receive them. Frequently have I met people abroad who, after greeting me, have said: "I have been in your home, Mrs. Havemeyer, and have enjoyed seeing your pictures." For our collection as well as our house had a far greater reputation abroad than here, and strangers were deeply impressed by the work of Mr. Colman and Mr. Tiffany.

Of actors I received many, and they were always delightful and entertaining, always welcome, and they left a feeling of friendliness which pervaded the house long after they had gone. I cannot speak of all, but there are two who linger with sharp outlines in my memory, one for his exquisite French, and the other for a funny little episode connected with his visit.

Coquelin *aîné* came frequently to my house. He was a welcome guest, and in his own original way loved art sincerely. He was strong, virile, compact, with a voice like a clarion call or, with the soft pedal, like the whisper of the wind, and a face that nature in her happiest mood had designed expressly for comedy. The humorous lines about his mouth, the inquisitive tip of his nose, the innocent questioning arch of his eyebrows, all said "comedian" as distinctly as it could be expressed by the human countenance or even

95

51

by a Greek mask. He could enunciate more words with one breath from his lusty lungs than any actor I ever heard. His recitation of the ballad in *Cyrano de Bergerac* echoes in my ears as I write these lines, and his rendering of the lines from *Les Précieuses* was, in its way, as dainty and as delicate a bit of art in declamation as anything the nineteenth century produced.

96   When Coquelin was in New York, Henry Irving was also fulfilling an engagement here, and while the latter's plays were wonderful achievements of artistic production, in my opinion Coquelin was far the greater actor of the two, relying for success on the legitimate means of expression and diction. They both played Mathias in *The Polish Jew*, which I think was conceded to be Irving's greatest role, or at least as great as *The Lyons Mail*. Yet even here in a role little fitted to him, Coquelin excelled Irving in many ways. Irving by the limitations of his art had to depend largely upon the mounting of the piece and the elaborateness of the details for the success of the play; while Coquelin trusted to his art, his diction and his interpretation of the part for his success.

Both were interesting performances! Irving, with remorse gnawing at his heart even as the curtain rose, never for one moment ceased to express that emotion but rather increased it through fear and apprehension as the drama developed. Coquelin, on the contrary, presented cunning and commonplace gloating and triumph with no thought of remorse, for even when bells ring they do not greatly disturb him as they do Irving. Only when he sits alone in the firelit kitchen rubbing his hands exultantly, and the door opens and a real Jew enters and asks for shelter, does he fall down in a shuddering heap on the floor and give that muffled yet piercing shriek that sends cold chills down our backs and makes us catch our breath in terror.

I found Coquelin a man of intelligence and poise who could thoroughly appreciate himself without becoming tiresome. But he had mannerisms off as well as on the stage. He had a way of kneeling on a chair and speaking in a very dictatorial way about art, for he had the misfortune of owning a few pictures and thinking he owned art itself. When he wished to emphasize his remarks, he would snap his thumbnail against his teeth, which I considered rather bourgeois although I had often seen him do it on the stage.

He was of the people, he knew it and what was better, he wanted it to be known. How he loved France! The tricolor was all about him, and with all the strength of his great heart he loved his country and countrymen. I recall the last time I saw him—he was working for his fellow actors, organizing and performing in a great fête at the Trocadero; and he died in Paris a few weeks later.

SIR JOHN HARE

The other actor whose visit lingers like a cameo in my memory is Sir John Hare, about whom I made a very funny error. He was an Englishman and, I believe, considered one of the best actors in London, doing such plays as *Lord Quex* and others which required very careful delineation and diction. He had brought us letters from Edwin A. Abbey, and as evenings were impossible for them, I invited him and Lady Hare at once to have a cup of tea with me. I was waiting for them in the library, and I remember that Mr. Havemeyer came in and I asked him to wait and meet them at the same time, explaining who they were.

"And what is he like?" asked Mr. Havemeyer.

"Oh, a tall and manly man, large and imposing," I answered. "I saw him in London years ago, when he was acting in the old comedy of *Men and Acres* with Ellen Terry, long before she went to be leading lady for Henry Irving. You will like him, he is handsome and well built."

At that moment Sir John and Lady Hare were announced. A very dignified and beautiful woman approached me and behind her was a small, a very small man, such a tiny man, a veritable husband "no bigger than my thumb"—he more nearly approached his wife's elbow than her shoulders. But he had a mobile interesting face and flashing black eyes and his manner was charmingly free and easy. Mr. Havemeyer gave me a look which I still recall and which almost robbed me of my self-possession, for I too was struggling with my own astonishment, and I was almost tempted to ask what had happened to him since I last saw him. I soon found out that it was all my own fault and that I had mistaken the Mr. Hare. There were two actors of the same name, and I had never seen this one before, hence my mistake. Mr. Have-meyer with his usual frankness gave it all away, and they were so amiable that I recovered from my embarrassment and we became good friends and enjoyed a number of pleasant visits together. He had a very successful season in New York and I frequently had the pleasure of seeing him act. For a long time after this incident, if I tried to tell Mr. Havemeyer who was coming to see the pictures he would say:

"Is it another Mr. Hare?"

100   MRS. THEODORE ROOSEVELT

Although I met many railroad men, I knew few of our statesmen. I rarely accompanied Mr. Havemeyer to Washington, for we agreed that one bird should mind the home nest; but I watched closely that storm-and-stress period 101   which followed the tragic death of President McKinley and brought Roosevelt back from the sidetracks to occupy the presidential chair.

I prefer to leave Roosevelt to the historians. His record in the Spanish War, his attack upon the trusts, his unearthing of the Sherman Act as a weapon of attack, his appeal to the Supreme Court which found the law so impossible of interpretation that they left it hanging by the thread of "reasonable doubt," his shooting trip in the West while the "Roosevelt Panic" of 1907 was devastating Wall Street, his Bull Moose effort to destroy the Republican Party in the campaign of 1912—all these are facts for history, not for me to deal with. I saw him often; it was never necessary for me to meet him.

I was requested to receive Mrs. Roosevelt, and needless to say I at once opened my doors to the first lady of the land. It happened that I was obliged to receive her on one of my reception days, for I was notified of her coming only the previous evening, not in time to arrange for a special reception. I remember that I was asked to speak on the telephone with the President's sister. She told me that Mrs. Roosevelt was in New York and asked permission to bring her to my house the following day, saying she knew it would give Mrs. Roosevelt the greatest pleasure to see my pictures. I answered that I was expecting guests the following day, but she assured me it would make no difference and promised me there should be no formality, no guards, no "in waitings" so to speak, not even a Secret Service man in attendance.

I had heard many remarks about Mrs. Roosevelt's attitude toward society during her husband's administration, such as that she wished to establish an aristocracy in the White House, that she demanded the distinction of royalty, that she required the privilege of bowing first before anyone dared bow to her, that even the President's sisters stood up when she and the President were present—and many other things which I wished to forget, and remember only what

Mrs. Saint-Gaudens, the sculptor's wife, herself a welcome guest at the White House, told me. She said:

"Mrs. Roosevelt's position is very difficult. She wrote me recently that her present life was not an easy one."

I could readily believe it and felt great sympathy for her in spite of any silly ambitions. We who could do as we pleased without the fear of criticism, what could we know of the difficulties of being in the public eye, morning, noon and night; of planning receptions and dinners, of placing each one according to his rank, probably placing many higher than their ranking; of pleasing this one, of placating that one; of being a good mother to her children, a capable mistress of her mansion, and the first lady of the land *par-dessus le marché*. No, no! We could have little idea of her work, her weariness, or her perplexities. If the bows of deference or standing in her presence could add to her enjoyment or lend to her triumphs, I for one felt she was entitled to them. I knew I should have failed had I been in her place, and I truly wished to give her pleasure when she visited my home.

Mrs. Roosevelt came in so quietly that I had greeted her and had led her into the library before anyone knew she was there. Of course, introductions were out of the question, but several of her old friends were calling on me. I remember that two of them called her by her Christian name when referring to her later. It was very easy, however, to steer Mrs. Roosevelt from one apartment into another without having her meet any of my guests, and leaving her free to enjoy what she came for—a sight of the pictures.

You must remember this was the first time I had been called upon to receive a President's wife, and the notice of the visit was too short to allow me to be prompted as to how to conduct myself; therefore it was hardly to be expected that I should go through such an ordeal without a mistake—

and I didn't. I found my Waterloo in the library during the first few moments of Mrs. Roosevelt's visit. Some evil star prompted me to say:

"Mrs. Roosevelt, would you not enjoy it more if we left you quite by yourself to look at the pictures?"

Mrs. Roosevelt looked at me gratefully and answered: "Indeed, I should like it very much."

Thereupon, the President's sister and I drew aside and began chatting together. I noticed that she was leaning against the back of a chair, and, forgetting the rules, I motioned her to be seated and I sat down myself. The President's sister refused in such a way that I realized at once the break I had made. All the tales I had heard about formalities rushed into my mind and I arose at once. Think of me sitting—and in an easy chair at that—while my presidential visitor stood! I glanced at her. My Waterloo was not a complete rout, for the President's wife, happily for me, stood with her back toward me and her eyes glued to a Rembrandt! I arose—on any less distinguished occasion I should have said that I jumped up—and blessing that Rembrandt, I stood pressing my high heels tightly together lest I should again be guilty of such an act. I rattled and rustled the train of a beautiful French gown, hoping Mrs. Roosevelt would hear it and know that I was "on duty" or "in attendance" as the phrase may be.

I cannot recall that Mrs. Roosevelt took the slightest notice of it or of me either, or of any of her friends there— not even of Mrs. John Milburn; although it was in the Milburn house that President McKinley died, whose death made her husband President of the United States. She was there for a purpose, and she accomplished it. When finished, she said good afternoon, by the code—without thanks, be it understood—on the steps of the gallery, and vanished from my sight, and from my life so far as I can remember.

That was my one White House visitor, a small, trim, neatly dressed woman who said no word I can recall nor gave expression to any impression she received. Whether she enjoyed her visit I cannot tell, for she never recognized my courtesy, not even through her secretary; nor did the President's sister ever thank me for showing my pictures to the President's wife.

HELEN KELLER

I have written of actors, statesmen, authors, but under what head shall I classify one rare guest whose visit made a memorable afternoon in my recollections of my library?
103　　She was Helen Keller, blind and deaf—a wonderful girl who triumphed over all her misfortunes, sustained as she was by another woman almost as wonderful as she, Miss
104　　Sullivan, her teacher, her guide, her friend. I was asked to receive the blind girl, as Helen had taken a great fancy to
105　　my daughter Adaline, whom she had met at a friend's house, and she wanted to meet her friend's mother. She also longed to have the privilege of passing her hands over my marble statues and bronze Venus. It was her only means of comprehending and enjoying objects. I remember that I was in
106　　the gallery with some musicians. My sister happened to be with me and I requested her to go down and receive Helen Keller and her friend. I mention this as it has to do with Helen's wonderful sense of feeling. When my friends heard who was below, one of them, a fine pianist, said to me:

"Oh! I should love to play for her." I smiled. "But she cannot hear you," I replied.

Still, strangely enough, Helen loves to stand by a pianist and feel the vibrations of the chords, just as she delights to go to the theater for a play she can neither see nor hear, to have Miss Sullivan hold her hand and with those lightning touches explain to her what is going on upon the stage.

"Wonderful," replied my musical friend, "I am so anxious to see her and I wish I could play for her."

We went below. As I went forward to greet Helen Keller, my cousin, Mrs. Mary Mapes Dodge, who had brought the blind girl to my house, stopped me.

"Wait a minute," she said, and she took my hand and put it into that of Helen Keller.

"Mrs. Peters," said Mrs. Dodge, as Helen laid her hand upon her lips, so she could understand what she said.

Helen was thoughtful for a second, she pressed my hand gently with that wonderful touch, and then answered: "No, it is Mrs. Peters's sister."

Mrs. Dodge looked triumphantly at me. "Would you believe she could be so sensitive to touch?" she asked, and, as you may believe, we were all too astonished even to express an opinion.

Helen was the heroine of the afternoon. Being blind we felt we could gaze upon her as much as we liked. I even caught sight of my maids looking at her cautiously from behind the curtains; one of them said to me afterwards: "What a wonderful face she has! It makes you happy just to look at her." And she spoke truly. The buoyancy of hope beamed from Helen's countenance. To encourage others seemed to be part of Helen's religion. Some time later when she was a student in Radcliffe College, she wrote me:

"Dear Mrs. Havemeyer, I don't know why I try so hard to get through college, but I feel that if I can accomplish the hard task it will encourage others who are as unfortunate as I am to do the same thing."

The way Helen Keller conversed with you was to put her middle finger upon your lips and her thumb under your chin, and as you spoke, she slowly repeated the words, her face radiating as she caught their meaning and her body full of quick staccato movements, as the brilliant mind framed an answer almost before the words had left your lips. Her understanding anticipated your thoughts and her bright wit was ever ready with a repartee. She was graceful, poised, and self-possessed. Imagine a blind, deaf girl sitting among a group of friends, holding a cup of tea with its difficult spoon and its dangerous contents, eating a cake full of soft cream without an accident while she entertained us all in the merriest way. That very day a musician from London had called to see me. His name was William Shakespeare. Someone said to Helen Keller that Mr. William Shakespeare had called that afternoon and had just left. Naturally she looked incredulous, for her blue eyes although slightly altered were expressive. Finally, when told who William Shakespeare was, she said softly: "Poor man! what does he do with his name?" When asked about college, for she was preparing for college at that time, she said: "I use a typewriter for my examinations." When asked if the work was hard, she replied: "Oh, no, the typewriter does it all." "But how about the languages," persisted her questioner, "for instance, how do you manage with German?" "That is easy," quickly replied Helen gaily, "I change the shuttle." For an hour or more she entertained us without a shade of embarrassment or a trace of fatigue. Animated and graceful, glowing with happiness, she fairly radiated the golden rule and love to all. Surely the dear Christ had in her misfortune laid His hands upon her head, and given her the blessing of a world within when disease had closed her eyes to the world without. Later from Radcliffe she writes me how much she enjoys Spenser's *Faerie Queene* and she adds: "I read over and over again about the pretty white charger." Yes! that was a memorable afternoon, rarely had my library sheltered a more interesting character.

Miss Sullivan discovered one of my old maids peeping at Helen Keller from behind a door. The soft-hearted creature was wiping her pitying eyes. Miss Sullivan said to her: "You need not weep for her! I have never seen her unhappy in her life." What a record! What an example! If, ah! if only some of those on whom the baskets of the gods have showered every gift could say as much, could only profit by the blind girl's life!

Yes, Helen was well worth knowing. It was a great pleasure to lead her to the marbles of the Renaissance and watch her pass her soft hands over the face of the Madonna and feel the outlines of the infant Christ. Her pleasure was evinced by the caressing touch when she passed her hands over the Venus of Milo and over the symmetrical spheres of the Greek helmets. What a pleasure to think that art—my art—had put something new and something beautiful forever into that blind girl's life.

Dear children, for whom I am writing these recollections, never forget how blessed you are and when an opportunity offers, try to equalize the sum of human happiness and share the sunshine that you have inherited.

Helen was interested in everything that touched her sex and was herself an ardent suffragist. I once asked her to speak for our cause and I at once received an answer telling me how she regretted that a lecture trip in the Far West prevented her coming. It was as usual a typewritten letter but she wrote that for the first time she had signed her letter. It was pathetic to read her noble words and then see the irregular block letters of her signature. I was chairman of the meeting that afternoon and the letter had a great success for I sent my little granddaughter to show it to my audience, and I believe the sight of that signature and the thoughts it awakened caused more than one to consider suffrage and the effort we were making to emancipate women. Although Helen Keller came again to my home, I shall always prize my recollections of that delightful first visit.

109

110

111

CHAPTER VII

A Great Actress of Japan

SADA YACCA

112   IT was an epoch-making moment when the New York band of Japanese enthusiasts saw Sada Yacca, a renowned actress from those wonderful islands in the farthest waters of the Pacific Ocean.

113   When Admiral Perry sailed into the harbor of Yedo, the Tokyo of today, and freed Japan from the thralldom of the double sword, he not only opened to the world a treasure of art but he also revealed to us an equally wonderful people. Some wag facetiously remarked, when he heard of the coming of Sada Yacca, that before Japan had been known as a "Perry and a paradise," but now we could speak of it as "paradise and her peri." The gates which for many centuries had shut in the remarkable islands had been opened, the Mikado after many struggles had established his sovereignty, trade relations were firm and friendly, and now Sada Yacca had arrived in our midst to give us an idea of the Japanese drama. Her real destination was Paris and the world's exhibition of 1889, but as she was obliged to cross our continent, New York was to have the first opportunity to see her.

Great was my wonderment when I learned they had actors in Japan, and greater still when I heard we were to see them. I was also told they were quite unlike the singsong chanters of Chinatown's continuous performers in San Francisco.

62

Excitement ran high among the little New York group who had listened to Fenollosa tell them of Japan's marvelous civilization and of her great actors and actresses. Sada Yacca was already assured of an audience which would have to compensate her by its appreciation for the meagerness of its numbers. In those days you would not have been obliged to hold up your fingers many times to count all who were interested in Japanese art. 114

How well I remember every detail of that first night. In memory I can recall each incident of that performance. I can see that tiny theater, the only one available for Sada Yacca and her troupe, and that only because it was too small, too badly ventilated and unattractive to be of use for any other troupe. It was indeed a meager audience, one or two of us here, three or four of us there, five or six on the balcony and seven or eight restlessly walking about, disconcerted at so great a choice of seats, not knowing which to select. Frequently they would stop to greet friends and ask them what they thought it would be like? There was not a spectator above the first balcony, and the proscenium was in total darkness. It was a very social affair, however, as each little group knew the other little group. There were heart-to-heart talks from the orchestra chairs to the balcony seats and from the balcony seats back to the orchestra chairs, for each had heard some bit of gossip about the wonderful Sada Yacca and each one was anxious to contribute his quota of evidence and hearsay.

The playbills—I wish I had kept one—although miserably little thin sheets, were a tragedy in themselves and promised us shudders and shivers enough: vendettas, Japanese Medeas, Lady Macbeths, and Juliet in a geisha garb, historical episodes, the catastrophes of love and "other novelties" were to be presented upon that memorable evening and the following ones. It almost seemed as if we should have a big contract upon our hands to see the season through, but we all agreed then and there that we would stand by the enterprise to the bitter end, and that if the "following ones" meant performances, they would see us in our places unless we melted away during this first evening—for the heat of the theater was almost insufferable. It goes without saying that there was no music. I doubt if we would have recognized the renowned samisen, and we were so attuned to our own conversation that we preferred to hear ourselves talk, and a merry time we had of it!

I can see it all as if I were again taking part in the event. After a while we began to wipe our faces and to look at our watches. Are we growing tired? Heaven forfend! not we enthusiasts! but the wait is certainly becoming interminably long and we are growing proportionately warm. We could not request the ushers to open anything for there wasn't anything to open and the ushers had long since left the theater in disgust at finding that they were not of the slightest use. We were flushed with laughter over the sallies of our own wit, and we could not substitute those miserable little woe-laden programs for fans. If, in technical terms, a manager had wished "to feel" that audience it is safe to say he would have found the prevailing sentiment to be heat or impatience. However, we did enjoy it, heat and all—for is it not full of pleasant anticipations and shrouded in mystery, which only whets our imaginations?

But hush!—and we did—the curtain is stirring. It does not go up however! Is it possible that someone is simply coming out to speak to us? To tell us Sada Yacca is ill, that the forty ronins are in a free fight, that there isn't money enough in the house to pay the curtain raiser? What in goodness' name is the matter? Are we to be turned into the cold night in our steaming condition? Possibly the troupe is as warm as we are and is clamoring for cold drinks!

Whatever it is, let us have it and have done with it. And we get it. The baize curtain is pushed out— not more than ten inches and out of its folds, Matsuki! By the gods of Japan what does it mean? What can Matsuki have to do with that performance? He is only a dealer, whom we all know well—too well most of us—yet there he stands in a gorgeous kimono far too big for him, and smiling like a merry god. As he stands there he suggests Bret Harte's hero of the card pack. Bland and unembarrassed he steps before us and folding his hands naïvely over the brilliant embroidery of his kimono, he makes a queer little bow and invites our attention.

Instantly the ones and the twos in the orchestra sit erect, the threes and the fours in the balcony twist around and face the speaker. There is a general attitude of "give him a chance, but at this temperature let him beware and cut it short." Alas, how misguided can human nature become. We were wishing to cut short one of the features of the evening. To hear that little Japanese talk with the small amount of English he possessed was inimitably funny. His effort to find expressions adequate to the lofty subjects he was to treat put our sense of humor beyond the control of our politeness. We laughed and he laughed with us, repeating his bow at each outburst of applause and continuing— when he could get a chance—to put us *au courant* of what we were about to witness.

"Ladies and gentlemen," he begins, "you will see a very melancholy love history. In the first act Mme Sada Yacca gets a visit and she is much pleased and she sings and dances to it, which is very beautiful. In the second act, which is the last, she is most restless because she is alone, and she goes to see her friend and when she gets there she finds another lady in her place. She is very mad about and—and—she goes—goes goes"—he cannot find the word and he draws his kimono tightly about him and in a stage whisper he says: "she goes *hanya*—crazy, and then the fun begins." With a timid gesture as if hesitating whether he should say more, he suddenly decides to make a gamut of little staccato bows almost to the ground, and disappears.

In a minute the curtain goes up! Let me first say that Sada Yacca is a great actress, beautiful, graceful, and gifted with true tragic force. Her very presence was a delight, her mobile face lighted up, her form was tall and lithe, and the rhythm of her movements and her gestures were in harmony from tip to toe. She danced with consummate art, her hands were as flexible and expressive as her feet. Her features changed and the infinite variety of her form as she turned and swayed made it possible for her to describe the most beautiful lines with the flow of her kimono. She flashed its gorgeous colors in our eyes, she swirled and posed her graceful form, her lovely arms delighting us with their continual variety of expression. While our vision still vibrated with the rhythm of her constantly changing movements, she quickly dropped one kimono only to flash another color scheme before our eyes, this time pale and delicate like the soft sheen of a moonlit night, and as suddenly her movements became slow and languishing, gentle and amorous. The appassionato had changed into a cantabile con sentimento; her heart was now speaking to the man she loved. Could the art of expression go further? Yes! for again she dropped her kimono. It disappeared almost without our perceiving it, and in another one with a scarlet lining the brilliant finale began. The other movements expressed individual sentiments, this one was the glorious abandonment of self, the avowal of her love, the expression of the caress, the plighting of an eternal troth, the tying of the tragic knot which henceforth could never be loosened again, and prepared us for the development of the plot.

We were all breathless as the curtain fell, the enchantress had held us enthralled, the ones and twos of the orchestra looked speechlessly at the threes and fours of the balcony. We felt it had been accorded to us to sit in the inner temple, and we realized that here also the Japanese were supreme in their art. The faithless lover had been well portrayed by a distinguished member of the troupe. He stimulated his ladylove's performance, and if he gave any sign of his perfidy, it was too subtle for us to perceive it.

We waited impatiently for the second act. Now be it known that as Japanese plays are usually full of action, the intermissions must be long enough to give the actors time to rest. When the curtain rose, however, Sada Yacca gave no sign of fatigue. In another splendid robe she tripped lightly across the stage and entered her lover's house. As she crossed the stage she stopped just long enough for us to see how fresh and beautiful she was, how joyous and full of love and hope, in order that we might be appalled by the contrast when she reappeared. What a picture she made! Distraught with frenzy, shaking with jealousy and bowed with grief. Her long black hair is undone, her face pale and drawn, her crisped hands have lost all their grace as they grasp a sword, or rather a long stick. The angel has become a demon. You would scarcely recognize poor Sada Yacca, she is the incarnation of fury uncontrolled. We know such rage must have a victim, and out it comes—her rival. The next few minutes are as tragic as any I have ever witnessed upon a stage. Sada Yacca attacks her rival and fairly beats her to death, and then she kills herself. Her cudgeling is like a broadsword duel, and the movements of her body as she deals her murderous strokes are magnificent; with lightning rapidity she passes from one position to another, never forgetting the grace of her lines nor the beauty of her pose. This scene must have been far more difficult and exhausting than her dancing. As her rage is appeased her vengeance turns to grief. After her tragic climax she portrays with exquisite skill physical exhaustion, heartbreaking despair, the ebbing of her vital force, until, as she sinks upon the ground with every muscle relaxed, nerveless and drooping, her eyes glazed and her features fixed, you feel how truly she welcomes death.

It is all over! the green curtain has fallen and we draw a deep breath. Little did we dream when Matsuki said, "and then the fun begins," that we should see such a tragedy. The heat of the place was forgotten, there was no laughter nor talking. We sat there quietly waiting, yes, wishing to wait, before seeing another piece, for we felt we could stand no more. We had again taken a deep draft from that inexhaustible well of Oriental art and we knew that that evening would always have a special place in our memories.

When Matsuki appeared again, it was to announce the drama of *The Forty Ronins*, a historical play of ancient Japan. Sada Yacca did not appear in it, but Kawa Kama, Japan's greatest actor, had the leading part. Matsuki availed himself of every word of English he knew to tell us the plot of the play and to impress us with the heroism of the ronins. Matsuki said:

"When I first saw this play and realized how these industrious men loved their country and would die for it, I was so excited that the perspiration pushed from every pore!" He disappeared after that rhetorical effort, and we saw him no more.

When the curtain rose, Matsuki's industrious heroes were already on the stage and certainly they gave the impression of being noble men! The play was full of mystery, of interest and of action; the battle scene one of the most wonderful I have ever witnessed. I can recall nothing comparable to it, not even in our greatest Shakespearian re-

116

vivals! How they produced such an effect upon that tiny stage is a mystery to me. A cold blue light just outlined the trees. You felt—rather than saw—that the banks of the river were high and the waters deep. The anxious messenger hurried across the bridge, and stealthily gave the word to his comrades hidden behind the concealing bushes. The dark blue shadows and the very stillness gave a foretaste of the tragedy that was to come. The sudden glint of armor can be seen moving rapidly behind the thick trees. You detect the faces of warriors in their fierce helmets, stealing along upon the river's edge below, or above upon the bridge; then comes the tramp of feet, the war cry! the clash! The bridge is full of men, the swords flash, the daggers are drawn, the warriors grapple with each other, and the corpses are tossed below. The struggle is intensely tragic, deadly and determined. It is still, so still that you can hear the clash of the armor as the combatants close in upon each other, and the thud of the bodies as they fall upon the ground. The forty ronins fought like forty thousand men and I doubt if any of us there ever forgot that terrible battle on the bridge!

What a lesson it was in artistic realism! A lesson that was not lost upon our managers. Plays with Oriental settings became the rage, and before the season was over we managed to interest many of our friends in Sada Yacca and her troupe, although I am not certain that her season was a financial success. My friend, Miss Cassatt, wrote me that Sada Yacca was so popular in Paris that visitors at the exhibition of 1889 would remain from one performance to another, and that often Sada Yacca would be obliged to repeat a piece during an evening in order to accommodate her many spectators. She must have filled her beautiful kimono sleeves with gold napoleons.

117

CHAPTER VIII

Tea Jars and Potteries

118, 119 So Matsuki said my library ceiling was made out of tea jar
120 covers, did he? He said Sir William van Horne told him so,
did he? Well! I don't believe Sir William van Horne ever
told him any such thing! Sir William van Horne knew better, as I told him all about my ceiling myself." I said all this
121 sharply to Mr. Ushikubo of the Yamanaka Trading Company, a merchant who sold us our first tea jars and con-
122 tinues to sell them to me today.

"I heard you had not kept them," said Mr. Ushikubo, "and
it would have been a pity as the tea jars are much more
valuable with their covers. The tea ceremony means old
traditions and old associations to the Japanese, and the tea
jars with their covers and their stands command a very high
price in Japan today."

"Good-bye," I said hurriedly, "I am going right home to
count my tea jar covers and I will let you know the result."

It was not a difficult thing to do. I had always carefully
kept every box, case and document, and I felt angry at what
that clever little Matsuki had done to assail my reputation
as a collector. In a few days I again sought Ushikubo and I
felt a thrill of triumph as I saw his stupefaction when I told
him I had counted 475 tea jar covers.

"Is that enough?" I asked exultantly.

"Oh! Mrs. Havemeyer," he answered, "is it possible?

70

That is wonderful. Do you know you have a great fortune in them?"

"I know the fortune is done up in lots," I replied, "each lot carefully tied, and you can come see them at your pleasure."

"And have you those gold lacquered stands and boxes we sold you long, long ago?"

"Certainly I have," I answered, "why not?"

His eyes grew large and he became excited and said: "Please wait a minute." When he returned, he had a catalogue in his hand and he showed me the price a tea jar with case and stand had brought at a sale in Japan the previous year. I kept my poise, but I confess it staggered me. Four hundred and seventy-five such possibilities sickened me. I wanted to go home and protect my little tea jars, that came from prince and daimio and tea ceremonies with their associations and traditions. I wanted to have them free and uncovered to enjoy their beauty. I even hoped my little jars were conscious how precious and beautiful they were. Although I well know the value of a dollar, the commercial valuation of a work of art thrust upon me always disgusted me.

The tea jars of Japan reveal a refinement of art little known to the western world. In China the potter's art seemed to decline as the taste for porcelains developed in the Ming and Ch'ien Lung dynasties, and from the high hill where the celebrated kaolin was found originated a new style, beautiful, polychromatic and later decorated— yes, even to the question mark of good taste.

Not so in Japan, the potters of these islands clung to the traditions of Korea and to those of China. The islands of Japan are divided into many provinces, and every province has its furnace, every furnace has its genius, every genius has his school and so on ad infinitum. The potter's was a

noble profession and no artist, no matter how great his
reputation in other productions, hesitated to put his hands
into the soft paste and turn the humble wheel. Koyetsu,
Kenzan, Korin and the great Ritsuo were familiar with the
secrets of the kiln and the witchcraft of the wheel. Potters
had their kilns in every province and there existed a rivalry
among them that stimulated them to the greatest efforts, to
the highest perfection of their art.

No doubt Japanese potters learned much from the classic
tradition of China, but these toilers by the sea had made
their art less classic, more plastic and personal, had given
it the individual mark whether in color, form or touch, until
with a little observation you can recognize the style of a
province, the clay of a kiln, the mark of a potter or the seal
of a glazier. They did not seek the profound expressions as
the Chinese did, they were content to turn to nature for their
models. These richly endowed Japanese extended their hand
and plucked a flower from the clinging vine, and the delicate
lines and exquisite proportions were soon baking in the fiery
furnace; a seed pod gathered from the ripened bush gave
them another thought and another form; a shell picked out
of the soft sand made a potter's heart tingle with delight as
he felt it in his soft palms and then made his wheel reproduce
the pearly tones and delicate tints of the floating seaweed.
There were no fetters of any kind; nowhere in the wide
realm of art could an individual work so fancy-free as in the
islands of Japan.

The potters, like the metalworkers, were relieved of the
burden of livelihood. They were the retainers of the princes
and of the daimios, whose word of commendation was all the
reward they sought. They had no identity—with few excep-
tions—but the name of their kiln, generations of workers;
from father to son, from son to after-son, the secrets of the
kiln were passed down and new secrets added.

Untrammeled and free they were in the production of their kilns, and yet the result was so characteristic, so individual, that it is not necessary to look for stamp or for seal. You may take the object in your hands and feel the surface of the glaze, the wheel marks at the base, the turn of the lip, and you, or rather one who has collected, can nine times out of ten mention the name of the province, and often the name of the maker: Oribe, Takatori, Izumo, Seto, Kaga, etc., etc., 126, 127 or the name of Ninsei or Koyetsu, each with its own cachet of form, sign and color. Individuality was a sacred right to them. Their effort was to outdo, not to outcopy, their rivals, and they potted from the depths of their souls, seeking inspiration from the beautiful objects nature had placed easily within their reach—the lovely fir tree, the ever-varying bamboo, the garden plants and flowers; they coaxed the birds of the air to lend them the color of their plumage, and the fish of the sea to show them the glint of their pearly scales. No one who has not seen a collection of Japanese pottery can form any idea of their art.

How well I remember my first acquaintance with a tea jar! I think it was in 1884, and as usual, done in Mr. Havemeyer's grand style. My husband said to me one morning:

"A case of tea jars will arrive today. You'd better unpack them; make a selection; take out what you want and put the rest in the storeroom."

"But what is a tea jar?" I asked innocently.

Mr. Havemeyer looked at me curiously, as if amused that my question could puzzle him, and then said frankly:

"Well, I don't know much about them myself. They are little brown jars that hold tea. I guess that covers it, but they are very beautiful, so soft you want to hold them in your hand, and so lovely in color you cannot but admire them; just sober dark brown—but wait and see. I know you will enjoy them—and do as you please with them." He left

me for the excitement of Wall Street while I remained at
home and did just as I was told—and then as a perquisite for
my labors, I did a little more. Be it understood that my
labors were usually well paid for by the pleasure they gave
me, but there were occasions when my curiosity asserted
itself and then I did as I pleased with a result that always
confirmed me in my own judgment.

I opened the case and was surprised to find it contained
innumerable small boxes. I opened these small boxes and
found they contained each another box inside. Upon opening
the second box I found it had a silk bag and upon undoing
the silk bag my little "brownie" revealed himself to me.
Like a child with a toy I soon had rows of brownies about
me, while the little boxes were in a heap upon the floor
beside me. What pretty, dainty things they appeared to me!
Soft clay bearing the mark of the wheel, with here and there
a drip of dark glaze—or a metallic *soufflé* covering the entire
jar. There were cool dark browns relieved by a splash of
most lovely shaded blue or a glow of yellow, or—or—or—
indeed I cannot tell you of all their dainty forms or solemn
tones; rows of tiny jars as varied as the smile of as many
lips, or varied as the twinkle of as many eyes. Never shall I
forget that morning with my tea jars, those little jars which
were taken from their many wrappings upon some grand
occasion when princes knelt before them, when they crawled
into the sequestered room and joined in the solemn tea
ceremony.

I selected a few of the tea jars which pleased me best, I
put the rest away, and to this day many are still in that case,
and for this reason: Mr. Havemeyer began collecting tea
jars in his usual way, and dozens—yes, scores—came to my
care, most of them superlative specimens, for they were
selected with ever-increasing knowledge and taste from still
greater numbers the dealers brought to our market. After a

time, I became familiar with my tea jars. I was no longer confused by the blue splash of Satsuma, the soft greens of Banko, the wonderful white of the rare Hagi, the infinite variety of the brown Seto, the brilliant yellow of Izumo and the tender pink of Raku.

There were but few collectors in the field and it was a long time before anything approaching a classification of our heterogeneous collection was made. Professor Morse of Salem was our greatest authority upon the subject. He had gone to Japan to investigate deep-sea mysteries and had been lured by the beauty of the kilns into becoming a collector of Japanese potteries. His collection is today in the Boston museum. I can see Professor Morse as he stood many a long day before my tea jars ferreting out the enigma of province, clay, kiln and maker. Often he would say to me how much he owed to Mr. Havemeyer, as it was he who taught him the true worth and beauty of Japanese pottery. The professor was madly bent upon copying every mark and seal and he would work day in and day out at our collection, leaving cigar ashes in his trail, which he carefully deposited in the tea jars and vases and sometimes, in *flagrant délit*, a stump of a cigar found its way there and the scent would give him away. I recall a conversation between my husband and the professor one day; Mr. Havemeyer lost patience with his constant examination of seals and kiln marks.

"Professor," he said, "don't you ever get tired looking at the bottom of those jars? Why don't you look on top and admire them for what they are, and not for what they are made of? That mark that you are everlastingly sketching upon a piece of paper doesn't affect their beauty, but it prevents you from seeing it."

"But damn it, Mr. Havemeyer," said our profane professor, "don't you know I am writing a history of Japanese pottery?"

128

"Well, write away if it amuses you, I don't care a hang,
only do not get your history as upside down as you do
your jars."

On one occasion when Mr. Havemeyer and I were in
Boston looking at the professor's collection, my husband
said to me as we stood before a cabinet containing specimens
from a certain province: "Did you ever see such an arrangement? Isn't it just like Morse? He puts that magnificent
vase beside those others not fit to cook in. Who is going to
look at a lot of stuff like that just to see one fine thing? Those
who know a good thing won't do it, and those who don't
know will never learn by any such arrangement. Educate
the people to know what is beautiful and they can do all the
classifying they want to later."

By following his own instructions Mr. Havemeyer soon
outclassed the professor as a collector. His quick eye would
detect a bowl by Ninsei however hidden in the pell-mell of
an auction room. If a fine bit was up, as the hammer fell it
was usually "Henry Henry," the name he bought under, or
if he did not attend himself, being too busy in his late years,
he had a novel way of procedure. He sent someone from his
office with instructions to buy—"Then I know I'll get it,"
he said laconically.

I recall a funny anecdote my brother-in-law told about an
auction sale. Mr. Havemeyer wanted only one piece in that
sale, a pink vase with a peculiar luster. He gave his order to
Mr. Kirby, our noted "Christie" who knocked the art of
Japan into the very hearts of the American people. There
were others after this beautiful vase; Sir William had come
from Canada and had given his order to "Miss Rosie," Mr.
Kirby's first aid. It was a lively tussle according to accounts,
the tens flew by into hundreds and the hundreds almost into
thousands, when Mr. Kirby, becoming nervous at the extraordinary price for such a small vase, whispered to my

brother-in-law what to do. "Follow instructions," was the reply, "you know Mr. Havemeyer." Again the figures snapped out in the still room. Perhaps because Mr. Kirby was so staunch and renewed the attack with vigor he won the day, for Miss Rosie weakened and gave it up, and the vase was ours. There was great applause as usual, for is there anything short of a prize fight that the public likes better than a rally in an auction room?

Long years after, Sir William came to see my collection. He looked so eagerly over the shelves that I asked him if he was looking for any particular vase.

"Yes," he answered, "a small pink vase with metallic luster which I tried to buy years ago."

"Come down to my sitting room, perhaps we shall find it there," and I led the way to the cabinet that was "like a Rembrandt."

"There it is," exclaimed Sir William, "how beautiful it is! I must tell you how I lost it. It will interest you."

We sat down and he told me the following story—a real collector's story. "During one of my visits to New York I stopped in at a dealer's on my way to my lawyer's and saw this vase. I asked the price and he said sixty dollars. I refused it for you know, Mrs. Havemeyer, in those days sixty dollars would have been considered a high price for such a vase. I continued my way to my lawyer's who, you know, is a collector also. I spoke to him about the vase and he said to me: 'You left the vase?' 'Yes,' I answered. 'You have done an unwise thing,' he said. 'Mr. Havemeyer too walks down Fifth Avenue on his way to his office.'

"His words kept recurring to me all the morning, and as I ate my luncheon I determined to return at once to the dealer's and buy the vase. I went there as fast as I could and asked to see the vase. 'I am very sorry, Sir William,' said the dealer, 'the vase is sold. Mr. Havemeyer stopped on his way to his office and bought it.' Your husband was a great collector and never lost a fine object for the sake of bargaining."

Another friend told of Mr. Havemeyer's kindness: he was at an auction one afternoon and the bidding became lively between Mr. Havemeyer and a dealer. Suddenly Mr. Havemeyer called out:

"Are you bidding for M. or for yourself, Moore?"

"For M.," was the answer.

"All right," answered Mr. Havemeyer. "He can have it," and he walked out of the auction room.

Mr. Havemeyer had two great essentials for a collector. He had the flair and the nerve. Often when friends would say to him: "Mr. Havemeyer, how did you manage to collect such beautiful things—even with a fortune, how did you do it?" my husband would avoid answering, but I knew the question could have been answered with one word, "nerve."

I recall that our first acquaintance with Mr. Charles Freer was through an incident at the auction room. It was after the great Dana sale. We learned through Yamanaka that we had bought a piece of pottery on which Mr. Freer had set his heart and which he keenly regretted. Mr. Havemeyer asked the number of the piece and turning to me he said: "We don't need it, let him have it." Of course I acquiesced, and Yamanaka took the piece to Mr. Freer. About a year later I attended a sale, and I noticed that someone behind me was buying largely but for some reason did not seem to care for the pieces I bid on. Rejoicing in my good luck and not wishing to attract attention by looking around, I continued to buy until the end of the sale, and as I left the room I saw that Mr. Freer had been sitting behind me. Years afterward, when we had become old friends, he spoke of my husband's kindness and I thanked him for his.

Before I close this chapter, I will tell you my recollections about some bowls we owned. If I met a collector he would say to me: "Mrs. Havemeyer, you own the wonderful bowl with the leaf on it?" etc., etc. When in England I visited the splendid Eumorfopoulos collection the owner said to me: "Some day I hope to go to America to see your Temmoku bowl with the leaf on it. I have a fragment of one something like it. I must see yours." All the connoisseurs who came to New York would beg for an opportunity to see it. Time and time again Mr. Freer would hold it in his hands, put it down and stand off to admire it, caution me never to sell it, saying that no such bowl as that would ever come out of China again.

"How do you know, Mr. Freer?" I would ask.

"Because I have sent men to explore the place and the kilns," he answered, "and they report that nothing is left; and there is nothing like it in any collection in China."

Several very wonderful bowls came into our collection in those early days. Whether Mr. Havemeyer knew they were Chinese or not I am not sure. He probably did, but I am quite sure he would have bought them had they been Hindustani or made in the South Sea Islands. There were bowls that had to figure in every exhibition; but it is not of them I want to speak but to tell you an interesting anecdote about a Temmoku (Chinese) bowl I owned. I cannot tell when the modest little brown bowl with browner grittings as decorations first appeared in our collection. Mr. Havemeyer always bought the best but I doubt if *he* was conscious, when he bought that bowl, that one of the great art treasures of the Orient was passing into our possession. The little bowl received its meed of admiration, especially from my brother-in-law Mr. Peters, whose collection of T'ang and Sung potteries was second to none, save possibly that of Eumorfopoulos of England. I recall how Mr. Peters

132

133

would take the little Temmoku bowl in his two hands, his thumbs touching, as collectors do, and carrying it to the window, would call my attention to its many, many beauties, the form, the size, the paste, the tooling, the edge or lip, the design, the simplicity, the style and above all the color.

"Did you ever see such a bowl as that?" Mr. Peters would say time after time to me as he stood holding the treasure in his hands. "And you never will again," he would add emphatically, "for there isn't another bowl like it in the world."

"Oh! come now," I would rejoin just to excite him, for I loved to hear him extol a piece, not his own, but for the love of art, and I knew he was a great, if not the greatest authority on the subject in America. "Oh! come now," I would say, "don't go too far; it is fine I will admit, but you will see some day there will be another."

"And some day, you will find there will not be another! Mind what I am telling you. You will not see another." And he was right. We lived to see his prophecy realized and in this way it happened.

Mr. Ushikubo came to me one day and told me that a member of the Yamanaka firm was on his way to America with a very celebrated Temmoku bowl supposed to be the most splendid example in existence. The firm knew that Mr. Havemeyer owned a fine Temmoku bowl, and he honorably begged the privilege of comparing the two bowls in order to settle the question. I gave my consent and appointed the following Sunday morning for the contest or the examination. I hoped Mr. Peters could be present but he was unable to come.

"But mind you," he said as we parted, "yours is the best. There could not be two like yours and I know the other, it is larger, the paste is not so clear and warm and the wheelwork is greatly inferior."

"Have you seen it?" I asked hastily; he seemed to know all the points so well.

"Only a print of it, but you wait and see." Mr. Peters's perception of objects was phenomenal if not uncanny. I waited and I will tell you what happened. Sunday morning Mr. Ushikubo appeared, also the bearer of the bowl and several associated members of the firm. We proceeded at once to my library and, making it as light as possible, I opened the glass cabinet and took out my little Temmoku bowl. I placed it directly in the sunlight where all could see the bowl and I invited my Japanese visitor to open his case so as to compare the bowls. As I looked at the bowls, I confess I felt dizzy, queer, what you will—for Mr. Peters's words rang in my ears. If he had stood by me, he could not have compared the two objects more correctly and more justly than he had done from memory and through intuition.

My visitors looked and looked and compared one with the other, asked my permission to take my bowl in their hands. They examined by touch as well as by sight; they were long and deliberate; they ran their fingers about the rim, about the base, and ever and always would they take up my little bowl, examine it and as they put it down, they would look at each other, shake their heads and smile at me. There was no envy, rancor, or visible disappointment when the opinion was given.

"Madame, yours is the best." That settled it, the little stranger that one day had quietly come into my collection was champion, was acknowledged the best and by the highest authority. It was a memorable moment! we were all intensely interested in the subject.

I opened the case containing my collection of Temmoku 134 bowls, about twenty in all, and allowed my visitors to examine them at their leisure. I showed them the Temmoku bowl with the leaf upon it and the plum blossom modeled 135 in the paste, the bowl Mr. Eumorfopoulos says he is coming to America to see, and again I listened to speculations as to how that leaf had been produced. Everyone admits it is a marvel and each one would like to fathom the mystery of its production. Was it a real leaf baked in the paste? Was it colored under the glaze? Or was it a "happening" of the burning of the kiln? I have never shown that particular bowl without evoking conjectures as to the manner of its production.

I showed my guests my rabbits'-hair bowl with lines on it as fine as the rays of light and glazed as thick as precious stones. I showed them the raindrop bowl and the other Temmoku bowls, all I possessed, and finally when the sun had passed from one window to another toward the west and I felt a weariness coming over me, I placed my little bowl in its accustomed place, regardless of the question in the Japanese eyes. My eyes answered his and said:

"No, indeed, I couldn't think of it! No price could tempt me to sell the little stranger who came to me many years ago. He offered me all the charm of his art and never once boasted of his superlative beauty. He had all the modest simplicity of the truly great."

Later, I went to see Mr. Peters and told him all about the visit. "Mine is the best," I said, "but how did you know it? The lip, the rim, the paste, the design, everything you said about it they found true. How did you know?" I asked impatiently.

"Good gracious! you can't forget," he answered just as impatiently. "And there is only one," he added knowingly, "don't forget that!"

CHAPTER IX

Visit To Italy

1901   136

I NOW come to the most interesting period of our collecting. It took us abroad into lands little frequented by travelers in those days; into out-of-the-way places, where no
one would imagine art treasures could be found; into unknown bypaths where, high among the hills, a painter had
left a Madonna to hang unknown and unobserved in the
little chapel among the trees; into palaces which had been
adorned by works of the great masters; into the villas of
the *signori*, or into the tiny apartments of the impoverished
nobility, where just an heirloom or two remained unsold.
It brought us in contact with people of many nationalities,
with collectors and with critics, with gentile and with Jew.
It enabled us to penetrate into some vast estates where the
dealer had not been permitted to apply his rake.

It took us to Italy, and to Spain, that treasure house of
art where on the arm of a collector I would be conducted to
view some of his marvels of Flemish art, or with a grandee
enjoy his Goyas and tapestries. Dukes and duchesses were
kind enough to permit us to view their treasures. In Madrid,
we were received by the greatest swordsman in the king-   137
dom, and by that visit acquired "La Bella Librera" by Goya,   138
while we ferreted out with the help of an infanta's godson
the more important picture of Goya's, "Las Majas al Bal-   139
cón." We went to the foothills of the Italian Alps and

83

climbed the steeps at Bergamo to seek in a lonely villa a Moroni or a Veronese. We spent several days in Brescia hunting for examples of the same masters, and made many a hurried visit to Belgium or to the Netherlands, when we caught the scent of an important work of art. As the French say, Miss Cassatt had the "flair" of an old hunter, and her experience had made her as patient as Job and as wise as Solomon in art matters; Mr. Havemeyer had the true energy of a collector, while I—well, I had the time of my life. We had all the pleasure and interest we desired, and probably saw more than falls to the lot of many mortals. There were no maids nor valets, no couriers nor trunks, no "Ritzes" to bother us, just light luggage and hand-bags, an outfit that could adjust itself to any timetable, be transported by any conveyance, or be accommodated in any hotel.

On that first trip in 1901, we were a party of four: Miss Cassatt, Mr. Havemeyer and I, and then my sister—a woman of strong character, a fine traveler, and of a very good-natured disposition, all excellent qualities for such a journey. The whole trip was unexpected; it happened in this way: Mr. Havemeyer came home one afternoon in January and said to me:

"I am tired out; I want a change; I can leave my business now for three or four months, and I want to go to Europe. Will you go with me?"

"The children!" I gasped, for the suddenness of it startled me. "How can they leave school?" as the idea of leaving them behind never entered my head.

"Of course they cannot go," answered my husband positively. "They should not leave their school; your mother will come and remain with them. I really need to go, but if it makes you unhappy—"

"No, no," I answered quickly, "it can be arranged. Mother

will take good care of the children, and anyway, they will want us to go. What do you propose?"

"This," he answered, and took some steamship folders out of his pocket. "The 'Augusta Victoria' sails on January thirtieth for a southern trip, she stops at Madeira, Gibraltar, Algiers, Naples and Genoa, and then goes on to the Holy Land. I propose to go as far as Genoa, then leave the ship and ask Miss Cassatt to join us; we will travel through Italy, Sicily, and possibly through Spain if we have time. You have ten days before sailing, let me know your decision in the morning, and I will engage cabins and cable to Paris."

I had had plenty of experience in "striking camp" quickly and I knew my husband needed the trip and deserved a good holiday. Long before the ten days had passed all was arranged, and when the hour of parting came, I was ashamed to appear tearful before my children, who were very cheerful and sent us off with many good wishes and the promise of a weekly cable. The "Augusta Victoria"— she later went down in the Russian-Japanese War—was a steady ship, but I was a poor sailor in spite of my thirty voyages across the Atlantic, and I had a miserable time of it until we reached Madeira. I think it was the very first of those southern voyages that afterwards became so popular. The Hamburg American Line was trying out a new enterprise and wherever we went we received an ovation. Our band—a really fair one—played gaily as we reached a port and when we left Madeira, our first stopping place, with the band playing and flags flying, we were honored by a display of fireworks as we sailed along the coast. It was equally entertaining at Gibraltar and Algiers and I think I should have felt sorry to leave the ship, but that I knew I was to see Miss Cassatt and also, that on the last night on board I was treated to a spell of bad weather, which made me realize that the sooner I reached land the better. We

sailed into the harbor of Genoa after a miserable night, and
in the bright sunlight of early morning, from the upper
deck, I could see Miss Cassatt walking impatiently up and
down the wharf. It was not long before we were together,
talking so eagerly that Mr. Havemeyer jollied us and suggested that my sister was suffering from the cold and that
we should go to the hotel, have breakfast, and determine
our plans. Of course, we ladies said we had no definite de-
sires, but I assure you we were greatly astonished at Mr.
Havemeyer's next remark.

"If it will be agreeable to you ladies, I should like to run
141   up to Turin, and see the 'black Rameses.' "

I remember how we all laughed. Why, as we were going
to the Vatican, and with the Bargello so near, should we go,
in the bitter cold of January, to Turin to see an Egyptian
statue? But Mr. Havemeyer had a very positive way of
knowing what he wanted, and why he wanted it, and we
were soon convinced that it was the best way to begin our
tour. After breakfast, we set out to see Genoa, and the Van
Dycks, many of which afterwards found their way to the
United States. We went to several dealers for we had already determined to seek pictures in every city we visited.
I may state at once that although we had many experiences,
we never bought any of our Italian pictures through a
dealer.

We started the next day for Turin—oh, how cold it was!
Everyone told us it was the coldest winter ever known in
Italy, but we did not believe it then, nor do I believe it now,
for I have spent several other winters there in that "sunny"
land that were just as cold, and one can suffer from the cold
in Italy, I assure you. In Turin, even in the hotel, our breath
looked frosty as we huddled close to the porcelain stove in
the dining room and tried to eat with chattering teeth. My
sister was disgusted; she had come to visit the "sunny

south," and was obliged to wear her fur-lined coat continually, declaring she had to sleep in her wraps and overshoes in order to keep warm. The museum was the most desolate place I ever saw. We were its only visitors, and the guardians, hugging their meager braziers, looked sullenly at us, as if we were responsible for their misery in having to be there on such a day. When we asked our way, we received short answers but we soon found our statue in spite of their scanty instructions. There he sat, superbly grand, with an immense crown, and with but little raiment—just as he had sat centuries and centuries before upon the warm sands of Egypt. It was the work of a master; you wanted to look into the brain of the man who could have held a composition as great and intricate as that in his mind, to feel the hand of the workman who could have modeled the majestic repose of those calm features.

"Isn't it lifelike?" said Miss Cassatt softly. "You feel if you touched it, it must be soft like flesh."

"It was worth coming to see," said Mr. Havemeyer emphatically.

He studied it long and carefully, and several years later if I, alas, had not prevented him when an opportunity offered, he would have bought a statue in Egypt which is now 142 in the Kaiser Friedrich Museum in Berlin—I deserve a black mark to my record as a collector. Miss Cassatt and I often wondered at Mr. Havemeyer's capacity to absorb a work of art, and have it guide his judgment in future purchases. He was certainly as eclectic in his judgment of art as in his taste for it.

"What made you want to come and see this?" asked Miss Cassatt.

He answered: "For many years I have wanted to see Egyptian art, and it occurred to me this would be the easiest way to see some fine examples." Then turning to my sister, he added, "You are frozen, aren't you, and would like to go south?"

"Yes, I would," she answered positively. "I came for a southern trip and I hope we don't stop before we reach Naples."

But we did; we made one stop. Miss Cassatt induced us to go to Milan as it was so near, and see the Luinis, the Veroneses and the Moronis, as she was very anxious we should have a Moroni in our collection. After visiting that splendid gallery, Mr. Havemeyer also became keen to acquire good examples of their works and included Mantegna in his list, a painter whom he admired more and more as he became familiar with his works. We visited all the dealers in Milan and found one fairly good Moroni, the portrait of a man in a green coat and a dark hat. I mention this not because we bought it, for Miss Cassatt convinced Mr. Havemeyer it was not up to his standard, but because I shall refer to it later to show the subtle practices of some Italian dealers. (I must not take too much time telling you about our trip.) After Milan, we sped rapidly southward, stopping to thaw out my sister in the sunny gardens of a comfortable hotel in Naples, while with Miss Cassatt we visited the museum—we were greatly disappointed that pending alterations rendered it impossible to see the pictures.

But the museum recalls an experience in my life, and I should like to say something of early impressions. I have often been asked if I thought it did any good to send young students abroad either on finishing school or during vacation, to visit the galleries in order to get an idea of art. This was the fashion in my day, so that question I always answered:

"Yes, let them see the best pictures at the earliest possible age. Youthful impressions are very vivid, and if the young students are intelligent it may have an important influence upon their lives and will give them a standard to help their judgment." I recall that I took my children at an early age to see the magnificent Shakespearian productions of Henry Irving and Ellen Terry—so young were they that it was   143 advisable to give them a nap in the afternoon in order that the little tots could remain awake—with the result that ever afterwards a Shakespearian play was their delight, and their standard in judging other productions.

To relate my own experience, I was just fourteen when I first visited the Naples gallery, and I can still recall the impression it made upon me. I was almost fifty years of age when Mr. Havemeyer brought me a photograph of a beautiful nude and said we could buy it. I looked at it carefully   144 and can still remember the effect it made upon me. I was conscious I had seen it, and I felt almost dizzy in my effort to place it.

"Where is it?" I asked.

"In Florence, in a private gallery," answered Mr. Havemeyer.

"No," I answered; "it is in Naples, and it is Titian's 'Danae' "; for in a flash my memory brightened like a developed film and I again saw the picture hanging in the gallery just as I had seen it when I was fourteen years of age.

"Nonsense," said Mr. Havemeyer. "It is in Florence; I have H.'s letter."   145

"Nevertheless, it is Titian's 'Danae,' and *is* in Naples. You go to Braun's, and ask for the photographs of the Naples gallery and see if I am not right."

He did so, and the next afternoon came home with the photograph, and said he could scarcely believe I could have remembered it so long and have placed it so quickly, when I had seen it only once and at such an early age.

"It made a great impression upon me," I answered.

The picture which was offered to Mr. Havemeyer was a copy of the period of Titian's "Danae," and a beautiful picture. I saw it later in Florence. You may imagine that I was disappointed I could not see it in Naples when we visited the museum that wintry morning.

We hastened on to Sicily. Out of consideration for Miss Cassatt, who also was not fond of rough seas, and for me, we took the train to Reggio and crossed the Straits to Messina—alas, after the great earthquake in 1908 there was little left of either Messina or Reggio—and we soon found ourselves in beautiful Taormina. Of all the colonies in Sicily I believe the Greeks must have loved Taormina best, and here they built their loveliest theater. As we entered it, Miss Cassatt drew back astonished, and stretching her hand towards the distant horizon, said:

"Didn't they know how to build? What a background for a play!"

"Yes," said Mr. Havemeyer, looking at the old monastery that was now the hotel, "I should think with this magnificent ruin close by those old monks could have done better."

"You should read Diderot," answered Miss Cassatt; "he also thought we might still have art as fine as Greek art if it had not been for Christianity with its draped angels and its martyred saints."

From Taormina we went to Syracuse, which was rather depressing. The dirty activity of a seaport town was not suggestive of Grecian splendor, of galleys and fêtes. It was difficult to imagine the harbor full of magnificent ships with red marble baths waiting for the Tyrant at his pleasure. There was too much of the Tyrant in Syracuse! He was associated with the temples, he was in the theaters, you had to listen to his "ear," etc., etc. Even today, he seems to dominate the place to the exclusion of the more interesting Archimedes and the pretty Arethusa, which nymph, in whom I was interested on account of her beautiful coins that Mr. Havemeyer had given me, I thought lived in a grotto that was most unattractive—it was dark, damp, green and shiny, totally unfit for the delicate creature who caught up her lovely tresses in a net and allowed three sparkling fish to play in her golden hair. We were content to move on and take that splendid railroad journey between the mountain heights to Girgenti, through the romantic gorge where, according to accredited mythology, the drama of the fair Proserpine, Ceres's daughter whom the wicked Pluto whisked off to the nether regions, was enacted.

At Girgenti another thrill awaited us: even in the broad daylight we were not allowed to go beyond the protecting walls of the hotel on account of brigands. We were obliged to have an escort to go see those marvelous temples on the borders of the sea. The sun shone in dazzling brightness on the white marble columns and the perfect proportions were outlined against a cloudless blue sky.

"Do you think there could be anything finer in Greece?" queried Miss Cassatt.

"Some day, let us go and see," answered Mr. Havemeyer, and we did; but for the moment, Girgenti was Greece for us, particularly in the evening when after dinner we perched ourselves safely in our balconies, where no bandit could approach, and looked across at the far-stretching Mediterranean, and admired the great temple of Concordia standing in its majesty in the solemn white moonlight. 146

"And a thousand years shall be as a single day," I repeated as we gazed at those ancient splendors of long ago.

We left "ancient Greece" and sped to Palermo; in almost the twinkling of an eye we were again living in the time of the great Roger of Sicily and his fair Juliana. Miss Cassatt

and I entertained our companions with Lenormant's description of that extraordinary man and his brilliant court.
147 We knew the three volumes of *La Grande Grèce* almost by heart.

"It is the last word on travels, and ought to be translated into every language," said Miss Cassatt. "Did you know it inspired George Gissing's *By the Ionian Sea!*"

We visited the Palatine Chapel, perhaps the finest bit of mosaicwork in Europe, unless it be the Mosque in Constantinople, and certainly it is the most perfect. I cannot describe it to you, dear children; go and see it for yourselves. While we were in the chapel we saw old Mr. Agnew, the uncle of the present members of that celebrated house in London. Mr. Havemeyer looked him full in the eye, but did not bow. I saw him, Mr. Agnew, flush up and quickly
148 turn away. Mr. Havemeyer had bought only one picture from him, but that was just one too many. They angled for many years, with offers of exchanges or to get us into the net again, but I am happy to say without success.

Miss Cassatt and I formed a great desire to travel by automobile through the places Lenormant describes in *La Grande Grèce*, but a year or two later, when I received a visit from Marion Crawford, who had lived many years in southern Italy, I asked him if it would be possible to motor through Calabria. He told me it would be absolutely impossible, as the bridges would be unsafe for an automobile. He was delightfully interesting about Sicily, however, and
149 had just written *The Rulers of the South*, which he told me he considered his best work.

We left Palermo on a stormy day and when we reached Messina the wind was blowing a gale, the waves were running high and the ship was dancing like a cockleshell upon the angry waters. Miss Cassatt and I huddled together, making a poor attempt to conceal our fear from my sister and Mr. Havemeyer, both of whom were excellent sailors, and were making fun of us.

Mr. Havemeyer approached us and said: "You don't care much for this, do you?"

Miss Cassatt smiled faintly, but I answered stoutly: "Indeed we don't, and I hope we don't cross tonight."

"But look at the hotel; would you like to pass the night there?" asked my husband.

"Anywhere," I answered, "but on that boat."

The next moment, to our great relief, word was called out that the ship would not sail, and joyfully we hurried to the hotel and found they had already anticipated our arrival. Our dinner smelled savory enough and they cooked it right in the court of the hotel. We could see the chef turning the chickens before a bright fire, and all looked cheerful and warm. The hotel was not bad, even for those days, and we passed a comfortable night and embarked early the next morning for Reggio, where we had to pass the day as there was only the night train for Naples. Mr. Havemeyer and my sister made themselves comfortable before a bright fire, while Miss Cassatt, who was always hunting for old glass or old rings, and I started out in quest of antiquities. After visiting all the shops in the principal street, we found just two interesting objects—a gold coin which Mr. Havemeyer was too drowsy to go and see, and a communion cup, one of the most beautiful specimens of early renaissance silver we had ever seen.

Miss Cassatt pressed my hand and said under her breath: "Isn't it beautiful? How much do you suppose they want for it?"

I immediately asked the price.

"Ninety francs," answered the man, and he appeared very anxious to sell the cup.

We told him we would return later and went directly to

the hotel to get the money from Mr. Havemeyer. I shall not forget how he and my sister laughed when we said we were negotiating for a communion cup.

"What in heaven's name will you do with it?" he asked.

"I don't know, but it is beautiful and delicate in design and wonderfully preserved."

"Well," said my sister, "I think you both are crazy enough about rings, but a communion cup! I must say I think *that* the limit of a collector's folly."

Nevertheless, Mr. Havemeyer gave us the money, but we never got that communion cup. When we returned to the shop, the owner had finished luncheon and was very much the worse for the wine he had taken. He would have sold it to us, probably to get more wine or to gamble, but his wife appeared furious at her husband for offering it to us at such a price, telling us it came from an old Sicilian church and was worth its weight in gold. Hot words passed between husband and wife with every indication they would become hotter, so Miss Cassatt and I left the shop—and the communion cup, of which we were never to hear the end.

We walked down to the shore where, in the glow of an early sunset, with the great wind clouds scuttling by, we watched the huge waves beating against the rocky shore and looked across the Straits at Mount Etna which was smoking ominously—it was an imposing sight. The chill of the afternoon made us shiver. We took each other's arm in order to brace ourselves against the sudden gusts of wind that swept by us; we watched a few ships tossing outside the harbor, and a certain terror crept over us as we realized what nature had done in a fiery mood.

"It's terrible," said Miss Cassatt. "Think what may happen at any minute and yet the people live here apparently unconcerned about the awful possibilities. Do you remember Lenormant's description of the Calabrian earthquake in

1663? What a description that was! The best I ever read. It seems those who lived through it never smiled again. Do you recall the poor man who was caught among the falling timbers of his house, and they robbed him, while still alive, of the silver buckles off his shoes as his feet stuck out between the beams; or the poor woman who was rescued after five days, still holding her dead baby upon her knees, and when asked how she managed to survive answered, 'I just waited.' "

"Let us go back to the hotel," I said. "This is uncanny; I am thankful I do not live here, I should not have a peaceful moment."

Not many years later it came, that awful earthquake of 1908, almost wiping out Messina and Reggio, and Miss Cassatt and I recalled that afternoon, when we stood at the water's edge and almost prophesied the catastrophe that would destroy both cities in a moment's time.

Possessed of a melancholy that made our voices low, we slowly retraced our steps to the hotel, and were soon en route for Rome. Let him who takes the railroad to escape the miseries of the sea beware! The rocks and the tide are not the only Scylla and Charybdis of Calabria, and in the choice of two evils, let him take care lest, like a pessimist, he choose them both. Miss Cassatt and I were both carsick and seasick, wretchedly miserable, capable of naught but a sense of suffering, until morning brought hope into our hearts—hope that Naples and a change to better cars would give us relief and bring us soon to Rome. I overheard my sister and my husband saying something in a low tone about the advantages of traveling by sea; I know they were disgusted, but I felt that my side of the argument was too weak just then to admit of discussion, and it required all my strength to aid Miss Cassatt and to collect my own hairpins for the speedy transfer to the Roman train.

What a delight it was after such a journey to find ourselves in a comfortable hotel salon with an interesting piazza
beyond, the dome of Saint Peter's in sight, the consciousness
of the Holy City, and hot coffee and rolls steaming upon the
breakfast table. We forgot our journey and our guidebooks,
and not even a reference to anything Roman, from the Punic
Wars to the seven hills, was made during that delightful
repast. If any voice of our social quadrangle had suggested
a plan, it would have been voted down by the three remaining corners before utterance had reached our thoughts. Our
hearts beat in thankful unison that this was not our first visit
to Rome. If we did not care to know how many bricks were
used in the original Baths of Caracalla, we could omit the
addition, as we could the sight of the catacombs and Saint
Clement's, and even pass the Forum without feeling obliged
to crawl upon hands and knees under the big stone which a
blinding flashlight showed us covered the grave of Romulus
and his little brother.

The delicious coffee, the pleasant fire, and general sense
of welfare soon restored us to normal. The afternoon was
still bright when my sister announced that, providing a
comfortable carriage could be found, she would watch the
sunset from the Pincio. Mr. Havemeyer decided upon a
brisk walk, while Miss Cassatt and I, with an unforgotten
grudge against the previous night, remained together as
companions in misery should do.

150   "They want to discuss the Boer War," said my sister to
Mr. Havemeyer. "They had to stop last night, just as they
began about 'the American mule'—you know, it means two
hours at least. They will not miss us."

However, Miss Cassatt and I felt too peaceful for war,
but we did dicuss art and decided we must see Veronese's
"Europa" at the Capitol, a picture whose beauty so capti-
151   vated Mr. Havemeyer that it resulted in our placing four

examples of the master in our gallery. Also, we determined to see all the Domenichinos in Rome, and even to go to Bologna and see still more of them if possible.

"Degas admires Domenichino so much and wonders he is so little known," said Miss Cassatt. "It upsets me terribly to see all this art," she continued. "It will be months before I can settle down to work again"—a paraphrase of the familiar words among the painters of France: *"J'ai perdu chemin."*

Apart from our many visits to the galleries, we did little but amuse ourselves in Rome. The great object of interest of course was Velazquez's "Portrait of Pope Doria." It was a disappointment. It is so badly hung, in a small alcove like a tiny chapel, where it is impossible to get the proper distance from which to view the picture. The faded green stuff upon the walls hurts it, and for some reason it appears oily and greasy. We were prepared for a sensation upon beholding this celebrated masterpiece of the great Spanish painter. The sensation did not come, in truth we preferred the portrait of his Negro slave, which we had seen in London and which Velazquez did to get his hand in before undertaking the portrait of the Pope.

"Don't let Mr. Havemeyer regret it," said Miss Cassatt to me. "It does not impress me at all as it did; I wonder why!"

I hoped that my husband would not be disappointed that this picture, which he longed to possess, was beyond his reach. Should we ever own Greco's "Cardinal"—the portrait said to have inspired this one? Would we have cared to acquire Velazquez's "Doria"?—I believe not.

Of course, while in Rome we could not neglect the dealers; not that we expected to find anything but it was interesting, and as our quest was pictures, who could tell but that we might stumble upon some odd stone, which in

turning up might reveal a work of art. Entering a large
establishment in Rome, we attracted, by our renewed requests for something better and better, the attention of the
padrone himself, and Miss Cassatt who was our spokesman
tried to convey to his mind what we were seeking. It was
impossible to misunderstand her and the *padrone* finally became interested.

"Ah, I understand what you want," he said. "Nothing
here would do for Mr. Havemeyer. I know his collection
and I also know of one picture that he should have, just one!
It is very fine—a Moroni, but it is not here. It is in a collection at some distance. If you will give me two days, I will
send for it."

When we returned at the end of two days, there was an
air of solemn mystery about the place. We were received
and conducted through room after room and attendants
whispered mysteriously as they passed us on. At last, we
reached the inner sanctuary where the veiled easel stood
that held the masterpiece. The *padrone* rubbed his hands
as he greeted us, and would have dilated longer upon the
merits of his picture had not Mr. Havemeyer's impatient
gesture decided him to throw back the curtain, in order to
show us his wonder and to enjoy our astonishment. He was
not disappointed. We were astonished. The figure, the
green jacket, the jaunty hat, were all familiar. My husband
looked bellicose, and I feared what might happen. In appeal I pressed Miss Cassatt's hand, who without pity for
that clever "Ananias" said distinctly:

"No, it will not do. We refused it several weeks ago in
Milan."

The dealer was pathetic in his discomfiture but I doubt
if he ever realized what we thought of him or of Italian
dealers as a class. We hurried Mr. Havemeyer from the
place.

We stopped in Bologna long enough to see the later painters of her school, and devoted most all our time to the wonderful Domenichinos. Miss Cassatt's remarks inspired us with her own and some of Degas's admiration for the great master, and although galleries are not improved by the dullness of a rainy day, we pigeonholed some valuable impressions in our memories before we had to take the train for Ravenna.

My sister and I had not visited Ravenna since the days of the bandits, when we were young girls and together drove there in a tumbling, rumbling sort of conveyance which recalled the last days of Marie Antoinette or Mme Roland, protected by guardians, two on each side, who kept looking anxiously about until relieved of their responsibility by passing us on to the next relay, who in their turn sullenly took their places. Heaven alone knows why we undertook to visit Ravenna; our only excuse was our youth and the enthusiasm of a first visit to Italy, an enthusiasm which made us determined to see Dante's tomb, notwithstanding that we scarcely knew whether he was a Guelph or a Ghibelline, or had written more than the celebrated and much quoted doorplate to the Inferno. We did see the lonely grave and the bandits did not get us. I think we were always proud that we had seen something of Byzantine art.

Alas, Ravenna today is a vast mosaic workshop. Everywhere we were confronted with scaffoldings, and it was necessary to watch our feet and feel our way; our ears were filled with the dull thud of the hammer and our eyes and nostrils were full of dust. The visible parts of the Baptistry and the tomb of Galla Placidia were ablaze with color and the new black marble eyes of the many figures gazed vengefully down upon us. They are doing their best to restore the mosaics, but Ravenna will always remain but a beautiful fragment, a reminiscence of Byzantine art. We were very glad that we had seen it however, for it was here that Mr. Louis Tiffany found his inspiration for our white mosaic hall and the ten pillars at the entrance of our gallery, which many have thought as fine as anything in Ravenna.

After a visit to San Vitale and a drive to the Mausoleum of Theodoric in the gray twilight which left the landscape sad and shadowless, we took the train for Venice, mounting into something which, when it rattled off, left you in doubt whether you were in a train or in a wheelbarrow. But what did it matter! We had some bologna sandwiches bought under the shadow of the leaning towers, and they proved to be excellent. The sights of Ravenna had pleased Miss Cassatt, who was in fine form. We talked of the iconoclasts and of Roger of Sicily and his Juliana, of the Saracens and their art. We argued about art and its origin, about the origin of all art. Was it along the sandy desert of Egypt, among the Babylonian hills, by the borders of the Yangtze, or in the mountains of Persia that we could trace its source? What human bee carried the fructifying pollen from country to country? How responsible were the caravans for the finding of the same design in lands so widely separated? Did these caravans carry the Chinese fret that we find on the hand mirrors into Greece, and the grapevine back again into China? Did Persia first find the brilliant field flower and bake its splendid colors upon her cups and plates? Who first discovered the burning gold and ruby red of the iridescent glaze, the Greeks in Fosta, or the Persians among their hills? Shall it be proven that Homer sang of real mortals and shall the shield of Achilles be found in the palaces of Crete?

Those bologna sandwiches were very stimulating. We did not forget the Tartars and even Kubla Khan, with their wonderful kumiss mares who were both transport and commissariat all in one. Would Kubla Khan ever have conquered China if he had not been able to move his men with such rapidity? Then why, we questioned, did all these sources of art later flow into the great estuary of Constantinople, in order that she, in her turn, should open her gates and let the flood flow westward into Europe, carrying the Byzantine into Italy and into Sicily, and the Gothic into western Europe, the Saracenic into Spain? Often have I discussed the subject since, but never without a pleasant thought of that evening when we nibbled the specialties of Bologna and were jounced and jigged in the bitter cold as we went towards Venice. It was late when we arrived and we almost perished with cold on the canals. We were glad enough to reach the Danieli, and so eager for the warmth of a hotel and a good bed that I, for once, forgot to grumble about our rooms; a fact not overlooked by my husband, who evinced his appreciation of my thoughtfulness by a compliment to me at breakfast the following morning.

Alas! It was not our first visit to entrancing Venice. We could not have that unique pleasure; we could not breathe more deeply, nor quicken our souls into tingling more delightfully; we had no desire to feed the birds of St. Mark's, nor tip the beggars on the piazza. Neither the lagoons nor the bridges actually thrilled us. We had not the desire of our artist friend to lie on the steps of the Ponte Vecchio, and inhale the sunshine. The ambitions of old Marco Polo did not stir our souls. We did not want to go abroad; if he wished to go sightseeing, why let him; he was not appreciated in Venice, and even in his day they did not care to have him tell them of his travels, and they let him knock in vain when he returned. No! on a bright Sunday morning—*dolce far niente* for us. My sister and Miss Cassatt arose late and wanted little besides hot coffee, a newspaper, and afterwards to be let alone. They maintained that as it was Sunday they were entitled to a day of rest, and there was noth-

ing for me to do but make the best of the situation. I wrote
to my children, and as the morning dragged along, looked
out of the window at the red noses of the children trying to
keep warm in the sunny corners of the cold piazza.

When *déjeuner* was announced, I noticed a restlessness
about Mr. Havemeyer. By the time we had had our coffee,
an idea occurred to me which I communicated to my husband. He disappeared for a time and then returned to announce that "we," he and I, intended to do Venice on foot,
to walk in every possible street, to cross every bridge on
every possible canal. It was fun to see the astonishment of
our comrades. Their idea of happiness was more warmth,
more wraps, to say nothing of more rest, and I doubt if
they believed we were serious, until they saw us starting
forth with an old white-haired guide. When Mr. Havemeyer had asked for a cicerone, the proprietor had sent for
this man to show us the way, because many years ago, he
said, he had done the same service for Ruskin. Although he
stooped and every now and then gave a little hacking cough,
he was alert to all the opportunities the occasion offered,
and on that crisp Sunday afternoon we saw Venice as we
had never seen it in all our previous visits. The fascination
of its hithers and thithers, the queerness of its nooks and
corners, the dodging of its canals, the spanning of its
bridges and the circling of its ins and outs made our feet
light and our hearts merry. We peeped through windows,
gazed upon curious towers, or admired iron grilles as we
passed along, recognizing, either through our own perceptions or at the suggestion of Ruskin's "ex-official guide,"
old bits of architecture, old courts of buildings, that had
been used in romance or written of in short stories. Of
course we ended our journey in the rio di Santa Caterina, in
order to have a look at the lovely saint above the altar.
Long, long we looked, and greatly did we enjoy Veronese's

admirable picture, little dreaming that in the near future, we should own a fine example of that master's work. It was here our poor old guide had a coughing spell, and I thought he should walk no longer, so we took a gondola and did it all over again by water, reaching the hotel long after dark, to find the other two angles of our *partie carrée* hugging a fire and quite as content with their afternoon as we were with ours.

It took several days more to see our favorite sights again, for apart from other great pictures, we had to have a long look at Carpaccio's "Ladies feeding their dogs, while ₁₅₄ bleaching their hair in crownless hats, upon the roof of a Venetian villa"—a picture Ruskin calls "the greatest picture in the world." Please refer to Ruskin!

Another long day for San Marco, a pagan temple for a Christian god, another for the Palazzo Ducale, for in spite of the many on the Grand Canal, there is only *one* Palazzo Ducale. How beautiful its staircase—no wonder Mr. Tiffany copied it for our hall and united it there, as in Venice, _{155, 156} with Byzantine art by wonderful mosaics.

Then we had to go to the Campo SS. Giovanni e Paolo, by the church, to take a still longer look at the grandest of all equestrian statues, Colleoni, the greatest general of them all. I wondered if Verrocchio and Colleoni had equal parts in that great achievement. And Verrocchio! Was the "deed outdone in the doing"? Did he absorb of the joy he gives, I wonder? How could he have measured that dignity so high, placed so much distinction in the air, beat high courage into bronze! No need for me to ask. There it stands and must speak for itself. Art has no need to hawk her qualities to the gaping crowd! Better for her to be still, unless some echoing heart catches and repeats her soft, low message of beauty and of inspiration. Yes, it was a long look we gave to the helmeted hero of the piazza. I have thrills of pleasure

157   when I think that his distinction is, in part, reflected in our
       gallery, for a Veronese portrait we bought shortly after-
       ward was a relative of the great general—like him a Col-
       leoni of Bergamo. Those valiant fighters were the heads of
       great families, grand *signori* in Italy in Verrocchio's day.

         Want of time alone forced us to leave Venice. We reluc-
       tantly entered a bobbing transport, piled high with bags
       and boxes, and again braved the discomforts of a cold rail-
       way journey. Ferrara had little to interest us, and even our
       short stay there was uncomfortable, as the *albergo* where
       we had to stop evidently deemed it a duty to remain in the
       same century and in the same condition of dilapidation as
       the great brick *castello*. However much we may admire
       renaissance art, we do not care for bedrooms of that period,
       or to eat a tart in ruins, or eggs as old and as musty as the
       story of Francesca. It was with a sigh of relief that we made
       an early start for Mantua. There we found an entirely dif-
       ferent atmosphere, an air of comfortable luxury pervaded
       the place.

158   We had but to close our eyes to conjure up a picture of
       the past; to see the indolent, sumptuous Isabella, a pearl
       net holding the waving auburn hair, the folds of velvet con-
       cealing the dreaded stoutness; cultivated in mind, brilliant
       in conversation, passionately fond of art, living her golden
       hour in all the luxury at her command. We could see her
       surrounded by her court, amusing herself with her dwarfs,
       listening to the music of her lutes or to the verses of her
       poets. True daughter of Italy! Mantua was her home and
       Italian courtiers were gay companions. Let "Sister Bea-
       trice" set forth in gold brocade and crimson cloak to meet
       the King of France! She craved no pageant that the streets
       of Mantua could not offer her; no festivities that could not
       be held in the halls of her great *palazzo*. She preferred the
       little *camerino*, "Paradise" as it was called, with its wonder-

ful carvings, its incomparable proportions and the delicate designs of its decorations. A bijou of renaissance art was that little *camerino*. Here she could listen at her ease to Italy's poets, lending her keen intellect to help the turning of a rhyme, or her fine ear for the phrasing of a melody— pleasure-loving, art-loving, life-loving Isabella. When satiety dulled the perceptions, or fatigue made the velvets weigh heavily on her limbs, she could wave aside the lute players and the poets and let a handmaiden throw open the doors, and go down the tiny staircase to seek diversion from the dwarfs below. Was it a whim that made her build their apartments as if for dolls—to make them comfortable and happy so that they would be able to amuse their beloved Duchess? A radiant star was in the heavens when this easy-going d'Este was born. All must be happy about her, luxury must surround her, sweet sounds must beguile her, and art —great art—must ever meet her eye. Here she lived, this true daughter of the Renaissance.

Alas, when we opened our eyes again, we saw no Isabella; no ladies, no lutes, no dwarfs, only empty halls, gray walls, a dreary loggia, a dark lake and lonely piazza—what a pity that only the mind of a traveler can see visions. We hate reality when she rudely shakes us out of our trance and bids us look about. In Mantua reality woke us rudely, and we went to the Palazzo del Té to see Giulio Romano's "Horse Show," a fine exhibition of life-sized quadrupeds in every conceivable attitude, a veritable tour de force of foreshortening; one could almost smell the sawdust and the hay. Mantua was in no way responsible for any of our works of art. Isabella's treasures had long since been dispersed, so we made our way to Padua.

If you repeat the words "Padua on the Bacchiglione," you will fancy you hear the ripples on that tortuous stream that winds in and out its many streets, just as when you speak up sharply the word *bersaglieri* you can fancy you hear the quick tramp of feet and see the tossing side-feathers of Italy's sturdy soldiers.

For us, the interest of the place centered in the church of Saint Anthony and in Donatello. We lost no time in reaching the Piazza del Santo. Again we admired a tribute to a great general—the statue rises high in front of the church, he sits firmly upon his bronze horse. He is Gattamelata, the proud warrior of a proud republic, who looks triumphantly over Padua. Donatello had been hired from Florence to do the statue, to place a victor over the fair city of Padua. One naturally thinks of the equestrian statue of Colleoni in Venice, but we need not compare the two Florentines, Donatello and Verrocchio! Verrocchio and Donatello, that's all. Why compare them any more than their Colleonis and their Gattamelatas; each did his work and each did it well—what more!

Within the church there was much to interest us and in a remote way to affect our collecting. Mr. Havemeyer was much impressed by Donatello, by his marble screen with its free, vital, forceful figures; by Donatello, the great interpreter of moods in action; and we eventually owned an example of his work. As we drove away, Miss Cassatt made a remark which impressed me.

"Donatello," she said, "in his statues, took all he could absorb of classic art, and besides put into them the note of the Renaissance. Be it as they say, that all original European art ends with the Gothic, that the Renaissance is only an imitation of the classic, still it had its masters, and into that era of the Renaissance they pressed a very living personal evidence."

We crossed and recrossed the Bacchiglione many times, always looking up and down to admire its beautiful curves, before we reached the station and we left the city, dull and

monotonous as it appeared, with regret. Time pressed and
we had to reach Florence, the Mecca of our wanderings.

Cold, snow, frost, ice and wind!—that was the Florence
we found in 1901. The cold was everywhere. It covered the
plain, it mounted the hills, it grayed the Arno, it entered
the hotels, it emptied the churches, it impudently sought
our beds, it crept into the very marrow of our bones. We
fussed and fumed and sent a malediction after the winds
that swept and moaned about San Miniato. We crossly
clung together as the wintry blast almost swept us from the
Ponte Vecchio. We looked at the huge square walls of the
Bargello, without the courage to enter. The Palazzo Vecchio made us shudder and even the pictures could not lure us
within the cold galleries of the Uffizi. We felt a peevish disappointment that sunny Italy should prove so cold that
wintry March. We huddled around the porcelain *stufa*, the
scanty brazier of the hotel, and only when time pressed did
we collectively find will power enough to make us face those
March winds. However, there was a star rising on that
bleak horizon that we little dreamed of and it was to point
the way to many a work of art which eventually was added
to our collection.

One afternoon Miss Cassatt and my husband agreed to
go to a large dealer's, and at dinner that evening we learned
the circumstances which had made their visit interesting. I
listened eagerly to their tidbits of conversation.

"How ill he looked," said Mr. Havemeyer, "and alto-
gether disgusted with his job. When he saw you he appeared embarrassed, as if he feared you would not care to
recognize him."

"I knew him so many years ago," answered Miss Cassatt,
"but his face puzzled me at first. He was an artist then, doing small things, *putti*, etc., and seemed rather successful.

He married an Italian woman about the time I left Italy, and I never saw him again until today. He did indeed look ill and very poor, didn't he?"

Then there was an explanation. At the dealer's Miss Cassatt had met an old acquaintance who had evidently been forced to give up art and take a position as salesman at the dealer's.

Suddenly Mr. Havemeyer said as if voicing a reflection: "If he has lived so long in Florence, he should know something about art, and also where good things might be found."

Miss Cassatt gave Mr. Havemeyer a penetrating glance, for she caught his meaning at once.

"We can ask him when he calls this evening," she answered quietly.

I know Mr. Havemeyer and Miss Cassatt; they had caught a new scent and I was delighted when Mr. H. and his wife were announced. I saw a man past middle age, discouraged and weary, a wife much younger, courageous and merry—two human beings, one almost dead, the other very much alive. For the first time we met the man and the woman—for she did more than her share—who were to secure for us some of the finest pictures we ever owned. They were very ready to talk, and Miss Cassatt adroitly found out the circumstances of their life. They had lived all these years in Italy; he had traveled much, and was perfectly *au courant* in art matters and not only knew all the galleries, both public and private, but also was familiar with every inch of ground where a work of art could be found. The vivacious little wife could turn her hand to anything, was *persona grata* with the nobility of Florence, or wherever she could make herself useful to the *signori*. When many others would fail, she could wedge an opening with her twinkle and her smile. They lived in a miserable cupola, a sort of afterthought on the roof of a great high building, "suicide house" it was called, she told me cheerfully, on account of its height and because it stood upon the edge of the Arno. From time to time during our long friendship, I had glimpses into a brave little heart and learned to know of her struggles and of the good fight she had made: how useful to the Italian poor were the government-controlled *monte di pietà*, and how, on one occasion, her gold wedding ring had to be used to drive away the wolf who was howling at the door. I admired the valiant little black-eyed woman, who said naïvely:

"I could not let *il mio Arturo* starve."

It was not difficult for Mr. Havemeyer to examine and cross-examine them, and Miss Cassatt expressed her approval as he proceeded. By the pleasant glow of our fire the preliminaries were arranged. In due course of time, he was to give up his present position and to work for us alone, while his wife, who could express herself very well with the use of an occasional Italian word, told us she could take us to see something at once. She knew very well *palazzi* where pictures hung, which, if they could be allowed to depart in silence, would be given Godspeed as they left for the western world, while the ducats would be eagerly taken to fill the empty pockets and pay the pressing debts. Not later than the next day did La Signora appear to tell us that she would, with *molto piacere*, take us to see a collection and the pictures were all for sale.

A collection—"all the pictures were for sale"—you must remember this was many, many years ago. In the western world buyers were few and marketable pictures still fewer. Rembrandts could be counted on the fingers of one hand. So far as I know, great Italian pictures by even fewer digits still, and examples of Spanish art by almost none at all. We felt the keenest interest as we sallied forth into the bitter gray of that cold afternoon. I should blush to write what were my hopes, for only then did I begin my novitiate of picture hunting; visions of great finds haunted my thoughts and I was considering a choice of which masters I should select. When the *vettura* drew up before a shabby building, too far from Florence to be a *palazzo* and not far enough to be a villa, we followed La Signora and soon found ourselves in a large dark room, which, when some wooden shutters were thrown open, we found contained many pictures, most of them as dark as the room.

"I don't believe they could give them away," said my husband in disgust, turning to leave, but I caught his arm and, glancing at La Signora, I asked my husband just to make believe for a few minutes.

At an exclamation from Miss Cassatt, we turned around to see what she had found. From its hinges upon the wall she had swung a huge frame directly across the window and was looking at a portrait. As we gathered about her, La Signora said:

"That is by Paolo Veronese; it is a portrait of his wife."

We saw a middle-aged, portly woman, her yellow hair drawn back after the fashion of Veronese's time, and dressed in lilac and silver brocade; she sat holding her handkerchief in one hand and her dog in the other.

"See here," said Miss Cassatt. "This is very fine"; and she pushed the frame towards us a little to give us a better view.

My sister, who thought beauty essential in a portrait, did not like it and made fun of the full chest and tightly drawn bodice, while my husband seemed inclined to share her views; nevertheless, Miss Cassatt held firmly to her opinion and studied the picture carefully; she knew a work of art demanded truth as well as beauty. I fear we did not take Veronese seriously that afternoon, but the next morning at breakfast, Miss Cassatt began in her earnest manner:

"I've been thinking of that Veronese all night. My! my! my! the way that brocade is painted and the lace with the gold stars over the chest! Do you know, it is magnificent. The Venetians *were* full-busted, and *did* wear tight bodices. In all that rubbish I don't believe they know what a picture it is. If you don't like it, Mr. Havemeyer," she added, "I will take it myself, and sell something to pay for it when I return to Paris. What do you suppose they will take for it, ten thousand lire do you think?" Then turning to me, she added, "Let us go to the gallery at once and see if we can find any better portrait by Veronese, or any other painter there."

We spent a wonderful morning at the Uffizi. Miss Cassatt talked art to me as I have rarely heard her. She spoke of Veronese, of his composition, of his style, of his brilliant color and luminous shadows; she compared him favorably to Titian; she called him the father of modern art, and advised me to go to Treviso, probably in the Villa Manfrini, and see there another portrait of his wife, where he has painted her at the end of a gallery looking through a doorway. Then Miss Cassatt tried to find a Bronzino she could compare to ours.

"See how hard, how conventional they all are," she said.

"No, my dear, if Bronzino did your portrait he was a far greater painter than when he painted those."

Later Mr. Havemeyer joined us and at once we had to go and admire Botticelli. Mr. Havemeyer had seen the "Birth of Venus" for the first time.

"What a picture," he said emphatically. "It is worth the whole collection."

We smiled, for we very well knew what he meant. For the moment, it *was* the whole collection for him. He could see nothing else until he had absorbed it. He had to take it from the walls and press it close to his heart to stamp it upon his memory, in fact make it his own. It was pleasant to listen to him as he spoke his enthusiasm, to see his soul revealed in his eyes. It was singular that a man without technical knowledge could be so convincing in his appreciations, but he had an exceptionally keen and sensitive perception of truth and beauty. Many years after, in speaking of his love of art, Miss Cassatt said to me:

"He learned with leaps and bounds; there will never be another collector like him."

Mr. H. and La Signora took us again to see the "robust" Veronese, cautioning us as we entered to look at it all we pleased, but not to admire the picture openly. This time we saw it with other eyes, and Mr. Havemeyer listened with respect, if not with conviction, when Miss Cassatt said it ought to be in our gallery. With a sigh that it could not be his admired and coveted Botticelli, Mr. Havemeyer began negotiations. If he could not have Botticelli's "Birth of Venus," why not consider a Veronese! Mr. H. was told to ask the price, and when he did so, his answer produced much amusement for the laugh was at Miss Cassatt's expense. No, it was not to be had for ten thousand lire; she would have to repeat her multiplication table nine times and more ere she reached the sum demanded.

"*Che, che, che,*" said H., his favorite expression. "*Pazienza, molta pazienza*; wait; don't make any offer, you must leave it to me. I know these people and their ways."

Well, it required two years of "*pazienza*" before we owned that picture. In our letters we always referred to the portrait as "Venice" to conceal its identity, a precaution probably unnecessary, as at that time Veronese was not *à la mode*, even the *galleria* not caring to purchase it, which made it easy to take it out of Italy. When at last it reached Paris, Miss Cassatt wrote to congratulate us, and added:

"I have taken H., who traveled with it to Paris, to the Louvre to show him some pictures there, in order that he may know what we want."

Rather ambitious, was it not, but when one considers our Lippi, our Del Sarto, our Raphael and others, it must be conceded that she not only knew her agent but judged well of the opportunities that would offer. 162

I do not know whether this was the first Veronese in America or not, but frequently I have heard exclamations of surprise that we owned such a masterpiece, and many a critic has said it was our finest picture and second to none that we possessed.

Before leaving Florence, and through Mr. H., we secured another work of art, a marble "Madonna and the Infant Christ" by Mino da Fiesole. With much secrecy H. conducted us to a *palazzo*, and there in the wall, where it had 163 been since the artist's time, we found this lovely Virgin and Child, a more realistic work than the one we bought in Paris from Gavet, a French collector. The Madonna smiles and so does the infant Jesus. She is the mother of the lovely boy, rather than the Virgin holding the Christ. It is in higher relief and less classic than the other but it is more alive and vital, and two charming angels hold a crown above the Madonna's head. We found the same composition in the Bargello, but coarser and in gray stone. It is marked *scuola da Mino*, etc., and may possibly have been a copy by some pupil. In this same collection was the Saint George, and the 164 head of John the Baptist which commanded great admiration in the art world and was sold later for a fabulous price. I have never heard our marble doubted, except by one dealer, a veritable "Thomas" in his line, with much method in his doubting, although we had no intention of selling it; as against this one opinion, I have heard it extolled by many competent critics. Never shall I forget the vision of poor H.

tugging hopelessly with ropes to get this marble up the narrow winding stairs to the little cupola on "suicide corner" where it was to remain until forwarded to us some time afterward.

165   Several years later, we purchased through H. our Donatello, a stucco in low relief of a Madonna and Christ with angels. It was one of those lovely architectural altarpieces, with a frieze and side columns which the sculptors of the Renaissance loved to make for the little chapels in the Tuscan hills, whether as an order from the *signori* or from the nuns of some nearby convent. These sculptors of the Renaissance delighted to work in the plastic stucco, and delighted still more in the lovely tone which they could give to it; for many reasons they preferred it to marble. If Donatello could have known what would happen when his Madonna passed our customs, I think his shade would have returned from Hades to point a finger of scorn at our government. The stucco arrived at our port, and imagine Mr. Havemeyer's surprise when notified that his Donatello relief had been entered and taxed as *earthenware*! Forty-five per cent duty was to be levied upon it.

"But it is sculpture," said Mr. Havemeyer, "and art besides; I will bring sculptors, experts, who will prove that what I say is true."

In vain! that particular, specially developed intelligence that one finds in the customhouse would not listen. The best sculptors, the highest authorities of this country asserted that the stucco was art, the finest art that mind could produce, and should come in on the fifteen per cent basis, at which rate art was taxed at that time. These Dogberrys held high court and the verdict was:

First, it was not sculpture because it was not marble but a sort of clay, hence earthenware, and secondly, it was not sculpture because "you could not walk around it"; ergo, it was not sculpture, and if not sculpture it could not be art, and ergo again, it must be earthenware; therefore write it down earthenware and tax it forty-five per cent duty in order to protect the crocks and pots of productive New Jersey. There is quite a volume written about the customs tax of our Donatello, which I am keeping as a curiosity. Perhaps some day the Madonna may go into a museum, and if it ever does, these Dogberry reports of the U. S. customs duties go with it, for the amusement and enlightenment of future generations. If not appreciated in America, this funny bit of art history is greatly relished in Europe, I assure you, where they deride and laugh at our gross ignorance in art matters. 166

By the time we made our second visit to Florence, H. had proved his ability as an art hunter; he had already bagged several fine pictures, the Raphael, the Del Sarto, etc., and was now on the scent of something quite extraordinary. There were many difficulties in his path, however, and we should be obliged to follow this trail with the greatest precaution; not only was the family who owned the treasure divided and at swords' points through legal entanglements, but we had the dealers to count with, for the picture was nothing less than a Filippo Lippi, one which the dealers would buy at a high price or which any museum would be proud to acquire. 167

My husband immediately said: "Let us see it."

Whereupon H., staggered with apprehension, whispered like a low tragedian: *"Che, che, che, piano, piano, pazienza,* we shall have to go far, far up into the hills to see it, and no one must know where or when we go."

Mr. Havemeyer seemed little impressed with H.'s mysteriousness, and answered: "I don't care where it is, we must see it."

The situation appealed to me, it would be exciting; we

were not only to hunt, but to hunt in a drama, and each one would have a leading role. It was arranged that the smiling, twinkling Signora was to provide luncheon, which she could easily do as they now lived in a pleasant apartment with a tiny little charcoal arrangement, which she heated period-ically and called a fire. H. was to prove he knew the ground by making all necessary arrangements for the journey, which was to be partly by train, partly by *vettura*, partly by foot and, judging from his anxiety and uneasiness, partly by nothing at all, by which he meant failure. We made an early start upon a heavenly day. La Signora's infectious de-light, the well-filled luncheon basket, to say nothing of a bottle of Chianti which H. carefully guarded himself, grad-ually dissipated H.'s apprehension and he became genial and almost boyish, revealing quite a new side to his char-acter. It was a new experience for Mr. Havemeyer and for me to start from a remote corner of the station in a shabby third-class train that jolted along in an unknown direction with a lot of noisy passengers, who seemed to have every-thing their own way. We dragged along for an hour or two, winding in and out, passing streams and slopes until we reached the foothills of Tuscany. H. had us all ready to de-scend for half an hour before it was necessary; he had had repeated conferences with the guard, whereupon he would motion to us to be seated again, and at last rushing up to us, as if charged with dynamite, yelled to us to *"uscite, uscite,"* out, out as fast as possible. This was totally unnecessary, for that languid locomotive had not the least thought of starting while it had any possible excuse to stand still. I believe to this day that the only reason H. made us get out was that he spied, up the road beyond the station, a rickety old yellow basket cart on two wheels such as children use with a pet pony; to it were hitched two enormous horses, which from lack of grooming, from the wide difference in matching up and from their patient stillness as they stood facing the high hills, must have been pressed into service from some neighboring plough. La Signora and I were finally handed into it and wedged, our knees together as we sat facing each other in this *vettura*, while the gentlemen squeezed in beside us. With their weight, down went the cart and up flew a long stick which had been extemporized as a pole, fortunately without breaking the vehicle or in any way disturbing our noble steeds. We descended and made another start. This time the gentlemen got in first and La Signora and I squeezed in after. This produced a better balance, which, however, was again disturbed when the driver took his seat upon the rim of the basket, and the improvised pole dropped almost to the level of the horses' backs. There was now only one other combination left. Again we descended; La Signora and Mr. Havemeyer sat by the driver and H. and I sat by the rear door. This cater-cornered arrangement was rather embarrassing on account of our limited knee space, but as it produced a better balance that had to be overlooked. With wraps, luncheon, and the Chianti tucked in as best we could, and with Mr. Have-meyer's arm tight about me lest I should fall out, we mo-tioned the driver to start.

"*Avanti, avanti,*" called H. to the sober-faced youth who acted as ploughboy-driver, but not yet were we to start.

Whether the angle from the bit to the back of the harness gave the reins an unfamiliar tug, or whether the horses re-belled against the unusual work, I do not know, but the only thing that moved, and moved vigorously, when the driver jerked the reins, was the horses' tails. Perhaps it was a necessity, for there were plenty of flies. The youth got the brunt of it, for the tails slashed his face, and he cursed out his quadrupeds by the Holy Mother and all the saints. Mr. Havemeyer did not like it a little bit, but La Signora put up a good fight. With the butt end of the Chianti bottle she beat the horses' flanks. Impatience spurred my husband to the rescue.

"Those beasts will have to start; get out, H.," he said, "and give the cart a shove, then we'll pull you in."

That proved successful; probably thinking they had struck a furrow, as in the ploughing days, the old nags started, each for himself in his own particular gait, and from start to finish they were never neck and neck again. What a ride it was! For the first hour we had all we could do to keep in the cart and adjust ourselves to its peculiar motion as we climbed the hill. By that time we were up far enough among the hills to be attracted by the beauty of the landscape, and we thought less of our discomfort. The intense dark green of all the woodland slopes, their sharp outline against the pure blue of the clear sky, the well-defined shadows and the brilliant sunshine, the streams that sparkled in every crevice of the valley below, revealed at once where the Tuscan artists had sought their backgrounds for their Madonnas and their saints. I thought I could detect familiar scenes in the works of the Florentine painters from Lippi to Leonardo, and as the horses now settled down to their task and tugged slowly up and up, there were constantly new vistas to be seen, first on one side and then on the other.

In all, three hours were consumed in our climb. Luncheon was eaten en route. It was excellent, and we found a trickling stream which was *molto sano* and we could quench our thirst with safety, for we did not care for wine, and H. found himself the undisputed possessor of the bottle of Chianti. This disturbed him for a time, as it was hard for him to be convinced that we really preferred water to wine and that our refusal to drink of his bottle cast no reflection upon the quality of his grapes. Suddenly, with a twist and jerk which almost sent me rolling down the mountainside, the youth headed the horses into a grove of thick pine trees and then as suddenly pulled them to a standstill, or rather they stopped themselves, not from an unwillingness to proceed, for they had shown their sturdiness with admirable endurance and willingness of mind, but because they could go no further as the woods were too dense.

H. now instructed us in our various roles. We were *all* to be wine merchants; we were to walk up the remaining distance and go into the sheds and wine cellars we should find at the top of the mountain and we should sample the Marsalas and the Astis which would be offered to us. We now knew why H. was so perturbed when we refused his Chianti; he was afraid we would not taste the offered samples. Mr. Havemeyer was convulsed with laughter at the idea of my sampling wine.

"Go on, H.," he said. "I suppose we can spit it out; but what the devil did we come up here for anyway?"

"*Che, che, che,* Mr. Havemeyer, you don't know these people, the trouble they can make; some want to sell and some don't. No one must know we have been here, there would be lawsuits and they would want fabulous sums for the picture, and perhaps they might even tell the dealers." To express the possibilities, he flung his arms about his head as if he suddenly had found himself in a wasps' nest.

We, the little quartet to be known as "the wine merchants," started up the hill. It was good to stretch our cramped limbs, and we really had not very far to go. We soon found ourselves on a broad plateau; a long white stucco villa, with fascinating arcades and *torrelle*, was just where it should be to command the magnificent view of the surrounding hills. The villa had been there for centuries, while later additions, not helping the original design, had attached themselves from wing to wing until they reached a large low building, which probably ashamed of its ugliness had twisted itself behind them and was partly concealed by tall pine trees. This last building was the wine cellar and within it we went, to be greeted by a tall fine-looking man in shirt sleeves, evidently not afraid of work and as evidently expecting us. He gave H. a cordial greeting and was rather deferential when we were introduced, while to prevent any embarrassment or explication he proceeded at once to tap a hogshead and offer us a glass of wine. I can vouch for the quality; it was not bad. When H. saw me taste it, he "anticked" in ecstasy and finished his own glass. My husband gave a hearty approval, whether sincerely or not I do not know, but he was cautious in the amount he took, not knowing where the farce would end. With H. as interpreter, we chattered about vintages for some time, and then it was necessary to taste more wine and sip of many other glasses, until at last we resorted to the sampler's privilege and rolled the wine about our mouths and deposited it upon the ground.

The third act of the drama was now approaching. A subordinate, and there were many all watching us suspiciously, gathered up the glasses and the master-of-the-wines led us about the place. We had to admire the view toward the north, toward the south, toward the east and toward the west. We stopped at a truly beautiful garden and examined the old marble benches and statues, beaten black with the assaults of winds and clouds and storms, marble figures crumbling under the weight of years; flowers that were pathetically pale and sparse and vines that went marauding everywhere. We passed the long low villa and while the wine-master gesticulated his apologies that he could not open the doors for us, he passed on to the other additions and stopped before a chapel, where with a furtive look toward the subordinates still standing gazing at us from the wine cellar, he drew forth a key which was hidden in his blouse and, unlocking the door, he pushed in the two wings and we at last stood before the object of our visit.

It would be hard to describe our emotions for the reason that we had to conceal them; not a word was spoken, but forgetting caution, Mr. Havemeyer and I pressed forward to the altar, for above it hung the picture, Filippo Lippi's "Madonna." Against the landscape of the morning sat the Virgin holding the baby Jesus, while two saintly boys pressed against her knee to look up into the lovely Infant's face. Perfectly preserved, fresh as if just painted, it made us fairly catch our breath with delight. Instinctively Mr. Havemeyer with his familiar gesture passed his hand caressingly before the Virgin's face, which was like a petal of a flower, for she bloomed in youth and beauty, while tenderly pressing, in holy mother love, the divine baby to her breast and smilingly looking down upon the little saints. With the exception of a tiny spot upon her hand and one upon the cushion of her chair, there was not a touch, not a blemish nor a crack. The high dry air had carefully guarded its treasure since it left the convent studio. The old profligate must have had a heavenly vision when he did that altarpiece; he was painting a "Madonna della Misericordia," of whom he would stand in need when brought before the judgment seat. The little saints should plead for him, and the Holy Babe would save him. So absorbed were we that we forgot how long we looked until H. told us it would not be wise to remain any longer. Contrary to his habit, Mr. Havemeyer did not even ask me if we should buy it; that question had already been decided in both our minds ere we left the chapel. Still without any show of emotion we continued our inspection of the place, and finally said good afternoon to our cicerone at the wine cellar. Mr. Havemeyer and H. managed to have a few words together in transit, but that was all that anyone could observe; those words might have had reference to the wine or the magnificent view.

Arriving at the station, through H.'s neglect to consult a timetable we were forced to face the prospect of a night in camp, or as Mr. Havemeyer said, he would prefer a night "without a camp," for under the trees was an acceptable alternative for any shelter those miserable stucco inns could offer. There was no possibility of getting anywhere with horses. Ours were exhausted, and every other beast in the place had done a hard day's work. The sun was low, the air was becoming chilly, wraps we had none, and for "calorification" there was only the Chianti left. H. was frantic, and even La Signora's fortitude failed to keep her twinkle going. It was Mr. Havemeyer who cheered and encouraged us for having "bagged our game" so to speak, we should show stout hearts and make the best of things, for after all, there might be worse things than a night in the Tuscan hills.

Scarcely had the words left his lips when we heard a whistle, a line of smoke curled round the distant hill. H. sprang into the station and brought us the joyful news that a "mixed" train was approaching; but the tickets! We had first-class tickets; we should waste them, think of the expense; and he would have crossed the tracks to change them, had not Mr. Havemeyer held him back.

"Would you lose your life? Never mind the tickets, man!" he said. "I pay for them; get aboard the train and help the ladies."

We hustled into the train, and mixed indeed it was. Half of one car had a few benches in it, peasants and babies and monks were huddled in together and stared at us in unfeigned wonderment. It reeked of warm humanity and garlic, otherwise it was interesting. The poor are good-natured and kindhearted, and their pleasant chatter, where it did not rise to the confusion of a din, was not disagreeable. I was touched at the way they always made room for another peasant with her baby and her bundles, and the comparison was not favorable to my English-speaking brethren when I thought of my own experiences in Italy.

Before we reached Florence nearly all the passengers had disappeared, and H., who did not wish to be burdened with the bottle, offered the last glass of Chianti to a young Capuchin, who had scarcely lifted his eyes from his breviary during the journey. He refused it with such a gentle gesture, but his solemn face flushed so painfully, that I was tempted to rebuke the indiscreet tempter. Mr. Havemeyer did it for me.

"H.," he said, "throw that infernal bottle out of the window and never mention Chianti to me again."

Of course we got the Lippi. How it all came about, I cannot tell. It had to be wrapped in mystery. I know there was a stalwart youth who went up the mountain ostensibly to paint, that he carried an easel and a great huge cape and a box of colors, that he knew the master-of-the-wines and had permission to enter the chapel, that one day the picture disappeared and that there was a lawsuit, which was finally settled and everyone was satisfied, even to the old lady who made all the trouble, and that everyone, as in the fairy tale, lived happily every after. That painting has hung in my gallery over twenty years.

It was hard to leave Florence, but there were reasons why we should move on, and we turned our steps northward. One evening we were chatting in the pleasant court of a Milan hotel when H. suddenly appeared. We knew he had something to propose, so we drew our chairs closer together in order that we might not be overheard. He told us

169 he had heard of another Veronese, a full-length man's portrait, and furthermore that of a Colleoni who was a relative of the great general, and like him was born and bred among the mountains of Lombardy. The owner had become poor and obscure, he added with a depreciatory shake of his head, which meant we were blessed by the owner's misfortunes. The owner would sell the picture probably at a low price. It was to be seen not far from Milan, only at Brescia, to which place, thanks to its being on the main line, we should find an excellent train service. H., who loved to gossip over family traditions and the history of pictures, gave us further alluring details and we decided to go and have a look at the portrait. Unfortunately, the day was gray and my husband was threatened with a headache. When we arrived in Brescia, H., who was the vaguest and most casual mortal I ever saw and never knew whither he was going and rarely from whence he came, found that the villa was situated several miles beyond the town, which would preclude our lunching at the hotel, and that only by taking a carriage and eating station sandwiches could we manage to go to the villa and return in time to get the afternoon express back to Milan.

We started, but for some reason the spirits of the party appeared to be as gray as the day. Bread and sausage did not help my husband's headache. We fell into a mood of sullen silence from which it was pleasant to be aroused, even by a knocking at the gate and the clanging of a bell, for the custodian was expecting us and had caught sight of the carriage. He wished the gates to be open as we approached, so that he might at length see someone drive up to the great door, as the *signori* used to do in olden times. When inside the great gate, we found ourselves close to the hills, which made a wonderful background for the villa of which there was little left but its lines and its proportions; the paint and stucco had been battling with the elements for many a year. It was pitifully dreary; one felt that even a parasitical carp would not care to swim in the basin of the fountain that lay in the center of the once splendid gardens, now how changed; what flowers could bloom, or what heart beat normally in such a place! Your ears listened to a windy dirge and your nostrils scented decay. Ugh! This was no place to live in, at least not now. I shuddered to think what would become of me were I obliged to call that place my home. As the Italians say, it would *tocca mio morale*.

We entered the villa and the air of the long dark hall was foul with the smell of mold. We passed through several cheerless, unfurnished apartments, turned an angle in the hall and passed through as many more; had there been another repetition, I think I should have turned and fled, but at last we reached an enormous room, which was very cold and dark. Not until all the wooden shutters had been thrown open could we distinguish a fireplace at the distant end, around which were grouped a few chairs and a solitary table. This must have been the living room, for in the others they could not have lived. H. led us to the fireplace and pointed to the chimney above. Now that our eyes, cat-like, had grown accustomed to the gloom, we could see that there was a picture there, but it took several minutes before we knew it represented a young man standing upon the terrace of a garden with a greyhound beside him. On looking closer I could perceive the striped sleeve of the stiff jacket, the hilt of a gold sword and a hand extended towards the dog, also green stockings with low shoes. The outlines were firm and masterful, but where was Veronese's light touch and brilliant color? Alas, they were missing, and we frankly spoke out our disappointment. Mr. Havemeyer would not consider the picture and didn't even ask

to have it taken down from the chimney for a closer inspection, and he was inclined to reproach H. for his temerity
in bringing us there to see it. He was now suffering from
headache and he hurried us away, for I believe he felt as I
did, that the pleasantest part of the visit would be our leavetaking. We entered the carriage and again passed through
the iron gates.

It was easy to see that H. felt humiliated. He thought he
had such a fat prize for our net, a Veronese! a Colleoni! and
at such a moderate price. The honest man never developed
into a dealer, nor could he, living with the paintings of the
Renaissance on every side and within easy reach, realize
that art could hold up her head and say:

"I am a first necessity; all else may be cheap, but I shall
ever be in demand. My present owner's fortune may
crumble, his title may vanish, his manhood deteriorate, but
I shall survive and with proud prestige of fame, pass on
from generation to generation, from one great land to another, bearing regardless of race or time my message unto
all mankind."

Poor H. said very little and the subject of "The Boy and
the Dog," as we called the picture, was dropped. The sequel, however, is interesting. For a year or more we kept
up a three-cornered correspondence about the Colleoni
portrait, H. in Florence, Miss Cassatt in Paris and we in
America. He was very desirous that we should own the
picture, and finally wrote that upon taking it down he had
found it covered with dirt and smoke, that there was a thick
deposit of soot upon it, which when removed revealed
Veronese's brilliant coloring.

"Unfortunately," he wrote, "the owner now wants much
more for his picture"; but added with his abnormal love of
mystery, "I have accidentally learned certain facts, which
under no consideration can I tell you, but which I believe,

when the right moment comes, will let us buy the picture cheap."

The moment came about a year afterward. Mr. Havemeyer brought me a cable from H. It read: "Will you give a little more for the Boy and Dog?"

"What shall I answer?" asked my husband.

This meant that he threw the responsibility of buying or of not buying it upon me, but as I was backed by Miss Cassatt, I stoutly replied: "Answer 'Impossible to increase offer,' and await results."

The next day came another cable saying: "Boy and Dog yours; cable funds."

"The funds" represented just twenty-five thousand lire; less than five thousand dollars for a full-length portrait by Veronese! I doubt if the *Memorials of Christie's* ever recorded a greater bargain! H. took the "Colleoni" to Paris, and Miss Cassatt showed it to a few friends.

"Roger Marx, the French critic," she wrote me, "says 170 Velazquez never did anything finer than the dog, and the drawing of the legs is marvelous. Compare it with a Van Dyck and you will realize what you possess, and as for the face, you know Veronese loved to paint bullet-headed boys."

At last it arrived in America, and with a richly carved frame of the period it now hangs in our gallery, twenty-five thousand lire for the painting and ten thousand for the frame!

Long afterward we were again speeding through Italy. this time in an automobile. It was about five o'clock in the afternoon, and we were approaching Modena. We slackened our speed to wind slowly through the narrow streets of the town. At the Piazza Grande Mr. Havemeyer, ever a man of quick perceptions and prompt actions, saw a café; he put his hand on the chauffeur's shoulder and called out:

"Ferma."

The Fiat came to a sudden stop at the very foot of La Ghirlandina, and the little man at the wheel looked around in astonishment to see what *could* be the matter.

"*Caffe*," said my husband, smilingly, "*buono caffe*; I want some. Don't you? *Dato voi* some. It's *qui—li*, over there, see," and he pointed to the arcade with the little tables invitingly arranged for visitors. As we descended we stopped to have a look at the beautiful campanile, and then proceeded across the square. When approaching the arcade, H. said to me:

"Do you see those men there? It was at that very table I found the owner of the Veronese, when I received your message. When I handed him your cable, he told me with an oath to 'sell the picture.'"

The gray villa will grow grayer, its walls will crumble and even the gates may fall from their hinges, but its art will ever survive. Veronese's "Boy and Dog" is one of my most admired pictures.

171 Through H. we obtained many other pictures: some with a history like that of our fourth Veronese, and others without any history at all. There was a Madonna of the Sienese school from a chapel in the high hills beyond Massa Carrara; also a Madonna and Child from another convent chapel which had to be demolished, a wonderful Del Sarto; a pair of portraits of the Cologne school, strange to say found in Italy, but from the Demidoff Collection and still in the heavy black frames which he invariably used; a lovely Fra Diamanti, whose conservation was my despair, for that irresponsible monk had used a panel for his picture and painted his Virgin across the grain of the wood, which in our climate meant continual cracking, and however well repaired the cracks were always visible to the eye of its anxious custodian.

172 Then there was the Raphael portrait which came to us

directly from the Altoviti family. With it came an important volume, which tells of the intimacy of the painter with the young Altoviti and of their resemblance to each other being so great that at one time there was a doubt whose portrait it was. There is in the Munich gallery a portrait, catalogued "by Raphael" and apparently of the same person. Florentine tradition tells us of a lawsuit about its authenticity, discontinued only when the family treasury was exhausted, and which perhaps is best settled by comparing photographs of the two pictures, or better still by placing them side by side. Vigée Le Brun in her memoirs speaks of 173 the Florentine portrait, and says that besides the copy of it which she made herself there existed other copies. On a recent visit to Munich I found that they no longer attribute the portrait to Raphael, but to Giulio Romano. All this may prove interesting in the future, but be that as it may, to many Raphael the draftsman is greater than Raphael the painter. I was never very enthusiastic over my Altoviti portrait.

After a visit to the high Bergamo and to the low city, in a fruitless hunt for a Moroni, we came to the parting of our ways and with regret said farewell to H. and his affectionate Signora, who that day had no merry twinkle in her eye, and we returned to Paris.

CHAPTER X

Visit To Spain

174 LEAVING my sister comfortably settled in Miss Cassatt's apartment in Paris, Miss Cassatt, Mr. Havemeyer and I started forth for Spain. It was a tiresome journey with a necessary change of carriages when one reaches the Spanish frontier, and we found we had to travel over a hot and dusty plain in order to reach Madrid. I became accustomed to Spanish ways, however, and thought nothing of the return 175 trip, when I carried a small Greco in one arm and some 176 Hispano-Moresque plates in the other, all of them done up in newspaper. There were no Ritz hotels there in those days, for which I am devoutly thankful, for if we had not gone to our comfortable hotel in the Puerta del Sol, Miss Cassatt would have perhaps missed meeting the Infanta's godson, through whom we were to find one very important picture. We settled in our hotel in Spain; we began at the beginning, and a good one it was, the Prado. Mr. Havemeyer always maintained that after the Spanish War we should have demanded the Prado as an indemnity instead of taking over the Philippines, and he lived long enough to know that he was right. We did not need the Philippines, and the Prado would have been inestimable to us as a young nation, young in an art sense. The gallery was a revelation of art; I think its contents the greatest and most creditable monument to the art-loving Charles V and his descendants,

the many Philips. Is there any other gallery where you see so many masterpieces, and from so many different schools? Apart from Velazquez, who with his "Meniñas" and his "Hilanderas," his portraits and his dwarfs, his "Don Baltazar" and "The Surrender at Breda," would make it a gallery unique in the world, where can you find three out of his five full-length portraits by Titian, sixty Rubenses, including that marvel of portraiture, his "Marie de Médicis"—a painting so lovely in its transparency and in its charming grays that it seems fairly to have been blown upon the canvas—or another portrait that can rival it, "Queen Mary" by Sir Anthony Moro? Where will you find finer examples of Flemish art, or greater masterpieces of the Venetian school than those two gems of painting, "The Finding of Moses" by Paolo Veronese and Andrea Mantegna's "Death of the Virgin"? Can you think of a finer Zurbarán in any gallery than the "Vision of San Pedro"? Or of finer Murillos and Riberas than those in the gallery in Madrid? Goya has now added his fame to the Prado, and with his "Royal Family" and his "Majas" has lent new interest to that wonderful museum. One might well say, as Miss Cassatt did, that the resplendent gallery offered an "orgy of art."

We went there many times and my husband had the joy of discovering what was for us a new master—Greco. No great composition of Greco hangs in the Prado, but some of his best portraits are in the gallery and it was these por- 177 traits that first attracted Miss Cassatt and Mr. Havemeyer to Greco. Back and back we went, and always the fascination of that painter threw a spell over us. We could not resist his art; its intensity, its individuality, its freedom and its color attracted us with irresistible force. We determined to see every work of his in Spain, for we knew of few else-where, as the one in the National Gallery in London, or

178   the very inferior one in the Louvre, gives no conception of Greco as a painter. As usual, Mr. Havemeyer wondered if we could not obtain one, and he appeared delighted when one morning Miss Cassatt and I said we were going out in quest of a Greco.

"You had better add a Goya while you are about it," said my husband.

"Perhaps we may, who knows," laughingly answered Miss Cassatt, and out we went.

179
180   That was the first step, but it led to Greco's "Cardinal,"
181 and to his great and only landscape, as well as to twelve Goyas, some very important ones. First, we went to a photographer's and bought a photograph of every Greco and Goya we could find, and adroitly managed to find out where some of them could be seen. That morning we learned of Señor Cossio for the first time; he was writing a life of Greco and a catalogue of his works. We went to see him and it was he who told us that after the "Burial of the Count of Orgaz" he considered the portrait of the cardinal Greco's greatest work and that he should use it
182 as the frontispiece of his book. I think it was he who later arranged for us to see the "Cardinal" and judge for ourselves. We made a good beginning that morning, and were directed to an apartment where we could see two Goyas. We found the *calle*, mounted the narrow stairway until we reached the fourth floor. A lady answered our ring and very willingly offered to show us her two Goyas, the por-
183 traits of her ancestor, "La doña Zárate." One was a half-length portrait of the Zárate, painted when she was young and full of health; she was dressed in black with a veil over her hair, her cheeks were full of carmine and her eyes dark and brilliant. The other, far smaller, was evidently painted only a few years later, for the poor thing was still young, but the dark eyes were sad, the bright cheek had

paled, the white fiend had clutched her; she no longer wore the black veil, instead Goya had painted her with great tenderness and delicacy as an invalid, and a soft bit of white covered the loosely gathered hair. We listened to her sad story and then Miss Cassatt felt, for Mr. Havemeyer's sake, we should talk business, and asked the price of the pictures. Now if anyone thinks that in Spain he can get a price on a picture, or negotiate a sale at a first interview, he is a novice at the game, that is all. We lost these pictures because we were novices. Of course the owner hesitated, and we made a fatal mistake: we named a price.

"Would you take twenty thousand pesetas for the two?" asked Miss Cassatt.

That was just what our friend was waiting for, she wanted to know our ideas about price in order to fix her own; if we had said ten thousand francs, the result would probably have been the same. Needless to say, she flatly refused, and we went away.

"I should not have made an offer," said Miss Cassatt to me when we were again walking through the little *calle*. "Now she will ask five times as much."

And surely enough, a note was brought to us that very evening saying the owner would consent to part with the two portraits for one hundred thousand pesetas. Just five times our offer as Miss Cassatt predicted, and a ridiculous price for Goyas in those days. However, the dealers later saw their chance; they bought and boomed Goyas. I saw a number of years later a woman's portrait by Goya that I had refused at twenty-five thousand pesetas in Madrid; it was for sale at a New York dealer's at a price over double that number of dollars. As to the two portraits of the Zárate, one, I am told, went to an Irish museum at the price of eight thousand pounds, and the other I saw at a dealer's, and the price asked was forty-five thousand dollars. When I heard it, I wondered if they had been bought at the price they were offered to us.

I recollect that on that morning, as we were returning to the Puerta del Sol, Miss Cassatt's quick eye caught sight of a painting that had been placed in the doorway of an "antiquity" shop. There were many such shops in the street and we knew the locality was a dangerous one for us.

"There he is," said Miss Cassatt to me, and I, thinking she meant Mr. Havemeyer, looked quickly around and answered:

"I don't see him. Where is he?"

"There," replied Miss Cassatt. "That 'Christ' there, that small picture. It is Greco surely, no one else could have done those hands, look!"

I looked, and surely enough there was a small picture about twenty inches by twelve, a Christ holding the cross, a study probably for the painting called "El Espolio," which we learned to know so well later in Toledo. The long slim fingers of the Christ were pressing the cross to his bosom, and the wan face, expressing intense pity, seemed human in its suffering. We stopped and examined it carefully. I waited for Miss Cassatt to pass judgment upon it, for I knew her knowledge and artistic sense would guide her, and I paid no attention to the voluble salesman who had come forward, having seen his line stir and knowing he had a nibble.

"Yes, my dear," said Miss Cassatt finally, and in the unmistakable way I knew so well. "That is a Greco, or I am mistaken, and a fine one. Do you suppose they are so plentiful that they can be found like this? I wonder how much he asks for it?"

"Shall we negotiate?" And as she nodded, I asked the price in French, and the salesman with consummate art answered in Spanish.

Inferentially, I judged it was too dear, so I shrugged my shoulders, shook my head, and made a motion to go, whereby I drew forth such a flow of Spanish that by the time he had finished, Miss Cassatt's previous knowledge of the language had gradually returned to her, and with the air of a true Castilian she concluded the bargain I had begun. Fifteen hundred pesetas; a peseta then was worth about seventeen cents, so my Greco cost me a little over two hundred and fifty dollars, and I carried it in my arms, frame and all, to the hotel to show it to Mr. Havemeyer. Apparently astonished that we should admire Greco, the dealer insisted upon showing us another, one more precious, hidden in a dark back room. It was a Saint Peter in a brilliant green robe, holding the keys upon his arm. Miss Cassatt greatly admired it also, but it would be so hard to carry, it was much larger, more important and to a dealer's mind worth a great deal more. Miss Cassatt decided she would not take it, as it might upset her in her work, and we let it pass. Eight years afterwards, when we were again traveling in Spain, my daughter Electra bought the picture in Vitoria, after it had gone around and about Spain until its wooden case was dark and travel-worn.

As we were, so to speak, to open the market for Grecos and Goyas, at least in the United States, I may as well cite here a curious letter about Greco which I still possess, and an equally curious incident about negotiating for one of Goya's portraits. The letter, which was from the Infanta's godson, offered us a set of the Virgin, the Christ and the twelve apostles, an order which Greco repeated several times for the rich monasteries of Spain, for the sum of twenty thousand pesetas. Fourteen Grecos for less than four thousand dollars! Mr. Havemeyer consulted me, and we, not knowing how rare Greco's paintings were and thinking that we had but to wait to find more Cardinals and more landscapes, declined the offer. We also decided that it would prove too large a contrast to hang fourteen religious pictures in our gallery at once. Now for the other side of the picture, to show how Goyas were afterwards boomed and how fantastic became the pretensions of their owners. An old friend of mine, H. C. Frick, who has one of the finest collections of paintings in the United States, once said to me:

"If ever you hear of a Goya that you do not care to purchase, will you let me know, as I am very anxious to secure one?"

I said I would, and as I frequently had pictures offered to me through private parties, it was not long before I could offer Mr. F. a splendid Goya which I considered too high priced for me. It was the portrait of the Spanish actress, "La Tirana," considered finer than the one we had once refused and which is now in the Academy in Madrid. This one is a half-length portrait. La Tirana is dressed in white, has luxuriant black hair and is holding a paper in her hand. I showed the photograph to Mr. F., and gave him all the details. Unfortunately, he was negotiating for a Velazquez at the time and felt poor. I do not wonder, for he told me what he paid for the Velazquez, and I should think the price would make not only an individual but a government feel bankrupt. Mr. F. examined the photograph long and thoughtfully, and then asked the price.

"Two hundred thousand pesetas," I answered.

"That is very high," he said.

"Yes," I replied, "when you think we bought our 'Wellington' for twenty thousand pesetas, and the pair of 'Sureda' portraits for less than fifty thousand."

"I like the picture," he said, "but it is very dear."

"True," I said, "but fancy what a dealer would ask for it, if he could get hold of it. They have turned the heads of

the Spaniards about their Goyas. I met one duke in Madrid 191
who told me he would not sell the portrait of his grandmother for less than one million pesetas. I really advise you,
Mr. F., if you want a fine example of Goya, to take this
one. I do not think you can get one finer or cheaper."

"Very well," he answered, "I will take it."

"Shall I cable?" I asked.

"What for?" he questioned a little crossly.

"Oh, I always buy by cable," I answered. "There is no
telling what might happen if you wait to write. It is a habit
I learned from Mr. Havemeyer."

"Well," he answered, "there's no need of cabling at that
price. They will be only too glad to sell, I think."

"As you like," I replied.

Mr. F. brought me the draft, and I sent the letter, but
before it could reach Spain I had another cable saying the
owner had withdrawn the picture and now wanted a much
larger sum. Legally they had a right to do that, as no cable
had been sent, no money paid down. I took the message to
Mr. F. and you may imagine his astonishment and his
disgust.

"I see now what you meant by cabling," he said, "but I
thought they would grab at that amount of money."

"Yes," I said, "it is better to conclude a bargain at once.
Most of those Goyas have several owners, and as soon as
one party makes a price, the others think they should ask
more, and unless they are legally bound it is impossible to
tell what may happen. A 'million-pesetas' grandmother's
portrait is a legacy worth fighting over."

Mr. F. took his disappointment very amicably, but although he later bought two Grecos he never owned a really 192
great Goya. I realized how fortunate it was that we had
made a start in buying Spanish art on that April morning,
even if our first purchase was only a small picture by Greco. 193

Needless to say, Mr. Havemeyer did not think much of it, nor did he hesitate to say so. He made several remarks at dinner which rather piqued Miss Cassatt and me and were perhaps the very reason that he afterward acquired so many examples of Greco and Goya. If anyone about him had any determination or ability, there was no one like Mr. Havemeyer for getting a lighted fuse into it.

After spending some time in Madrid, Mr. Havemeyer began to grow restless. He was a mighty sightseer and, unless there was something to interest him especially, he did not care to remain long in a city. The Escorial was being prepared for Holy Week, and we could not visit it; he had seen the churches and the Armoria and almost knew the Prado by heart, so he made arrangements for a little *tournée* in the south of Spain. Miss Cassatt announced her intention of remaining in Madrid. We did not guess her real reason at the time, which was to hunt for a Greco, and she let us believe she was tired of traveling and had spent so much time in Seville in her youth that she had no inclination to go there.

"I am going a lot to the Prado while you are away," she told us. "There is much I want to study there."

As we said good-bye, I did not dream that by the time we returned, she would be in full scent of Greco's "Cardinal," and have located Goya's "Las Majas al Balcón" with the result that it afterwards came into our collection.

It was easy to reach Toledo but very difficult to find Greco's great painting. How well I remember that afternoon when Mr. Havemeyer first saw the "Burial of Count Orgaz." We started out on foot. To walk is *de rigueur* in Toledo, the horse is a *rara avis* there and rarely to be seen on those stiff slopes and in those narrow streets. The Toledan climbs from the Tagus to the cathedral and slides or slips from the cathedral back again to the Tagus. He browses on the bridges and he smokes in the Puertas, the women carry their clothes down the steep hill to wash them in the river below, and the *pequeños* Toledans laugh and chatter, tumble and roll, after the fashion of Spanish children. This afternoon, the high wind clouds gathered and rolled over the lofty city and darkened the Alcázar, making its outlines sharp as a silhouette against the sky. Toledo looked to me just as it did in Greco's time, when he painted his only landscape which we own and which is called just "Toledo." In this picture, the city is perched high in the clouds and is painted like a miniature, while the Tagus flows broad and even at the foot of the mountain, and one can see the men on the same bridges, and the children, also the women washing, just as we saw it all on that memorable afternoon.

197

With only a few hours' acquaintance in Toledo it was not an easy task to find Santo Tomé; Toledo with its intricate streets and its unfamiliar half-Spanish, half-Moorish aspect made it difficult to find our way. We dodged in and out, only to find ourselves at our starting place again. We entered a shop to inquire our way, but not understanding much Spanish, we found the instructions of little use and we gyrated in the tortuous *calles* of the city, not wishing to seek difficulties by descending the hill which we knew was very dusty and Mr. Havemeyer became tired and disgusted. Manlike, he neither cared to inquire the way himself nor to have me do it; the number of corners we turned kept mounting up, the sun shone fiercely hot upon us and we grew warmer and warmer.

"Let the blamed thing go," said Mr. Havemeyer crossly; "I am tired of it all. Why don't they hang their pictures where people can find them without going through all the filth of their dirty town? I'm going back to the hotel."

"Oh, don't," I exclaimed, for I knew we were to leave that night for Seville, and to the first passerby I said pleadingly:

"Santo Tomé, *donde*, Santo Tomé?" and to my joy, he politely turned to show me the way. There, right around the corner, not a hundred yards from the spot where we had stood so discouraged, was the church of Santo Tomé. It stood there so simple and so quiet in comparison to the Moorish buildings, so unlike a church that I doubt if we should have known it even if we had passed before it. With a bow on his part and thanks on mine, the Toledan left us and we entered the church.

It was then that my husband's real admiration for Greco began. He could not, nor could anyone, stand before that composition and not be stirred to the depths of his soul. You feel your being furrowed with the intensity of your emotion. The religion of goodness lies revealed. The heavenly hosts, the Church and the laity all depicted upon one canvas with an unparalleled prodigality of talent. The translated, the living and the dead; devotion, grief and tenderness blending in overpowering conviction; and such portraiture! Marvel of marvels! You stand speechless before the art of it. The expression of the saints, the still life in the picture, the crackling brocades heavy with golden embroidery, the movements of the angels, their lightness and charming naïveté, the countenance of the dead Count, the way his armor is painted, the group of portraits in white ruffs which would have baffled any other painter; its technique, its color, its harmony and its execution make it a chef d'œuvre, which no other painter perhaps could have achieved and few others would have attempted.

We did not speak for a long time. I saw my husband was struggling with a big proposition, was wrestling with a mighty emotion, and was doing it with all his might. As for me, I was just equal to making a feeble effort to remember something about it. It was a long, long time before Mr. Havemeyer moved or spoke. Finally, he heaved a sort of sigh as if expressing a thought to himself, then turning to me, he said, so very softly that I realized how deeply he was stirred:

"One of the greatest pictures I have ever seen; yes, perhaps the greatest."

He then proceeded to tell me his impressions, and it was very late when we left Santo Tomé. On the way to the hotel, Mr. Havemeyer suddenly said, still thinking of Greco:

"Why don't they have his pictures in every gallery in Europe? That man makes you think. Who knows anything about him?"

That question has been asked me time and time again as visitors have stood before the "Cardinal" and the landscape of Toledo. All that the years have revealed of the painter is that, born in a Greek isle, he made Toledo his home after passing his novitiate in the Venetian school; that he lived luxuriously and had musicians play for him while he ate, that he quarreled with everyone who gave him an order and that he was probably as eccentric as geniuses are apt to be. Our hats must come off, nevertheless, for he was a genius, a great one! Several years afterwards, the Marquis de la Vega Inclan bought the house that Greco was said to have lived in, in Toledo. The Marquis told me he had put many interesting things into it, among others a set of the apostles and the Christ, possibly those that were offered to us, and had hung a photograph of Greco's "Cardinal" beside a photograph of Velazquez's "Pope," to show how much Velazquez had been influenced by Greco, when he painted his "Pope Doria."

That night we had more experience in the Spanish mode of traveling. I was curious then, and I am curious still, to know how they make their timetables in Spain. It seemed

to me then, and it seems to me still, that they start a train
from the north of Spain and let it go to the south, stopping
at the various places at any time it happens to arrive there
and leaving on the same casual schedule. There were no
sleeping cars on the train at that time, and we were forced
to take an ordinary coach; not that the sleeping cars were
any more comfortable than the coach when we did find
them. We went to the station and waited until *the* train,
there was but one, came along; we got into a day coach,
glad to find two empty places. Bracing against each other,
we resisted as best we could the jolting and tumbling over
a rough road, learned that it was considered a good run if
we arrived only two hours late, and joining the panicky
confusion of the other travelers tumbled out onto the platform of Seville, wondering where the charm of Andalusian
life came in. Mr. Havemeyer's memory was so filled with
the beauty of Greco's masterpiece, "The Burial of Count
Orgaz," that Seville had to stand an unfavorable comparison with Toledo, and it was only after a day's rest and a
sight of the Alcázar and the incomparable Giralda, that it
commanded its just admiration, and he admitted that the
houses with their comfortable patios interested him, and he
was willing to submit to the indefinable charm of the Calle
de las Sierpes. We went to the splendid cathedral and he
told me he thought the Gothic art of France and Spain impressed him more than anything he had as yet seen of Moorish art. I told him about Murillo's "Saint Anthony"; how
200   it had been stolen and through dear Mr. Schaus's efforts—
from whom we obtained our "Gilder"— had been found in
a New York pawnshop and returned to Spain.

"Just where we are now standing," I said; "I remember
seeing it when it was sent back to Seville. It was resting
upon an easel and someone was repairing a hole which had
been made in the canvas."

"That was during your first visit to Spain?" he asked.

"Yes," I answered laughingly; "so long ago, it makes me feel very old. It was at the time of the earliest war; I remember we were in Madrid when Alfonso XII made his entry into the city and we attended a bullfight given in honor of the occasion."

"And the bullfight?" he questioned.

"It was horrible," I answered; "a wonderful feat of skill and agility, I admit, but why eviscerate poor blindfolded horses for the delectation of the Spanish taste. I assure you I couldn't manage even a cup of simple consommé at dinner that evening. Wait until you see one."

He did. It was in 1901, after the Spanish War. I tried to dissuade him from going, for knowing how impulsive he was I feared he might make a scene. I begged him to remember he was in Spain and that a bullfight was a national diversion, and at least to remember I was with him and, if he didn't like it, just quietly to leave the place. That is just what he did. He saw one bull killed which, being a coward, was dispatched in hot haste, but the second was a fierce, wide-horned, ferocious beast which ripped open horse after horse that was forced into the ring. I was looking nowhere and trying to swallow the disgust that was rising in my throat, when I felt a heavy hand laid upon my shoulder.

"Come! Let us get out of this," said my husband. "I wish we had licked them twice as bad as we did."

Fortunately, it was said in English, and I doubt if anyone understood him although he took no pains to conceal his sentiments. The *espada* had just killed his victim, and there was a great uproar and hats and cigars were thrown wildly into the ring. In the confusion we made our escape. Often afterward I heard him express his opinion of a Spanish bullfight and I sometimes, with a sense of fair play, would ask him if he would like to see a celebrated illustrated book of English sports which my father owned, or recall a prize fight which some friends once induced him to attend.

Although we enjoyed all that Seville could offer in the way of art, I think it would be necessary to live there for a time in order thoroughly to appreciate it. It is the Andalusian life that one wants to know; one must attend the *ferias*, the fairs and the religious fêtes, one must drive on the *paseos* and the alamedas, and on that unique promenade, Las Delicias, one must frequent the Calle de las Sierpes, one must know where the Andalusian sings and dances, one must visit the Giralda at sunset, one must enter the cathedral at the quiet noonday hour and beg the organist to fill the great edifice with heavenly music that floats through the building with an effect you will never forget, one must see the Guadalquivir at flood tide as it winds about the city and flows on to the sea, carrying great ships on its tranquil surface; you must do all that before you really know Seville.

201   Many years later, I returned to Seville and with time and letters to help me, I learned to know it well.

I am writing memoirs and not a book of travels, therefore I will hurry on just as we did, leaving Cadiz, because we found it would be impossible to see Goya's other painting
202   of the "Majas al Balcón" which we hoped to buy from the Montpensier family, but which later, and after we had purchased Goya's larger and more important one from the Bourbon branch of the family, was sold to one of the Paris Rothschilds.

A short stop at Cordova left nothing in my mind but the memory of a mosque, a wonderful one, and we soon found ourselves perched in the Washington Irving Hotel on the Alhambra Hill. We yielded to the enchanting loveliness of the place, enjoyed heavenly moonlight nights wandering through the courts and portals of that wonderful Moorish palace, going back to examine in the daylight that exquisite Alhambra vase which fairly fascinated Mr. Havemeyer and which in form and color the subtleties of Saracenic art had rendered incomparable.

It took some time "to do" Granada, but it took Granada very little time "to do" us. What collector escapes being "done"? If he is not "done to death" he may be thankful. As collectors our Waterloo awaited us in Granada. The bait was thrown to us and we, as many another traveler has done, swallowed it. I often repeated to my husband an axiom of my wise old Irish nurse, who used to say to me: "Believe nothing that you hear and little that you see."

In art, I should say, believe nothing that you hear and still less of what you see, and then pray the gods to protect you. It is hard to destroy the faith of a collector, however, or dampen the ardor of an enthusiast; but I believe he who relies on his own judgment, or on the appearances of things, or in the proofs of seals or dates, or on style, or on the texture of fabrics or the composition of color, or on any other test under the sun, will in ninety-nine cases out of a hundred be taken in. I firmly believe there is nothing under the sun that cannot be imitated, and with such consummate deceit that it is necessary to know the art of the imitator to discover the imitation. If you wish to enjoy the subtleties of deceit, to enter the inner sanctuary of art's legerdemain, or to learn the mystery of mystification, seek them all in the revelations of art imitation, and if one has philosophy enough to surmount the disappointment, he cannot fail to be amused at the clever shrewdness of the master thief when the fraud is revealed. This experience is not easily acquired, sometimes it is very costly and we, like everyone else, paid for our knowledge. I have learned that the patina of a painting can be neatly rubbed off with the finger tips and then the canvas can be touched up and glazed over so that an amateur can work over it as he would over a jig-saw puzzle, without being able to discover anything wrong. An old expert comes along and helps you out, takes the stretcher from the frame, places it flat in the full sunlight, lays bare to your unsuspecting vision the places that have been "treated" and the difference between the old and the new. Your eyes open and you wonder how you could have missed observing it all for yourself. Yet, my friend, don't be elated. The next picture will have another set of snares ready for you and I wager you will trip into them as lightly as if walking upon smooth grass. An old master can abso-lutely be done over equal to new. The fumes of alcohol re-move the varnish; they also remove or coalesce the paint underneath but that does not daunt the restorer, who usually for that sort of work is a young audacious novice who is sure he knows it all. Then the colors are restored, "values strengthened"—the novice loves to do that—the flesh tints are brightened; of course he has studied the "style of the master"; the drapery is vivified, the still life "fixed up," and when the sacred sentiment, the beautiful harmony and the subtleties of the shadows have been disturbed, cor-rected, restored, then the whole picture is glazed over with coat after coat of varnish and sold under the bewildering effect of the "wet sponge" held in the hand of a suave and plausible salesman by the name of "Judas." I recall lately having been shown by a proud dealer a "wonderful find," a Vermeer of Delft, of "such and such collections," and when I saw it, I confess I was thrown off my guard, and exclaimed:

"How wonderful!" when I should have asked: "Is that it?"

The same things go on in every line of art. Pass your hand over some old Persian or Chinese pottery; you will suddenly feel that it sticks a little, you can detect the smell of varnish; you will know it has been repaired, possibly recolored and glazed, or put on a wheel and the lines absolutely preserved for a new decoration, or the leaping tigers in relief have been recast and new ones put on where missing. The wonderful old Venetian velvets are woven today and tramped over by diligent feet until worn as threadbare as their much sought-after originals. It is a well-known old dodge to put fine shot in woodwork to imitate wormholes, and old nails are carefully preserved and used in the so-called renaissance furniture, and the imitation of Queen Anne, Eastlake and Colonial is a farce. Moorish plates and tiles can be reproduced to deceive all but the expert, marble can be colored with tar oil to resemble the old Greek statues —in fact I believe the Greeks did put tar oil on some of their statues. The frauds in old metals and the imitations of precious stones are all too well known to need mention here. It is amusing to compare the number of Stradivarius violins there are in the world with the number known to have been made in Cremona by the great Antonius. However, as a church fair is more successful through its chances and its raffles, and a watering place more interesting when the *petits chevaux* go around, so I suppose the interest in the quest of art objects is enhanced by the element of danger, of trickery and of fraud, which must be constantly met and counted with. As all art countries have been raked over and over again, as the demand is greater than the supply and prices are constantly advancing, ask yourself what the natural result must be.

Our turn came, and we were "done" in Granada, but for years we lived in happy ignorance of it and many a time I pointed in pride to my beautiful Moorish tiles from the villa of Charles V at Guadix. After visiting the Alcázar at Seville and wandering through the lovely halls of the Alhambra, we were naturally attracted by the beauty of the walls with their wonderful tiles. Sauntering out for a walk on our last afternoon in Granada, we stopped in one of the numerous antiquity shops to try to find something to take with us. One shop which had an attractive old sign seemed promising, and we asked if they had any tiles for sale. Of course we were at once taken in hand by the adroit *padrone* and shown the ordinary line of supply.

"No good, no good," said Mr. Havemeyer; "we want something better."

We were led a few steps farther into the gloom of the dusty shop and shown a different grade with a very much increased price.

"No good, no good," repeated Mr. Havemeyer; "something better, show us something better."

Again the goods were changed and the prices advanced without daunting my husband. He would not look at them. He wanted something fine, something better. The blue vase of the Alhambra was still dazzling his eyes. Our Rachel, seeing he was beyond *her* branch of the business, transferred us to the real *padrone* in person, a very shrewd Rebecca with an extremely subdued Isaac. They, Rebecca taking the lead, put us through our pretensions, though I saw at a glance she was a little disturbed by Mr. Havemeyer's persistence and disregard of price. At last, after a side consultation with Isaac, Rebecca led us still farther into the gloom and showed us some wonderful old furniture, whereupon she was made to quail before the expressions of Mr. Havemeyer's impatience and wrath, which he emitted with vehemence in polyglot that convulsed me with laughter. Poor Rebecca, in all her experience she had evidently never met his like before and her head was turned. She fled into a darkened corner and returned with several photographs and some glass negatives in her hand. The discovery of the year was revealed to us in subdued tones.

"If Señor didn't mind the price, they could perhaps buy this villa of Charles V at Guadix, but hush! hush! no one must know it or the government would interfere and any Spaniard who had a dollar to invest would come at once to secure the treasure."

My husband inspected the negatives and the photographs and passed them on to me. They represented several rooms partly covered with tiles and partly with panels of Moorish stucco and carved woodwork, and doors were placed in around the rooms so as to be easily photographed. Furthermore she had a few specimens to show us, and they were lovely. Old or modern they were lovely, a gold luster tile for the dado and a smaller one above, the castle and lion of the coat of arms of Castile and León and the motto "Plus Ultra" for the border. I was delighted and I advised the purchase, an investment of several thousand dollars. All were to be packed and delivered in New York. We took the samples, photographs and negatives; I have them yet—the negatives were part of the plan to make us think they had been just taken and that no one had seen the tiles yet. They told us they did not want any photographs struck off, as Rebecca was afraid someone might see them, etc., etc. The farce was well played and we, poor innocent Reubens, were as unconscious and pleased as if we had discovered America again.

In parenthesis, I must assert they are extremely beautiful and well worth having, even if Charles V did not authorize his Moorish workmen to put them in his villa at Guadix. He probably did have the originals and the copies are still in my home and can prove that he had excellent judgment and taste. It took two years for those tiles to reach us. Rebecca was evidently in no hurry to have them made and was using our money to good advantage in the meantime. They finally arrived, were inspected at the customhouse and pronounced false by experts, not that that proved anything, but we paid the duty as we had done before on a veritable Donatello, and part of the 250 cases were used in the addition we were building to our home and the rest were stored in our stable. It was only several years later when I became much interested in the "expert" business, that I found out that they manufactured tiles, fabrics, furniture, etc., in Spain of any period and of any amount. Nevertheless, such tiles, judiciously placed in a summer home, are more beautiful and effective than anything else I can recommend to replace them, and I hope Rebecca still continues her infamous trade and that her victims' homes are improved by the results of it.

Only one other purchase did I make that day, and Mr. Havemeyer almost spoiled my afternoon by his interference in my bargaining. I saw a fine bishop's ring in old gold of splendid workmanship; I asked the price, intending it as a present to Miss Cassatt. The price was high and I immediately assumed a superb indifference to its beauty. Mr. Havemeyer bought a few things and then the dealer returned to the ring.

"Wouldn't Madame have it? Such a bargain! It could never be found again," etc., etc.

"No," I said; "I didn't particularly care for it. It was only gold; there were no stones in it; I was looking for rings with stones; I might consider it at a small figure."

I mentioned less than half the price asked. Up went the arms of the dealer and down went the ring on the counter. He couldn't think of it. At his price he was losing money on it and at mine, well! he might as well put up the shutters. I maintained my indifference, shrugged my shoulders and walked out of the shop.

"But," said Mr. Havemeyer to me when once outside, "it was a fine ring, don't you really want it?"

"I intend to have it," I replied.

"Nonsense," said he. "He won't sell it at that price. It's ridiculous to think of it."

"Do come on, please," I said. "Walk up."

"But listen to me," insisted Mr. Havemeyer. "You know you overdo things. You can't expect a man to sacrifice his goods just to please you," and he hesitated again.

"Come on, do come on!" I pleaded. "Walk along there. You see," I exclaimed, for as I spoke someone called me. The dealer with the ring in his hand was running after me.

"Madame must take it. She must have the precious ring, no matter how much he suffered through the transaction."

Just to tease my husband, I hesitated still and made him insist upon my taking it. At last I reluctantly gave in and allowed Mr. Havemeyer to hand him his money. The dealer was simply overjoyed to get it, and Miss Cassatt was delighted with her present. Was it genuine? I don't know but I am sure my dealer was overjoyed at the sale. I cast a glance at my husband and although he was smiling, he said grimly:

"All the same, I think you overdo it."

"Nonsense," I replied. "You are still thinking of the blue vase of the Alhambra. You can't have it, dear; we have seen it and our souls possess its beauty and through our memory it is ever with us, think of that; and that is the great joy of traveling. Through our memory we have all the enjoyment but that of possession. The great pyramids, the black Rameses, the Praxiteles at Olympia, the art of Byzantium or the Gothic cathedrals of Europe are stored in those tiny cells of our mind and can be reproduced at pleasure upon the sensitive film of memory. What a joy! What a blessing to be allowed to possess even so far the great works of art."

Knowing Miss Cassatt would be expecting us, we returned to Madrid and to the Puerta del Sol with a sense of homecoming. We found her waiting for us at the door of the *albergo*, not only delighted to see us but eager to tell us of her experiences during our absence. How well I remember our dinner that evening over which we lingered late, listening to all she had to say. She had met the Infanta's godson and had had a peep at some of the pictures we were later to possess.

"You may be sure I missed you," said Miss Cassatt, "when I tell you I was even glad to see Mr. and Mrs. X. who arrived here the day after you left."

"Did they have all their traveling literature with them?" I asked.

Miss Cassatt gave a characteristic gesture. "Yes," she said, "more than ever. I went with them one afternoon to the Prado, and as we were driving home Mrs. X. suddenly started up and said to her husband: 'Oh, Ned, we must go back! I forgot to look at the grays in Saint Catherine's dress. He,' and she mentioned some author on art, 'says we must notice them, they are so charming and transparent.'"

We laughed, and Mr. Havemeyer remarked:

"When will people observe with their own eyes!"

"Well," continued Miss Cassatt, "I have met someone whom I think we shall find really worth-while. You will like him; he speaks English and does not appear like a foreigner."

"Does he know where to find a Greco?" queried Mr. Havemeyer, who was never in doubt as to what he wanted.

"Yes," answered Miss Cassatt. "I have seen one, a magnificent portrait by Greco, a full-length seated portrait of a cardinal in splendid red robes. I believe he had something to do with the Inquisition, and he has let fall a letter he has just been reading; he wears huge tortoise-shell spectacles as they did in those days!"

"What!" exclaimed Mr. Havemeyer, "spectacles in a portrait! I would not consider it. They must be terrible."

"No," answered Miss Cassatt, "they look perfectly nat-

ural. A great painter always knows how to preserve the
relations of things; you forget the spectacles and see only
the glance of the eyes. Besides," she added, "you know very
well a man of the cardinal's age could not read without
glasses."

Still Mr. Havemeyer was not convinced and asked what
else she had done.

"Well, I went with W. who you see has the Infanta for a
godmother, and knows the nobility and where the Grecos
and Goyas are to be found. He took me to see the 'Cardinal'
and a wonderful landscape by Greco, a view of Toledo; both   205
were right here in Madrid and W. thinks, if we keep in the
background, he can in time manage to get both of them. I
asked him about a picture of Goya I remembered seeing in
Spain many years ago, some women on a balcony. He knew   206
where it was and we went to see it; it took us all day. When
we arrived at the place we found the picture had been stored
away, but W. managed to have several cases opened and I
saw the Goya and another Greco, a huge altarpiece, 'The
Ascension of the Virgin.' It is perfectly splendid in color;   207
I think it must be an early work, for it is so Venetian in style
and composition. We also saw a charming Holy Family by
Murillo, which, if you don't object to Holy Families, I
should advise you to take."

"I think you have done remarkably well," commented
Mr. Havemeyer. Miss Cassatt was delighted.

"But that is not all," she continued. "We went to Boabdilla and I saw some astounding Goyas, portraits of the
Bourbon family. W. says we shall have to wait for those,
that they will be difficult to get as they belong to several
brothers and there will be complications, but he promises a
portrait of Wellington by Goya, one that he knows we can   208
buy almost at once. He also promises to take us to the
Marquis de H. tomorrow, to show us another Goya, a por-

209   trait called 'La Bella Librera.' You know it," she added,
        turning to me, "the one we bought a photograph of the day
        we saw the Zárate portraits."

        Of course I remembered it, and we talked on and on until
        very late. It was a memorable evening and we made many
        plans, some of which matured and some of which did not.
        Sooner or later we secured most of the pictures she men-
        tioned, except the Murillo which Mr. Havemeyer did not
        care to buy, and the Bourbon Goyas which we never saw in
        Spain, but, by a curious incident, years later we saw them
        in Italy. I recollect that just as we were leaving Florence
        one morning in our automobile H., our Italian friend, sud-
        denly said to us:

        "Would you care to see a portrait by Goya, a little sketchy
        thing with feathers in her hair?"

        "No, go on," said Mr. Havemeyer, who was impatient at
        any delay.

        But I protested, and we finally went to the villa, and
        when we saw the picture Miss Cassatt was too astonished
        to speak for a moment, and then she said: "The Boabdilla
210   Goyas!"

        Through an Italian marriage they had found their way
        into Italy and we saw the splendid picture of Don Luis de
        Bourbon and his family and a portrait of the little Princess
        of La Paz, full-length and, as H. had described her, with
        some "feathers in her hair." We were never able to buy
        them during Mr. Havemeyer's lifetime, and after his death,
        when they were offered to me, Spaniards' heads had been
        turned and the prices were prohibitive.

        As for Greco's "Ascension of the Virgin" which Miss
        Cassatt unearthed that day in the Bourbon Palace, every
        American who cares to can judge for himself the merits of
        this picture for it hangs today in the Art Institute of Chi-
        cago, and I am going to write about it frankly, giving prices

and details. A few years later when the time was ripe, Mr. Havemeyer, on account of W.'s sudden death, was obliged to request M. Durand-Ruel of Paris to go to Spain and negotiate the purchase of Greco's "Cardinal" and Goya's "Las Majas al Balcón." While in Spain for that purpose M. Durand-Ruel wrote Mr. Havemeyer that he had seen and would be able to buy a fine Greco, the "Ascension of the Virgin," for one hundred thousand pesetas. He added that as he did not have that amount available, would Mr. Havemeyer provide the cash and allow him to buy it for Mr. Havemeyer's account, promising that if for any reason we did not care to have it he would take it off our hands, as he was sure such a picture would not go begging and that he could sell it. Mr. Havemeyer did as M. Durand-Ruel requested, but when I learned that the picture measured fifteen feet without the frame, I knew it would be an impossibility to hang it properly in our gallery and I asked my husband's permission to offer it to our Metropolitan Museum. His answer was:

"You can do as you like; you know what they are."

No, I did not know what they were until I received Mr. Samuel Avery's answer; as a trustee he declined the picture at the price we paid for it, one hundred thousand pesetas, about seventeen thousand dollars, because, he wrote: "through Mr. William Laffan, they had secured a finer one." The "finer one" still hangs in the Metropolitan Museum. Anyone can now compare the two Grecos. The price of the "finer one" is a matter of record and was many thousand dollars more than the price of the "Ascension of the Virgin." I was keenly disappointed and wrote at once to Miss Cassatt about it, and also told her my husband had relinquished the picture to M. Durand-Ruel. She wrote to the directors of the Art Institute of Chicago and the picture went there. Eventually Mrs. Sprague, a friend of mine, gave the picture to the Institute in memory of her husband. She was much interested in its history and what I told her about it. I was ever thankful to be a collector on my own account. I also remember Mr. Edward Robinson, director of the Metropolitan Museum, telling me how the Boston museum acquired Greco's portrait of "Fray Paravicino," which we had refused because as Mr. Havemeyer said:

"Why buy a monk when you have a cardinal? Better wait for a fine woman's portrait." Alas, the Spaniards were not Hollanders; Greco was not Rembrandt, and they painted cardinals, saints, monks, anything but women in his day.

Mr. Robinson said to me: "I was in Italy when I heard of this portrait by Greco and I was so afraid you or Mr. Havemeyer might have heard of it, I could scarcely wait for an answer to my cable, fearing the Museum might lose it."

I sympathized with him in his anxiety and forgot to mention that we had already passed it. We eventually bought Greco's "Cardinal" and his landscape of Toledo, "Las Majas al Balcón," and the "Portrait of Wellington." This was the only one we bought directly through W. for two reasons: first, we bought it within a few months, and secondly, he was accidentally killed while hunting the following year. His tragic death was a great loss to us and I am sure our collection would have been far richer in Spanish art if he had lived.

There is an interesting little history to the "Portrait of Wellington," as there is to most of the Spanish pictures we bought. It seems the Spanish Duke of Montalava was a great friend of Wellington's and it was he who asked Goya to paint the portrait for him. When it was nearly finished, Wellington became dissatisfied with it and insisted that it did not resemble him and that Goya must change his face. He counted without his host; Goya was first, second and for all time a painter, and cared nothing for Wellington, nor Waterloos, nor anything else but his art, and he hotly replied that he would not change a brush stroke on the portrait. Words ran high and weapons were drawn, but fortunately the two great men were separated before they could do greater harm than to express their opinion of each other. It must have been most interesting for the onlookers; I wish I could have seen Goya tossing his artistic little nose in the air in defiance of Wellington's red cloth and gold braid, while the General drew his decidedly hooked nose down as he pursed his lips firmly in disdain of a creature who could only paint bad portraits and had never shouldered a musket. Goya would neither change the portrait nor allow Wellington any longer to pose for him. He walked indignantly off with it, threw a cloak about a model and finished it in his studio. In the corner of the canvas Goya put "A. W. Terror gallorum"; he was at least generous. When we bought the portrait, we received from the Duke's family where it had remained since it was painted, the documents certifying to what I have written, and later M. Ricardo Madrazo again verified the story and said it was his grandfather who separated the two men.

214

No matter what fortune you can command, buying pictures is no easy matter. It took three years to negotiate for "Las Majas al Balcón," and four for Greco's "Cardinal." Mr. Havemeyer became so disgusted and tired with the red tape and the delays that he did not care to hear them mentioned. I recall that we were reading one evening in our library, when suddenly my thoughts were directed to the Cardinal and I felt impelled to say to my husband:

"I think we shall get our Cardinal soon. I don't know why, but I just feel it."

"Don't mention Cardinal to me," answered Mr. Havemeyer. "I am sick of the whole subject."

The next day, when he returned from the office, he came to me and said: "What made you think last night we should get the Cardinal?"

"I don't know," I answered. "It was a sudden impression that came to me."

"Well," he answered, "it is curious. I found this cable on my desk when I reached the office this morning. The Cardinal is yours."

215 "Las Majas al Balcón" for some reason went to Paris, and remained a while with Miss Cassatt and was greatly admired by the critics who dropped into her apartment to see it. When she finally shipped it to us she wrote:

"Roger Marx congratulates you on the possession of this Goya which he considers very fine, and says it is extraordinary for Goya to paint the women's faces as if they were miniatures."

The acquisition of the "Bella Librera" was also an affair of several years. W., as he had promised, took us the following day to see it, but when we entered the room where it hung I saw Miss Cassatt start in surprise, and leaning towards me she whispered:

"What a disappointment! Is it covered with dust, or why is it so dull?"

The courteous old Spaniard extolled the merits of his picture which he was very willing to sell, but Miss Cassatt lost no time in making W. understand that it did not interest us in the least. We made some polite remarks about it and admired some fine old furniture he showed us and then we left.

"W.," said Miss Cassatt as we drove away, "if that is a Goya it is unlike anything else he ever painted, and I don't believe it is a Goya."

W., whom we found perfectly straight, said frankly that he knew little about pictures, but thought it very possible that the owner had sold the original and had put a copy in its place.

"Some of the nobility," he added for our information, "are very poor and will do almost anything to conceal their poverty. At times when they have to make payments to the government, they are willing to sell a picture and it is then I propose to make them an offer if you want anything."

We found W.'s surmise correct. We had seen the copy. 216 We bought the real "Librera" in France several years afterward and learned that one of the conditions of the sale was that the owners should have the privilege of having a copy made to fill the empty space. We had to give the same privilege when we bought the "Cardinal" and several other Spanish pictures, and I sincerely hope no future art collectors may be deceived by them. As for the owner of the copy of the "Librera," he may have known what he was talking about, but we noticed on entering that he had had a very good luncheon with plenty or too much wine. We must forgive him, for some time later our one Velazquez was to be found stored away in the attic of a nobleman's palace of the same name. I do not know if it was the same nobleman or not, nor do I care.

We never secured but one example of Velazquez, a picture that was the admiration of Degas and of Miss Cassatt and also had the seal of authenticity of Raimundo de Ma- 217, 218 drazo who bought it for us through a dealer called Berringham. It is just a head, a fine head of a cavalier looking over his shoulder, probably a fragment of some larger composition lost in the fire, for the date of the burning of the Alcázar was found upon the heavy coarse canvas which Velazquez used and is known in most of his pictures. The painting had to be transferred to a panel to preserve it, but a small piece of canvas with the date, etc., is glued upon the back of the panel. I have never heard its authenticity disputed.

Raimundo de Madrazo stood before it and said to me:
"It is certainly a Velazquez; no one but he could have done
it. It was probably part of a large and important composi-
219   tion like the 'Breda' painting. I wish Beruete could see it."

M. Beruete also told me he wished he could see it before
he finished his Velazquez catalogue, but unfortunately he
never did for he died a few months later. As Miss Cassatt
said, the drawing of the eyes and the modeling of the mouth
bear witness in themselves that it is a Velazquez. While
writing of this great painter I may say W. took us to see
the Duchess of Vallambrosa's Velazquez. It took some time
to open the tightly closed shutters and make it possible for
us to breathe in the musty rooms, but we finally saw it. I
do not need to describe it for upon her death the Duchess
220   left it to the Prado, where it now hangs. It was for sale then,
but we did not admire it sufficiently to buy it, although it is
a fine production in his early manner but without the seduc-
tiveness of the famous "Los Borrachos," which is also one
of his early works. At the Duchess's villa we also saw two
other full-length portraits. Several years later, after the
death of the Duchess, I went with my daughter and M.
Ricardo de Madrazo to the villa and saw them again. M. de
Madrazo told us that a record of Velazquez had been found
wherein he acknowledged the receipt of so many *scudi* for
two portraits. Several years afterwards I read in the New
York papers in huge headlines of the sale of two Velazquezes
from the Duchess of Villahermosa's collection.

They were quickly bought for a fabulous sum and later
left by will to the Metropolitan Museum by B. Altman.
221   We also bought a Patinir while in Spain, for the indefatigable Miss Cassatt had more than one string to her bow
in hunting for pictures and told us to expect something
quite different from Velazquez and Goya. Before long a
pale, sickly little man appeared at our hotel carrying a

canvas. As soon as I laid my eyes upon him I was ready to purchase whatever he brought, if only to give him the means of a good meal and the wherewithal to take care of himself.

"You see," explained Miss Cassatt to Mr. Havemeyer, "your wife has so often spoken of Patinir that I thought she might care for this picture; it is certainly very fine."

The poor little man uncovered his package and sure enough I saw a beautiful example of that early Flemish master. The bright green, the conventional background so wonderfully drawn, the clear atmosphere and the still life were done with such perfection as only the followers of Van Eyck were able to do it; a charming Madonna, naïve even in her gorgeous dress, held the infant Jesus upon her knee. It seemed to me more important than any of the eight I knew so well in the National Gallery in London. The little owner knelt as he told us all about it and showed us exactly where the tiny altar lamp had done some damage to the picture, which had been deftly restored. He seemed very modest about its beauty and its worth. His price was twenty thousand pesetas, a peseta in those days was worth much less than a franc, about seventeen cents of our money. It was not the first nor the last altarpiece which we bought and which had changed misery into a fortune for its owner. We passed without remark the price and were only interested in the value of the painting itself. It was the first time we had to decide upon a fifteenth century painting and we felt our disadvantage, as Miss Cassatt frankly admitted she had never seen a Patinir before. As ever, she was equal to the occasion.

"Why, let us go to the Prado; there must be one there. All Flemish art is represented there; it is the great gallery for them."

The picture was too primitive and the whole transaction scarcely big enough to interest deeply Mr. Havemeyer,

222

and as the day was very hot, he refused to go and showed little interest in the affair.

"Of course we'll go," said I, "and Señor Moreno can wait here until our return."

In a few minutes we were at the Prado and found two fine examples of Patinir there. After examining them carefully, we determined that the one at the hotel was quite good enough to buy, in fact, in some respects was better than those in the Prado, so we returned to the hotel and completed the purchase. When did I see such a delighted expression on a man's worn face as that on our little dealer's, when he realized he had really sold his Madonna and possessed twenty thousand pesetas? I was glad too, for he was really sympathetic and I hoped it would prove lucky money for him also. It did, and in after years I often went into his fine shop in the rue Laffitte in Paris and was always received with the greatest distinction. He never failed to tell me how that sale in Madrid was the beginning of his good fortune.

Although W. took us to villas and palaces where we saw many other pictures both Spanish and Flemish, I think I have mentioned all we acquired through him, for the poor fellow's untimely death put an end to further transactions.

Everyone who collects Goya must have a portrait of the Queen and one of the Duchess of Alba. The royal lady and the beautiful Duchess were rivals and I was told as a bit of Spanish gossip that the Queen, wishing to keep Goya as her own special painter, sent the Duchess away from court to the south of Spain, whereupon Goya, who had no intention of giving up his romantic diversions to sit all day before his easel painting her ugly Majesty, packed his portmanteau and promptly followed his more interesting and beautiful Duchess to the south of Spain, where he spent several years

painting her over and over again. Two of her portraits were   223
offered to us, one in black with a veil over her hair and pointing with her finger to the ground, where at her feet one sees
Goya's signature. She is not so attractive in this portrait,
nor very young either, and we passed it. I believe it is now
in the Hispanic Society in New York City. The portrait we
purchased is of an earlier date. The Duchess is still beautiful and still young. She is dressed in blue and is seated in a
chair of the period, which is partially covered by her cloak.
She holds a guitar by her side and looks languorous and
lovely, as if she had been singing the soft romances of
Andalusia to her lover. She leans back in her chair resting
her cheek upon her hand; as if to please herself, she stretches
out her limbs and one sees her exquisitely pretty little feet
peeping from beneath her delicate gauzy gown. I often
wondered if all Spanish women had the exquisite hands and
feet Goya loved to paint in his portraits, or whether, with
an artist's license, he did them according to his own fancy.
The coloring, the youthful freshness, the charm and the
attractive grace of the portrait are captivating, and I think
with certain visitors it was the most popular Goya I possessed. The casual observer is often confused between an
attractive portrait and one of intrinsic merit.

Fortunately for us, our portrait of the Queen was as much   224
a portrait of a costume as it was a likeness of Her Majesty,
in fact, we really bought it because the costume was so
wonderfully painted and made one forget the distasteful
arrangement of the hair, the cruel black eyes, and the ugly
features with the hideous mouth and heavy chin. We bought
the picture from Théodore Duret, the French art critic. I   225
don't know where he obtained it, but often and often did I
puzzle over that costume, wondering where the Queen of
Spain found such an exquisite yellow gown to wear when
Goya painted her portrait. When we were deciding whether

to purchase the picture or not, Miss Cassatt observed:

"Well, Goya never did a finer bit of painting than that dress."

"All right," said Mr. Havemeyer. "We'll buy the dress, and take the Queen with it."

Only a year ago I found out about that "yellow dress" and in a very curious way. I was dining one evening with Mrs. Dean Sage, the wife of the gentleman who presented me with a copy of the *Memorials of Christie's* which I mentioned in my opening chapter, and the conversation turned upon the quality of literature suitable for our different stages in life.

"At my age," said Mrs. Sage, "I want to read books that I can forget."

We laughed at her philosophy, and I asked her how she managed to read such books when she found them, for we knew she lived among wonderful books and possessed the finest library in America.

"Yes, I do find them, but rarely, I admit," she answered.

I mentioned a volume I had just begun, the *Mémoires d'une Femme de Cinquante Ans*, and I said I thought it might serve her purpose as it was interesting and made no great demands upon our mental reserve.

"True," she answered quickly, "that is exactly such a book as I referred to. I have just read it. Don't you find it diverting?"

"Very," I answered; "so far as I have read it, but I have scarcely finished the first volume."

"You will enjoy it more and more," said Mrs. Sage, "particularly where the author describes her life in America after her escape with her family from France. She lived for several years on a farm near Albany, which Mr. Van Rensselaer let her have. I was so interested that I drove to the place and found the house, etc., all as she described it, but in a very dilapidated condition. She was certainly a wonderful woman; read how Napoleon insisted upon having her at court after her return to France."

I returned home and eagerly began reading the volume and, lo and behold, to my great astonishment I found a description of Marie Louise, the Queen of Spain, and the yellow dress. Mme de la Tour du Pin was a remarkable woman, half-English, half-French, lady in waiting to the unfortunate Marie Antoinette, an *émigrée*, refugee, during the Reign of Terror, the admiration of Talleyrand and of Napoleon, who insisted that she should grace his court and who showed her many favors during his reign, and later, after the restoration of the Bourbons, the duchess par excellence selected to receive Louis XVIII upon his return to France. When the King and Queen of Spain were taken captives by Napoleon, he detailed Mme de la Tour du Pin to be lady in charge of Her Majesty, Marie Louise, during her stay in Bordeaux. I cannot do better than to allow the Duchess to relate the incident of the yellow dress in her own words, and will endeavor to translate literally the passage in which she described it. She writes:

"When Charles IV of Spain and Marie Louise, his wife, arrived in Bordeaux, the Emperor commanded that I should serve as lady in waiting to the Queen during her stay of three or four days in that city. I arrived at the palace at eleven o'clock and M. Dumanoir, who was to present me to her Majesty, said to me as we entered the apartment of the Queen:

" 'Pray, don't laugh!'

"But indeed, I had great difficulty in restraining myself, for I saw a most unexpected and surprising sight. The Queen of Spain was dressing and stood in the middle of the apartment before a large mirror. She had on only a narrow, short percale skirt and wore, on the blackest, driest and skinniest neck I ever saw, a gauze kerchief. Near her stood the King and several other gentlemen whom I did not know. M. Dumanoir presented me to the Queen, who asked him twice to repeat my name; then she said something to the King in Spanish and he answered that I bore a very noble name. Afterwards, the Queen while finishing her toilette conversed with me and told me that as she had been unable to bring anything from Madrid, the Empress had given her several gowns. In fact, they brought her one of Josephine's to put on, which I recognized at once in the exquisite taste of the Empress. It was made of *yellow crepe* and lined with *satin of the same color*. I felt a sensation of disgust as I witnessed this spectacle of the Queen's humiliation. I no longer had a desire to laugh; I felt more like crying." Mme de la Tour du Pin then relates the history of a few days of court functions, given to entertain Their Majesties, and concludes her chapter with:

"Such is the story of my few days in the service of King Charles IV and the horrible woman who was his queen."

I am convinced that Marie Louise desired Goya to paint her in Josephine's gown feeling sure that it was the last word in Parisian fashions and that the gown, if not the Queen, might attract some admiration and thus gratify her ruling ambition.

Three other Goyas were connected, not with this visit to Spain but with a later one, for I returned eight years after with my daughter and was able to see, through the kindness of M. Ricardo de Madrazo, nearly all the great Goyas in Madrid. After seeing the fêtes and *ferias* in Seville, we came to Madrid for I hoped I might be able to secure another Greco, the portrait of "Saint Ildefonso" at Illescas. We took a dusty motor ride there in order to see the splen-

229

did picture, and at one moment it seemed as if it would come to our collection, but the usual collusions and combinations started and I was obliged to relinquish the idea. It was a disappointment to me for the reason that just before Mr. Havemeyer's death we were considering two other pictures by Greco, which had been in a chapel in Toledo. They were an "Ascension of the Virgin" and a "Saint Martin." We saw only the photographs at that time, 230 and although after my husband's death they were still offered to me, I, feeling little interest in art, refused them both and they passed into the collection of Mr. Widener of Philadelphia. M. de Madrazo took us again to see the Boabdilla Goyas, at least to see those that still remained in Spain, and I so much admired the portrait of the little Countess of Chinchon, that I at once bought the other portrait of her 231 done for her husband, the Duke of Olivares, in the same dress and hat, when it was offered to me a little later. The one in the Boabdilla Palace was covered with white mold which I regretted to see as I knew it could not be removed without injuring the picture. Usually the Spaniards take good care of their pictures, but this villa seemed to me unusually damp and a bad place for paintings. Some day, I suppose, these pictures will be restored and sold as wonderful examples of Goya's work. We also saw "La Marquesa de la Solana," one of Goya's best portraits, but unfortu- 232 nately not the portrait of a beautiful woman. I think it was not a success as a "seller" for I afterward saw it in Paris and it was again offered for sale. For some reason, "La Marquesa de Pontejos," with her *bouffant* skirts, her quaint 233 attitude and her shepherd style of Louis XVI, did not interest me. I enjoyed far more the little "Condesa de Haro," 234 one of the loveliest portraits Goya ever painted. It fairly breathes life, and the pretty creature is so entrancing in her youth and grace, and it is executed with such a light touch that the very petals of the rose in her hair appear to move and the lace to vibrate that rests upon her delicate shoulders; you feel portrait painting could go no further.

We spent a delightful morning viewing the art treasures of the Duke of Alba, and from his palace went directly to see the Goyas belonging to his grandmother, one of the greatest and most respected duchesses of the realm. The young Duke received us and appeared to enjoy chatting with us and telling of his ancestors whom Goya had painted. There was one of a charming woman in a thin light dress, such as Goya delighted to paint, which fairly stirs with the atmosphere which this painter of realism knew how to put into his pictures; and another of three young girls, an interesting group, although not one of his great works. The Duke told us that Goya, who had a sense of humor, as a joke painted one of his aunts or great-aunts, who had never been known to read a book, seated holding a volume in her hand. When I expressed my admiration for the arrangement of the many objects in the long glass cases, which we examined as we passed through the apartments, his face lighted with pleasure and he said eagerly:

"It was my mother who arranged all these cases. Everything was in confusion before she married my father, but she spent several years classifying and arranging the objects. She completed it just before she died," he added and took up a photograph of a young woman with serious dark eyes and, showing it to me, said: "That is my mother's photograph."

I said something that pleased him, but I did not dare ask why she died so young. I wished she might have known how much pleasure her labor gave to me. I examined a splendid set of Moorish armor taken by the ancestor of the young man who stood at my side, and I read a letter that poor Mary Stuart wrote to his many-times grandsire, the great

Duke of Alba, pleading with him to intercede in her behalf with Elizabeth of England, and for the first time since I had been a collector, I realized what was the true sense of possession. That letter of the Scottish Queen was a personal appeal to the great Duke, who with her had made history, and it was still in his family. The young Duke could take it up and consider what *he* would have done if the appeal had been made to him. That letter would stir the same blood that was moved by the perusal of it centuries before by his grandsire, and it seemed to me that the young man by my side could not return it to the case with the feelings of a collector only, as if it had come from this or that collection, or had a price mark attached, but that blood would tell and he must have felt the thrill of past pride as well as of present responsibility, that he would have to remember that he was another Duke of Alba and a grandee of Spain. I tried to express this to him and I think he understood, for he told me with much animation how the great Duke had captured the armor and had worn it as well, and spoke of other members of his family, and I recall he seemed to have an especial affection for his grandmother who was a sister of the Empress Eugénie. I left feeling much impressed with the splendors of Spain myself and wondered what the Spanish nobility thought of me as a collector. The humor of it was irresistible, and I remarked to M. de Madrazo:

"What a 'collection of ancestors' I have!" I said laughing. "I scarcely know their names and I could not tell whether they fought with the Moors or the Spaniards. I have portraits of Spanish ancestors, Dutch ancestors and Italian ancestors, and I could furnish portraits of the progenitors of many families that have settled in the United States, and yet I could not mention a fact of their individual history. Art cares little for escutcheons; pedigrees are forgotten, the long titles are lost and today the 'ancestors' are known rather by a signature modestly drawn in neutral tones in the corner of the portrait."

M. de Madrazo laughed too, but I fear as a Spaniard it was hard for him to appreciate my point of view, and we had already arrived at the palace of the Duchess of Fernán-Nuñez. Here I saw another side of a grandee's life. I also had a glimpse into the heart of a noble woman, for in order to see a certain picture we were permitted to enter the Duchess's private apartments. They appeared to me comfortable and homelike, a place where a mother lived and thought of her dear ones. A little roof bower was just beyond the bedroom, where in the cool evening air she could look up at the stars and take courage for the sad day that had to be lived on the morrow, as one dear one after another died and left her mourning alone—several of her daughters died in early youth. By another door one entered a boudoir, where I saw books, a work table and many photographs. Likenesses, alas, that were far sharper in the memory of the poor Duchess than in the photographs before her, for here I learned the sad cause of the early death of the Duke of Alba's mother. The same photograph which I had seen in the morning stood here upon a table and several others of her taken when she was younger, yet even in these one was impressed with the dark earnest eyes. She was the oldest daughter of the house. The handsome man with the same dark eyes was the late Duke, and another photograph of a lovely young girl was of a younger daughter who also had met an untimely death. I expressed my sympathy for the poor mother to M. de Madrazo, and he told me what a wonderful woman the Duchess was. He said:

"Her receptions are the finest in Madrid; she receives downstairs in those apartments we passed through, where you saw the tapestries and the palm gardens and the Goya portraits. To see her as she receives the nobility of Spain, herself one of the noblest of them all, you would scarcely believe it was the same person who lives here mourning for her husband and her daughters."

We left these sad apartments to go see the Goyas again. There were two fine full-length portraits, a man and a woman both in Spanish costumes, the portraits of the Count and Countess of Fernán-Nuñez. Strangely enough I pre- 235 ferred the man's portrait. It was full of movement and life and beautiful in color. However, both were fine, a pair of portraits to be proud of. I trust the family were as proud of them as ancestors; I have no doubt they were.

When Goya painted a *fine* man's portrait, he did it as the saying is, "to the queen's taste," yet he was far more successful in his portraits of women, and I think one of the most beautiful I ever saw was the portrait of the Marquesa de Santa Cruz. I can recall only a few other portraits by Goya 236 as beautiful as this one. When we arrived at the palace, the Count Pié de Concha offered me his arm and led me up the broad staircase and into a large room where the portrait of his grandmother, the Marquesa de Santa Cruz, hung. You felt how susceptible Goya was to beauty. He must have been under a spell when he painted this lovely girl of eighteen. Goya probably had it all his own way in arranging the portrait for he posed her as a muse reclining full-length upon a divan. One arm is extended over the back of it, and she is holding a lyre in her hand; the other arm is extended over a soft pink drapery which covers the divan. It is a bit fantastic in composition, but entrancingly beautiful in color and execution. She has a grape wreath upon her hair, through which I believe she could pass her fingers if she chose to do so, in fact, it is all so lifelike, so realistic, you stand before it breathless in wonderment waiting for her to stir or to move those soft black eyes which look at you with the innocence of a child. It appeals to all the senses;

the lines are like lovely harmonies, the color makes you think of sweetness, you recall the fragrance of a flower as you look at the lovely creature and long to touch the gauzy lace that covers the graceful form. There is Goya's own pink—as only he could paint it—in the drapery over the sofa, and never before had he been so prodigal with his rosy tones.

The Duke allowed me to look at it for some time and then he said: "It is the portrait of my grandmother."

"I wish she were mine," I answered quickly.

He smiled and said: "Ah, madame, I would let you have it, if I could, but what can I do? I cannot sell my grandmother, can I?"

Words flew to my lips but fortunately I held them back, still I think he read my thoughts for he said graciously:

"Ah, perhaps some day when I grow old."

I, of course, caught the cue and hoped he never would grow old and that his beautiful grandmother would smile at him for many a year to come. Reluctantly I turned from the splendid portrait and said good-bye to the kindly Duke, but as soon as we had left the door, I turned to M. de Madrazo and said:

"M. de Madrazo, you must get me a portrait like that; indeed you just *must*."

The good man smiled and said he would try; in fact, he hinted he had something in view but was not sure he could get it. He had succeeded in securing a child's portrait for my daughter, a Goya which she prized very much and which she now has in her home and can show to her children to-day. It is the portrait of Juanita Mazarredo, a pretty little Spanish girl dressed in white, with pink bows; she has sparkling black eyes; one hand falls by her side and the other is tugging at the end of a black belt about her waist. M. de Madrazo also found me the only Goya child's por-

trait I own. It is the portrait of Manuel Cantin Lucientes,   238
a cousin of Goya's, and here is what M. de Madrazo, the
best authority on Goya I know, said:

"Goya, returning to Saragossa at one time, evidently
wished to paint this young cousin in a hurry, so he seized
upon the first thing that came to hand, and it happened to
be a fifteenth century panel with a painting of the Virgin
and Child upon it; the top is arched as if it had been made
for an altarpiece. Upon this panel Goya painted the good-
looking young boy in the costume of the period, in a gray
coat, a soft white shirt and a vest of 'Goya pink,' the pink
that only he could paint. Through the color, in a certain
light one can detect by looking carefully the outline of the
Christ Child's leg, and above, the nimbus of the Virgin.
The impetuous Goya did not take time to clean the panel
thoroughly. There is another defect in the picture, the
panel is split just to the right of the boy's face and it has had
to be cradled and the crack retouched. Still it is one of Goya's
interesting children's portraits, and he was not always successful in painting children. Beruete in his catalogue of
Goya's works gave a description of it."

M. de Madrazo kept his word about finding me something important. He was at the *albergo* in the Puerta del Sol
late one afternoon, and I, thinking he had come to say good-
bye, as we were leaving in the early morning for a visit to
Catalonia, received him at once. He entered hastily and
asked me if I could possibly accompany him to see a very
beautiful Goya which he had just managed to have sent to
Madrid in time for me to see. I answered I would go at
once, and we rattled along in a little *voiture de place* and
were soon in front of a modest-looking house in a rather
deserted street. We climbed some winding stairs and for
the first time met the Marquis de la Vega Inclan, who
showed me an easel on which rested "La Princesa de la

239 Paz." I could scarcely believe my eyes, but there she was just as I had seen her in the Boabdilla Palace, only this portrait was half-length and Goya had varied the color of the bow in her bonnet and had painted it green instead of blue. I must have looked incredulously at M. de Madrazo, for he said to me:

"It is a repetition of the portrait in the Boabdilla Palace and was painted for her husband the Duke of La Paz. It comes from the descendants of the Olivares family."

The chair, the light dress, the folded hands, the portrait ring, the fluffy hair, the pretty bonnet were all there. The movement of the head was the same; there was the same gentle expression in the eyes and the same sweet maternal sentiment in the face. The movement was exquisite and Goya expended all the art of his greatest period in its execution. I looked at it long and carefully and left feeling my journey to Spain had not been in vain.

"Why did you not show this to me before?" I asked M. de Madrazo, when we were alone again in the fiacre.

"Because," he answered, "M. de la Vega Inclan had sent it to Paris and I was afraid he could not get it back before you left. I did not wish to disappoint you."

"Do you mean to say," I persisted, "that that picture was in Paris, and they let it go again! Don't tell me Paris is an art center if they did."

M. de Madrazo explained that it had been there only a short time for, feeling sure that I would want it, he had persuaded the Marquis to send for it. Of course, I bought it and when I returned to Paris and showed it to Miss Cassatt, she was delighted and exclaimed:

"*That* is fine, *there* is style; it is wonderful," and looking at its elaborate Spanish frame of black and gold, she continued, "When a picture can stand a frame like that, you may be sure it is fine."

Yes, it was certainly fine and Miss Cassatt's remark about its being able to stand such a gorgeous frame recalls another incident about the portrait. When I returned home with the picture, it was accidentally placed in a small room, which was hung with old Chinese satin of soft yellow, while the furniture and curtains were of black plush. Mr. Colman and I once had a conversation about decoration and the difference between the effect of harmony and contrast in a room. I asked him if such a strong contrast as black and gold were possible, and he replied it could be made very beautiful and that he would decorate such a room for me. I do not need to speak of the room, nor to enter into the details of the yellow stain he made for the woodwork and furniture, of the wonderful designs in lead relief decorated in dull gold, of the yellow glass he used, or of the blue tint he gave to the black plush curtains on which he applied some large yellow medallions of Chinese embroidery. All this belongs rather to the history of my home than to the story of the picture. Yet, when I saw the "Princesa de la Paz" in that room, I felt I could not take it out of it for it looked so well against that yellow background. I at once hung it in the black and gold room and there it hangs to this day, and is a striking illustration of how a background can help a picture. The following little story will further explain what I mean.

One day, I was receiving a number of friends, among them a well-known collector, Mr. Frick, who brought with him a dealer, M. Knoedler, from whom he bought most of his pictures. After going through the gallery with my guests, I stopped to converse a moment with a friend, when I heard my name called and turning found Mr. Frick and some other gentlemen standing before the "Princesa de la Paz." As I entered I heard Mr. Frick say:

"No, it cannot be the same portrait; if it had looked like

240

that, I should certainly have bought it," and turning to me, he continued, "Mrs. Havemeyer, please tell us where you bought that portrait. It, or one just like it, was offered to me in Paris last year. Can there be two, for surely it was not this one."

"Yes," I answered. "Although there is another portrait like this in Spain, I surmise it was this one, for I bought it from M. de la Vega Inclan in Madrid last year, and I knew it had been offered for sale in Paris."

Mr. Frick looked disgustedly at M. Knoedler, who evidently had shown it to him in Paris. He hastened to excuse himself for causing Mr. Frick's disappointment. He said to me that although it certainly was the same picture, it looked very differently when Mr. Frick saw it, as it had no frame on it then, and that Mr. Frick must have seen it in a bad light, and added as a most conclusive reason for rejecting it, that the Spaniards asked far too much for it and he mentioned a price, which although more than I paid did not seem to me exorbitant. I was quite aware that he hoped I would follow his cue and mention the amount I paid for the portrait, but I did not care to gratify his curiosity. Poor Mr. Frick, he must have felt his disappointment, for I found him a short time afterward leaning against my library table looking at the Rembrandts, and he said to me sadly:

"If I had a homelike place like this room to hang my pictures in, I should enjoy collecting. Mine do not look as yours do here."

"Perhaps your ceilings are too high, or your backgrounds are not right," I answered, feeling truly sorry for him, and added, "such pictures as you own must always look well, you mean they might look better. When you build," for he was about to begin a lordly home with an immense gallery on Fifth Avenue, "let me give you a few suggestions about backgrounds."

But to continue—admiration for my portrait of the little Princess grew until my head began to be turned and I gave to the picture the credit which should have been given to its surroundings, the appropriate background, the frame, the light, even the glow from the golden carpet beneath it. However, truth will out, and never more emphatically than in art. The following spring I decided to lend my Spanish pictures, my Grecos and my Goyas, for a certain cause. They were to be exhibited at the Knoedler galleries on Fifth Avenue. I went to the galleries to place the pictures and I will only say the background was little better than red. It fairly hurt me to see my paintings hung against it. Poor little Princess, what a change it made for her! She faded and paled like a drooping flower. Even the elaborate frame which she stood so well could not sufficiently protect her from that dreadful background. She sank back and seemed to disappear in timid embarrassment. Although I was shocked as I gazed upon the dainty royal lady, I made no remark but began comparing the other paintings. How differently they all looked; I could scarcely believe they were the same pictures that had left my home that very morning. The portrait of the Cardinal in his magnificent red robes was the only one which was not greatly injured by that background. The exhibition lasted for three weeks and I was rather curious to know how these Spanish pictures would be appreciated hanging in this gallery. I found that it was the least complex, the most easily understood picture that was the favorite, the portrait of the beautiful, seductive Duchess of Alba. The honors did not go to the Cardinal, nor even to the famous portrait of the Countess of Giocoechea—a portrait that a popular critic said he thought "as fine as a Velazquez," a remark which another critic overheard and replied: "Why not say, as fine as a Goya?" My Princess, Olivares's pathetic wife, did not receive her just meed of admiration, and I was glad when I could again hang her against a background which suited her so admirably. Colonel Payne always insisted that my Princess was finer than his two Goyas, a pair 244 of portraits of Señor and Señora Ignacio Garcini that I had lately secured for him through M. de Madrazo, and I always answered him with:

"Bring them here first and compare them on the same background."

I think I have now mentioned all the Grecos and all the Goyas that we actually bought in Spain. M. de Madrazo had in a measure replaced the Infanta's godson, although I am persuaded that had the latter lived, our collection would have been far richer in examples of Spanish art. He, W., had a marvelous way of finding pictures and when found, of knowing how to secure them. Our last day in Madrid in 1901 is an illustration. I remember that he came to say good-bye to us about an hour or two before our train left for Paris. Mr. Havemeyer and W. spoke about the financial part of buying pictures and then my husband added:

"And, W., if you find another Alhambra vase, don't let it pass."

"Or some Hispano-Moresque plates," I added.

"Oh," said W., who spoke English extremely well, "if I had known you wished for those I could have taken you to a palace where you could have bought some off the walls. Their owner has to sell; he needs money badly."

"Why not go there now?" said Miss Cassatt.

W. consulted his watch and thought we had time. Mr. Havemeyer declined to accompany us and begged us not to be late, and then, to our amazement said, for he had always maintained he would not consider the bespectacled Greco:

"And go buy your old cardinal with the glasses."

We looked at him incredulously, but I knew he was again,

as he had done many times before, only deferring to Miss Cassatt's sound judgment. Therefore, it was W. who started the entering wedge for the purchase of the "Cardinal," although we did not get the picture for several years after his death. We left Mr. Havemeyer at the hotel and met him an hour later at the station. He found I now had two large packages to carry to Paris, the small Greco in one package and two Hispano-Moresque plates in the other, one with a copper and the other with a moonlight luster. We had selected them hurriedly and the owner had taken them from off his walls to give them to me. I learned in later years that it became a fashion with dealers to sell plates off the walls in the same way, and although we did not then know that His Majesty Charles V could have walked from kingdom to kingdom through tiled corridors of modern manufacture, yet Mr. Havemeyer was suspicious of my plates, and it was not until such an expert as "Manheim" of Paris had passed upon them and had said that they were not only genuine but very beautiful, that I consented to place them in my dining room where they hang to this day.

CHAPTER XI

Gustave Courbet

1917

THERE were three painters who had but to shut their eyes and look within to know who was the supermaster, who taught them; had but to think of the delicate retina which received impressions to realize that the Creator of those marvelous retinas, He who had endowed each with a vision far beyond that accorded to most mortals, was alone responsible for the masterpieces they achieved. I do not deny that each had to work, that each had to study, but I do not think that any earthly teacher could have given Velazquez, Rembrandt, or Courbet axioms or formulas that would have enabled them to produce "Las Hilanderas," "The Night Watch," "L'Enterrement à Ornans," or "Le Combat de Cerfs." These painters were guided by an unerring vision. They saw the truth and the reality of things; they perceived the values of light, and felt all the subtle harmonies of color. They looked and painted; they made things real and living because they saw them real and living, and they found the way to put the living impression of their retina upon canvas, to delight and astonish an admiring world while art shall last. I dare not undertake a treatise on painting, and so much has been written about Velazquez and Rembrandt that I will content myself by telling what I remember hearing of Courbet, as told to me by those who knew him well, and by describing some of the many pictures we own and how we happened to collect them. Although I never met Courbet, although I never even saw him, I believe Courbet is the most real and living personality to me of any of the modern painters whose works hang in our gallery.

Just as I think of him, I feel his elemental force, his savage tenacity of truth. All this is well expressed in one of his portraits, the one where he leans his fine head against one hand and puts the other hand to his hip; he throws a glance over his shoulders; as he looks at you through his half-closed eyes the defiant lips seem to say: "Carry me to fame or to the devil, mistress art, thus I am and thus I remain." Or again, in "L'Homme Blessé," in the suffering mouth and drooping eyes you feel a great struggling in fulfillment of his destiny; with placid courage and without fear he is passing into the great unknown.

I see him, *le bon garçon* of the simple *bourgeoise* family who lived among the white cliffs of Ornans and the ragged rocks and dark chasms of the Loue, where the *fils* went to paint. I see the big-hearted loving boy making his dash for liberty, and when he held his treasure, which was as the breath of his nostrils, to his heart he cherished it there through long years of constant struggle and chagrin, concealing his heartaches and his disappointments under a gay, debonair indifference, sacrificing the warm blood of his youth and all the force of his manhood upon the altar of his muse. Thus I see him, the joy of his friends, the leader of his clique, the strong powerful child of nature, defiantly asserting his right to liberty in art, as well as liberty of soul. I don't wonder he felt the irresistible desire "to pull" at something, for in those days there was much "to pull" both in art and in politics, and all the world must give credit to Gustave Courbet that there was no ulterior motive in soul, no thought of self-advancement, if he "déboullonned" when

247 he helped get the cords ready. He pulled for the pure love of liberty, and when his passion for that one treasure laid him low, led him into Ste Pélagie—where his great heart beat so wildly against his prison bars that the good doctor gave him colors and canvas to quiet his rage, and he painted those pictures of flowers and fruits that today are cherished in Europe's great museums—and finally, when his enemies made him suffer and die an exile from his beloved France, he made no murmur; he proclaimed his faith and his innocence, and then the government to its lasting shame, robbed him of almost all the labors of his life.

He continued to work to the very last, honorably trying to pay his cruel fine, and dying in the cheerless room of his Swiss exile with loving words upon his lips for his heart-broken father, and regretting that he could not see once again his beloved Ornans, his home, and hear the Loue as it splashed over the jagged rocks of the lovely chasm. Posterity must judge whether his was the artist's life, or the martyr's life. Fate wove them closely together for Gustave Courbet, and yet he bore his trials with the true spirit of his race, joyous and brave, tender and defiant, fully appreciating his own worth and readily acknowledging that of others. When all has been said of Gustave Courbet, one must admit he was a true Frenchman at heart, loyal and proud, a banner bearer of the tricolor. I remember that 248, 249 Théodore Duret told me that Thiers once wished to meet Courbet, thinking he would see a rough, uncouth *bourgeois*, and that he was greatly surprised to find a well-dressed, refined man when he entered his salon, thoroughly poised and self-reliant, who not only understood the subject of the conversation but was able to express himself with great clearness and dignity.

Courbet's nature, rather than his life, is expressed in his works. He has great breadth of stroke and feeling, great nobility in his compositions, less analysis but deeper sympathy, intimate appreciation of the humble toilers of France, and a brutal disgust of hypocrisy. Courbet, the great exponent of realism, was never tempted to paint either religious or philosophical subjects. I do not recall one, for the "Retour de la Conférence" is purely a satire, almost a caricature, and no religious thought is suggested. 250

Courbet was essentially a painter of nature. Nature was his mistress, and he interpreted nature with amazing facility with broad brush strokes, or dashes of his thumb or the use of his palette knife. Like Manet, he loved a large canvas. I remember no really small picture by Courbet. Nearly everything he did was from life, and life-size. "The Studio," containing one of the best groups Courbet ever did, is perhaps 251 the largest picture a painter ever attempted. Evidently stimulated by the thought of other great compositions of the world, possibly "The Surrender at Breda," or "The 252 Night Watch," he desired to do a large modern composition. He paints his vast studio replete with light and air; on the right he groups his literary and artistic contemporaries, on the left is a page from his *"comédie humaine"*; it represents pathetic figures from the social scale, and there is a satire of the Academy in a manikin of many angles posing as Saint Sebastian; Courbet is painting at an easel in the center group, while a nude model looks over his shoulder and an adorable youngster stands by looking up at the master—as large in style as it was in canvas. When I saw the picture, it served as a curtain to the stage of a small theater in a Parisian home. Courbet, the exquisite classic model, and the painting of that urchin's back, which challenges even Manet, compose a group which could give a name to the nineteenth century. I remember that it was once offered for sale, and Mr. Havemeyer thought he would buy it and take out the center group, for the rest of the picture was never finished, but—a composition is a composition —my husband could not make up his mind to do it, and decided not to buy it.

Courbet loved to stand before his easel, surrounded by an admiring crowd, when he would say in his proud self-reliance: "See my trees grow." And then the palette knife and thumb would move rapidly over the canvas, producing the impression which his retina—no one knows when—had indelibly stamped upon his memory.

All traditions, all conventionalities he tossed to the winds. He jeered at the *a b c*'s of studio plodders; he acknowledged no teachers; he disregarded the ordinary adjuncts of the formal compositions and hated the rules of the Academy. A red curtain might be needed to throw out the flesh tints for other painters' nudes, but not for his. His nude lies upon the bed and leaves her clothes just where they fall as she takes them off; the light comes in through the window just where it will, the hair falls as it likes, and the brilliant para-keet is held upon the lifted hand, and pants and talks at its own sweet will. There is the subject of one of Courbet's great pictures. He wanted an academic for the Salon—an academic that the *cancan* of his detractors would have to call an academic. Do you wonder the jury gasped, that they were indignant, and refused it? Courbet took it back with a defiant laugh upon his lips, but rage was devouring his heart. In the loneliness of his studio he fought the disappointment of his hopes, but not for one minute did he dream of sacri-ficing his art to the narrow views of a jury! No, not if hunger stared him in the face, and indeed, he often did feel her fangs in his quivering flesh. Oh, no! Liberty and truth for him, the treasures he prized above his life! His academic might be refused at the Salon, but it would live in the art world, and after all, someone would give him a bit to eat or he would go hungry—such is the pathetic history of one of the great-

253

est nudes the world has seen, "La Femme au Perroquet."
And how it is painted! Pearly, pulpy flesh, delicate modeling of tone after tone, bathed in air and light, the rich glow,
the luminous shadows, and oh, the way the clothes are
painted and the daylight comes through the window! Why
do we think of Rembrandt and the skill of the great Hol-
lander? Why? Because it is truth; it is nature pure and
simple caught spontaneously upon the intricate network
behind those wonderful eyes. It is mine; how proud I am
of it!

What a memory the man must have had! In more than
one picture, the figures are painted in one place, Germany,
and the landscape in another, Ornans. I have a charming
picture of a nude, the figure was done in France and the
landscape was painted in the beautiful woods of his villa in
Switzerland. We see the nude's back, as the model faces
the stream and reaches out her hand to feel the dripping
water as it trickles over the rocks and bushes. "Le Combat
de Cerfs" was also partly done in Germany and the great
woods, where the bucks are fighting and the frightened
deer leaps away into the background, were not painted until
Courbet returned to France. He writes: "I must go to L——
for a landscape." Think of what a mental strain it must
have been to have taken up that composition again, and to
have continued it after having let it drop for a length of
time!

Look at his marines, or his pictures of coast and water;
at his "Wave" or his many waves, the one with the boat in
the Louvre which I would advise as many as can to compare
with Whistler's "Wave"—for Whistler liked to be with
Courbet and had the intelligence to learn from him, but he
never could paint a wave as Courbet did. No painter ever
put more depth or weight or salt or wind into a wave than
Courbet did; no effect of atmosphere was neglected, from

the dramatic downpour to the opalescent beauty of a summer's evening. I have one of each and as I view them, I am convinced that few aspects of the sea escaped his eager eye.

258   I recall that I bought one day two marines; one "La Roche Isolée," where the great boulder looms up in the foreground, slimy and green as the waves wash over it with the rising tide and then receding leave it incrusted with barnacles, and the seaweed clings to its base affording a home for the mussels and the little sea life. How did he manage to put his horizon so far away that the vast melancholy of the sea is expressed so strikingly, how did he put his clouds so high in the arched dome? They float far above you, and leave you a lonely speck upon the shore. When Courbet painted "La Roche Isolée" did he feel as I do when I look upon the lovely picture, or did he paint the scene just as he saw it, knowing nature would express the sentiment through his "honest brush?" I have often asked myself that question and many more when I study Courbet's pictures. The other picture that I bought that same day was a beautifully transparent and exquisite bit of summer calm —just a stretch of shore with opalescent ripples lapping against the sand and the sky scarcely touched by a cloud. Again I ask how could Courbet, except through the medium of memory or vision, leave the strong contrasts of dramatic effect, and paint a picture of such tender, subtle harmonies? His eye, of course, is responsible.

He must have been a wonderfully rapid painter, and always busy, for wherever he is he is working. At Ornans, on a visit to his family, it is another picture of his favorite

259   grotto, the "Source of the Loue," or a sketch for the "Enterrement." If he is on a visit in Saintonge, it is the lighthouse on La Pointe de Vallières that attracts him; and after a long afternoon of work he greets the friends who come to fetch him with a merry laugh, and suggests a supper of

oysters and wine and then a little exercise with oar and row-locks to aid digestion, lustily pulling his share and hugely enjoying the discomfiture of his companions, who find their lack of headway is due to their neglect of casting off— through the influence of wine and oysters, they find they are still fast to the shore. Or when upon another occasion they find him with his huge canvas in a tiny donkey cart, both cart and donkey about to disappear down the sharp mountainside, as Courbet, holding on to his precious day's work, loudly calls for assistance. It is always work, work, work.

I love to fancy the rollicking, genial Courbet and the dainty, keen-witted Whistler, comrading together for a summer on the coast of France; the one painting away regardless of the other, unable to change one jot or tittle of his large style or broad strokes of his own manner; the other, with all his perceptions struggling like antennae, feeling the methods of Courbet, analyzing the systems and theories, taking this, rejecting that, as he did in later years when Oriental art came to the western world and attracted his attention. The broad humor of the one and the delicate wit of the other must have made a delightful combination for their friends.

I own one picture by Courbet painted at that time. It is called "La Belle Irlandaise," and is the portrait of Johanna 260 Pfeiffer. The Irish beauty's wavy chestnut hair falls about her face and shoulders, and she is looking at herself in a mirror which she holds up in her hand. Evidently the beautiful red hair and the peculiar complexion that usually accompanies it attracted Courbet and he painted her on a canvas large for what it represented, as she is painted life-size, but rather small for a Courbet. There is no attempt to make either a composition or a portrait out of it. When Courbet does a portrait, there is no mistaking it; it is a

portrait. As soon mistake a Rembrandt, whom Courbet recalls in many of his portraits; the light shadows, the fleshy
envelopment, the life and the expression of anatomy insist
upon the resemblance, and make you recall Rembrandt
when you look upon Courbet.

I have several portraits. One, for which I share Degas's
261   admiration, is that of Mme Brayer. I believe she was a
Polish exile, married to a Belgian who lived in Brussels. I
remember that Mr. Havemeyer, Miss Cassatt, and I made
a one-day trip to Brussels in the *grande vitesse* to see it. We
found it in a modest apartment, and the portrait of the poor
exile hung in a frame that beggared description; for years
afterwards, the very mention of that frame brought expressions of fierce indignation from Miss Cassatt. Even
the color of the gold was bad; the heavy moldings of the
frame flopped over the moldings of the room. It crowded
the other pictures hanging upon the walls; even the lovely
woman seemed to shrink away from it, and the delicately
folded hands, hands which Degas said were like Rembrandt
—you see Degas was in line on Courbet's resemblance
to Rembrandt also—lay folded upon her knee, as if she
had to hold them there in Christian resignation instead of
struggling to get free from that gilded scaffolding that
surrounded her. It was a beautiful, ideal countenance, expressing the pathos and the suffering of her race. Courbet
must have felt the tenderest respect for the noble woman,
whom he placed in a simple pose in her quiet dark dress,
the low lace collar at her throat fastened with the large
brooch of Queen Victoria's time.

Théodore Duret, art critic, thought this Courbet's finest
portrait, as painting goes, but here Miss Cassatt always
disputed with the critic. She gave ample justice to the painting of "Mme Brayer," but insisted that the portrait of
262   "Louise Colet" was more spontaneous and a greater work

of art. Those little journeys were always filled with pleasant reminiscences for me, and there were plenty of them,
and as on this occasion conversation did not lag. Duret was
the friend of all the impressionists, as well as of Courbet and
of Whistler. Duret was a great authority on French history
as well, and Miss Cassatt and he chatted while I listened,
and Mr. Havemeyer would occasionally make some opportune remark that would suggest another side of the question.
They would discuss whether France would have been the
France of today without Jeanne d'Arc, or the force and object of French colonization, or even in those long past days,
suggest the possibility of the present war. Whistler's portrait of Duret hangs in our Metropolitan Museum. I had   263
long been familiar with it as it always hung in Duret's
apartment, and often I had wondered if the portly old gentleman who always ushered us in with friendly words could
ever have been the sprightly young man of the pink domino,
whom Whistler reveals to us with opera hat in hand, an
habitué of the masked balls and gay reunions of Paris. I met
Duret only during his later years of discretion and fancied
the pink domino part of Whistler's portrait an accessory of
the studio that he loved to paint and had hung upon his
friend's arm as a joke. Still it is possible that Duret—my
Duret, the eminent critic—was young once upon a time.
"Qué tal!" Goya would have said, and Goya was apt.

I have said I never met Courbet, yet nevertheless, there
was a beginning to my acquaintance with him as a painter.
I remember that, when I was a young girl scarcely more
than fifteen years old, a lady came to visit Mme Del Sarte,
where I was a *pensionnaire*, and I heard her say she could   264
not remain to tea because she was going to Courbet's studio
to see a picture he had just completed, and then she spoke of
him as a painter of such great ability that I at once con-

ceived a curiosity to see some of his pictures. For some reason, I did not see any of his pictures for several years. There
were probably few to be seen in Paris as they were usually
refused by the Salon, and poor Courbet—or Courbet, too
poor—had few exhibitions. It was not until 1881 that the
full splendor of Courbet's talent was revealed to me. Alas,
he was dead, leaving little money and few pictures behind
him, for the government had ordered many of his great
works to be sold to pay the fine he was condemned to pay
for his participation in the pulling down of the Colonne
Vendôme.

Well, in 1881 some friends and admirers planned an
exhibition of Courbet's works in the foyer of the Théâtre
de la Gaîté. How well I remember that exhibition; the catalogue with a brief introduction by Burty lies beside me on
the table as I write. As a result of that exhibition one of the
loveliest pictures Courbet ever painted has hung in our
gallery for many a long year. It was called "La Branche de
Cerisier Anglais" and I saw it for the first time at that
scantily attended exhibition in Paris. As usual, I owe it to
Miss Cassatt that I was able to see the Courbets. She took
me there, explained Courbet to me, spoke of the great
painter in her flowing, generous way, called my attention
to his marvelous execution, to his color, above all to his
realism, to that poignant, palpitating medium of truth
through which he sought expression. I listened to her with
such attention as we stood before his pictures and I never
forgot it. She led me to a lovely nude, the woman drawing
the cherry branch down before her face, and I recall her
saying to me:

"Did you ever see such flesh painting? Look at that
bosom, it lives, it is almost *too* real!" And she added, "The
Parisians don't care for him. You must have one of his
nude half-lengths some day."

And "some day" I did; the very one she referred to, but it took me many years to accomplish it, and even when I finally possessed it I almost lost it again. As it has to do with Mr. Havemeyer and was the second Courbet we pur- 266 chased, I must leave it for a moment and go back and tell of our first Courbet, the one we lost and which today hangs in the Louvre. This Louvre Courbet was part of the Secrétan 267 collection which was sold in 1889. I called my husband's attention to it, and for the first time he saw a Courbet. He did not appear to be favorably impressed by it; I understand why not now. He was excited over the other pictures in the exhibition, many of which he intended to buy, and could not give the attention to the Courbet which it deserved. I recall that I expressed a desire for the splendid "Landscape with Deer," and Mr. Havemeyer said to me:

"Surely you don't want that great big picture."

"But I do," I answered, whereupon he said:

"Come over here and look at the De Hooch. That's the 268 sort of thing to buy."

You see, Mr. Havemeyer's expressions show that he had not yet reached Courbet, but, as Miss Cassatt said, he learned more quickly than any collector she ever knew, and true to her estimation of him, my husband reconsidered his Courbet decision before he reached the North Cape, and sent us a telegram to "Buy the Courbet"—the only formula he ever used at auctions. Alas for us! The picture had been sold, knocked down to the Louvre, where Mr. Havemeyer saw it upon his return to Paris. He immediately told Durand-Ruel to try to get him one as fine.

"Easier said than done, my good husband," said I, and true enough, we succeeded in finding only one Courbet for sale during that visit in Paris. Our first purchase therefore was some cows in a meadow, fine, but not a remarkable 269 Courbet, except that it led to many another picture by the great painter. Now to return to the nude, "La Branche de Cerisier Anglais"; I think it was the following year that Durand-Ruel asked me to drop in and see a Courbet he had just received from France. Imagine my astonishment when I found myself looking again at the lovely half-length nude that I had seen with Miss Cassatt at the Courbet exhibition in Paris.

"Is that for sale?" I almost gasped, and I gave an order to send it to our home so Mr. Havemeyer could see it. I was disappointed when my husband looked at the picture, for I saw that he disapproved of it, and I know that we had agreed *not* to buy any nudes.

"Surely you are not going to buy that," he said.

"I should like to," I answered.

"I shouldn't do it, if I were you," he remarked shortly and left me.

I kept the picture for a day or two, feeling firmly defiant, and then I returned it to Durand-Ruel. A few days later Mr. Havemeyer said to me:

"What did you do about that Courbet?"

"I returned it to Durand-Ruel," I replied.

"I knew you wouldn't want it," he said, quite pleased.

"But I do want it," I had to answer. "I want it very much! It is one of the loveliest pictures I have ever seen, and if I had it I would keep it right there in my closet and not hang it in the gallery at all, but just go there and look at it all alone by myself."

The next day the Courbet came home with word from Durand-Ruel that "Mr. Havemeyer had ordered it sent home to Mrs. Havemeyer," and that is the way the half-length which I saw with Miss Cassatt when I was a young girl, and which she said I ought to have "some day," found its way into our collection. It was not long in becoming a favorite with Mr. Havemeyer, even among the many other

Courbets we eventually collected. Often and often have I watched my husband lead some friend up to that picture, and I have heard him say:

"Next to the Rembrandts—my favorite!"

It did not take Mr. Havemeyer long to recognize Courbet as a great painter. When we visited the exhibition, One Hundred Masterpieces, in Paris in 1900, he stood before Courbet's "Les Casseurs de Pierres" as if rooted to the spot. In fact, he stood there so long that Miss Cassatt said softly to me, pointing to Mr. Havemeyer:

270

"He is bowled over by that Courbet."

My husband, who caught the remark, quickly replied: "I am. I wish I could buy it. Let us find out who owns it and try."

But here follows the secret why art flourishes in France. The people love art, the people know art, the people buy art, the people live with their art. We followed that picture to its owner and it took us to a farriery, and the farrier would *not* part with it at *any* price. Brave farrier! Would there were more of you! Then, we might have art as the Greeks did, not as it is, Greek to most of us today.

After Mr. Havemeyer's death, I did not buy pictures for a few years and lost "Les Casseurs de Pierres" and never saw it again until I went to Dresden and found it in the museum there. Several years later, Duret found in an old French family, where it had hung since it was bought, probably for a few hundred francs, a Courbet of about the same period as "Les Casseurs de Pierres" and expressing the same sentiment of the hardships of toil and poverty. It is called "Les Rémouleurs," and represents two men in worn garments and heavy shoes grinding knives; one turns the wheel and the other holds the blade firmly upon the stone. It has the same touch but it has not the wonderful light and shade of "Les Casseurs," but it is a strong paint-

271

ing and recalls the former in its rich color. It was painted in 1849, the year before "Les Casseurs," and I needed the picture in my collection as many of my Courbets were painted after 1850.

Mr. Havemeyer never forgot that "Landscape with Deer" which he lost in Paris at the Secrétan sale in 1889, nor did he allow Durand-Ruel to forget it, and one after the
272 other we bought "Les Chiens de Chasse," a painting of two dogs in a wood, which resemble those in "La Curée" ("The Quarry"—dead game), "La Source de la Loue," one of the finest of Courbet's paintings of his favorite grotto at the source of the river Loue, and one which I think was painted just before the sixties; and then, after an interval, through the success which attends the ardent collector, Mr. Havemeyer obtained "Le Puits Noir," a landscape which rivaled the one he lost, being possibly more juicy and verdant, more suggestive of the charm and solitude of the forest and of the mossy brook, than the one which hangs in the Louvre.

273 Of Courbet's two large hunting scenes, both with a huntsman in red and dogs, I own one, "After the Hunt." For a long time we hesitated to buy it on account of its size, but I finally found a place for it, for I could not resist the "last word" in painting a hunting scene; I could not resist the fine execution of forest and figure, of dogs and game. Old Jordaens never put greater action and life in his best canvas than the dash of the dogs as the huntsman holds up the game towards them. The horn still hangs about his neck, he has thrown his cap upon the ground, and he enjoys, as a huntsman would, in the cool forest air the result of his morning's work.

From the day I first saw a Courbet with Miss Cassatt, in
274 the foyer of the Gaîté Theater, about thirty-five Courbets have fallen to our share of the great painter's works. At

least there were three persons who admired this descendant of the great realist of Venice enough to buy without stint any of his fine pictures. Miss Cassatt was ever ready to recommend, Mr. Havemeyer to buy, and I to find a place for the pictures in our gallery. Of our minor Courbets, we have several, including snow scenes, a huntsman whose horse scents a blood spot upon the snow, marines with landscape, a wave (from the Dollfus Collection), "La Trombe" a dramatic view of a downpour on a rocky coast, one of his several pictures of the great trees of Fontaine-bleau with a glowing sunset throwing their mighty outline into relief; "La Femme au Chat" whose title should be reversed, for who has ever excelled the painting of the cat? —the cat that plays by the boy in "The Studio"; in still life several pictures of blossoms done at Ste Pélagie, also several of apples, and a picture of asparagus and berries in a white bowl executed when he was in prison in Bordeaux, according to Duret from whom I bought it. I have always regretted that I have no great flower or fruit painting of Courbet. Several years ago, through my own stupidity, I lost a beautiful flower picture, "Les Pivoines," and later, through someone else's stupidity, I lost one of Courbet's best fruit pieces. The first picture, "Les Pivoines," is now, I am told, in a German museum, but the second I was able to salvage, but at a very high price.

Courbet will always live and be known as a great painter of nudes. No one knew better than he did that his métier required a tip-to-toe knowledge of the nude, and even in his earliest years, in the great studio at 89 rue de la Harpe with his favorite model he covered canvas after canvas with studies of the nude, acquiring a facility of flesh painting which in later years enabled him to produce "La Source" (1863), "La Femme au Perroquet" (1866), and many another nude as lifelike and as warm as if his delicate fingers felt the soft modeling, instead of transfixing the vision of his eye with rapid strokes from his broad brushes. How he worked over the difficult task, until he knew his formulas and could make the red corpuscles circulate in the tender tissues, even over the white shirt which he substituted for the old red curtain of the *dames* of long ago. The French girl of Paris was his model, and is it our affair if he mixed a little romance with his colors? We see the same features again and again; they were indelibly stamped upon Courbet's retina for years, and then the film of memory shifted and other features took their place and served the painter who died a bachelor, with love and romance crushed out of his sad heart in his weary exile.

Several of Courbet's nudes are in our collection: "La Branche de Cerisier," our debut in collecting; "La Femme au Perroquet," which was about to be returned to France by the Durand-Ruels in those enlightened days when a heavy duty was hanging about art like a millstone and crushing progress and civilization alike. I begged Mr. Havemeyer to buy the picture, not to hang it in our gallery lest the anti-nudists should declare a revolution and revise our Constitution, but just to keep it in America, just that such a work should not be lost to the future generations nor to the students who might with its help, and that of other pictures, some day give a national art to their own country. Mr. Havemeyer at once consented, and for many a year "La Femme au Perroquet" has hung in the Metropolitan Museum. We bought another lovely picture of the same model, a strange combination of sea and nude painted in 1868. "La Femme à la Vague" it is called, a woman sitting in the surf with her arms clasped over her head; she braces her back against a rock as the sea foam froths about her bosom, she looks toward the approaching waves while

279

280

we enjoy the splendid sea which rolls beyond, and a tiny boat on the distant horizon impresses us with the vastness of the ocean. How often have I heard pseudo-artists inquire with the tone of their voices pointing interrogation points as a musician would handle his staccato:

"Isn't that arm slightly out of drawing?"

"Surely," someone once answered such a question. "But you see, it is unusual to find an elbow in a marine."

Another nude, but not of the same model, is "La Femme au Chien," very delicately painted with evidence of the use of the palette knife in the background, and the way the little white poodle is painted excuse enough for the tender adoration of its mistress, who leans forward to caress it. "La Source" was once offered to me, but on Miss Cassatt's advice I did not purchase it. However, I did buy about that time one of the most beautiful of Courbet's nudes, through Durand-Ruel. It was in 1915 and the owner wanted to sell it during the war, so I bought and paid for it at once by cable. It is also called "La Source—Vue de dos"—probably for the lack of another name, as Courbet's efforts seemed to cease when his picture was finished. For in his time, "La Femme au Perroquet" was called by him an academic, and he would say to his friends:

"I wonder how *ils* will like that?" *Ils* was his generic name for the Institute, the Jury, the Ingrists—for everyone, in fact, who lagged in the traditions of the old school.

My "Source" represents a woman facing a streamlet that tumbles down over some moss-covered rocks in one of his loveliest and loneliest landscapes. She stretches out her arm in order that the water may trickle over her hand. Her back is toward us and she looks, as we do, into the dark green woods frankly enjoying the sunlight that sparkles on her back, revealing the same modeling, the same drawing, as one sees in the more celebrated picture of "La Source,"

281
282

where the model is seated upon a rock and turns her back toward us and stretches out her left hand to reach the dripping water and only a part of her profile can be seen. Courbet has evidently used the same model for both pictures, caring little for her features, but selecting a model that would give him an opportunity to do a nude as only Courbet could do one—with large firm strokes and a brilliancy that startles you. My nude is pearly and gray and the half-tones luminous and bewitching.

I think I know most of Courbet's nudes, they are realistic and frank, but never vulgar; he never even, like that crushing cynic Degas, treats them with brutal force nor reveals the degradation of their class. I have often thought how repugnant the vulgar, sensuous suggestions of the genre painters of this time must have been to a fearless truth-loving nature like Courbet's—a bachelor all his life, but loving a dash of romance to cheer him in his hard struggle. You always feel his deep sentiment for women, his tender respect and his love for his sisters, which they reciprocated with an ardent admiration for his talent and a devoted effort to help and pose for him—as one sees them in many of his pictures from "Les Cribleuses de Blé," and "Les Demoi-
283 selles du Village," to "L'Enterrement," where in various attitudes they express the grief of Ornans. This great painting of Courbet's, "L'Enterrement à Ornans," is like Rembrandt's "Night Watch," a series of portraits and an expression of all phases of his art.

I think Courbet was greatest as a portraitist. He showed a predilection for portrait painting from his earliest years when, lacking models, he painted himself in a series of
284 splendid pictures, as in "L'Homme à la Ceinture de Cuire," now in the Louvre; with his head leaning against his hand, again in the Louvre; in that wonderful portrait, "L'Homme à la Pipe," in the museum at Montpelier; or in "L'Homme

Blessé"; or again, as the "Violoncelliste," and many others. The "Violoncelliste" was once offered to me, but the great realist had frankly painted it as he saw himself in the mirror; when finished, he was a left-handed 'cellist, and my son, who played the 'cello himself, advised me not to buy it and I passed it, although it was a splendid piece of painting. I did not pass, however, the "Violinist," a portrait of M. Proma-yet, one of Courbet's fine portraits and one which reveals his analogy to Rembrandt.

285

Another portrait of Courbet's that has long hung in our gallery is known as "Le Suisse." Whether a collector or not, I cannot say, but "Le Suisse" was evidently an amateur who had a studio where Courbet often went to paint, pos-sibly to economize on models, for many a day the poor painter had not a sou in his pocket and was obliged to ac-cept his only real meal a day, his dinner, from his kind-hearted companions; the other meal was some dry bread in the morning, which he ate in his studio, and then set to work. Many a time wealthy picture buyers have stood be-fore this portrait of "Le Suisse," where the intelligent eyes look keenly at you and the thick hair is brushed erect above his forehead, and have rhapsodized over the "ideal life" of an artist and the alternate one of sordid luxury, as if the ideal painter brought forth his masterpieces while borne by many wings through Elysian fields and the rich stood chained to the easy life of the commonplace. Ah, the good Suisse could have told them of the agonies of producing, of the hardships of an artist's life, and often have I cast glances of appreciation at the good man, whose protégé tried to express his gratitude to his friend by making for him one of his finest portraits. It was done in 1861, when Courbet was *en pleine vigueur*.

When I had regained my courage and was once more buying pictures, I found myself one day with Miss Cassatt in the Galerie Petit looking at a collection that was to be auctioned off the following day. It was the most dreadful lot of trash I ever saw; the paint would have served a better purpose if it had been applied to the side of a house. Miss Cassatt said to me:

"Isn't it astonishing that there are people in Paris who will buy stuff like that?" And then added, "Ah, there's one Courbet."

For we had come to see a Courbet that in some mysterious way had been put into that collection. Perhaps the collector fancied a resemblance to someone he knew, or a friend, who was a better judge than he, had advised the purchase. I do not know, but it was there; and there I first saw "La Femme au Gant," the portrait of Mme Crocq, and I bought it the following day. It is one of Courbet's full-lengths. But why describe it! There was no make-up to it, no coiffure of a *dernier cri*, no heavy stiff brocade which Velazquez, making a virtue out of a necessity, loved to paint, no voluminous chiffon and bits of ribbon blowing like a brig in a storm, but a gentle woman seated placidly in a chair. Mme Crocq is a Frenchwoman, with bright eyes and fine smile, dressed as she probably dressed every day of her life. Her hair is parted on her forehead, drawn back and fastened I am sure by her own deft fingers. In a simple black silk gown, with a green shawl which falls lightly upon her arms, she is seated by a table and leans against it. Her feet in bronze slippers rest upon a footstool; she has drawn on one glove, an easy-fitting one, and in the other hand she holds a large handkerchief, such as French women carried in those days. Her friends will always see her in her own pose and the familiar environment of her home, and strangers will not care who she is but will admire a portrait of a woman by the great painter of realism. The harmony of the picture is exquisite. Could anything be finer than the painting of the black dress,

286

the green shawl, or the bronze slippers? And if the light is treated differently from that of the portrait of the "Violinist," it is as Courbet saw it, in its beautiful half-tone and rich depth of color. I was a happy woman when Miss Cassatt called the next afternoon to tell me the portrait was mine, and shortly afterwards it found a choice place in my gallery, where it hangs to this very day.

And now I have but to mention one more portrait by Courbet—and why I was to be its fortunate possessor, I do not know. Miss Cassatt says it is destiny. If so, I am very grateful to "destiny," and would like to whisper several other secrets in her ear. However, it truly seems as if chance sometimes throws things your way, and certainly it was chance that put the portrait of Louise Colet into our collection, to be the admiration and despair of painters. A picture always singled out by those who know, as being a chef d'œuvre of portrait painting. I remember that Miss Cassatt came to our hotel one afternoon and said:

"Duret has left a Courbet at my apartment for you to see. Your wife may like it," she said, turning to my husband, "but I doubt if you do. It is the portrait of a woman, and resembles your sister-in-law (referring to a beautiful Hungarian who married Mr. Havemeyer's brother); it is very quiet, the only color is the blue sky and her red cheeks. No doubt Whistler saw the white cuffs on the black riding habit, and the white gloves; he should have looked longer at them, before he did *his* woman in a riding habit. Will you come up to the apartment and have a look at it?"

As we drove to the rue Marignan, Miss Cassatt appeared more anxious than I had ever known her about our liking the picture; she almost seemed to apologize for taking us to see it, and said:

"I hope you will like it, but it is quite different from anything you have seen of Courbet's"; and again: "I think you will like it," turning toward me, and then added: "Well, it is not dear anyway, only fifteen thousand francs, and if you don't like it, I will buy it myself."

These are her words as nearly as I can remember them, and they were impressed upon my memory for I distinctly remember my inward determination to approve the picture, if only to allay her apprehension. When we entered the apartment, she said:

"I put it in the dining room," and I turned and entered it, the dining room, at once, and I recall exclaiming as I entered:

"Well, I don't see anything the matter with that! Do you see anything wrong with it?" I queried, as I stood looking at it with Miss Cassatt and Mr. Havemeyer beside me.

Mr. Havemeyer frankly expressed his admiration, and then Miss Cassatt's eyes sparkled and she glowed with enthusiasm, and we had a grand hour of it. I think Miss Cassatt feared we would not understand and admire it as she did, for ever after neither the portrait of Mme Crocq nor that of Mme Brayer could shake her conviction that "Louise Colet" was the finest woman's portrait Courbet ever did, and time and criticism have confirmed her judgment.

Finally, just to let mother earth know we had not entirely forsaken her and were not wandering in the clouds, I said:

"It is a bargain, of course we will take it, won't we?" looking at my husband.

"That settles it," he answered smiling, and turning to Miss Cassatt, he added, "Will you tell Duret to have it packed and shipped?"

But that was not to be for a long time, for, for the first time Miss Cassatt said she would like to make a study of the picture, and the portrait remained some time in France. Miss Cassatt told us that Mme Colet had many friends, and a reputation in letters, and I afterward learned that Courbet, like a *bon camarade*, while doing a good service for a friend challenged the beautiful "Amazone" to a séance, and the portrait was the result, he himself escaping without a scar upon his heart.

How shall I describe the portrait? A woman in a riding habit holding a whip in her hand, scarcely more than the "yellow primrose," but it is one of those rare spontaneous productions which are not often repeated, even in the career of a great painter. It is a masterpiece of technique, light and harmony, and Courbet the realist, who always painted just what he saw, felt the allure of his fascinating sister and painted her in all her charm and beauty.

Mr. Havemeyer and I collected over thirty Courbets and our good fortune as usual was due to Miss Cassatt, the godmother who took me to see that exhibition in the foyer of the Gaîté in Paris, and said to me:

"Some day *you* must have a Courbet."

CHAPTER XII

*W*histler

289 WHISTLER never visited my home. I do not recall even his ever having visited America. He was a firm and solid graft upon English soil. As an artist he hailed from no man's land but tastes and habits made an Englishman of him. However, he was well represented in my library, for upon the shelves of the large table lay the original set of

290 Venetian scenes which he exhibited in the "white and gold" room in the Fine Art Society, London, setting the critics by the ears and publishing their criticisms in his catalogue and adding his own witty answers to them.

It would make as interesting a page as any in *Christie's* were I to relate the many offers I have had to sell this interesting set of etchings. Mr. Havemeyer bought it one afternoon for a few hundred dollars when he dropped in at a dealer's on his way home and saw them for the first time. Mr. Havemeyer never bought a painting by Whistler, but he greatly admired his water colors and his etchings and of each he owned many fine samples.

My acquaintance with Whistler, not with his works but with Whistler himself, began when I was a girl in my teens,

291 I think it was the year after I bought my first Monet and my first Degas. I was passing the season in London with my mother and a friend of hers, and we visited an exhibition in Grafton Street. It was the first time I saw Whistler's

work, and I cannot at this moment recall all the portraits or "Nocturnes" he exhibited there, but I know I was deeply impressed with the portrait of "Little Miss Alexander" which I believe was shown there for the first time. At any rate the portrait created a furor with the public and with the critics and also with me. The critics led the public like the poor *tête de mouton* that it is, and one could hear in the gallery passing from picture to picture its silly remarks based upon the morning criticisms in the leading dailies.

The fascination of the little Alexander girl's portrait appealed to me very much; the movement, the color, and the originality of the composition interested me and almost involuntarily I remarked:

"I wish I could have an example of Whistler's work. Do you suppose it would do any good to write to him?" I addressed my remark to my mother's friend. Smilingly, she answered: "We can try," and we did, with the result that we presented ourselves a few days later at the White House in Cheyne Walk and were immediately admitted into a room I shall never forget.

Although we sat down, I do not recall any furniture in the room, not even chairs; I was so impressed with the lovely yellow light that seemed to envelop us and which began right at the floor and mounted to the ceiling in the most harmonious gradations until you felt you were sitting in the soft glow of a June sunset. Two objects in the room arrested the eye: near the window stood a blue and white hawthorn jar which held one or two sprays of long reedy grass, and in the center of the room there was a huge Japanese bronze vase; it loomed up in that mellow light with the solemnity of an altar and might have been dedicated to the lares and penates of the household. It seemed to me no Grecian home could have been more beautiful or more classic. I have since been many times in Whistler's re-

294   nowned Peacock Room, but I assure you it impressed me far less than this one did when I was ushered into it on that May afternoon.

Whistler entered almost immediately. Instantly I felt a flash as I looked at him and an impression was printed forever indelibly upon my memory. I gave a second glance and I was persuaded that Whistler had made that room as a background for himself. He was a black Loge against the yellow light. I cannot think of him otherwise, Loge the fire god, restless, excitable, with a burning intelligence concentrated in his piercing black eyes, a personality with a power to focus itself beyond resistance, a power that enjoyed the shock it produced, and a gay spontaneous irrelevance. He certainly was a Loge incarnate, a fire who emitted the sparks he swallowed and laughed as the shower fell upon the public whom he held in such contempt. I assure you I was thrilled as I shook his hand and felt at once that I could anticipate a new experience. Strange to say I immediately was at ease and had no fear of him whatever. I made a direct statement of my errand. I said: "I have thirty pounds to spend and, Mr. Whistler, oh! indeed I should like something of yours. Have you anything you would like me to have?"

He stood still just a second and looked at me, and I looked at the white lock in his intensely black hair. "Why do you want something of mine?" he asked.

"Because I have seen your exhibition and—because Miss Cassatt likes your etchings," I answered.

"Do you know Miss Cassatt?" he asked quickly.

"Indeed I do," I answered. "She is my best friend, and I
295   owe it to her that I have a Pissarro, a Monet, and a Degas."

"You have a Degas?" he asked looking at me curiously.

"Yes," I said, "I bought it last year with my spending money. It is a beautiful ballet scene and cost me five hundred francs." I added earnestly, for I always wanted price understood, "I have just thirty pounds—that is all I can spend, so please tell me if it is impossible."

"No, it is not impossible," he answered kindly, "let us go into the studio and I will see what I have," and he led the way into the studio, which I don't need to describe as everyone knows what a studio is like, with its easels and hangings, its enormous windows and spooky lay figures and messy old stuffs and its many portfolios.

Whistler went directly to one of the portfolios, and when we were seated he began taking out the pastels he had done in Venice when he was there and had brought back with him to use as notes in making his Venetian set of etchings; pastels of doorways, of bridges, of "Nocturnes," of churches, of anything he could use when he returned to London and did the set of etchings that has become so famous. I sometimes wonder if he ever knew that Mr. Havemeyer bought the original set which was exhibited in the white and gold room, and in white and gold frames! I wonder if perhaps his dealer told him, or perhaps Charles L. Freer, who knows? I had to exclaim, "how fine!" as he drew out a pastel of a doorway.

"You like that?" he asked, so quickly that again I thought he was Loge.

"Oh, so much," I answered. "You have done so little and yet it is just Venice as I remember it."

Whistler placed it against the portfolio, and taking out another he said: "Don't you like that brown paper as a background? It has a value, hasn't it? But it sets the critics by the ears, you know they think I'm mad." He gave a little laugh and took out another pastel and I saw by his expression that it recalled something to him. He continued: "Do you know the critics hate me so they are using themselves up trying to get back at me? Why, the other day I

297   saw Harry Quilter sitting in front of me at a funeral. He
knew very well I was there but he would not notice me so I
just leaned over and touched him with my wand, and what
do you think happened? Why he went home and died!"

It was a fact, poor Harry Quilter had died suddenly just
after the funeral, but how could Whistler laugh and be so
funny over such a gruesome jest!

298   Whistler finally selected five pastels for me. I put them
in a row upon the floor and knelt down to admire them. I
fumbled in my pocket until I found my pound notes and I
deliberately shook them out and handed them to him saying:
"Are you not ashamed to compare them with these?" and
I gave a proud wave of possession over my lovely pastels.

Whistler appeared to be amused at my disdain of his
mercenary instincts. He told me he had done those five in
Venice and did not expect to sell them. "I call that 'Nocturne,'" he said, pointing to the brown paper background
on which there was a bridge over a lagoon, "do you like
the name?" It was Venice enveloped in the beautiful mystery of night.

"It is just the title for it," I acquiesced. "I have been there
myself, have stood upon that bridge and have felt just what
I *guess* you felt! Do you know that lovely American word?
I got it from our Yankee dialect." I was ashamed I had said
"guess" but I feared Whistler might think me sentimental.

"I guess I do," answered Whistler, lightly falling into the
dialect himself, "and I guess I'd better put the title of each
pastel on the back of its frame, and you can tell them 'over
there' what they mean."

Friends, here I must write a few lines as strange as anything in *Memorials of Christie's*. Those five pastels, framed
as Whistler framed them, with the title upon each back
written in Whistler's handwriting, and with his butterfly
signature as well, are today, after these many, many years,

hanging in the C. L. Freer Collection in that splendid museum he built in Washington and gave to the American nation. I kept them in my home for over a generation and then, knowing how much Charles Freer would appreciate them, I gave them to Whistler's dear friend that they might do honor to both in that national museum in our capital.

I remember that Oscar Wilde and a friend came in and that Whistler served us a cup of tea very deftly and very daintily. I wondered how he managed to do it, and he joked all the time with Oscar Wilde, who it seemed to me was quite equal to Whistler in repartee, but not in the knowledge of art. I asked Whistler, when he appeared quite comfortable and happy after one or two cups of tea, to tell us about his art. Of course I did not put it just that way, but said something about the "Little Miss Alexander" portrait that, I think, pleased him, for he began talking about his methods and his inspirations. It was another Whistler, quite firm, quite earnest. For the first time I heard of the harmony of the palette. "Even when you begin," he said, "the portrait must be upon your palette and beware how you change it, or you will have to take another canvas and begin all over again." I remember how quietly we sat, how eagerly we listened; it was a golden memory. For at least an hour he spoke eloquently and earnestly about his profession.

These memoirs, if wanting in literary merit, are at least strictly truthful, and after so many years—more than a generation has elapsed since that afternoon—it is still vividly bright in my memory, and although I do not dare try to repeat all Whistler said, I know that to this day I break a lance in his defense when anyone accuses him of flippancy or insincerity in regard to his art. He may have played to the gallery, because, forsooth, he understood *cœur et âme* the British public. He loved to be Loge to his critics and to see them sizzle and squirm as he showered the sparks of his witticisms about them, but to his muse his attitude was ever dignified and noble and respectful. Like every mortal he had his limitations, and where he failed it was an honest failure, where he succeeded success was the result of an equally honest effort. There was much light and shade in the life of Whistler, both as artist and as man. No one appreciated this better than he did, but he said to himself, "Let them who will, judge me as they please; it is not for me to hang my heart upon my sleeve, for dogs to bark at, and to give my testimony to a world I know to be no better than I am."

One evening in our hotel in Jermyn Street my mother became restless and determined she would sit up no longer for Whistler's promised visit. It was after eleven o'clock, and I was still begging my mother's friend to wait "just a little longer" when Whistler was announced, and as gaily and cheerily as any troubadour he walked in and greeted us, with his wand in one hand and the bundle of pastels in the other. He appeared unconscious that the hour was late. He had evidently enjoyed a good dinner at his club or an amusing piece at some theater, for he was in a merry mood and entertained us for an hour or two. He showed me the pastels and he called my attention to the frames.

"You see," he said, "the frame is a very important matter and I had to have the gold changed several times before I was satisfied. I have also had the title of each pastel put on the back and added the 'butterfly.' You know my signature of course?" he added, "but you don't know about the sting," and he explained that at times he signed the butterfly with the sting and at others without it, but always for reasons best known to himself—and the critics.

Again lest my memory betray me, I do not dare try to repeat all that he said that evening, but I know that he touched upon every subject of interest in London at the time, artistic, theatrical, and literary; and only when I knew it was fast approaching two o'clock and I felt I owed something to my mother and her friend, I frankly said:

"Mr. Whistler, I think it is time for you to go." He did not take it at all amiss but said naïvely: "Is it late?" and as I laughed at him he rather made an apology for his bad habit of turning night into day, and bade us goodnight.

I never saw him again although some years later I came in touch with his past, but I did not see him. I hate to write it, but it was when he married, and through that marriage turned out into the cold world a poor woman whom he should have treated better. Berlioz did better in like circumstances, he dryly wrote when he contracted his second marriage: "*Je le lui devais.*" At that time Miss Cassatt wrote that the poor creature had appealed to her and she was sure, with the experience she had had in printing Whistler's etchings, she could find work enough to do in Paris and could support herself. Of course I sent the money, and "Maud" did very well. Many, many years afterwards, with Mr. Havemeyer and Miss Cassatt I attended a concert in Paris; the first piece had already been played, when Miss Cassatt suddenly called my attention to a lady and gentleman entering the box next to ours. I looked and saw a beautiful woman, exquisitely dressed, elegant and dignified. I noticed her furtively during the concert, and I saw she was a little uneasy and avoided looking in our direction, and she and the gentleman left before the end of the concert. As she passed out Miss Cassatt leaned towards me and said: "That was 'Maud.' She has married a rich man and lives in luxury on the Champs Elysées."

300

I fear that she was not happy, that Loge had dropped fire upon her heart and burned all the joy and brightness out of her life. Wicked Loge! Perhaps he could not help it, and I am sure he suffered too.

Long years afterwards, during one of Mr. Freer's visits
our evening chat turned upon Whistler. He spoke of Whistler's life after his marriage and gave me the impression
that it was happy. He told me Whistler was devoted to his
dying wife, and read me a letter he had received from him
just after her death. Whistler wrote of his loneliness and
wondered if he were left because "he was not yet fit to go."
He referred to the singing lark which Mr. Freer had pro-
cured at great personal sacrifice in the hills of India, and
which, on account of her fondness for birds, had given her
great delight as the end approached and the suffering increased. Mr. Freer also told me of Whistler's long illness at
301   The Hague, when his brilliant mind flashed with irresistible
vivacity, and his sharp wit was expended perhaps upon the
merits of his breakfast, perhaps upon his desire to have his
friend Freer draw up a will as he wished to have it, whether
it was legal or illegal. It was sad to hear of the flickerings
of a great intelligence as it burned low in the wasted earthly
tenement. Mr. Freer with all his efforts could not conceal
what a devoted friend he had been to Whistler and it made
me sad to hear of the end in London, dramatic to the last.
302   Mr. Freer said: "I was exhausted when the end came and
I thought that when finally the coffin was placed in the
studio I could go and rest. But when a member of the
family begged me to remain and receive those that might
come during the afternoon, I could not refuse and remained
alone in the silent studio. Before long the bell rang and I
opened the door. A woman's voice asked if she might be
permitted to see Whistler's face. As she raised her veil and
I saw the dark eyes and the thick wavy hair, although it was
303   streaked with gray, I knew at once that it was Johanna, the
Johanna of Etretat, 'la belle Irlandaise' that Courbet had
painted with her wonderful hair and a mirror in her hand,
during the summer he and Whistler had spent in Etretat

together. She stood for a long time beside the coffin—nearly an hour I should think. I noticed she was richly dressed and I felt the world had gone well with her. I could not help being touched by the feeling she showed toward her old friend."

"Did Maud come?" I asked.

"Yes," answered Mr. Freer, "the same afternoon. She had come all the way from Paris and was very much affected as I uncovered Whistler's face for her to see him. The Church and the press claimed the last chapter in the life of this great artist, but could one see behind the veil, he would have known that the real drama of his life was bound up in the love of three devoted women."

"Tell me something about his art and his work," I asked, and Mr. Freer sat thinking a few minutes before he began:

"Whistler had about given up painting in brilliant colors when I first met him. I believe it was his appreciation of Oriental paintings that led him to abandon his brilliant palette. He had made a close study of Chinese portraits and was probably actuated by a similar impulse to express the character of his sitter; he tried to have the body only a vehicle for the soul, making his portraits more intense and vital. He ever after sought softer tones and greater harmony, until some of his portraits, like 'Rose Corder,' are as somber as some of my Chinese monochrome portraits." 304

I asked, apropos of portraits, about that of "Little Miss Alexander." "Yes," answered Mr. Freer musingly, "that is undoubtedly his greatest portrait; but it will never be for sale," he added regretfully as if thinking of the gift he had made to the nation.

Mr. Freer then spoke of Whistler and his etchings. He said: "Nothing would induce Whistler to consider an illustrated catalogue of his etchings. 'Freer,' he would say to me, 'you know I will not have illustrations, who could do them?' I promised him to prevent such a catalogue if possible and now I know such an illustrated catalogue is impossible without Miss Birney's consent and mine as well, for we have some etchings that have never been edited."

305

It grew late! It seems to me the wings of time are always swifter in the evening hours. I felt that I must consider my invalid friend and ask no more questions, although even after he rose to leave me he turned at the door to tell me of two Whistler paintings he was negotiating for at that very moment.

CHAPTER XIII

Manet

ONE must turn over a new page in the history of art if one wishes to know anything of the painter Manet, that apostle of light and air. Gay, debonair, fearless, lightly carrying the opprobrium of "impressionist" upon his shoulders, he sauntered along the boulevards, answering the jests which were flung at him from the habitués of the cafés as he passed by, with a repartee or a prophecy which caused his merry critics to tip back their chairs lest their sides be oppressed by the laughter he evoked. He tripped lightly through his span of life, threw magic juice into the eyes of his derogators and said with Puck when he found he was not understood: "Oh, what fools these mortals be." Like the light-footed Harlequin, he rapped right and left at the art world of Paris, took its breath away; and when the art world would strike back, it heard only the echo of his laughter. He had already disappeared to paint another picture which would set those stupid Bottoms by the ears, those dull bellowsmakers who had no more idea of his art than Shakespeare's tinkers and tailors had of Pyramus and Thisbe. Like those they could not have told his art-lantern from a moon.

Manet's portrait by Fantin-Latour shows us a rather effeminate face with merry blue eyes and a sensitive smiling mouth, and anyone who understands physiognomies cannot look upon that delicate nose with its flaring nostrils

306

215

without knowing that its possessor was artistically endowed to the highest degree.

Manet felt the fire within, and realizing the folly of the modern studio life for him, he started forth to see things for himself and to paint nature as he saw it, brilliant with life, gay with color. This magician of the brush loved to startle Paris with his legerdemain. Paris never could tell what would come out of that wonderful studio, come forth from under the prestidigitator's silk handkerchief or out of his silk hat. One day would appear a canvas as big as ambition could stretch it and Paris stood aghast before "Le Déjeuner sur l'herbe." The Parisian public turned their thumbs down, held their hands before their faces, while the conservative Dogberrys filled the reviews with stupid appreciations meant to be stinging criticisms, and then hurried to the clubs to enjoy the bons mots and the jests the new creation called forth. Manet laughed and shrugged his shoulders. "My fête is at Bougival, yours is in Italy," he said to his critics. "Go to the Salle Carrée, go look at your Giorgione and admire his fifteenth century fête, mine is of today and I can wait for my public."

He kept his critics waiting for his academic, that painter's crux by which he must stand or fall. They thought they would catch him at the bridge, but lo, when Manet brought it forth and stood at the bridge with single sword to defend it, there wasn't a Gracchus or a Roman who dared attack him. What could they say of it? Nay, what could they think of it? Was that a nude, an academic? Surely, no. For never had they seen one like it. Yet who in the wide world or in Paris would have dared present such a composition or would have courted such difficulties in the doing, as Manet did when he painted his "Olympia"? A nude woman lies upon a white sheet, a black cat is at her feet, a Negress leans over her couch and offers her a bunch of brilliant flowers wrapped in white paper such as one sees in the Parisian flower market. Never before had a painter put a nude in contrast with such blacks and such whites! Who but Manet could have done it? The critics gnashed their teeth at the problem he offered. "It can't be done," they cried, "it is not art!" "Why not?" said Manet who enjoyed the fun. "There are Negresses, and black cats, and flowers in white paper, and nudes on sheets." And he added, snapping his fingers: "I have done it, it is my academic, and what is more, one day it will hang in the Louvre." It hangs there today and fate with mocking irony has placed it as a pendant to the academic and conservative Ingres. Thus Manet left his critics stampeded at the bridge and quietly returned to his studio to prepare a fresh surprise for them.

This was Manet the modern, who was to fill a new page in art's history with a long list of remarkable works.

Strange to say, I never met him. I recall that when I was a very young girl I went to see Miss Cassatt at Marly-le-Roi. Her villa joined Manet's home and his fatal malady made him very ill at that time. After luncheon we walked over to his villa to ask after him. Mme Morisot met us at the gate and at Miss Cassatt's inquiry sadly shook her head, saying that he was very ill and that she feared the worst. Mme Morisot walked back to our villa with us and I recall that she was a charming, intelligent woman, and that she and Miss Cassatt were very friendly and talked of art matters, and spoke of the pity of young American girls wasting their time in the Parisian studios. "It would be far better," said Mme Morisot, "if they would go to some city where there were a few good pictures, like Nantes for instance, or Lille, and study quietly there." That is all I remember of the conversation for Mme Morisot left us hurriedly to return to poor Manet.

I think it was in 1883 that I was in Paris when two of

312   Manet's works were exhibited at the Salon. They were "Monsieur Pertuiset Hunting" and the portrait of Rochefort, the editor of *La Lanterne*. I saw these pictures many times and always regretted that I did not understand French better, for if I had been able to catch the meaning of the phrases and jokes that they called forth from the daily visitors, I could have filled my notebook each afternoon with witty remarks and observations which, in view of Manet's place in art today, would be interesting to my readers. There was always a crowd before these two pictures, there was tittering, elbow nudging and shoulder shrugging with much laughter and vociferous exclamations of "Ah, ah" and "Ma foi" and "Oh, lá, lá." The public made frank fun of the lion hunter but the portrait of Rochefort came in for the largest share of ridicule. One day I saw a young man, a student probably, draw his companion away saying: "You must not go near it, don't you see his face is just about breaking out with smallpox."

       Little did Manet care, however; he was busy with his brushes and with his magic, finding his own long narrow road to fame, studying nature as he saw it, forgetting the shadows and seeking the light, throwing atmosphere around his figures, ever and again seeking new difficulties to overcome, and creating new pitfalls for the *boulevardiers* and the critics in order that he might laugh at their perplexities and enjoy their efforts to expound each new creation.

       One picture which set all the wiseacres' heads awagging
313   was "Le Bal de l'Opéra" which soon entered our collection. Was there ever such a picture! Surely Manet had never drawn anything so incomprehensible out of his magician's hat before. Hat! Why the whole picture was hats. Hats ad infinitum! High hats, low hats, black hats, silk hats, queer hats, hats such as Parisians wore with dress suits to the Opéra, hats with springs, hats open, hats shut, hats in

the hand, hats on the head, hats tilted, tipped, tossed, thrown upon the head, hats on straight, hats on crooked, hats on the crown, hats on the ear, hats on the forehead, hats down over the eyes, hats at one angle, hats at another. The foyer of the Opéra was just a sea of hats. They filled the vestibule, they lined the stairway. Men in hats crowded the entrance of the Opéra and mingled with women in dominoes and with the soubrettes in bright costumes. And the background, what could the critics say of that? "May the saints of the Academy forgive him," they cried. Never had art or artists from the days of Phidias down produced such a background—the marble of the great stairway. Yes, just some marble, toned by the lights from the dome above with a yellow luster, impossible to describe, that was the background and it threw the mass of hats into relief. A woman's leg ending in a pretty shoe was thrown over the marble stairway to let us know that the frolic was going on above as well as in the scene before us.

How the critics whistled and hissed, packed the reviews with articles upon the virtues of the old school and the villainies of the new one, found the masked ball (which they attended night after night) indecent and a menace to society, and all because they saw it for the first time represented to the life. Manet let them whistle and wail. "Write on, ye learned Dogberrys," he said, "and much good will it do you. I shall have the last word after all. It is a masked ball and ye know it well and it is as I saw it and not as ye see it."

"Le Bal de l'Opéra" fell to our share of Manet's works. We bought it in 1894 and the purchase of it marked one of those dramatic occasions, when two amateurs clash in the transaction. Our purchase of "Le Bal de l'Opéra" was a disappointment to Count Camondo who desired to see the picture in his collection, which is now in the Louvre; just as his buying Degas's "Pédicure" (a marvel of a picture) was a disappointment to us—a rare happening, but one which does occur in the art world.

I learned that in order to paint his "Bal de l'Opéra" Manet had spent a winter in studying black hats. He invited acquaintances to come to his studio in order that he might make a study of their hats. He would drop in at a fellow artist's studio and ask to be allowed to make a sketch of his hat. Friend Goncourt came in for a little chat and was immediately pressed into service and requested to keep his hat on. Duret's hat was painted, the family hat was painted, Manet's own hat served as a model. And you may be sure that when Fantin-Latour painted his friend's portrait which now hangs in the Art Institute of Chicago, Manet wore a high hat.

I hung "Le Bal de l'Opéra" in my gallery for a time, but I found that there were many of Puck's foolish mortals still posing as art amateurs in America. I took it down and hung it in my own apartment, where I have studied and enjoyed it, hour after hour, year after year, until I have learned to consider it one of Manet's best if not his greatest work.

Everyone who knows Manet's works, knows what a great painter of still life he was and it is a curious fact that we, who probably own more of his figure pieces than any other collector, should have selected a still life as our first example of the artist. To be a great collector one must be open to conviction and the following anecdote will show you how Mr. Havemeyer began collecting Manets with a still life and ended with the "Gare St. Lazare" and "Christ with the Angels." One morning, I think the year was 1889, Mr. Havemeyer as he bade me good morning, said: "I think I will stop in with Mr. Colman and see the Durand-Ruel exhibition at the Academy. They have some impressionist

pictures there, they will probably shock Mr. Colman."
"Not at all," I said, "you will both be intensely interested
and if you find any Manets there, be sure and buy me one."
My husband said he did not think there was any likelihood
of his buying a Manet, but when he returned in the afternoon and greeted me, he said quietly: "I saw the exhibition this morning. There were two Manets in it, one a boy
with a sword and the other a still life. The still life was very
fine and I bought it for you, but I confess the 'Boy with the
Sword' was too much for me." "I must see it," I answered,
and then, an unusual thing for me to do, I asked the price
of the "Boy with the Sword." "Oh, I think they asked
$3,500 for it," answered Mr. Havemeyer carelessly. I add
that as a dainty bit for a new *Memorials of Christie's* of
modern sales, or for the amusement of the amateurs who
will go on buying Manets at varying prices for many years
to come. Often did Mr. Havemeyer refer to our mistake in
not buying the "Boy with the Sword." It was at first a little
difficult to understand Manet's method of modeling in
light, but my husband learned quickly to appreciate him,
and the rapidity with which he collected many of his greatest works is the best proof I can offer of my husband's intelligence. The "Boy with the Sword" now belongs to the
Metropolitan Museum of Art and is considered one of the
finest pictures in the gallery.

We began very modestly, buying some of Manet's
smaller pictures first. One is an "Interior," with Mme   317
Manet seated by a table and a young boy, her nephew I
believe, seated near her. Manet must have taken his family
to some watering place, for the large window is open and
one has a beautiful view of the distant sea. It is full of atmosphere, very harmonious and not at all difficult to understand.
He evidently had gone away from Paris and forgotten his
critics for a time, or he may have been just "resting on his

oars," "keeping his hand in" as painters say, while his
mind was busy with some important work. The other one,
318   no larger than the first, shows an enchanting bit of garden
where Manet's brother-in-law has thrown himself upon the
grass, and seated close beside him is his wife dressed in the
favorite white; they are watching the baby carriage which
is placed in the shadows of the trees. It is a picture full of
charm and sentiment, of home life and refinement, executed with admirable skill and showing Manet's mastery
of light and shade. Mr. Havemeyer, who was feeling his
319   way, also bought a flower piece, some roses in a glass vase.
The color is cool and transparent and the delicate petals
tremble and quiver; one has fallen off and lies beside the
vase. It is a little bit of art such as an amateur prizes as a
precious thing and would not part with ever.

Nevertheless, to collect Manet, the great Manet, Manet
the magician, one must not consider dimensions, must not
measure canvas by the rule, but must take whatever comes
forth from his workshop, must accept the creations of the
master. Miss Cassatt and I helped Mr. Havemeyer through
the ordeal of deciding upon a large Manet by just buying
one "big one" for him ourselves. On a wintry morning,
during one of her very rare visits to America, Miss Cassatt
and I were taking a walk together and as we passed the
Durand-Ruel gallery she suggested we should drop in and
see if they had received any new pictures. After greeting
us, M. Joseph made a remark to Miss Cassatt which I did
not hear, but I heard her exclaim: "What! He returned that
Manet 'Marine' to buy a Whistler. Mercy sakes, what is
art coming to?" and turning to me she added, "Horace W.
has returned his Manet 'Marine.' Do let us go see it, for
you will surely want it."

We went into the gallery and there hung Manet's "Ala-
320   bama," a superb picture which I carefully examined while

Miss Cassatt related to us the exciting and interesting details about Manet's painting of the picture. "Manet was very much excited over the 'Alabama' affair," she said, "and actually went to Cherbourg to paint this picture. He had scarcely finished it when the battle with the 'Kearsarge' took place just outside the harbor. Manet witnessed the battle and he told me it was one of the most exciting moments of his life. He had never seen a naval contest and it was a great experience for him to see the attack and sinking of the 'Alabama.'" With a characteristic gesture she continued, "Look at that water! Did you ever see anything so solid? You feel the weight of the ocean in it. You must buy it, my dear, Mr. Havemeyer must not lose it."

I did buy it, and rather elated with my purchase, I said something that had been on my mind for many a long day. I pointed to Manet's "El Espada"—the bullfighter stands in the ring holding his sword, covered with the red cape, in his hand and doffs his cap, probably to the royal family, before attacking the bull. "I think we ought to buy that picture," I said.

"Why don't you?" quietly rejoined Miss Cassatt.

"I fear Mr. Havemeyer would think it too big," I answered.

"Don't be foolish," said Miss Cassatt, "It is just the size Manet wanted it, and that ought to suffice for Mr. Havemeyer; besides, it is a splendid Manet, and I am sure he will like it if you buy it."

"Very well," I said, "I will buy it, and now let us go home and tell him."

I think we enjoyed "telling Mr. Havemeyer" what we had done quite as much as we had enjoyed buying the pictures. I made a little bow and, imitating his manner, repeated the words he always said when he presented a picture to me. "Mr. Havemeyer," I said, "Manet's 'Bull-

fighter' is yours." He smiled so genially at us that Miss
Cassatt said to me quickly: "What did I tell you?"

But Mr. Havemeyer, not understanding what she meant,
said to me: "It no doubt is a very fine picture, but now, my
dear, it is up to you to hang it." Hanging it meant a lot of
work which I enjoyed, but I was obliged to change many
pictures.

When my husband saw how well the big Manet looked
in our gallery it was not long before he bought Manet's
322 "Majo," a life-sized figure in a Spanish costume of the
province of Catalonia. He has a pale face and brilliant black
eyes; he leans upon a staff and a gorgeous red scarf is
thrown over his arm. It is a strong portrait, done in Manet's
most characteristic manner, and it makes a worthy pendant
to the "Bullfighter." Shortly after, Mr. Havemeyer bought
the most important of our large Manets, "Mlle V. in the
323 Costume of a Toreador." It was painted after Manet's return from Spain, where he undoubtedly studied Velazquez,
and, I believe, determined to paint a large picture of a bullfight, which project was never completely realized but to
which we owe both our "Bullfighter" and "Mlle V." This
picture of Mlle V. is one of the greatest and most difficult
things Manet ever did. I hesitate to describe it, for I recognize my inability to give you an adequate idea of the beauty
of the picture. Mlle V. stands in the middle of the arena
holding in her hand a sword over which is thrown the tra-
ditional red rag, which Manet has made as lovely a bit of
color as ever left his palette. It is well that Manet left the
bull out of the picture, for were he as ferocious as any that
ever came from the Andalusian hills, he would probably
have crouched at the feet of this graceful *espada* and would
have licked the hand of his beautiful executioner, even
when she waved the bit of colored silk which Goya never
surpassed. A picador on horseback and three toreadors

stand in a distant part of the arena, and give us a hint that our magician has been to the Prado and has learned more sleight of hand from the Spanish wizard of Philip's reign who painted "The Surrender at Breda" and who revealed to Manet some of the wonders of his art.

But why should I go on? I cannot with words make you see the beauties of Manet's pictures nor feel his art—only, if ever it be possible, I advise you to see and study Manet for yourself. There is a Manet you can see, for it is now in the Munich gallery. I think it is called "The Studio." For many years it hung upon the walls of our gallery until one day—for some reason I never understood—Mr. Havemeyer asked me if I objected to his returning it to the Durand-Ruels. I never questioned my husband's decisions, and I acquiesced, of course. Manet's still life in the picture, and the boy with the black jacket and straw hat were lost to us forever; there was certainly nothing wrong with the black velvet jacket, but I often wished the young man in the straw hat could have been more intelligent and have made a more interesting central figure!

We soon bought another "Marine" painted just after Manet's "Argenteuil," now in the gallery in Brussels. Miss Cassatt calls it "the last word in painting" and told me that after having worked long and laboriously over the "Argenteuil" (which is about the same subject, a man in a sailboat) Manet was keyed up with the effort and training of the other picture and accomplished this one in a couple of days; did it in a white heat, like the race horse who makes a sudden dash and wins by a length, scarcely realizing the effort it has cost him. A still more striking illustration of this concentration of an artist's powers through which he produces the chef d'œuvre on which his fame will rest, is our "Blue Venice," a picture which Mr. Havemeyer bought for me from M. Durand-Ruel's private collection. In writ-

324

325

326

ing of this picture I must again quote Miss Cassatt who knew Manet so well and to whom he could speak of his work and its difficulties with the frankness of a fellow artist. She congratulated us when we bought this picture saying she considered it one of Manet's most brilliant works; it was so full of light and atmosphere and expressed the very soul and spirit of Venice.

"Manet told me," she said, "that he had been a long time in Venice. I believe he spent the winter there and he was thoroughly discouraged and depressed at his inability to paint anything to his satisfaction. He had just decided to give it up and return home to Paris. On his last afternoon in Venice, he took a fairly small canvas and went out on the Grand Canal just to make a sketch to recall his visit; he told me he was so pleased with the result of his afternoon's work that he decided to remain over a day and finish it. My dear," concluded Miss Cassatt, "that is the way Manet happened to paint your Venice."

Happened! Was not that a misleading word for Miss Cassatt to use? Happened! Oh no! a picture like my "Blue Venice" does not happen, it is created, created by the slow and painful struggle of production. From the moment Manet arrived in Venice every stroke he made, every touch of color he put upon his canvas, helped to create my "Blue Venice." Through every hour of discouragement it was incubating in the cells of his brain, and being nourished by his heartbeats and by the echoes of his sighs. Disappointment forcing him back to Paris! Oh no! it was forcing him to take that bit of canvas on that last afternoon and to go out onto the lagoon and to paint that masterpiece that had matured in his brain and was ready to come forth. He fastened his gondola to the big blue and white posts which give the name to my picture, and painted Venice as he saw it in that brilliant sparkling sunlight during the last few hours of his sojourn in the bewildering city. I think I see him painting there, wrapped in his work, forgetting how modern he is, sinking back into the centuries past as he paints the lagoons and the palaces of long ago. I think of him as he works, picturing to himself Venice in her grand old days when doges held their court in the Ducal Palace and encouraged their sculptors and painters to adorn the piazzas and the churches, giving orders for them to paint the fair women of that fair city. Who knows but that this living French modern may have evoked the shade of that modern of long ago, the shade of Veronese himself? Manet may have allowed the "father of impressionism" in renaissance Venice to have a look over his shoulder as the blue posts and the bright waters grew upon his canvas. Surely they had much to say to each other, this patriarch of realism and the magician of the boulevards.

"Do those posts look thus to you, Father Paul?" queries the modern. "Aye, my son," answers the great Venetian, "paint them as you see them and others will learn through your eyes. I had trouble enough in my day and criticism too, mind you." Upon hearing that, the modern drops his brushes, and turning to the venerable shade says quickly: "Critics! Father Paul, did you have critics? and in Venice long ago? Did they sit in the cafés of the piazza and cast jests at you as you passed by?" "Fie! my son," answers the shade reproachfully, "you a painter!—and mind critics! Go your way and think naught of them. A fool can criticize, it takes knowledge to appreciate," and he laughs in his shadowy beard as he adds, "I too had my critics." "But," persists the modern, thinking bitterly of the boulevards and his tormentors, "I painted a picture of a 'Bal' once and painted many men in high hats, high crowns to the hats just as I saw them there myself. I did not think them strange, but you should have heard the critics!"

327

"I have heard them, young man," says the venerable shade. "I hear them still," and he gives a sly chuckle as he thinks of the past and continues, "there was a young man in my day who painted some Venetian ladies on the upper terraces of their palaces, whither they had gone to bleach their hair; and they wore hats without crowns, for how could they bleach their hair if the crowns remained? But the critics! Santa Maria, the critics! This young man's name was Carpaccio; did you ever hear of him or of his work?" "Yes," rejoins the modern, "we all know him, and of that picture. A critic!—think of it! a critic—calls it 'the greatest picture in the world.' " "Ha! ha! ho! ho!" laughs Father Paul, "a critic says that! a critic, think of it; then they have learned something in four hundred years, those critics; and of me, do they say aught of me?" "Oh surely, Father Paul," rejoins Manet, as flushed with enthusiasm he works more rapidly than before, "they call you the father of the modern school."

The shade of the great master gazes earnestly for a moment at the painter and at his work, and then with a sigh he gently closes his eyes, and as he vanishes, Manet hears the words: "Modern! there is no modern, art is life! art is light!"

All this I seemed to see and to hear as I looked at my "Blue Venice"; indeed it would take many pages to tell you the delight that picture has given me. It is just a view of the lagoon with the blue and white posts conspicuous before the palace he paints; but it satisfies you that it is the Venice you saw, the Venice you know, the Venice you would paint; and what can art do more? It inspired me once to answer a guest who asked me if I would not prefer a string of pearls to a picture. "No," I said hastily, "I prefer to have something made by a man than to have something made by an oyster." If it was a good rejoinder, I take no credit for it;

it was my "Blue Venice" that fairly put the words into my mouth.

As I am not writing a biography of Manet, nor a history of his art, but am just jotting down as they occur to me, the recollections of how we acquired so many of Manet's important works, it would be almost impossible and it is not necessary for me to mention them in chronological order, for in the course of our collecting we bought early works late and late works early.

I recall that one beautiful autumn morning when Mr. Havemeyer and I were enjoying the few remaining days of a visit in Paris, Miss Cassatt entered the salon and said to me: "How would you like to have a portrait of Clemenceau by Manet?"

"Let us see it," I answered, "can we?"

"Certainly," she said, "I saw Clemenceau yesterday and he wants to sell his portrait. He says he does not like it, but I rather think he is hard up and wants some money. He really asks very little for it, only ten thousand francs. The picture is not completely finished, as you may imagine, with the combination of two such men as Clemenceau and Manet. Manet did not finish the still life in the picture, but he had forty sittings for Clemenceau's portrait and I think it is a very fine and interesting picture."

"Very well," I said, and looked at my husband who acquiesced.

We were soon at Clemenceau's home, a pretty villa out of the whirl of Paris, with an attractive garden, where we found the fearless statesman on whose broad shoulders had fallen the burden of premiership and who carried it as intrepidly as anyone since the days of Gambetta. It was shortly before the "Agadir" incident, when Clemenceau firmly encouraged the French president to *tenir tête* with

328

Germany, while gracefully offering "to relinquish his portfolio if he did not." At that time Clemenceau was not very
gray and he still resembled his portrait; Manet had painted
a very forceful Clemenceau. His black eyes look deter-
minedly from underneath his heavy eyebrows, and his head,
round and hard, appears ready to strike any other head,
however round and however hard that other head might be.
His arms are lightly crossed upon his chest and he plainly
says: "Yes this is my attitude, what is yours?" A vigorous,
middle-aged, keen, defiant Clemenceau, justly conscious of
his own worth, enjoying his power, admiring his own ability, and a little, just a little, proud of his wit.

We became friendly at once. I learned that in his struggling days, when he was at odds with the French government,
he had sought a home in America and had taught
French for many years in a school not over a mile from our
Connecticut home. He told me he did not like the portrait.
"I sat for Manet many, many times," he said, "but he could
never make it like me," and he took hold of the frameless
portrait and swung it around to show it to us.

"I don't care for it, and would be glad to be rid of it," he
continued. I thought it would be as well for the portrait to
be rid of him, for he switched it about so indifferently it
was a wonder he had not put a hole in it, or ruined it entirely. "Manet never finished it," said Clemenceau to Mr.
Havemeyer, "and yet I gave him forty sittings! just think
of it, forty sittings for one portrait!" He said it contemptu-
ously as if he could decide the fate of nations in far less
time, and turning the frameless canvas with its face to the
wall he said: "I shall never hang it anyway."

As if indifferent to the portrait, or the sale of it, he began
talking to Miss Cassatt. The subject of their conversation
was, of course, politics; church and state, I think, but I was
not familiar enough with the proposed "*séparation*" to be

able to recall intelligently what they said. I do remember that when that subject was rending France, there was a luncheon arranged in the rue Marignan, and Clemenceau met a French minister there, and that through the indiscretion of a priest to whom some papers and letters had been confided, Miss Cassatt's name seemed about to be drawn into the political quarrel, when Clemenceau in a brilliant article written to the papers averted from her the unpleasant notoriety by mentioning that the luncheon was given "at the home of a lady whose art was one of the glories of France." When Clemenceau and Miss Cassatt had agreed, or disagreed—it is sometimes hard to tell the result of a discussion in politics—we returned to the subject of the portrait and we bought it for ten thousand francs, the price at which Clemenceau said he would sell it.

Acting upon Miss Cassatt's advice I took another stretcher and folded back that part of the canvas on which Manet had indicated the table and the still life. This was very easy to do as the picture was oblong. No one will ever know, perhaps, unless they read these lines or someone else writes a record of the fact, that almost half of the original canvas of the Clemenceau portrait is neatly folded behind the stretcher, nor, furthermore, will they understand that it is hidden there because a great statesman and a greater painter after forty sittings could neither of them yield, and the tug of personalities prevented them from cooperating in an effort to produce a great work of art. The blood of our century beats faster and hotter than it did when Holbein painted. Our portrait of "Jean de Carondelet" which is so calm and poised, so firm and reposeful, shows the difference of temperament of the different centuries.

Besides the Clemenceau, we bought a woman's portrait in oil by Manet. It is not quite life-size, her hair is undone, she leans her cheek upon her hand and looks directly at you

out of the canvas. Alas, she is not beautiful, but could
Manet that master of realism make her beautiful when she
was in truth ugly? Oh no, but he painted her with all his
superb technique, in broad brush strokes and with his beautiful brilliant coloring. It is a painters' portrait and is always admired by them. I have even heard it extolled as
being better than "The Lady with the Parasol" which was
formerly in the Faure Collection in Paris.

Manet, as well as Degas, knew the value of pastel as a
medium for portrait painting. He knew what light and life
it gave to flesh, and his works in pastel are among his best.
Mr. Havemeyer bought several of Manet's pastel portraits.
One is of Guys, the caricaturist who did interesting aquarelles of many French types and who was a great friend of
Manet. Later we bought many of Guys's aquarelles and
drawings. Mr. Havemeyer bought a portrait of "Mlle Lemonnier" which many consider Manet's greatest achievement in pastel, and indeed it seems to defy art to go further,
for if he had blown those chalks on he could not have done
it with a lighter touch or with greater freedom. The face is
in profile, with full red lips and black hair in which is a deep
red rose, and Manet has made her so alive that the white
throat seems to palpitate and the blood to circulate freely
and the breath to dilate in the nostrils. I became accustomed
to the exclamations of admiration as visitors saw the portrait for the first time. By the side of this portrait hung
another of Manet's pastels, the portrait of a beautiful
blonde, her hair carefully arranged and with an elaborate
costume of the time. Her elegance had evidently impressed
Manet and it was most carefully done and highly finished,
"pushed" as the painters say. It was much talked of in its
day, and Madame clung to her beautiful portrait; it was
only in her old age that she decided to sell it and it came
into our possession. Our third and last woman's portrait is

that of a young girl with a retroussé nose and with a pretty
tipped bonnet, that carries out the line of the dainty nose,
on her head. She is perky and jaunty in her pretty clothes.
You feel she took pleasure in posing for her portrait and
was quite satisfied as the youthful face developed under
Manet's brilliant pastels. I admire it very much for it is full
of fire and life and youthful insouciance.

By far the best known and the most amusing of all our
Manet pastels is the portrait of George Moore, a onetime
dilettante artist and an alltime writer on art. He is best
known in England as an art critic but it is of his portrait I
would speak. There was a French dealer with an unpre-
tentious gallery near Montmartre, where we often went to
see some of the greatest pictures of the day. Pottier was a
favorite with the so-called impressionists and we bought
from him many of our important pictures. One day he came
to our hotel and it was easy to see he had something important to suggest. With Miss Cassatt, we started forth to
see pictures, going to a small apartment here, or a smaller
one there. The owners would take down some of the finest
examples of modern art and sell them to us, not so much
for the price, for they were usually well-to-do, but for the
love of collecting, in order to have money in hand so that
at the next exposition or the next opportunity they might
be able to make new purchases and again astonish their
neighbors with their judgment in art. I think it was on that
very afternoon that Pottier took us to see the "Casseurs de
Pierres" which Mr. Havemeyer tried to buy; but its owner,
a blacksmith, did not care to sell. I recall that we went to the
home of a dentist and bought two superb Degas's and as we
left the apartment Pottier said to us that he knew of a very
fine portrait by Manet which he thought might be bought,
but that it would be very dear—very dear, he repeated,
evidently fearful of the price the owner might ask for his

picture. "It is a wonderful portrait," he said, "a wonderful portrait of a very ugly man."

"Whose portrait is it?" asked Mr. Havemeyer.

"George Moore's," answered Pottier.

"George Moore!" exclaimed Miss Cassatt. "Can Manet's 'George Moore' be had? Let us see it by all means," and while we drove to a distant part of Paris, into one of its pretty suburbs filled with homelike villas, Miss Cassatt told us of George Moore and of Manet's painting the portrait.

"George Moore," she said, "painted a little, he went to his friends, he even boasted to me, that Manet had invited him to come work in his studio. I was surprised at Manet's doing such a thing, but when I saw the portrait I understood it all. While George Moore was studying in Manet's studio, Manet was studying George Moore and painting a portrait of him, and it was one of the finest portraits he ever did. He did George Moore for all time," said Miss Cassatt. "Of course, George Moore did not like it and said horrid things about it to me. I suppose George Moore sold it?" she asked turning to Pottier.

"Yes, it is here," answered Pottier as we drew up before an attractive house. "I think the parties will sell," he added in a low voice as we were ushered into the apartment, "but at a price."

We entered and among other fine pictures we saw George Moore's portrait. He certainly was not handsome, but all Manet's art was in it: it was the very epitome of characterization, the *ne plus ultra* of elimination. There was nothing upon the canvas but just the body and soul of George Moore laid bare, divested of all his self-complacency, of all his effort to produce effect. It could be none other but George Moore, for it suggested no other human being you had ever seen or could conjure up. No one ever had such hair; no eyes looked like his as they sought to see the hair above and dispute the superior right of the eyebrows; nose, mouth and chin fitted into the amusing oval. That was what we saw—a few features revealing to us all there was to know of George Moore. The jacket could be his only, no other would have worn it, and so was the cravat, it belonged to him just as much as did his hair or his eyes. With a vision as penetrating as Velazquez's, Manet had taken the features of George Moore and transfixed them forever upon canvas, using a little colored powder mixed with transcendent art. We looked at it long and silently, then Mr. Havemeyer turned suddenly toward Pottier and said:

"You say it is dear? How much do they ask for it?"

"Ten thousand francs," replied Pottier with a doleful shake of his head.

"We will take it," said Mr. Havemeyer decidedly, and the affair was concluded.

If it is any consolation, George Moore may know that his portrait attracted more attention than any Manet in our gallery. I grew accustomed to the exclamations I would hear as soon as visitors saw it. "Is that the 'George Moore' by Manet?" cautiously asked the amateur who had heard of it "somewhere." "That is Manet's 'George Moore,'" remarked the critic, who had heard much of it. "'George Moore'!" ejaculated the painter who knew it well. "Hello! Manet's 'George Moore' as I live," said the Frenchman almost to himself as he looked at it. Manet's genius had even enveloped the canvas, for he made every observer throw more light upon the character of his portrait, through the tone of his voice or by the exclamations he made. I never met, I never saw George Moore, but I learned many things about him from the remarks of those who knew him well. The echo of raillery and laughter in the casual observations made me certain that Manet's portrait was considered a huge joke on George Moore; what was amusing was that

he had sold it and it would forever be on view, and George
Moore would have to abide by it as a portrait of himself.
Would the portrait live through George Moore, or George
Moore through the portrait? That was the question that
caused a laugh whenever it was raised; would it be George
Moore's Manet or Manet's "George Moore"? If ever I
made a catalogue, should the name of George Moore be in
big black letters and Manet's name in little diamond, or
should Manet have the black letters and the name of George
Moore be in little script? What shall I do? Will George
Moore come to my gallery some day and give me his
opinion of Manet and the relative merits of painter and
sitter? Or will the great Judge, who sits with his hourglass
in his hand in the court of courts, pass judgment upon it and
determine which name shall outlive the other?

With "George Moore" ends the list of our Manet pastels, and to complete the list of oils I have only to mention
two more paintings well known to anyone acquainted with
Manet's works: his "Christ with the Angels" and his "Gare
St. Lazare." I persuaded Mr. Havemeyer to buy the "Christ
343   with the Angels" because it went begging both here and
abroad. I have said it and I repeat it, it went begging, and
let the public galleries explain it if they can, for if ever
there was a museum Manet, it seems to me it is his "Christ
with the Angels." Long afterward the Louvre bought
344   Manet's "Olympia," which had I been a little more persist-
ent, they would have lost; at that time Manet's "Christ"
was no longer in the market. When my husband bought it, I
knew it was not suitable for our gallery but I felt if it once
left our shores it would never return to America, so to
please me Mr. Havemeyer bought it, saying as he gave it to
me: "I really do not know what you will do with it." I hung
it in various places in our home, but I found it crushed every-

thing beside it and crushed me as well. Finally I concluded
it would be impossible to live with that mighty picture, to
look day after day upon the Christ supported by these pitying angels, to gaze upon the Redeemer offering the sacrifice of Gethsemane for the salvation of mankind. For several
years I put it away, but after my husband's death, when
Manet was better understood, I sent it to the Metropolitan
Museum, where it hangs beside the Manet Mr. Havemeyer
saw and rejected because it was "too much for him," the   345
splendid "Boy with the Sword."

The "Gare St. Lazare" Mr. Havemeyer bought to please   346
himself, for the painter had become an open book to my
husband and he recognized the "Gare St. Lazare" as one of
Manet's greatest achievements, the ripened fruit after many
years of growth, when, as Frenchmen say, he had "found
his way." Although he still clings to his straight and narrow path, he has a complete grasp of his method, he knows
his technique and models in light as few have ever done before him; he has that greatest of all qualities in a painter, a
marvelous vision that reveals to him nature as she is and
places him among the great names of all times. We see in
the "Gare St. Lazare" a very rift in nature. It is as realistic
as any picture Manet ever painted. A little child, a very
human little girl, returning from the park on a warm afternoon is attracted, as children always are, by the mysterious
steam engine that blows shrill whistles from nowhere and
rings bells without human hands. She peers through the
railings of the gare St. Lazare to see the black smoke that
trails above the tracks and disappears under the bridge beyond. Too interested to feel tired, she stands lightly against
the rail and is unconscious that her mother, probably fa-
tigued with her afternoon in the Tuileries, has sunk upon
the stone curb of the railing and rests there, quietly waiting
with her dog upon her arm. We see only the back of the

child; her dress is not pretty, her hair is not fluffy but is drawn up on the top of her head and held back from her temples by a black comb; her little hands grasp the iron rails and she does not care a fig for anyone, will not even turn her head that we may see her face, nor pose in the pretty way children are supposed to do when sitting for their portraits. She is just a natural little girl, doing just what a little girl naturally would do when she found herself beside the big gare St. Lazare where the trains were rushing in and out—she looks and looks and looks. You say, and many others say: "That is not a painting! How could anyone in their senses paint a child and turn her back toward us?" Probably no one else, in or out of his senses, but Manet could, and thereby he proves that he had more sense than others. He had the sense of fine perception, the sense of reasoning vision which saw the results, and the conviction that he could express it. He concentrated all his art, all his ability, on that which he wished to paint and was still able—what a gift to a painter—to eliminate all unnecessary details. No wonder he was so little understood by his contemporaries, who failing to understand made bold to jeer, while Manet putting his hands in his pockets nonchalantly walked the boulevards, listening to tattling critics and occasionally permitting himself the consolation of repeating to them: "Nevertheless, some day it will hang in the Louvre."

You ask me how we could have bought such a portrait? How we could have disregarded the silk stockings, the satin slippers, the best frock, the tortured hair, or the pretty bow? And again you ask, is that a portrait, what is the attraction in it, what made us want to possess it? What caused us to forgive Manet that we should never see the child's face? You ask why we paid for iron rails and steam engines we barely see? You tell us that the child is not even pretty and that the mother is positively ugly—only Manet's model in another dress—that even the doggie is unattractive, and you long to know why we put so much money into such a picture, when we might have had a gorgeous academic, an imposing English portrait, or some splendid Eastern scene, for the same price.

I answer art, art, art. It is there appealing to you, as it appealed to us. You must feel it. You must hear the voice calling to you, you must respond to the vibrations Manet felt, which made his heart throb and filled his brain, which stirred his emotions and sharpened his vision as he put his brush upon the canvas. Art, art, art, I say; you must try to see with Manet's eyes and comprehend how he can make a chef d'œuvre out of a homely story, or how others make a great symphony out of a simple melody. When Beethoven lifts our very souls on the wings of his compositions, we are not concerned about his chords and their resolutions, and care little whether the wood and wind are blown or beaten or whether the violins are held against the shoulders or grasped between the knees. We are listening to the message, and art is the interpreter. The "Gare St. Lazare" appeals to our inherent love of truth, and we look at the picture again and again because it might be our child, nay, it might even be ourselves when we were children, clinging to those rails and looking with the same interest on the busy scene below. It tells us of childhood—of all childhood—not only in Paris by the gare St. Lazare, but of any city where children exist and railroad stations can be seen. And then the execution of it! Where in art will you find a curve like the one which outlines the dress upon the child's shoulders, or see such light as that which creeps up to the yellow hair and models the lovely neck? Look at the pose of the head, the movement of the arm, the way the flesh of the little hand is pressed against the iron rail, see how atmosphere

and light envelop the two figures and give distance to the
scene below. Finally, notice the color! Did you ever see anything more beautiful and harmonious? Notice all these
things and many more and do not ask me why we bought
the "Gare St. Lazare"—the picture of a little girl who re-
fuses to be seen and turns her back upon us. We bought it
because we thought it a great picture and one of Manet's
best. I cannot look upon it, without thinking of the lines of
another great modern:

> "But each for the joy of the working, and each,
>   in his separate star,
> Shall draw the Thing as he sees It for the God
>   of Things as They are."

CHAPTER XIV

Edgar Degas

I<small>N THE</small> hour of birth, when nature bestows her gifts on the minds of mortals, with a subtle fuse attached, in order that in the heated energy of manhood they may scatter these gifts even unto those that did not breed the gifted owners, is it not possible that nature with a dainty caprice should divide a gift, bestowing one half here and the other half there, tempted by a humorous desire to see what each will make of the talent confided to him? Could it be that she thus divided of her bounty between the Anglo-Saxon, Samuel Butler, and the Latin-French, Edgar Degas, in order that she should see the fuse in the mind of one light the fuse in the mind of the other, and inspire Samuel Butler to write *Erewhon* and *The Way of All Flesh* and Edgar Degas to paint "Le Café Chantant" and "The Ballet Dancers"?

Philosophy, satire, psychological insight, and unbounded skill seem to have been the endowment of each. Theirs is no pleasant humor or gentle rallying. Their tools have sharp edges and cut deep, while the metal like a magnet guides them to the weakest spots. They pare off the rotten tissue and in many places leave the naked human truth to view. Neither sentiment nor the soft virtues guide their hands, for they work with nerves and sinews tense and taut. It has been said that Carlyle worked with a sledge hammer, it may

241

truthfully be said of Butler and Degas that they worked
with a flail. They thrashed humanity with right good will,
striking blows that separated the kernels from the chaff,
which they scattered to the winds lest it blow back and
blind us to our faults. No popular caterers they to the viti-
ated tastes of their easygoing self-complacent fellow men;
their recipes call for hot stuff that it burns to swallow, that
brings water to the eyes. They appeal to the human mind,
not to the human palate and they care little when the tears
flow; stern monitors, walking fiercely, fearlessly alone,
along the straight and narrow path. My deep admiration
for them both seems to unite them in my thoughts, but here
I must leave one for my task is to write of the other. So
much has already been told that I shall write only of my
personal recollections, of conversations with Miss Cassatt,
of visits to Degas, and how we collected many examples of
his work.

Although it is difficult to think of men whom we have
learned to appreciate, nay almost to reverence in their greatness, as having begun life in somebody's arms and in long
clothes like any other tiny creature, still, it is only just to
offer them the courtesy of a biography, and I feel like bor-
350   rowing the happy expression of Phillips Brooks, the bachelor Bishop of Boston, who when he held a little creature in
his arms to christen it returned it to its proud mother saying:

"That *is* a baby!"

Well! I suppose Degas was a baby once, but that has so
little to do with these memories that I prefer to write what
Miss Cassatt said, when I asked her one day to tell me
something about the early history of Degas. She said:
"Degas's great-grandfather during the Reign of Terror met
a friend one day, who as he passed said to him in an under-
tone: '*Vous êtes du nombre*' (You are one of the number).
The great-grandfather left France that very day and taking

his family with him he settled in Naples, where he made a living by selling pumice stone." I made an exclamation, "Pumice stone?"

"Yes, pumice stone," repeated Miss Cassatt. "Later he returned to France with his wife and son and the latter founded a banking house. This was Degas's father and he 351 married a daughter of the very last Spanish governor of New Orleans. Her sister married the Marquis of Rochefort. Degas made fun of his noble cousin and said that the Marquis drew down the curtains of his bathroom so that he could have the pleasure of looking at a coronet while bathing."

"That was just like Degas," I remarked.

"Exactly," said Miss Cassatt. "*Bon diseur de mots*, my dear, *mauvais caractère*. Degas had one sister who married M. Le Febvre, and four brothers, one of whom was a *mauvais sujet* and the family to save him from ruin gave up everything, the silverware and even the sister's dot were sacrificed. Now Degas's fortune in pictures which should realize several million francs will, of course, go to eight nieces and nephews." Here Miss Cassatt, probably feeling she had brought the biography down to the present time, stopped but I saw a look of reminiscence in her eye and a peculiar expression about her mouth, and I pleaded:

"Tell me some more about him."

"Oh, my dear, he is dreadful! He dissolves your will power," she said. "Even the painter Moreau said to Degas 352 after years of friendship, that he could no longer stand his attacks: '*Voyons, Degas, il faut que je mène ma vie! que nous ne nous voyions plus!*' (See here, Degas, I must lead my life! Let us no longer meet!)

"Degas said to me apropos of Sargent (John S. Sargent, portrait painter): '*Un facile peintre, mais pas un artiste*' (A 353 skillful painter but not an artist), and of another painter who would like to have been associated with us he said:

'*Il n'est pas assez méchant pour nous*' (He is not wicked enough for us)." And then after a moment's reflection she continued: "Think of this; one day a young painter seeing Degas in a color shop begged the proprietor to introduce him to the great Degas! 'Better not,' cautioned the proprietor, but as the young fellow insisted he presented him to Degas. Of course the youth was delighted, but after a few moments' conversation Degas turned to a picture which stood upon an easel and said '*Jeune homme, c'est vous qui avez fait ça?*' (Young man, did you do that?) '*Mais oui, monsieur*,' replied the young fellow, delighted that Degas had noticed his canvas. '*Je vous plains*' (I pity you) and he turned upon his heel and left the shop."

"He was indeed dreadful," I said sympathetically, but knowing Miss Cassatt was quite his equal in repartee I led her on to tell me more by asking: "How could you get on with him?"

"Oh," she answered, "I am independent! I can live alone and I love to work. Sometimes it made him furious that he could not find a chink in my armor, and there would be months when we just could not see each other, and then something I painted would bring us together again and he 354 would go to Durand-Ruel's and say something nice about me, or come to see me himself. When he saw my 'Boy be- 355 fore the Mirror' he said to Durand-Ruel: 'Where is she? I must see her at once. It is the greatest picture of the century.' When I saw him he went over all the details of the picture with me and expressed great admiration for it, and then, as if regretting what he had said, he relentlessly added: 'It has all your qualities and all your faults—*c'est l'Enfant Jésus et sa bonne anglaise*.' "

"Did no one ever hit him back?" I asked.

"Oh! certainly," replied Miss Cassatt, "but Degas never cared. When criticism was at its worst, he said to me: '*Ils sont tous jaloux de nous. Ils veulent nous voler notre art'* (They are all jealous of us, and wish to steal our art).''

"But," continued Miss Cassatt after a quiet moment, and I saw her face light up with a beautiful expression, "magnificent! and however dreadful he was, he always lived up to his ideals." Miss Cassatt folded her hands and I saw she had said all she cared to for the moment.

Yes, this great painter lived up to his ideals! He was a primitive of his own day, seeing things as they really were, depicting life in its terrible reality. Many things have been written and said about Degas, but the truest of all was said about him by Miss Cassatt. "He is a philosopher, and there it is," she said.

True, a Diogenes living in his tub if you will, hunting for and exposing hypocrisy, but always searching, analyzing, philosophizing. Unlike the group of impressionists with whom he associated himself in their exhibitions, he rarely painted out-of-doors. A Parisian in thought and temperament, he haunted the boulevards, the cafés, the opera, the race tracks. With an eye as keen as the early Italians for the reality of things, he observed and reflected and when the picture was produced it was not merely a *café chantant*, a ballet rehearsal, or a jockey with race horses. It was the subject treated from its profoundest depths to its minutest details.

Take, for example, one of his pictures of a *café chantant*. 356 It does not represent perhaps the attractive place we Americans recall on the Champs Elysées, but rather is a true record of what the *café chantant* really is. The dazzling lights are there, the gay crowd is suggested, but you cannot fail to see the crass banality of the scene. A woman stands upon the stage singing a popular song: "La Chanson du Chien." Look at her and observe the common type. You feel at once that she has crowded herself into the uncomfortable gown, that her gloves are a strange annoyance to her. There is nothing elegant about her pose. Her hands suggest the movement of a dog, and the gesture is done as only Degas could do it, with a flash of the pencil. The lines of the mouth as she bawls out the vulgar song, her exultant exaggeration, showing she is conscious of her power over her audience, all this and much more shows clearly what a *café chantant* is, what part it plays in Parisian life, the kind of creature it is that furnishes the amusement; and although you do not see them distinctly, you know immediately the class of pleasure seekers who are entertained by such a performance. Degas, the keen, subtle philosopher, reveals the *café chantant* as it is from its heart and core, from cause to effect.

The ballet interested the philosopher perhaps more than any other subject during his working years, and although he loved to pose the celebrated dancer Mlle Mauri upon the tips of her toes and make her gauzy skirts vibrate with the most enthralling harmonies of color, it was not thus that he cared to interpret the ballet. He preferred to portray the sinuous, sleek little creatures who came up from the heart of Paris with their mothers to present themselves at the opera and seek an entrance to the school which will enslave the best part of their young lives and make them the untiring pupils of "Pluque," the venerable *maître de danse.* You can see them to the life in a picture called "La Famille Mante" or in one which I own, called "L'Attente."

Degas painted them just as they were in character and in pose, relaxing tired muscles in easy attitudes in the foyer, exchanging coarse jests or indulging in the *cancan* of the *quartier*. The philosopher knew their bone and breeding and gave them to us no worse and no better than they were. It was his favorite subject, the difficulties fascinated him and he conquered them with almost incredible skill. His pencil

357

358

seemed like a live wire as he drew the floating figures or caught a fleeting gesture. As no other painter of modern times, he could put atmosphere around the rows of gliding forms and lift their fleecy draperies with the movement of the dance.

The main facts of Degas's artistic life are so well known I scarcely need to write of them. It seemed to me that he always lived in the rue Lavalle, and I remember how distressed he was when a few years ago the building had to be torn down and he was obliged to seek a new apartment. 359 He pathetically asked the Durand-Ruels to take charge of a large picture, a superb group of family portraits which had lain rolled up in his studio for more than thirty years and on which the dust lay thick, for no one was allowed to touch any picture there. His mother's wedding dress was kept in the top of an old piano that was never opened, and the moths had eaten their way into the very entrails of the horse which had served him as a model when he did his now famous "Race Horses and Jockeys." 360

That studio was a storehouse of art, for Degas was an indefatigable worker and he had lived in the same workshop for many and many decades, leading as Miss Cassatt has told me, the life of a hermit in its simplicity and frugality, extravagant only when he could find a pastel by La Tour 361 whom he greatly admired, or an Ingres drawing that he was always seeking and that might be useful to him in his work. I believe that only a few of his admirers were at any time welcome to his quiet apartment. On rare occasions he invited a few friends and a foe or two to a dinner which usually consisted of a beefsteak pie, his *pièce de résistance*, while over the feast he threw the *sauce piquante—très piquante*—of his caustic wit which frequently burned deep and hurt hard.

Long hours in his studio, short ones for recreation, a new

piece at the theater, a wrangle with a critic—poor critic—
a racial or political controversy: there was his life.

Degas, in his capacity for work, may be compared to
Balzac and George Sand. Balzac tells us he worked nineteen hours a day on his *Le Lys dans la Vallée*, losing his
profits as he persisted in polishing and correcting each line
and paragraph. George Sand apologizes for the lack of form
and continuity in her *Consuelo*, saying necessity made her
sit down at midnight with a pitcher of milk beside her and
write the number of pages that would enable her to support
the dying Chopin and the little family the following day.
How little we of the foothills know of the difficulties and
weariness of those that tread the narrow path that leads its
pilgrims to the high realms of great creative art!

I dislike to speak of Degas's idiosyncrasies, for it goes
without saying that he had some, in common with all great
men be they poet or painter. Napoleon loved his eight-min-
ute nap, Wellington was vain and longed for good looks,
Leonardo loved to play pranks upon his friends, Charles had
a fondness for old clothes, Rubens enjoyed his fine horses,
and within the month I have watched one of our greatest
naval heroes slyly take a digestive tablet after dining. Degas
indulged in fads rather, his imagination turned upon himself and his supposed infirmities. Miss Cassatt has told me
that sometimes he would greet her with his eyes closed,
fumbling as he shook her hand and telling her he was losing
his eyesight. He would grope his way about the apartment
feeling for the door of his studio, and then show her some
splendid glowing canvas he had just completed. At other
times he would take to his bed as if burdened with his years
and become irascible, impossible even to his friends whose
long devotion had taught them to bear with the foibles of a
gifted lonely man and forgive him offenses even before he
committed them. Genius, that strange bird, seeks wild and

lonely nests, and being much occupied with other things beats its wings and scratches with its claws in a desperate effort to make itself comfortable.

It is very sad to write of Degas's old age. With faculties dimmed, energy exhausted, wrapped in melancholy he paces the boulevards, day after day, hour after hour, and when someone stops to greet him he looks sadly up and repeats: *"Il faut mourir."* The last time I spoke to Miss Cassatt, 363 she said: "Mercy! what a state he is in! He scarcely knows you, he neglects his clothes, he takes no interest in anything, it is dreadful. With millions of francs still in his studio, they can do him no good; he is consumed with old age." Degas, the great painter, is fast passing from our world, but his name will be forever cherished by lovers of art.

I was about sixteen years old when I first heard of Degas, of course through Miss Cassatt. She took me to see one of his pastels and advised me to buy it. How well I remember 364 going with her to the color shop where it was for sale. Those color shops have launched more than one great artist, who later have made fortunes for dealers. The pastel was a "Répétition de Ballet." Old Pluque, the well-known *maître de ballet*, stood leaning upon his stick by the side scenes of the stage directing a rehearsal, the dancers were grouped about in various poses awaiting their turn while a *première* did a difficult *pas seul* in the foreground. The drawing of the picture was as firm as a primitive, the difficulties of planes and perspective handled like a master, while the effect of light and shade and the beauty of color were simply entrancing. It was so new and strange to me! I scarce knew how to appreciate it, or whether I liked it or not, for I believe it takes special brain cells to understand Degas. There was nothing the matter with Miss Cassatt's brain cells, however, and she left me in no doubt as to the desirability of the purchase and I bought it upon her advice.

Now it may seem strange, or a trifle extravagant to my readers of today, to make such a purchase, but if at the age of sixteen you had saved the sum of five hundred francs out of your spending money, probably you too would have thought twice before investing it in a Degas. Five hundred francs was a large sum for me to spend in those days, and represented many little economies and even some privations; also it was just half my art balance and I still wanted a Monet and a Pissarro. However, as always Miss Cassatt was firm in her judgment, and the "Répétition de Ballet" was bought. I did not know until long afterward how opportune the sale of the picture was for Degas, and then Miss Cassatt told me Degas had written her a note of thanks when he received the money, saying he was sadly in need of it.

The "Répétition de Ballet" was most appropriately framed by Degas, in soft dull gray and green which harmonized with the decorations of the scenery and the gauzy gossamerlike dresses of the ballerina. I mention this for two reasons. First, because Degas once told me he considered it an artist's duty to see his pictures properly framed, that he wished the frame to harmonize and to support his pictures and not to crush them as an elaborate gold frame would do. I wish he had repeated this more often, for the first thing I did to many a Degas that we purchased from amateurs was to remove the atrocious heavy gold frame which the owners probably thought gave the picture more importance, and to restore it to its original frame when possible or provide it with one Degas could approve. My other reason for mentioning the frame is to relate an amusing incident of a jury and the rules of our National Academy of Design in the early eighties. Degas's "Répétition de Ballet" attracted the attention of some members of the Academy and I consented to lend it for the spring exhibition. My sister and I dropped in at the exhibition one afternoon to see how the Degas looked among the American art of the eighties! We finally found our pastel skied upon the wall of a small room and alack! and alas! the delicate gray and green frame had been generously treated to a thick coating of brilliant gold bronze. We entered a protest at once, and learned that "the rules of the Academy exacted that all pictures exhibited should be provided with gold frames"; ergo the jury—there must have been one Dogberry at least among them—would not admit an Edgar Degas to an exhibition unless he submitted to their "golden" rule! Of course we were then only in the nineteenth century, and it was at least twelve years later before another Degas was exhibited in New York City. With infinite pains I had the frame restored, and today the pastel hangs in my gallery and interests many a visitor who wishes to see the first Degas and one that was bought for five hundred francs.

Mr. Havemeyer and I went several times to see Degas, usually in company with Miss Cassatt. I thought him a dignified-looking man of medium height, a compact figure, well dressed, rather dark and with fine eyes. There was nothing of the artistic *négligé* about him, on the contrary he rather impressed me as a man of the world. He made an etching of himself when quite a young man, of which I bought a copy at the Marx sale in 1914. Then there is a small portrait of Degas in ink which Guys made and which is owned by Durand-Ruel. Although I borrowed it for the exhibition I made of Degas's and Mary Cassatt's works in 1915 at the Knoedler gallery, I did not care for it; I felt a tinge of caricature in the portrait and it entirely lacked any expression of Degas's great mentality.

I recall one visit to the rue Lavalle, when after we had looked at several pastels lately finished, Degas opened a portfolio to show us some of his drawings. What treasures he revealed! Such immense talent and such endless labor! No wonder he produced works of such prodigious strength; he trained himself for his compositions, just as an athlete is trained for his feats of daring. I, for the first time, understood what he meant when he said: "Art is not spontaneous but the result of constant effort." Degas tenderly lifted the drawings one by one and showed them to us. We could see how greatly he prized them. They were the proofs of his great cases, notes from which he made his successes; each one on which he looked probably recalled some fine achievement to his mind. Mr. Havemeyer requested Degas to let him have some of them, but he seemed reluctant to give them up, unable to part with a single one of them. Miss Cassatt took up one drawing and called my husband's attention to it. It was the sketch for "Les Danseuses à la

370   Barre." It was done upon pink paper and the penciled squares could still be seen across the figure of the young ballet girl, who grasped the bar and extended her leg in a difficult attitude. It was a superb drawing and Degas watched us as we admired it. Suddenly, he selected two others, signed them all and handed them to Mr. Havemeyer. We realized we were the fortunate possessors, not only of his best drawings, but of those he wished us to have. No word of price was spoken. It was a solemn moment and all details had to be arranged by our kind intermediary, Miss Cassatt.

Another visit which is sharply engraved upon my memory was the occasion when we bought "The Designer of

371   Prints," a transaction that cost Degas Miss Cassatt's friendship for a long time, and strangely enough this time about a matter of price, for even Degas's ideas of a bargain were more picturesque than businesslike. For instance, he looked upon Durand-Ruel as upon a bank account, and I have in

my possession a *petit bleu* which Degas addressed one day to rue Laffitte, it read: *"Passez chez moi. J'ai besoin d'argent." Père* Durand-Ruel would kindly go to the rue Lavalle and supply his painter's needs. Well, on this memorable visit, Degas sold us a small oil painting called "The Designer of Prints" and the price was one thousand dollars. He asked to keep it for a time as he wished to add a few touches. He kept it nearly two years, and then told Miss Cassatt he would not give it up for less than three thousand dollars, as his pictures during those two years had advanced in price. In vain Miss Cassatt argued that he had sold the picture for one thousand dollars to Mr. Havemeyer and that he could not change the price. It was of no use! Degas was quite stubborn about it, and the idea was so fixed in his mind that he was entitled to the increase in value that at last Mr. Havemeyer yielded. We felt that we were perhaps very fortunate to get the picture back unspoiled, for Degas had a dangerous habit of retouching which sometimes spoiled a picture; hence M. Henri Rouart chained "Les Danseuses à la Barre" to his wall so the pastel could not be removed, and Durand-Ruel complained to me that Degas would frequently take a picture back to his studio to do some trivial thing to it, and it would never be returned to him again. "Degas's studio is full of such pictures," said the old gentleman to me. "He takes a picture to retouch and then goes on retouching and finally throws it aside in disgust. He seems unwilling to give us anything, but is always wishing to do better and better."

No one knew him better than we did in that respect. For a long time Miss Cassatt had spoken to us of a certain picture. She considered it one of Degas's best and she ardently wished us to have it. It represented a laundress ironing a fancy cap with a funny little iron such as they use in France. It was a picture upon which he had expended the fullness

of his art and which Miss Cassatt thought finer than anything that Count Camondo owned—yes, as fine as the
"Danseuses" itself! After infinite pains she traced it and
where do you suppose it was? Why in his studio of course,
a hopeless ruin! He had taken it to retouch and had utterly
spoiled it!

374   During another visit to Degas, I had an opportunity to
look around the apartment. I found a little vitrine containing the model of a horse and the remains of his celebrated
statue of "La Danseuse." Degas modeled it long ago—in
the eighties, I think—and exhibited it to the great astonishment of the Parisian art world. To some it was a revelation,
to others an enigma. The graceful figure was as classic as
an Egyptian statue and as modern as Degas! She is not
beautiful—just a model Degas frequently used—but the
knowledge of anatomy, the tense expression of muscle and
joint, the relation of movements, oh, I found it wonderful!
It must be seen, studied and understood to be appreciated!
The danseuse salutes her audience in a beautiful pose, her
arms extended and her head slightly raised, real hair is
hanging down her back, colored gossamer skirts are floating
about her, her feet firmly support her and yet she expresses
without effort the lightness and the spirit of the dance.

Here was a problem! All Paris said: "Has the soul of some
Egyptian come to our western world? Who has achieved
this wonderful creation? Whoever he is, he is modern to
his finger tips and as ancient as the pyramids!"

"Let them solve it as they will," said the proud Degas.
"What business is it of mine if they do not understand, I
do. Let them go their way, and I go mine. I have made the
long pilgrimage, I have kept the long lone vigil of the night,
I have drunk deep of the sacred fountain and communed
with the sacred muse."

But strange to say, some did understand. Artistic Paris

was taken by storm, ears tingled, eyes brightened and voices became animated when Degas's name was mentioned. Paris could scarcely maintain its equilibrium. Was ever such a thing heard of! A ballerina with real hair and real draperies, and one of the greatest works of art since the dynasties of the Nile! Degas became the hero of the hour! His name was upon all lips, his statue discussed by all the art world, while he, indifferent to public opinion, supremely conscious of his own worth, poured forth from the crucible of his wit those apothegms that burned the vanity out of men's souls. That is the painter Degas; for forty years and more has he labored for his art, never turning from the narrow path to accept any honors mere man may offer! No red ribbon flashes from his breast. He has worked for his muse alone, seeking only her smile, content with her approval.

Now "La Danseuse" lies in pieces! As I looked into the little vitrine, I remember how faded the gauze was and how woolly the dark hair appeared, but nevertheless I had a great desire to possess the statue, and as soon as I met Durand-Ruel afterward I requested him to interview Degas and find out if the statue could not be put together again for me. The answer came—"it might and it might not be done. There were hopes and there were doubts!" There would be work Degas could no longer see to do, that would have to be entrusted to another, but above and beyond other considerations, the statue was of the past for him and far away from his present line of thought, for after all we neither think nor work the same at intervals of forty years, and so after much hesitation and a great deal of advice, I finally abandoned the idea. However, I distinctly remember that when I called Degas's attention to the wax figure, it seemed to awaken pleasant memories and he became animated and began an interesting conversation with Miss Cassatt about the past, snapping sidelights upon the work of his contemporaries, and making personal allusions which I did not understand but which greatly amused Miss Cassatt. It is a great pity that she did not keep his letters, nor write down her impressions of Degas; no one understood him better and she was his compeer in intelligence and art appreciation.

I also recollect that it was during this visit that, an opportunity offered, I asked Degas the question—I blush to record it—a question that had often been asked me: "Why, monsieur, do you always do ballet dancers?"

The quick reply was: "Because, madame, it is all that is left us of the combined movement of the Greeks." It was so kindly said, I felt he forgave me the silly question and for not understanding him better.

375 He also spoke of his admiration for La Tour and said he loved to visit St. Quentin and see those wonderful pastel portraits there, and that he would remain weeks in Lille just to study the rich collection of drawings in the museum, and always to the profit of his art. It was a long afternoon and it was most inspiring to hear him talk, for he was in the mood and spoke very earnestly of the primitives and of their purity of line and color, of the greatness of Leonardo, and of his own admiration for Domenichino, whom he considered underestimated. It was a memorable visit, and as we drove away I said to Miss Cassatt: "Does Degas work on and on and never get discouraged?"

"Mercy no!" she exclaimed, "He frequently complains of having *perdu chemin* and then he goes away for months, sometimes to Lille but more often to Italy."

I was glad to hear her say so for it seemed to make him mortal again, and I hated to think of him chained, like poor Prometheus, to that lonely mountaintop for having stolen the sacred fire.

It matters little whether or not I recall the order in which we collected Degas's pictures, for like Brahms in music he began by doing his best, and his early works are among his greatest. Whether we admire the exquisite precision of his drawing, the light and air with which he envelops his compositions in the eighties and early nineties, or the broader touch and the glowing color of his later years, we can never forget that from first to last the eye of the philosopher is penetrating the innermost depth of his subject and that whether he works by analysis or synthesis, his vision reveals to us nature in its truth, its whole truth and nothing but the truth.

It goes without saying that of the fifty pictures in our collection almost all were bought about the time Degas painted them; many were purchased through Durand-Ruel, and others recommended by Miss Cassatt who watched their execution in the studio or saw them in the various exhibitions. Thus some of the earliest pictures by Degas we owned were ballet scenes. There is a small beautiful one of the seventies; some ballet dancers are seated upon a piano, resting in various positions. "La Famille Mante" is another; a poorly dressed mother "of the class," with her daughter dressed and waiting to be called for her turn, while another girl, a real little *gamine*, looks on with curious eyes, knowing her time is coming soon. This was a subject Degas repeated several times, as he did with the famous "Danseuses à la Barre." M. Henri Rouart bought the large "Danseuses" and Mr. Havemeyer bought the other. Rouart bought his from Degas and chained it to the wall to prevent Degas indulging his fancy to take it to his studio and "touch it up." Of "Horses and Jockeys," we have one in oil and an important one in pastel. When the "Milliner" series appeared, Miss Cassatt secured for us the large one—extraordinary in color—of a woman trying on a hat before a long

mirror. Miss Cassatt posed for this picture. The movement
of the hand that places the hat upon her head, and her pose
as she leans upon an umbrella is very characteristic of her.

I once asked Miss Cassatt if she often posed for Degas.
"Oh, no," she answered carelessly, "only once in a while
when he finds the movement difficult, and the model cannot
seem to get his idea." In later years, I bought another
382 "Milliner" pastel from the Alexis Rouart sale. It is not so
beautiful in color as the other but the drawing of the
modiste who is arranging a bonnet is very fine.

During a visit to Europe, Durand-Ruel allowed Mr.
Havemeyer to select a number of pictures from his private
383 collection. It was this privilege which placed several of
Degas's finest works in our collection. One is called "L'Attente." A ballet girl, waiting to be called, is seated upon a
bench and is leaning down to tie her sandal; by her side is
another figure, probably her mother. The latter is poorly
dressed and is also leaning forward, upon an umbrella,
which she holds in her hand in a difficult position. It is rather
somber in tone and subject, but is the perfection of art in
every detail.

There were two others, also pastels, rather high and narrow, perhaps suggested by the Japanese pillar prints which
had reached Paris in those days. One represents a ballet
girl in a very difficult pose: resting lightly on one foot she
extends the other as she throws her body forward and her
gossamer green draperies float around her, describing cir-
cles that might suggest an Egyptian bas-relief, and yet
fleecy and light, expressive of the movement that lightly
threw them up; the wonderful envelopment of air gives
them such buoyancy that one stands entranced at the marvelous skill that could produce such an effect and at the wonderful eye that could thrill you with such a piece of color. The
pendant is a ballet girl in yellow. I do not think it so fine nor

so interesting as the other. Strange to say, many years after, M. Joseph Durand-Ruel and I happening to be in the gallery together, he called my attention to these pastels of Degas and said his father had kept one pair and let Mr. Havemeyer have the other pair, and that in precisely the same way one of their pair was finer than the other. This fact led us into an interesting discussion, the gist of which was that no two compositions are ever alike or equal, there is always a "best" and a "second best." With all the technique and formulas that a painter can grasp, he cannot control the complexities that will arise in spite of his efforts between the thought that guides the stroke and the hand that executes it.

After that I think we acquired a pastel from a M. Viot in Paris, ballet girls in white seated upon a bench; and another 384 from Cottier and Company of about the same size, several ballet girls in a row—*vue de dos*—also in white and with red flowers. We have an oil of ballet girls on a bench and a 'cello 385 beside them; there is another pastel of the same subject. Ballets in blue, ballets in pink and green—of this series, and 386 it is of a later period, I have two: one a pastel and one a very important oil. The latter represents five ballet girls in various poses, and a man in profile by the wings of a theater. It is so transparent that many have mistaken it for a pastel.

It would take too long to describe fifty works by Degas in this short chapter so I will mention only a few more, most of which we acquired through private collectors. For instance, two of almost the same subject called "La Répétition," two important pictures of almost the same dimen- 387 sions, one done in pastel and the other in what artists call *gouache*, a preparation of color mixed with egg which keeps its transparency and does not grow dark. To an experienced eye, the two compositions bristle with difficulties which Degas had handled in his usual masterly way, and it is interesting to compare one with the other. We acquired them at long intervals: the first, we bought from the May sale with another also done in egg—ballet girls in a room, some standing in the light of a long French window, a very beautiful and brilliant composition, one of my favorites. The other "Répétition" came from the Sichert Collection and was bought in Paris many years later.

I recall an interesting afternoon when Pottier (an art dealer), came to our hotel and proposed that we should go see a Degas, one that the owner "might possibly part with for a price." It was not unusual for Parisian amateurs with moderate incomes to change their art treasures from time to time, particularly as the time for the spring exhibition approached and they knew of an American who would probably offer a tempting price for it, when *they* had bought it for a small sum.

"What is it?" asked Miss Cassatt keenly.

"A portrait," answered Pottier.

388   "The Taigny portrait," replied Miss Cassatt quickly.

"*Précisément*," rejoined Pottier.

"Of course we will go see it," said Miss Cassatt energetically. "It is one of the best things Degas ever did, one of the greatest portraits Degas ever painted. His cousin sat for it and it is like a primitive."

One could speak his mind before Pottier, and we were soon driving to a distant part of Paris where we found one of the most exquisite portraits I have ever seen. It was as if the hand had been eliminated from the production and the mind of the painter had transferred it directly to the canvas. It was, as Miss Cassatt had said, a modern primitive, pure in line, delicate in color and entrancing in its harmonious perfection. Probably suggested by Degas's admiration of La Tour, it is just the head and neck done upon gray paper, and then, as if it pleased his fancy, he traced another outline of the same face in an upper corner of the picture, in a way that does not appear strange to anyone familiar with the drawings of Leonardo da Vinci. We lost no time in letting Pottier know we approved of it, a fact which immensely delighted the good man who had true artistic instincts and perceptions himself, and delighted to please Miss Cassatt and Mr. Havemeyer, and he told us the price—*"Dix mille francs!"* he said—two thousand dollars! said Pottier timidly. Miss Cassatt, who was accustomed to the old prices, uttered an exclamation. "All right we'll take it," said Mr. Havemeyer promptly, and the affair was concluded. Ah! how many a picture was bought in the same decided way and how many a dollar was saved by doing so.

The nudes of Degas were a special admiration of Miss Cassatt's. She immediately selected a fine one for us. The 389 "cynic of the beefsteak pie" did not mince matters in painting his nudes and frankly exposed poor human nature in its vulgar banality, while his execution of each composition, which apparently exceeded each other in difficulties, was a revelation of his masterly handling of flesh, of interiors filled with brilliant stuffs, of the white lingerie of the dressing room, of the delicate harmonies and effect of light. The Paris art world was again taken by storm and divided between those who had learned to understand the philosopher and his art and those who reviled the "vulgar nudes." Later, I bought two more nudes, one from the Hayashi sale and one from Cottier and Company, but not until I finally secured the Roger Marx nude did I feel I had the best. For 390 many years had we admired this wonderful picture of a woman just out of her bath, seated upon a yellow divan, pressing her hands against her sides to steady herself while her maid lifts up her head and draws it back as she brushes the masses of heavy hair.

391   The memory of the Great War is associated with this picture, for I had just visited for the first time in many years the public and private galleries of Germany, from Munich to Berlin, from Berlin to Frankfort, leaving that city on a Sunday morning at six o'clock in my automobile in order to make the run to Paris in a day and be there for the auction the next morning. How well I remember my astonishment at the great military activity everywhere as we motored through Metz, through Saarbrucken, through Saar Louis, etc., etc. We crossed the border and saw the French in sad processions, placing wreaths on the crosses in the fields and by the wayside as they remembered and revered their dead on the anniversary of the battle of Gravelotte. I recall that as we crossed the Meuse and motored through Verdun I related to my maid the circumstances of the conflict and told her that the number slain at Gravelotte exceeded that of any previous battle in history. How little did I dream of the great struggle that was to begin within a few weeks! Could I ever forget it, that Sunday afternoon as I was hurrying along to buy my nude? I entered the auction room just in time to see the picture knocked down to me, and I knew I possessed one of Degas's finest pastels.

392   Among my oils I own a man's portrait by Degas. It is a portrait of M. Altès, the flutist of the Opéra; by only a few spare hairs does he avoid the charge of baldness, there is an oily quality to his skin and a suggestion in the eyes and about the mouth of constant blowing and puffing; otherwise the countenance expresses a genial resignation to hard work and to long hours, and I feel sure the kindly word the flutist always had for Degas led the painter to do his portrait. Degas put much spirit into this remarkable painting. It is a true character study as keen as any Rembrandt, and as usual,

a perfect piece of art. I hung the portrait in the gallery be- tween a Clouet and a Corneille de Lyon. In the subdued *393* light the low tones vibrate. You see the sharply drawn profile, the dark head, the inflated cheek. How beautifully it looked and how well it held its own; but not until a Frenchman visited my gallery, did I find someone who thoroughly appreciated my Degas—and my little joke with me. I must explain my little joke. It consisted in placing a Degas portrait between one by Clouet and one by Cor- neille de Lyon, and the great modern held his own between those of the Renaissance.

I have often noticed that sensitive artistic natures are very appreciative of a kindred art, even if they lack tech- nical knowledge of it. I believe Degas had such a nature and admired the beauty of the scroll handle of a stringed instru- ment as much as any violinist or 'cellist with all his knowl- edge of its workmanship. He loved to paint just such a scroll handle and did so many times, always making it prominent in his pictures. Among others I recall two oils, both scenes from *Robert the Devil*. One is in the Isagi Collection in the *394* Kensington museum and the other I own. It represents the scene of the graveyard where the ballet issues from the open tombs, but the orchestra is the real composition, it occupies the first plane; the sharply drawn profiles, the inflated cheeks, the tightly held instruments and above all in promi- nence the beautiful scroll of a 'cello or a violin! I have often wished I could have given Degas the pleasure of examining some of Mr. Havemeyer's instruments, for I know he must have been a connoisseur.

Mr. Havemeyer was the most generous amateur I ever knew. The pleasure he gave seemed to rebound to him again. He tried to make his friends enjoy art as he did. I remember he relinquished one of Degas's fine oils, just to *395* try to make his friend Colonel Oliver Payne appreciate

Degas as he did. Mr. Havemeyer had been instrumental in securing for the Colonel several fine pictures, a Turner, two Corots, and now he said to him:

"I advise you to take that picture," and needless to say the Colonel heeded the good advice and bought the painting.

For many a long year afterward, whenever the Colonel dropped in for a neighborly chat he would refer to his indebtedness to Mr. Havemeyer for allowing him to acquire the picture. After my husband's death the Colonel and I were looking at the "Foyer" and the Colonel said to me: "Your husband knew that I did not understand that picture. He often tried to make me appreciate Degas as he did, but he knew I could not do it. One day as we were looking at it together, he began telling me what a wonderful picture it was and trying to convince me how great Degas was. I don't know just what I said or did, but suddenly he stopped and said: 'Don't let us talk any more about it.' I fear I disappointed him; Mr. Havemeyer spoke very gently but there was something about him that struck me as unusual."

I knew, for Mr. Havemeyer said to me several times: "If ever you have a chance, get that picture back. The Colonel does not care for it and would rather buy one of the English school." The Colonel promised I should have it back but alas, he never let me have it!

Perhaps my last acquisition of Degas's works is my best and, as usual, I owe it to Miss Cassatt. One day I received a letter from her saying: "I advise you to buy one of the finest Degas. It is much in the style of a Vermeer and quite as interesting, very quiet and reposeful. It is a beautiful picture. A woman in black seated upon a sofa against the light, the model was a sister of Berthe Morisot, not handsome, but a Degas! The picture has never been shown and is far finer than the portrait Mrs. Gardner owns. I will send a photograph and the size. I have examined it carefully and

396

it is a very fine thing. I am sure you would agree with me—
a photograph won't give you any idea of it. Then, there is
another thing I am to see, another picture, small, danseuses, 397
very fine in execution."

When Miss Cassatt was on the scent, letters came
quickly. The next mail brought the following: "The little
picture was brought here this morning. It is no larger than
this full sheet of paper"—referring to her letter—"it is a
foyer like the Colonel's Degas and very finely executed. It is
a real tour de force. When Degas saw it, he turned away
and said: 'When I did that I had my eyes!' Of course that
was years ago, he could not see the picture now. Think
what his eyes must have been when he painted it! He attached much importance to it, and the owners expect to get
a great price. Both are fine paintings, not pastels."

Again, a few days later, I received another letter in which
she said: "I have just seen the owners of the two paintings
and they have come down in their price and brought something that they will add to the bargain. It is a fine drawing
—or rather a pastel with *gouache*—a woman in a green
dress with stripes, seated upon a sofa. The pink paper is
the background. I am doing this for you, dear! I really
think it is a chance and your collection of Degas ought to
be very complete with these two pictures and the pastel;
it, too, is a fine thing."

In a month or two the affair was completed, and the pictures on their way to me. The last reference to them in Miss
Cassatt's letters read: "I am anxious as to your impression
—not of the portrait, nor the pastel, but of the 'Foyer' on
account of its size."

What a purchase it was! This faithful friend, so true to
me, so interested in the collection, was as good as her word.
The "Foyer" is indeed a tour de force. I know of nothing
finer in the Dutch or Flemish school—different, yes! finer,

no! The picture is a small panel about twelve by seven inches—that's all. But what does it represent?—a large foyer, a room with windows and doors. In the center of it stands a long mirror, such as is used for ballet rehearsals, and a grand piano in front of which and leaning his back against it sits the white-haired violinist, with his instrument under his chin, looking at the ballerina who is taking a step before the mirror. Upon the polished floor he has placed his violin case and his high hat, into which he has stuck his roll of music. The inevitable sprinkler stands under the closed piano and in the room are no less than twelve ballet girls, stretching their limbs at the *barre*, practicing difficult postures, adjusting their sandals or leaning against the piano. And as if not content with the difficulties he had encountered, Degas paints the reflection of at least two ballerinas in different poses in the mirror! Think of it! Do you wonder that Degas turned sadly away from the picture and said: "I had my eyes when I did that."

I cannot adequately describe this wonderful painting, its drawing, the atmosphere Degas puts around each figure, the sentiment of the old violinist, the beautiful harmony of the soft gray tones. It is beyond my power of description. I can only hope it may always be preserved to delight and instruct both those who know and those who wish to know the marvels of art.

The drawing is evidently the portrait of a French woman, a *bourgeoise*—I could say—of the *bourgeoisie*, for could anything be more *bourgeoise*, complaisant, comfortable, conscious, content? She is stout and does not regret it nor seek to conceal it by modish tricks. She is rather graceful, and conscious that she is a Parisian born and bred, and perfectly satisfied to pursue her life of good works and good living.

Many an amateur would prefer to buy this picture, rather than the one Miss Cassatt calls "one of the finest of Degas," the portrait of Berthe Morisot's sister, a thoughtful young woman dressed in black, whose hands, with fingers idly interlocked, lie upon her lap as she leans against the cushions of the sofa. The light comes from an open door in the back of the room and there is a picture upon the wall. That is all, again, and Degas was not even prodigal of his paint, as you can see the canvas beneath it in many places.

Well! I paid a large sum for that picture and I do not regret it, not a farthing of it. I bought neither beauty nor glamor, no, nor still life, nor a great composition; nothing but art, just pure incandescent art, right out of the crucible; its author heated it over the sacred fire. It seems to me it is not a picture, it is not a portrait, it is an inspiration. Degas never did anything like it again. I doubt if he ever could, I doubt if *ever* any painter could do such a picture. It is forever! it is an art epoch in itself.

And now as I close this chapter where I have tried to write my recollections of this great man, I must end with a few sad words, for only today did I receive a letter from Miss Cassatt written at the close of the third year of the Great War, in which she says: 398

"Poor Degas is always the same. What a world it is! Oh! to get out of it without too much suffering!"

I thought of one of her favorite quotations:

> "We, in some unknown Power's employ,
>   Move on a rigorous line;
> Can neither, when we will, enjoy,
>   Nor, when we will, resign."

CHAPTER XV

Mary Cassatt

MARY CASSATT and I have been lifelong friends. She has been my inspiration and my guide. I call her the fairy godmother of my collection, for the best things I own have been bought on her judgment and advice.

399 A trip to Italy or one to Spain in those early days, when traveling in those countries meant dirt, dust, and discomfort, was as nothing to her if there was a good picture for us at the end of the journey, yes, or even the scent of a good picture that could be followed up with results. I have to smile today as I think of her many adventures on our behalf.

If ever there was a true artist, it was Mary Cassatt. Always steering toward the highest ideals, undaunted and unflinching, her hand upon the tiller, she has kept true to her course through all the storms of adverse criticism, of raillery and of discouragement. "There are two ways for a painter," she often said to me, "the broad and easy one and the narrow and hard one."

400 Although the year 1889, when I made my first trip to Europe after my marriage, was an important one for our collection, the most interesting event in it was Mr. Havemeyer's first meeting with Miss Cassatt. It resulted in a friendship which lasted through life, and in my hour of

401 grief, a cable was handed to me from her and I read the touching message: "I too mourn a friend."

It is difficult to express all that our companionship meant. It was at once friendly, intellectual, and artistic, and from the time we first met Miss Cassatt, she was our counselor and our guide. We corresponded constantly when we were apart and always traveled together when abroad. She was ever ready to go with us or to do for us, and rarely did we go to Europe that she had not traced some fine picture for us to consider, or had not skillfully laid a fuse into some rich mine of art for our benefit; occasionally the fuse was short, and a sudden upheaval resulted in a valuable acquisition, or the fuse might be long, burning slowly, and only after years of patient waiting would we see the flash and know we had unearthed a treasure.

Excepting only that of my husband, Miss Cassatt's was the most independent mind I ever met, and yet, strange to say, these two strong personalities never clashed; respect and admiration would have prevented any such misfortune.

I was only about fifteen years of age when I first met Miss Cassatt. In order to learn French I was living with the family of François Del Sarte, and Miss Cassatt was working in Paris after a year of art study in Seville and several more in Parma. I wondered how she had the courage to go to Spain in the days of the Carlista wars, or to Italy before the bandits were controlled, but she was resourceful, self-reliant, true, and brave, and no one had a better or more truly generous heart.

When we first met in Paris she was very kind to me, showing me the splendid things in the great city, making them still more splendid by opening my eyes to their beauty through her own knowledge and appreciation. I felt then that Miss Cassatt was the most intelligent woman I had ever met, and I cherished every word she uttered and remembered almost every remark she made. It seemed to me no one could see art more understandingly, feel it more deeply or express themselves more clearly than she did. She opened her heart to me about art while she showed me about the great city of Paris. She took me to the Opera, where, without depleting our pockets, she found a place where we could hear well and could enjoy the fine ballets that were attracting Degas's attention at that very time.

At the Théâtre Français also, she had a resourceful way of avoiding the queue and the interminable wait at the *guichet.* She merely said to the imposing gentleman who sat at the foot of the imposing marble stairway: "Madame D—c has our tickets," and lo! he would bow low and motion us to enter with a *passez Mesdames,* and we would mount to the second balcony, where the good-natured Madame D—c invariably had seats for us in the front of a box. When we were seated, the kind soul would go down to the *guichet* and settle for those mythical tickets at two francs each and accept a modest *pourboire.*

When traveling, Miss Cassatt was a very wizard and thoroughly knew a traveler's rights. In fact, I know her brother, the late A. J. Cassatt, owed much to her suggestions in perfecting the many details in the Pennsylvania system. Today it is hard to believe that there ever was a time when we had no cab service, no porters, no redcaps, no transfers, etc. All these novelties were imported from abroad, and most of them were first introduced through suggestions from Mary Cassatt to her "Brother Aleck."

The book of complaints, the call for the *chef de gare,* the right of a traveler to a continuous journey were all well known to her. I recall an incident in one of our journeys from Spain to Paris. When we left Madrid, Mr. Havemeyer, like many another tourist, in the rush of the Easter Fêtes had omitted to have his tickets stamped; in fact, he knew nothing about the necessity of stamping them. When we arrived at the frontier, the guards attempted to collect another fare. It was an old trick, and they had several other victims among the waiting crowd upon the platform. As we were on the French side of the border, Miss Cassatt at once demanded the *chef de gare*, who reluctantly appeared. Miss Cassatt said to him, "Monsieur, will you kindly stamp these tickets?"

I am sorry to say his sullen rejoinder made us suspect that there was collusion between the *chef* and the guards. He said to Miss Cassatt: "Madame, I cannot do it. These tickets were not stamped in Madrid, and it is distinctly printed upon them that they should be so stamped."

"Yes," quickly replied Miss Cassatt, "printed only in Spanish and in French. This gentleman speaks neither language. In order to be legal for him it should have been printed in English. Monsieur will kindly stamp them." And he did so, and it goes without saying that he had to stamp those of the other tourists, to the discomfiture of the guards and the delight of the travelers, who gave Miss Cassatt a hearty round of applause as she walked down the platform and entered the *train de luxe*.

It was really a liberal education to be with Miss Cassatt. Only the dullest mind could fail to retain her original and suggestive remarks, for they stuck like burrs in one's memory and pricked the imagination for many years to come.

Miss Cassatt was descended from Jacques Cossard, a French Huguenot who fled after the massacre to Holland and then sailed to New Amsterdam in 1668. The spelling of the name, she told me, had changed several times, but the armorial coat of arms had always remained the same—a crenelated tower. The family has always been identified with Philadelphia, but I remember Miss Cassatt told me that her grandfather was a banker in Pittsburgh, and that she was born in that city. 405

Shortly after I met her, her family—her father, mother,

and sister came abroad to be with her and ever made their
406 home in France. Her life ever after was an example of devotion to duty. She held duty high before [her] as a pilgrim
would his cross. No sacrifice was too great for her to make
for her family or for her friends. For years she put ambition
aside to devote herself to her invalid family, and only when
she had laid them to rest in the quiet tomb at Mesnil did she
again return to work and seek consolation in her art.
Today, she survives them all and lives alone, spending the
407 summers in a beautiful old chateau at Mesnil-Théribus. For
a short time in the spring and in autumn she lives in her
apartment in Paris, and the long winter months are spent in
a pretty villa at Grasse—Fragonard's Grasse—the land of
flowers, where she has a splendid view of the mountains and
the blue waters of the Mediterranean.

I often visited the family during our early friendship, and
I remember Mr. Cassatt as a very courteous, tall, white-
haired man with a military bearing. Her sister, Lydia, was
408 exactly as represented in Miss Cassatt's portraits of her
where she is sitting in an easy chair in the garden beautifully dressed, elegant, and indolent, [one] who graciously
allows her sister, the "Martha" of the family, to do a double
share in making them all comfortable and happy.

Anyone who had the privilege of knowing Mary Cassatt's
mother would know at once that it could be from her and
from her only that she and her brother, A. J. Cassatt, inherited their ability. Even in my day, when she was no longer
young, she was still powerfully intelligent, executive and
masterful and yet with that same sense of duty, that tender
sympathy that she had transmitted to her daughter Mary.

I think Mrs. Cassatt had the most alert mind I ever met.
She was a fine linguist, an admirable housekeeper, remarkably well read, was interested in everything, and spoke
with more conviction and possibly more charm than Miss

Cassatt. Even in her last illness, I recall sitting beside her holding her thin hand in mine, filled with pity for the poor sufferer and with regret that this world must lose such a remarkable woman. To poor Miss Cassatt the loss was irreparable. She struggled bravely. At times, like many another lonely soul, she sought to see through the mysterious veil that hides our dear ones and ever after was deeply interested in the science and development of psychic phenomena.

She must have found some hidden strength, for through a friendship of over half a century I could never see that Miss Cassatt grew old. Even in looks she changed but little. It was her personality that impressed and that ripened early. It merely deepened more and more as years passed on. After all, what matters the day of our birth? It is the day of our death that counts, and the memory of Mary Cassatt will last many years after she is gone.

She devoted her life to her art as devotedly as Degas did. She drew a charmed circle about her, and it took credentials of the highest order to be permitted to enter it. She had no time [and] no taste for visiting and could resist meeting princes and princesses with a nonchalance that was amusing.

"I have a right to refuse anyone, for I work from eight to ten hours a day," she would say when she refused a card. Yet when she did entertain, the occasion was not to be forgotten. She would then offer her splendid gifts as royally as a Queen of Sheba and her conversation and quick catching at thoughts was simply entrancing.

"It is no matter what she says," said an enthusiastic admirer, "it is the way she says it."

Although Miss Cassatt's taste was for a quiet life, she often entertained in her apartment in Paris. Her evenings "at home" were attended by many interesting people: diplomats, painters, critics, and writers. Her brilliant mind

was like a crystal with many facets. She discussed the Boer
War with her friend "the special envoy"; the destiny of
museums and art influence with the directors and the leading critics of the day; or realism in literature with some
young god of Parnassus. Her luncheons were delightful. I
remember one where church and state met at the time of the
409   *séparation,* and it took a Clemenceau to calm the resulting
agitation. He wrote an able article and referred to her art as
"one of the glories of France."

After one of her dinners, you would find her spellbind-
ing an admiring group of guests, herself a striking personality, beautifully gowned (usually in gray, always high
at the neck) her hair parted and waving on each side of a
broad forehead, large eyes whose glance came frankly
forward to meet yours, a wonderfully flexible mouth, and
410   a nose like Garrick's—remarkable in its modeling, and
with those sensitive flaring nostrils which I always said
made her an artist in spite of herself. Miss Cassatt's tall
figure, which she inherited from her father, had distinction and elegance, and there was no trace of artistic *negligé*
or carelessness which some painters affect. Once having
seen her, you could never forget her—from her remarkable small foot to the plumed hat with its inevitable tip
upon her head and the Brussels lace veil without which
she was never seen. She spoke with energy, and you
would as soon forget her remarks when she conversed as
to forget the motion of her hands. Not even to a Spaniard
need she yield anything in the matter of gesture or
expressiveness.

"I give myself out too much," she said to me one evening
as we drove home from a dinner and she became conscious of
her fatigue. Yet her endurance was marvelous. I have seen
her entertain a large house party until two in the morning
and be ready for another busy day after only a few hours' rest.

She never allowed her photograph to be taken and if any-one begged her for a snapshot she would quickly turn so that all the camera caught of her was the outline of her back or, at most, a little bit of profile.

The only suggestion of a portrait that I know of her is a small picture that I bought before my marriage. It is in gouache and represents a lady in a bonnet with her gloved hands lying upon her lap. Miss Cassatt told me she was her own model for that picture and did it looking at herself in a mirror. The hands are very characteristic, and she wore the same bonnet when she posed for one of Degas's *Modistes*.

As for Miss Cassatt being a pupil of Degas, it is not true, for she did not even meet him until she had known his works and felt their influence for several years. She wrote me only a few weeks ago and said: "How well I remember nearly forty years ago seeing for the first time Degas's pastels in the window of a picture dealer in the Boulevard Haussmann. I would go there and flatten my nose against that window and absorb all I could of his art. It changed my life. I saw art then as I wanted to see it."

After they met some years later, long years of friendship ensued, of mutual criticism and, I must add, of spicy estrangements, for Degas was addicted to throwing verbal vitriol, as the French called it, upon his friends, and Miss Cassatt would not have been the daughter of the French Cossards if she had not been equal to answering his taunts. She could do without him, while he needed her honest criticism and her generous admiration.

I have been amused, during the long years I have known them, at the little luncheons or dinners that have been planned by friends to effect a reconciliation. I recall one which took place in Paris. Degas and Mary Cassatt had quarreled over the Dreyfus affair. Degas was such an anti-Dreyfusard that he wrote to his lifelong friend Halévy, who was a Jew, not to put his place at the table as he could no longer dine with him on Sundays.

Miss Cassatt was perplexed whether or not to accept her friend's invitation to meet Degas at luncheon.

"By all means accept," said I.

"But this Dreyfus affair!" she objected. "I know he will anger me."

"Don't hesitate," I insisted, "go and silence him for once and for all time."

"But, Louie dear," she said pathetically, "you don't know what a dreadful man he is, he can say anything."

"So can you," I answered and she reluctantly decided to go. Just at that moment Matilde, her good maid, entered with a beautiful new gown over her arm.

"Wear that new gown," I suggested, "and enjoy the repose and assurance the conscious elegance gives you."

Needless to say, Miss Cassatt attended the luncheon while I impatiently awaited her return to learn what had happened.

"Mercy, Louie," she exclaimed, as soon as she saw me, "who do you think sat next to me at table?"

"Degas?" I queried, knowing from her tone I was wrong.

"No! Worse!" she answered, "General Mercier! Would you believe it? And they know how I feel toward him! I wanted to run away!"

"I hope you did nothing of the sort!" I said.

"Oh, no, I couldn't, on account of Degas! He has aged, dear, aged so very much it made me sad, but I was glad to see him, and he was very nice and did not say a disagreeable word."

"Of course, he didn't," I rejoined. How could he? Were they not old, old friends, good comrades, with the deep respect each paid to the other's talent lying firm beneath any momentary differences of opinion?

416 417

During that celebrated affair, Dreyfus did not have a more ardent or more able defender than Mary Cassatt. From first to last she fearlessly expressed her firm conviction of his innocence. And when his vindication came, no one rejoiced more sincerely than she did, for she felt, as she expressed it, France's honor was at stake.

She brought tears to my eyes one day as she glowingly related the following incident: "I was returning from town one evening just after Dreyfus was vindicated, but I did not know that Madame Dreyfus, who lived near me, was on the same train. As we pulled into the station, I noticed something unusual was happening, for every employee, high or low, appeared to be on the platform, and every passenger as they descended from the train joined the waiting line. Of course, I did the same, not knowing what it was all about. I soon found out, however. It was known that Madame Dreyfus was expected to return from Paris, and as she stepped out of the rear car every hat was taken off and not one word was spoken as the valiant woman, almost overcome, walked silently and erect down the platform, looking neither to the right nor to the left." I wiped my eyes and Miss Cassatt added, "I have never witnessed anything so touching in my life as that silent token of sympathy and respect for that brave and noble wife."

It is no wonder she quarreled with Degas over the Dreyfus affair, although on other occasions she would stand valiantly by and defend his work, a fact Degas appreciated even if he could not resist a little dart in his words of praise, as when he said of one of her compositions: "I won't admit a woman can draw like that!"

To appreciate how that remark could hurt, one must know that Miss Cassatt never admitted sex in art, and could never be persuaded to exhibit in any exhibition for women's work only. I have often, out of deference to her views, refused to lend her pictures on such occasions.

Miss Cassatt was one of the first to appreciate Degas's nudes, and she "tells a story on herself" apropos of the subject. She said: "Degas went to Durand-Ruel père and asked him to take his nudes, but the old man, who did not care for them, hesitated. 'But,' said Degas, 'they must be good, for Miss Cassatt admires them.' '*Pauvre fille,*' answered Durand-Ruel, '*mais elle n'a pas de goût*' (Poor thing, she lacks judgment), but I did not lack judgment," she added triumphantly, for the nudes were not long in becoming famous.

Brought up by such a mother, it would be impossible for Miss Cassatt to indulge in fads or foibles. She was practicable, self-reliant, and conscientious toward all, and one of her greatest charms was the contrast between her frank admiration for others and a timid, modest appreciation of herself.

"It is a liberal education to be with her," said one of our leading businessmen to me, and indeed it was, for, gifted with a marvelous memory, hers was one of the best-stored minds I ever knew. She stored her knowledge in the cells of an active, vigorous brain and ripened it as the bees do their honey in the comb. She thought deeply and reflected long, and her remarks were always pithy, apt, and full of suggestion. I once asked her, apropos of a certain subject, how she had arrived at such a conclusion. "Ah!" she replied, "when I take my walks and during the long evenings when I am alone, I have time to think."

Early in our collecting, when Mr. Havemeyer and I were chatting with Miss Cassatt after dinner, she suddenly looked up from her coffee, and holding the little spoon in her hand, she made a convincing gesture and said emphatically: "To make a great collection it is necessary to have the modern note in it, and to be a great painter, you must be classic as well as modern."

I at once thought of a beautiful painting which M. Durand-Ruel had allowed us to buy out of his own collection. Miss Cassatt had done a mother with her baby's head upon her shoulder, which we had always called her Florentine Madonna. It united the old and the modern just as she said it should be. 421

It seems to me, I could write a textbook on art only by repeating her aphorisms, her terse, sapient counsels on the science and the difficulties of the profession. For instance, in expressing a movement or a gesture, she would say you must make the cause as well as the result felt, or it will not tell the story.

I must go on and tell you more of my friend as I knew her, and later she can speak to you herself of art through her letters, for she wrote brilliantly and with such clearness that anyone could read them with delight.

Miss Cassatt was an ardent suffragist always stimulating me to renewed efforts for the cause. On the 2nd of August 1914, she wrote me: "The great drama is opening around us! How will it all end? Possibly in a United States of Europe!" And she added, "Work for suffrage, for it is the women who will decide the question of life or death for a nation." 422

Truth compels me to add that after a time she expressed grave doubts about our being able to control the destinies of a nation or in any way affect their future.

Miss Cassatt was never loath to consider a new thought or to investigate a new theory. Upon our oft-repeated visits to France, we would find her at one time a Kneippist, walking about the grass in her pretty chateau at Beaufresne, to bathe them [her bare feet] in the morning dew, and upon another occasion we found she had adopted a vegetarian diet, much to Mr. Havemeyer's distress and amusement. He frequently railed her upon it. One day, when we arrived tired and hungry in Bologna, I heard him say to Miss Cassatt, as 423 424 he offered her a bit of chicken: "Oh! do eat something solid, and stop chewing water." I think she soon gave up vegetarianism, for while eager to learn if there was any benefit in a new theory, she soon got to the bottom of it, and if she found a flaw in it the bottom soon fell out.

My first meeting with Miss Cassatt in Paris after my marriage is indelibly graven on my mind. I found her in bed with a broken leg. Her horse had slipped upon the pavement of the Champs-Elysées, and she sustained a bad fracture of the leg. The poor creature was forced to give up work and lie still for several weeks. She was very dear and cordial and as usual full of a new hobby. She had become enthusiastic over Raspail and was using his camphor treatment for her broken leg.

"You must get his book, my dear," she said to me. "Camphor! Nothing but camphor! Compresses of camphor, spirits of camphor, and pomade of camphor! It is wonderful! You know, it kept my mother alive for years. I am rubbed with it and done up in it every day. When they carried me up here, Matilde put a compress upon my leg and the doctor said we could not have done better. Raspail is, as you know, the 'Father of Modern Surgery.' I know I shall be well soon. Poor Aleck," she continued, "I hate to let him know about my accident, for he gave me that little mare, a dear creature and so gentle! She just slipped and fell, that was all!" Miss Cassatt could make no case out against the little mare, and she had the strongest convictions about medicine, Raspail, electricity, camphor, or plain Vichy! Each had its turn as her cure-all. Her wonderful physique and phenomenal capacity for work sustained her judgment, and no one disputed her belief in her various creeds or their healing powers.

It was then that she met Mr. Havemeyer and saw my children for the first time. Naturally, we talked art together, and she was much pleased that we admired Courbet and had bought one of his landscapes. "What a man he was!" she exclaimed. "Just to think he wanted to pull down the Column Vendôme and actually saw it fall. The Parisians are prejudiced against him on account of that, and he is not yet fully appreciated, but he is a great man in spite of his politics, and they will have to acknowledge it later." (This was the accepted view of the Vendôme affair in 1889.)

Then, turning to me, she said: "Do you remember the exhibition we went to see years ago in the foyer of the Gaité Théâtre? Wasn't it fine! Those nudes and half-lengths! I will look out for some for you! I would like you to have one or two good Courbets!" That was the beginning of her "lookouts." I don't think from that day to the present one she ever left her "watchtower," and her searchlight brought many a fine picture into our collection. 427

When her family came abroad to live with her, they finally made their home in the rue Marignan, and there she lives today in a charming apartment with windows both on the rue Marignan and on the rue François I. It was all cheerful and light and had an excellent exposure for painting. 428

How well I recall the little room she used as a studio! It was not half as large as the studio at Beaufresne, and tiny in comparison to the glass gallery where she worked in Grasse, but many and many a pastel was done there and the "placard" was full of canvases of pictures that were never finished, portraits that she kept for herself, sketches for compositions, or studies of children. It was a simple room and without any *artistique* effects. She selected it because it had good light. It contained little furniture but her easels and a few fine Empire and Louis XVI chairs which are familiar to any one who knows her work. I recall her drawing room and the tender green of the soft silk curtains, the rich brocades she had collected when in Italy or

429   Spain. Several [works by] Degas and a still life of Cézanne
       were upon the walls, and a *gesso* of Donatello was on an
       easel in a corner.

          How many pictures of ours at one time or another were
       placed in that salon or in the hall, waiting to be sent to
       America, or to be seen and passed upon by friends and crit-
       ics. Goyas and Grecos, Courbets and [works by] Degas,
       Ingres, and Chardin, all went to the rue Marignan, where
       Miss Cassatt could see and pass judgment upon them.

          In the dining room was a little cabinet of exquisite silver
430   and a fine Courbet upon the wall. Wonderful times we had
       in that dining room, true symposiums of intellectual
       refinement and free from any taint of bohemianism, won-
       derful evenings when Miss Cassatt and a few friends con-
       versed and the rest of us were delighted to listen.

          It was in the rue Marignan that Miss Cassatt developed
       her remarkable capacity for work. She inherited her energy
       from her mother, but its application to her work was all her
       own. I remember she said to me one day: "Why do these
       young girls come to me for advice? They have not the
       slightest notion of giving to art the devotion it requires. I
       say to them, 'Do you ever go to the Louvre and copy some
       of the great masters?' And they invariably answer, 'Oh, no,
       we can't, we are working in a studio, we have no time.'

          "'Degas does,' I answer. 'He will go to Lille for weeks or
431   to St. Quentin for months.' But what good does it do to talk
       to them? They will never arrive! Mme Morisot was right
432   when she said a young student should go to some provincial
       town where there are a few good pictures and avoid the dis-
       tractions and the snares of the studios of Paris." Miss Cas-
       satt was silent a moment and then continued: "I went to
       Seville when I was a young girl. It was horrid and I was
       alone, but I braved it out for a year. Then I felt I needed
433   Correggio and I went to Parma. A friend went with me; she

did not remain, but I stayed there for two years, lonely as it was. I had my work and the few friends I made. I was so tired when my day was done I had little desire for pleasure. Even now I work eight hours a day and afterward take my walk with Matilde, and in the evenings after reading a little I am quite ready to go to bed."

Miss Cassatt seemed inclined to talk and continued: "I doubt if you know the effort it is to paint! The concentration it requires, to compose your picture, the difficulty of posing the models, of choosing the color scheme, of expressing the sentiment and telling your story! The trying and trying again and again and oh, the failures, when you have to begin all over again! The long months spent in effort upon effort, making sketch after sketch. Oh, my dear! No one but those who have painted a picture know what it costs in time and strength!

"After a time, you get keyed up and it 'goes,' you paint quickly and do more in a few weeks than in the preceding weary months. When I am *en train*, nothing can stop me and it seems easy to paint, but I know very well it is the result of my previous efforts."

I have tried to repeat Miss Cassatt's words as nearly as I can remember them, for it is interesting to know how a painter works, and it may help some young student who is really serious and knows there is no royal road to fame.

Miss Cassatt always deplored the invasion of the French studios by Americans, who were lured to Paris by the fata morgana of thinking that a disposition for art meant a talent for art, and who were sure to fail after years of useless labor, or be lost in the contamination of the Latin Quarter. "How much better for them to find something to do at home," she would say to me. "I have worked for forty years and I feel I need forty more. Few have the courage to stand the strain."

434   I recall the time when she was interested in etching. Eight o'clock in the morning would find her in her gray blouse in the small pavilion over the dam that fed her *pièce d'eau* and where she had installed her printing press. There she would work while daylight lasted with the aid of a printer. She did her own coloring and wiping of the plates. It was at the cost of much physical strain for she actually did the manual work.

"I wonder all etchers do not do their own printing!" she said to me. "It makes a great difference, for no two impressions are exactly alike." Then she continued, "I love to do the colored prints, and I hope the Durand-Ruels will put mine on the market at reasonable prices. For nothing, I believe, will inspire a taste for art more than the possibility of having it in the home. I should like to feel that amateurs in America could have an example of my work, a print or an etching, for a few dollars. That is what they do in France. It is not left to the rich alone to buy art; the people—even the poor—have taste and buy according to their means. And here they can always find something they can afford."

Helas! Miss Cassatt did not continue etching! "The Durand-Ruels tell me there is not enough in it," she said to me rather bitterly. "They want me to go back to pastels." I bought an impression of her colored print of *The Girl with* 435, 436   *the Banjo*. The price was fifteen dollars.

Her generous nature was always seeking to help others or to do a kind action. I rarely met her that she had not just done a portrait for someone who could not afford to pay for it; or, if she had accepted an order to do a portrait of the daughter of the house, she would add a pastel of the younger sister. For example, when she made a beautiful 437   portrait of my daughter Adaline, she did a pastel of her in a large hat that was so successful that she kept it for herself. But long years afterward, she sent it to Adaline's daughter,

"Because," she said, "some day she would like to know how her Mama looked when she was a little girl."

Again, an eminent American physician was very kind to her brother when he was ill in Egypt. After her brother's death, she wrote me: "I was able to show Durand-Ruel a 438 pastel nearly finished which he liked and wanted very much, but my great desire to do something for Sir William Osler in gratitude for his kindness to my brother makes me keep it. Until I do that, I don't want to give up a pastel."

Even her *vendeuse* at her dressmaker's was remembered: "One of the best things I ever did," she said to me, referring to this pastel, "was the portrait of Mme—'s little daughter. Just think of it! she has made my clothes for over twenty years, and I wanted to do something for her."

I suggested to Miss Cassatt that it meant a good deal of hard work. "Of course it does my dear," she answered, "but who thinks of that? There is Roger Marx"—mentioning a 439 well-known critic—"he wants me to do him a 'little pastel' because, I suppose, he wrote something about me in his review."

"And you will do it?" I said, smiling.

"I suppose I will," she answered. "Poor man, he is very unhappy."

Like a true artist, Miss Cassatt shunned notoriety and was as inaccessible as Degas himself. She had no desire and no time for *réclame* of any kind. With fortitude, she could see her contemporaries push forward and seek popular favor, but she patiently continues to work.

When the red ribbon was conferred upon her, she wore it 440 for a year. After that I did not see it for a long time, and I asked her the reason.

"Oh," she answered, "it is etiquette to wear it for a year."

And again she said to me: "M. M. asked me to paint a picture for the Petit Palais, saying the government would 441 surely give me the red ribbon if I did. Did you ever hear of such a thing, my dear?"

"What did you answer?" I asked.

"Why, I told him I had had the red ribbon for several years, and he appeared much embarrassed."

"I may be able to do something that will live," she would modestly say. And with a tenacious hold upon truth, she sought to leave behind her a new chapter on maternal love and express the natural charm of childhood.

"I love to paint children," she would say. "They are so natural and truthful. They have no *arrière-pensée.*"

Of the artistic qualities of her work, much has been said and more will be written. I do not need to speak of them here. I shall write of Miss Cassatt only as our friend and the "godmother" of our collection.

Perhaps the best way to reveal her true self, her judgment, her perception, her courage, and her enterprise will be through her letters to me. And surely a correspondence which is well advanced into its fifth decade cannot fail to be interesting, as it paints her character in her own words and throws sidelights on many a bit of artistic history. There are so many of them it will be difficult to make a selection. However, I will begin with the letters she wrote about the first pictures we bought and continue as best I can to the present writing.

EXTRACTS FROM MISS CASSATT'S LETTERS

1890, Rembrandt and Courbet

When we were in Italy we were constantly at the house of an old friend of Mr. Havemeyer who was much interested to hear of you and your children.

Poor dear Italy! I thought it sad and much changed! I saw nothing there more beautiful than the Rembrandts Mr. Havemeyer has just bought. What a marvel the woman's portrait is!

Duret saw it with me and said he had never seen a finer picture. I wonder who the originals were! Certainly Rembrandt painted that woman before! Duret (a french art Critic) thought he had seen it in Cassel (The Dutch Admiral and his Wife, no name given in any catalogue).

The man who comes nearest to Rembrandt in modern times is Courbet. I was very much surprised to [find] Duret and I [are] as one about that. He spoke of Courbet eloquently enough to satisfy even me. When I hear people paying such prices for "Troyons" I wonder at them. I am sure the 444 reason Courbet is comparatively neglected is on account of his politics!

He had that large noble touch, which is so characteristic of Rembrandt.—Not that I think Courbet was as great as Rembrandt, but they seem to me to arouse the same artistic sensations, though perhaps not to the same degree. Do tell me whether you feel as I do about this. I know Mr. Havemeyer does not so don't tell him, what I say, only tell him that such a critic as Duret says that he has two of Rembrandt's finest por- 445 traits painted in his very best period, and the third is also a very fine Rembrandt of a later date.

The two Rembrandts were the portraits of a Dutch admiral and his wife. They were painted in 1643. They were owned by the Princesse de Sagan, who was amusing herself in Trouville and exacted that she should be paid in cash. Charles Durand-Ruel was obliged to come from Paris to pay her, and when he saw me he said: "*Ah, Madame je suis watte* [sic] *des billet de banque.*"

Miss Cassatt underestimated Mr. Havemeyer's judgment in art when she wrote about Rembrandt and Courbet, for shortly afterward I overheard my husband [say] at one of our Sunday musicals that next to Rembrandt he prized Courbet's *Branche de Cerisiers*, a beautiful 446 nude half-length, and he was keenly seeking Courbet's wonderful landscapes.

447   *Paris, 1890. Degas's rage! Duc d'Aumale, Sargent, Whistler, etc.*

448   I am going to do a decoration for the Chicago Exhibition.
When the Committee offered it to me to do, at first I was
horrified, but gradually I began to think it would be great fun
to do something I had never done before and as the bare idea
of such a thing put Degas in a rage and he did not spare every
criticism he could think of I got my spirit up and said I would
not give up the idea for any thing. Now, one has only to men-
449   tion Chicago to set him off; Bartholomé, his best friend is on
the jury for sculpture and took the nomination just to tease
him. By the way Degas thinks most seriously of finishing
450   your picture for you. However when we see his drawings and
his fine pastels, we forgive him everything.

There is a great movement in the art world just now. Exhibitions and important sales going on all the time. The Duc
451   d'Aumale bought a Filippino Lippi for Chantilly the other
day. The French are not going to allow everything to leave
France.

452   At the Champs de Mars, there is a portrait of Carmencita
by Sargent, which meets with the approbation of artists and
redeems his very poor exhibition of the last two years.
Whistler has a very lovely "Marine" and a portrait, not so
453   good. Have you any of his marines? —

You ask me about Degas's speech as to the "necessity of
454   art." He was answering Vibert.

Vibert was saying apropos of the first exhibition of the
455   French Society of Water Colors, which was inaugurated in
handsome surroundings, "After all Degas, pictures are *objets
de luxe.*"

"*Pas les notres,*" answered Degas. "*Les notres sont de première nécessité.*"

You must know that our exhibition had just closed amidst
éclat, although it was held in a modest apartment and a very
simple arrangement.

It may be interesting to read of her version of the now
famous bon mot:

Beaufresne

Durand-Ruel has just returned from Vienna where he saw a ver Meer von Delft, which he says is beautiful. Two million marks was asked or refused for it, I forget which. Col. Payne's Degas is more beautiful than any ver Meer I ever saw. Tell him that.   456

Col. Payne bought at my husband's request Faure's Degas—one of his greatest paintings ranking with the *Danseuses à la Barre.* Here is another letter, perhaps more intimate, but it reveals another facet of the brilliant mind as it sparkles in the warm defense of a cause, and she speaks in the defense of justice.

Boers, Dreyfus, Lenormant's La Grande Grèce, *Beaufresne*   457

Professor S. and Polly have just been here. He just from the   458 Kissingen treatment and has lost 30 pounds, which is no doubt to his advantage.

We disputed about the Boers. He was reduced to saying that they must be suppressed because they were immoral! I was obliged to point out that it would be difficult to go beyond the English Aristocracy in that respect. If there is one argument that drives me frantic it is that, the impudence of it! Justice be denied people because they are immoral!

In the Dreyfus business, when Picquart came forward in   459, 460 defense of Dreyfus, it was suddenly discovered that he was immoral. Degas, who is always brutal undertook to enlighten me, but the answer was easy—"a nice thing for Dreyfus, the youngest Lieutenant colonel in the French Army, if such were the practices of the officers." But enough of such unsavory subjects. Your books have come and I have been beguiling the stormbound hours by reading the first chapters. The outside is more attractive, but Oh! the difference in matter to the volumes I sent you! Do read in the 3rd Vol. of *La Grande Grèce,* the chapter entitled "Mileto" with the picture of the court of Roger of Sicily. There is word painting, but all the book is an enchantment to me. Thanks for these two volumes for they recall our never to-be-forgotten journey! We ought to have gone to see La Jina in Palermo.

I had sent Miss Cassatt Crawford's *Rulers of the Sea*,
which appeared shortly after our visit to Italy and Sicily,
461   while the three volumes she sent to me were Lenormant's
La Grand Grèce, the most interesting work on travel I have
ever read—a veritable last word upon the subject.

Many, many letters pertaining to picture buying were
exchanged and a run to Italy or Spain was no effort to this
dear friend and helper.

462   *Spain and "The Wellington Portrait"*
Your letter "retour de Madrid" came since I left, and also the
photograph of Wellington. It is really a good thing and not
dear. I think I did well to "manage" W. as he is about [all]
we have in Spain. Do you know he was actually offered a position at court? His Godmother is an intimate friend of an
Infanta. Don't talk to me about Monarchies! Give me decent
Republics. They may be corrupt! We know they are, but the
others are worse.

You must not be surprised at my going off to see pictures
for Mr. Havemeyer, I said I would and I meant it, besides it is
an excellent wit sharpener, good for an artist and all in the
day's work.

We bought the Wellington with its thrilling story and
Goya's testimony to the general's ability when he wrote "*Terror Gallorum*" on the bottom of the enveloping black cloak.

Miss Cassatt made one journey to Madrid to see and
secure some pictures for us. She was there but twenty-four
hours, no small effort when traveling in Spain was not as
pleasant as it is today. We owe much to her alertness and
decision. This letter speaks for itself:

463   Your cable came and I must explain why I said I thought it
would be better to see about the picture before September. All
the pictures W. spoke about are in private collections, where
they have probably been for generations, and the suggestion

was made by W. that although the owners would like money as it was the tax season, he thought any time would do. My opinion is to the contrary, I think that if you shake the tree, that you ought to be around when the fruit falls to pick it up. In other words, now that the idea of selling has been put into their heads, that if someone else offers to buy they will let the things go.

The letter refers to such pictures as the Greco's *Cardinal* and the landscape called *Toledo,* and *Les Femmes au Balcon* 464 by Goya, all of which we bought within a few years.

Now she writes of the *Ascension of the Virgin* by Greco, 465 which is now in Chicago. I have written how Durand-Ruel came to buy it, and how Miss Cassatt, after my effort to get the Metropolitan Museum to take it, offered it to Chicago, and it was at once bought for the Art Institute there.

I saw again the great Greco at the Durand-Ruels. Isn't it a shame they don't buy it for the Metropolitan Museum? I must try and get M. to speak to Mr. Morgan about it. 466

M.'s father and Mr. Morgan were partners, and again she writes of the picture:

I was sure you would like the Greco. Did we not work hard to 467 get it to America? It never would have gone there if it had not been for Mr. Havemeyer. Durand-Ruel has just sent me word that the sale is definite and he has received his first installment of the price.

She writes another word about the magnificent *Assumption* of the youthful Greco:

They are wrong about the Greco. It was not the woman who 468 gave the *Assumption* of Greco in memory of her husband that had anything to do with buying it. I had a finger in that pie. I urged Mr. Ryerson and Mr. Hutchinson to buy it and when they did they said they knew I would be pleased. Their method is to buy a fine thing and when someone wants to make a gift, that person reimburses the cost. A method I would like to see other directors of Art Museums adopt.

As our purchases of Goyas and Grecos drew attention to Spanish pictures, Miss Cassatt rather enjoyed the stir they caused in the art world in Paris. The paintings were usually sent to her apartment and remained there until they were shipped to us. She writes of the *Femmes au Balcon*:

469   I particularly wanted Marx to see the Goya. After expressing his great admiration, he said he was deeply impressed with the fact that the flesh was painted like a miniature whereas the rest of it was so broadly treated. You will see the point of this remark. It is always worth while to show him a picture for he says something new.

Another letter, after her trip to Spain, tells of her enthusiasm for her work and her desire to achieve something worthwhile:

470   All day long I work! I am wild to do something decent after all the fine things we have seen. Oh! if only I could! Goya's unhesitating firmness upsets me. You will surely get the *Librera*. Durand-Ruel picked up the photograph of the latter one day and said: "How Manet copied him! *Lola de Valence* is just this. If you get all these you will have more Goyas than any Museum outside of Madrid.

       From Spain she goes to Italy and is deeply interested in
471   the four Veroneses we secured through H. as well as the two
472   wonderful Holbeins we acquired, and the *Jean de la Caron-delet*, which we bought from the Duc de Trémouïlle, in whose family it had been since it was painted so many hundred years

ago. This letter gives an idea of procedure in her way of giving advice when the purchase of a picture is in question:

> I received a telegram to arrange a rendez-vous in the avenue Gabriel. I went to Paris the next morning and the first thing I did was to go to the Louvre and to carefully examine all the Holbeins there. Then to the Duc's to see yours. What could I do, but give it my most unqualified approval? I think it finer than any of the men's portraits by Holbein in the Louvre except the astronomer, and I prefer it to that on account of the wonderful and expressive hands. You will I am sure be delighted with the picture. It is a privilege to have seen it; certainly you and Mr. Havemeyer know how to spend your money!
>
> I have sent the money for the two Holbeins, I am sure you will be pleased with them and find them up to the mark.

473

474

These are my two wonderful Holbeins done in 1538 at his best period, when he made his second visit to England and was fond of doing portraits with his sitters holding a glove and with rings on their fingers. In my pair the woman holds a prayer book and has several rings on her fingers, and the man holds a glove in his left hand and has only one ring on his hand.

She is delighted with my Veroneses. I have already written about the part she played in acquiring the portrait of the painter's wife. She writes of it:

475

> Ever since I was staying with you, I have had an ambition to be instrumental in getting you a Veronese. I wish I could have been with you when you saw the portrait of his wife in your Library. In Italy they don't think her ugly, for her portrait exists at the Villa de Trevise, where Paolo has painted himself in a white costume and a gun returning from hunting, that at one end of the Villa when all the doors are opened, your lady stands at the other end with a green fan in her hand. The caretaker who showed us around waved her hand toward Paolo

and toward the other saying: *Ecco la sua Bella.* She was not quite so old in the portrait but just as stout. She ought to look well in the Library but it is hard to climb to Rembrandt's height. Oh! was he not the greatest painter that ever lived?

She goes to Italy and returns finding it much changed. She writes:

476   I saw nothing more beautiful than the Rembrandts Mr. Have-meyer has just bought. What a wonder the Woman's portrait is! Duret, Théodore—art critic—was shown them with me and he said he had never seen a finer picture. I wonder who the originals were! Certainly he painted that Woman (the Admiral's Wife) before! Duret thought it might be in Cassel.

The man who comes nearest to Rembrandt in modern times is Courbet. I was very much surprised to find Duret and myself as one about that. He spoke of Courbet eloquently enough to satisfy even me.

When I hear of people paying such prices for Troyons, I wonder at them. I am sure the reason that Courbet is comparatively neglected is on account of his politics. He had that large noble touch which is so characteristic of Rembrandt, not that I think he was so great, but they seem to me to arouse the same artistic sensations, though perhaps not to the same degree. Do tell me if you feel as I do about this, I know Mr. Havemeyer doesn't.

Mr. Havemeyer knew Rembrandt better than he knew Courbet; when he had assimilated Courbet, he always placed him next to Rembrandt. Miss Cassatt was deeply interested in the moderns of her time, but she did not over-rate them. Her enthusiasm was always tempered with judgment, and she was capable of giving a rational opinion about a purchase. Here is an excerpt of a letter apropos of a celebrated Manet, a boomed Manet:

Durand-Ruel wants to see me to talk about Faure's Manets to impress upon Mr. Havemeyer that the offer he makes is too low and he may miss the three he wants. Now Mr. Havemeyer has seen the pictures and therefore is perfectly able to judge for himself. I must confess personally I would not *faire des folies* for the *Bon Bock*.

477, 478

Later:

I am rather glad the Manet deal fell through, I think you ought to see the pictures again before deciding. For myself, I prefer the Courbet head I bought for Mr. Havemeyer to the *Bon Bock*.

The *Bon Bock* never seemed to go with our other Manets, and we never bought it.

When the war broke out in 1914, she remained in her chateau in Beaufresne until she was forced to leave it suddenly one morning as the Germans were within a few kilometers of her home.

479

Her letters at this period were very brilliant and interesting, although written under great difficulties, for she had already had several operations upon her eyes, and they were painful and bandaged most of the time. When she left Beaufresne she went to Dinard and helped the good mayoress feed the refugees who poured into the city from Belgium. We were all glad to help, and I have letters of acknowledgment from that dear lady, who, with French instincts for thrift and precision, accounted to me for every expenditure of every centime I sent. Here is one of her letters written from Dinard in 1914.

480

Your kind letters have all "dropped in"—the first written —the last to reach me. I was touched by your anxieties over my fate. Here I am still in this *bicoque* longing so much to get back to Beaufresne, but what the English call the "ding dong" of battle is still raging around me with dreadful slaughter.

481

Of course, every question is subordinated to the war, but never more than now was suffrage for women the question of the day, the hope of the future. Surely, surely! women will wake to a sense of their duty and insist upon passing upon such subjects as war, insist upon a voice in the world's government!

Again she writes:

482

We cannot move even from village to village, aeroplanes are flying over us, but everything has passed with quiet dignity. What Germany's vaulting ambition will cost her seems easy to foretell. "When the Gods wish to destroy they first make mad" would seem to apply to Germany's case. Will a United States of Europe be the outcome of this? I hope so. I am so glad you have the Rubens, but Oh! cherish the 13th century sculptures! Cherish your Gothic statues! I cannot bear to think of Rheims! Such an inheritance from the past destroyed! New generation[s] may replace those that are gone but what was left to us of those days is gone forever!"

483

She goes to see Renoir after she has been able to get to the Riviera. She finds him crippled with rheumatism, nearing the end but working to the last:

I went to see Renoir. He is failing fast. He said to me that Degas as an artist rose in his esteem every day! Just what you feel. In the meantime his mind gives way more and more!

In the "ding dong" of battle Degas passed away, but not without bursting upon the art world his greatest achievment whose vibration will stir it as long as art and art forms shall last. He left his sculptures, those lifelong companions of his artistic activities. He seemed to have led a dual art existence. His sculptures went hand in hand with his paintings, keys the one to the other, records and proofs, form and color! Again our godmother looked out for our

collection! I went to Paris and bought the whole collection 484
of seventy-two pieces, wonderfully reproduced by A.A.
Hébrard, Degas's ever faithful friend and helper. I bought
the first of the twenty-two sets Hebrard was permitted to
take. And No. 1 of Series A was soon in America, and I put
it at once on exhibition in order that the great artist should 485
again be honored and appreciated by a rising generation. I
must finish this short sketch of Miss Cassatt's life by quot-
ing one of her last and most eloquent letters about Degas's
sculptures.

> I think Degas will live better and longer by his sculptures than
> by his paintings. I think him a greater sculptor than painter. 486

Miss Cassatt said this to me at Beaufresne in 1921. Again
she said:

> Degas's statues are as fine, as great as anything the Greeks or
> Egyptians ever did. They will constantly increase in apprecia-
> tion and value. They are just as fine as his paintings.

Mary Cassatt deferred an operation upon her eyes in
order first to study Degas's sculptures. She said: "Degas
was not an etcher."

CHRONOLOGY

1847
October 18 Henry Osborne Havemeyer (known as Harry or H.O.) is born.

1855
July 28 Louisine Waldron Elder is born.

1869
Harry is admitted into partnership in Havemeyers and Elder, the family sugar refining firm.

1870
March 1 Harry Havemeyer marries Mary Louise Elder, Louisine's aunt. They have no children and eventually divorce.

1874
Louisine stays in Paris with her mother and two sisters. She meets Mary Cassatt.

1876
Harry visits the Centennial Exhibition in Philadelphia with Samuel Colman and makes substantial purchases of Japanese decorative arts.

1877
During another visit to Paris, Mary Cassatt takes Louisine to see a Degas pastel. Louisine purchases her first modern picture, Degas's *Ballet Rehearsal.*

1881
Louisine is in Paris and visits the Salon several times and later, in the company of Cassatt, attends the Courbet exhibition held at

the Théâtre de la Gaité, Paris. In the summer, Louisine is in London with her mother. They meet Whistler at his studio and Louisine acquires five pastels.

1883
August 22 Louisine Waldron Elder and Henry Osborne Havemeyer marry in Greenwich, Connecticut.

1884
July 11 Adaline, the Havemeyers' first child, is born.

1886
March 19 The Havemeyers' son, Horace, is born.

1888
August 16 The Havemeyers' second daughter, Electra, is born. Harry makes his first gift to the Metropolitan Museum: a portrait of *George Washington* by Gilbert Stuart. In the fall, plans are underway for the construction of a new residence for the Havemeyers at 1 East 66 Street, with interiors designed by Tiffany and Colman. The Havemeyers begin collecting paintings on a grand scale.

1889
Harry acquires Rembrandt's portrait of *Herman Doomer*. In June, the Havemeyers travel to Paris where Durand-Ruel obtains a number of old master and nineteenth-century pictures on their behalf. In August, the Havemeyers acquire their first paintings by Courbet. Later that month, Harry and the children meet Mary Cassatt for the first time. From this point on, Cassatt is on the "lookout" for new acquisitions for the Havemeyers. That summer they make several visits to the Exposition Universelle in Paris.

1894
The Havemeyers focus on acquiring modern French painting, purchasing works by Manet, Monet, and Degas.

1895
That summer, the Havemeyers travel to London and then to Paris. They visit Cassatt at her country residence, the Château de Beaufresne, at Mesnil-Théribus, about fifty miles northwest of Paris. In September, the Havemeyers purchase works by Degas, Millet, Daumier, Manet, Courbet, and Corot from Durand-Ruel, Paris.

1896

The Havemeyers donate a collection of Japanese silks and brocades and a collection of Tiffany favrile glass to the Metropolitan Museum.

1897

In September, the Havemeyers acquire a pair of portraits by Goya, marking the beginning of their interest in Spanish painting.

1898

Cassatt visits the Havemeyers in New York. In April, the Havemeyers purchase Courbet's *Woman with a Parrot*, and in May, they acquire Bronzino's *Portrait of a Young Man*. Before the end of the year, they purchase three large-scale works by Manet and Courbet's *Portrait of Jo (La Belle Irlandaise)*, all from Durand-Ruel, New York.

1901

The Havemeyers travel to Madeira, Gibraltar, Algiers, and Genoa where they are joined by Mary Cassatt. They travel throughout Italy. In Florence they engage the services of A.E. Harnisch to seek out unknown works in Italian private collections. From Italy they travel to Paris, briefly, and then onto Spain. In Madrid, they visit the Prado and make the acquaintance of Joseph Wicht, who arranges for them to see works by El Greco and Goya in private collections. In April, they purchase two Cézannes from Vollard's gallery in Paris and other modern French paintings through Durand-Ruel.

1903

Paul Durand-Ruel takes an active role on behalf of the Havemeyers in negotiating the purchase of works by El Greco and Goya, some of which are acquired over the next year. In March and April, the Havemeyers are in Europe, mainly in Paris, but also traveling in Italy.

1905

The Havemeyers travel out west to Colorado and California; they return to New York via Salt Lake City.

1906

The Havemeyers travel to Egypt, Greece, and Constantinople,

and then on to Vienna and Paris. They acquire Courbet's *Woman in a Riding Habit* from Théodore Duret. In the fall, the Havemeyer's travel to Colorado on a business trip. They stop in Detroit on the way to visit the collector Charles Lang Freer.

1907
January 1 Horace is admitted to partnership in Havemeyers and Elder. On February 7, Adaline marries Peter Hood Ballantine Frelinghuysen in New York. The Havemeyers spend April in Italy and France. On December 4, Harry Havemeyer dies from acute nephritis with uremia.

1908
Horace becomes Director of the American Sugar Refining Co. and President of Havemeyers and Elder. In March, Louisine travels to Europe. In December, Cassatt visits Louisine in New York.

1909
In February, Louisine travels to Europe with her daughter Electra and her sister Anne. En route she attempts to throw herself overboard and is suffering a "nervous breakdown" upon arrival in Belgium. They travel through Italy, France, and Spain. In April, Louisine purchases El Greco's *View of Toledo* from Durand-Ruel, Paris. On August 7, Louisine's first grandchild, Frederica Louisine, is born.

1910
February 8 Electra marries James Watson Webb. During the year, Louisine becomes concerned with woman suffrage.

1911
February 28 Horace Havemeyer marries Doris Anna Dick. In the summer, Louisine is in France and visits Cassatt at Mesnil-Théribus. She reestablishes contact with Theodore Duret, through whom she acquires, over the next years, several works by Courbet.

1912
December 18 At the Rouart sale, Louisine acquires anonymously Degas's *Dancers Practicing at the Bar* for the record price of f478,500 (about $95,700). This is the highest price paid to date for a work by a living artist.

1913

In New York, Louisine acquires Daumier's The Third-Class Carriage at the record-breaking price of $40,000. She also acquires works by Pissarro, Sisley, and Guys.

1914

Louisine begins to take a more active role in the woman suffrage campaign. She travels to Italy, France, Switzerland, and Germany in the spring. She purchases works by Cassatt and Degas at the Roger Marx sale in Paris.

1915

Louisine organizes the exhibition *Masterpieces by Old and Modern Painters* to benefit woman suffrage at M. Knoedler and Co., New York. She lends nearly half the pictures included and delivers a talk, "Remarks on Degas and Cassatt," at the opening. Throughout the year, she delivers many speeches on behalf of woman suffrage, campaigning vigorously in New York, New Jersey, and Connecticut. In the summer, she begins writing *Sixteen to Sixty: Memoirs of a Collector*, which she continues to work on for the next few years.

1916

Louisine acquires works by Courbet and Degas. She lends several pieces from her collection to the Metropolitan Museum's *Exhibition of Early Chinese Pottery and Sculpture*.

1917

Louisine gives the five Whistler pastels she purchased from the artist to Freer for the museum he intends to establish. In August, she is acknowledged by the French government for service in the war effort. Louisine writes her will.

1918

Louisine acquires Cassatt's *Girl Arranging Her Hair* from the posthumous sale of the Edgar Degas collection.

1919

February 9 Louisine leads a demonstration in Washington, D.C., the day before the Senate vote on the Federal Suffrage Amendment. She is arrested and while she is in jail, the amendment is defeated by one vote. She then embarks on a national tour to garner support for woman suffrage. In April, she lends sixteen paintings to the centennial *Loan Exhibition of the Works of Gustave Courbet* at the Metropolitan Museum. In May and June, the Woman Suffrage Amendment is passed in the House of Representatives and the Senate. Louisine travels widely to rally support for ratification of the amendment. In July, she writes a codicil to her will selecting works to be bequeathed to the Metropolitan Museum.

1920
In August, the suffrage amendment is ratified and becomes part of the United States Constitution.

1921
February 12 At the Grolier Club in New York, Louisine gives a talk "Recollections of Miss Cassatt and her Work." In August, shortly after her arrival in Paris, she purchases a set of bronzes by Degas cast posthumously at the foundry of Adrien A. Hébrard. The following year she buys a posthumous bronze cast of Degas's *The Little Fourteen-Year Old Dancer*. In the summer and early fall, Louisine remains in France, dividing her time between Paris and Cassatt's country house in Mesnil-Théribus.

1922
May 8 France decorates Louisine with the Cross of the Knight of the Legion of Honor. In June and August, Louisine adds second and third codicils to her will enlarging her bequest of works of art to the Metropolitan Museum. She publishes two articles on her activities as a suffragist in Scribner's magazine.

1923
Louisine makes an anonymous donation in memory of Oliver H. Payne to the Metropolitan Museum of Tiepolo's *The Glorification of Francesco Barbaro*. She publishes a tribute to her late friend Charles Freer.

1924
Cassatt breaks with Louisine in a misunderstanding over some print proofs due to Cassatt's failing eyesight. In December, Louisine is elected a Benefactor of the Metropolitan Museum.

1926
June 14 Mary Cassatt dies at Mesnil-Théribus.

1927

Louisine lends several pictures to the *Mary Cassatt Memorial Exhibition* at the Pennsylvania Museum of Art, Philadelphia. In July, Louisine presents Manet's portrait of *Georges Clemenceau* to the Musée du Louvre, Paris.

1928

In March, the government of France promotes Louisine to the rank of Officer of the Legion of Honor. Later in the spring, Louisine departs for Paris. She visits Cassatt's burial place, the family vault at Mesnil-Théribus.

1929

January 6 Louisine dies at the age of seventy-three in the company of her three children. The cause of death is arteriosclerosis complicated by bronchopneumonia. On January 29, the Metropolitan Museum of Art accepts "the munificent bequest of Mrs. H.O. Havemeyer" under the terms of her will.

1930

March 10–November 2 The entire Havemeyer bequest is presented at the Metropolitan Museum in the exhibition *The H.O. Havemeyer Collection.* After the close of the exhibition, the 1,967 objects in the bequest are distributed to the appropriate departments in the Museum.

ABBREVIATIONS

MMA = The Metropolitan Museum of Art, New York

NGA = National Gallery of Art, Washington, D.C.

SM = Shelburne Museum, Shelburne, Vermont

Numbers preceded by "A" refer to the appendix by Gretchen Wold of European and American paintings, drawings, pastels, and watercolors owned by Mr. and Mrs. H.O. Havemeyer as documented in *Splendid Legacy: The Havemeyer Collection*, published by The Metropolitan Museum of Art, New York, 1993, pp. 281-394.

NOTES

SUSAN ALYSON STEIN

CHAPTER I
SIXTEEN TO SIXTY

1. Louisine Waldron Elder Havemeyer, who was born July 28, 1855, began writing her memoirs in the summer of 1915, at age sixty (see note no. 16). She began collecting in her early twenties, with the purchase of Degas's *Ballet Rehearsal* (see note no. 291).

2. Dean Sage (1841-1902), American businessman in the lumber trade and avid fisherman, who, in addition to his distinguished library on fishing, a subject on which he was an authority, owned a valuable collection of first editions and manuscripts, including a first folio of Shakespeare. He married Sarah Augusta Manning in 1865. For his wife, see pp. 164-65.

3. Bernard Quaritch (1819-99), English bookseller, who developed the largest antiquarian book trade in his time.

4. José de Madrazo (1781-1859), as court painter to Charles IV in Rome, and subsequently to Ferdinand II, participated in the establishment of the Prado, and served as its director from 1838-57; his son, Federigo de Madrazo (1815-1894), followed in his father's footsteps, as court painter from 1850, and director of the Prado after 1860. For Federigo's sons, Ricardo and Raimundo, see note nos. 214, 217.

5. Louis La Caze (1798-1869), French physician, who in 1869, bequeathed to the Louvre his magnificent collection of paint-

ings, largely from the 17th-18th century; the bequest, considered the most important ever made to the Louvre in terms of the number and quality of its pictures, included such masterpieces as Rembrandt's *Bathsheba* and Watteau's *Gille*.

6. Manet's *Le déjeuner sur l'herbe* (Musée d'Orsay, Paris, R.F. 1668).

7. Velázquez's *The Fable of Arachne*, known as *Las Hilanderas* (or "The Spinners") in the Museo del Prado, Madrid (since 1819, no. 1775).

8. Leonardo's *Mona Lisa*, called "La Gioconda," was stolen in August 1911 and restored to its place in the Grande Galerie of the Musée du Louvre in January 1914. During this period, the Louvre acquired Corot's *Woman with a Pearl* (R.F. 2040)—a picture that Mrs. Havemeyer had wanted to buy—from the estate sale of the *Collections de M. Jean Dollfus* Galerie Durand-Ruel, Paris, March 2, 1912, lot no. 6.

9. Presumably a reference to the Parisian jeweler and collector, Henri Vever (1854-1942), from whose sale, *Collection de H.V.* (Galerie George Petit, Paris, February 2, 1897, no. 23), the Havemeyers would acquire Corot's *Bacchante by the Sea* (MMA 29.100.19 [A 106]).

10. The celebrated baritone, Jean-Baptiste Faure (1830-1914) owned nearly seventy pictures by Manet at one time or another; the Havemeyers bought eight Manets that were formerly in Faure's collection (A 344,

345, 348, 349, 350, 353, 356, 357). See Gary Tinterow, "The Havemeyer Pictures," in MMA 1993, p. 53, fn. 68.

11. Courbet's *The Stonebreakers* (Fernier 1977-78, no. 101) was owned by Louis-Alfred Binant, a Parisian art dealer and paint supplier, from 1871 until 1904, when it was acquired from his estate sale (Hotel Drouot, April 20-21, 1904, lot no. 19) by the Gemäldegalerie zu Dresden; it was destroyed during World War II. A smaller version of the subject (Fernier 1977-78, no. 102, now in the Oskar Reinhart Collection, Winterthur) was owned, until 1890, by Jean-Paul Mazaroz (b. 1823) an industrial sculptor and furniture maker, possibly "the blacksmith" in question. See also p. 193.

12. Daumier's *Man Reading in a Garden* (MMA 29.100.199 [A 178]), purchased by the Havemeyers from Durand-Ruel, April 9, 1890, for $240.

13. Daumier's *The Third Class Carriage* (MMA 29.100.129 [A 177]) was purchased by Louisine Havemeyer in February 1913 for the record-breaking price of $40,000.

14. Courbet, who worked indefatigably to protect works of art in and around Paris as chairman of the Arts Commission and was politically active as member of the Commune (the Paris municipality), was sentenced to six months' imprisonment at Sainte-Pélagie for his alleged involvement in the destruction of Vendôme Column in 1871. Facing the confiscation of his property and fearful that he would be imprisoned for debt as the court determined his financial liability for damages to the column, he fled France for Switzerland in 1873, settling in La Tour de Peilz, where he died in exile, in 1877.

15. For Mrs. Havemeyer's subsequent discussions of *The Duke of Wellington*, now considered Workshop of Goya (NGA 1963.4.1 [A 302]), see pp. 136, 153, 156f, and 290.

16. Ricardo de Madrazo wrote two letters to Mrs. Havemeyer in the summer of 1915

(on June 18 and July 28) in which he asked her to send a photograph of the Wellington portrait (A 302) on behalf of his friend Aureliano de Beruete y Moret. She sent photographs accompanied by a list of "all my canvases by Goya" to Beruete on August 15, 1915 (MMA/Havemeyer correspondence). The author's first monograph on the artist, *Goya: Pintor de Retratos* was published in 1916.

17. H.O. Havemeyer died on December 4, 1907.

18. In the summer of 1909, Mrs. Havemeyer sold two Cézannes, *Self-Portrait with a Cap* (A 71) and *The Banks of the Marne* (A 77) to Durand-Ruel for 15,000 francs; the gallery sold them for twice this amount, 30,000 francs, to the Russian collector, Ivan Morozov (both, Hermitage State Museum, St. Petersburg).

CHAPTER II
MUSIC ROOM

19. The Havemeyers' residence at 1 East 66th Street in New York, built in the Romanesque Revival style by architect Charles Coolidge Haight (1841-1917) was completed in the Spring 1890. The interiors, designed by Louis Comfort Tiffany (1848-1933) and Samuel Colman (1832-1920) were finished in the Spring 1892. The house was demolished in 1930; an apartment house was erected on the site in 1947.

For photographs and a description of the decor and furnishings of the music room, including Tiffany's extraordinary chandelier, see Alice Cooney Frelinghuysen, "The Havemeyer House," in MMA 1993, pp. 185-86.

20. Three rare Italian violins, two by Rogerius and one by Stradivarius, and a violoncello by Rogeri, were included in the American Art Association sale of *Important Paintings From the Havemeyer Estate*, held at the Anderson Galleries, New York, April 10, 1930, lot nos. 88, 89, 90, 91.

21. A quantity of Japanese lacquers— including 190 *inro* and some sixty objects, mostly boxes and largely nineteenth cen-

tury in date—as well as a selection of Chinese textiles were included in the 1929 Havemeyer bequest to the Metropolitan Museum; other pieces were inherited by the Havemeyer children, and a number were sold at auction. See Havemeyer 1931, pp. 237f, 287-88, 475-77; Havemeyer 1958, pp. 82-89, 119-120; and *The Estate of Mrs. H.O. Havemeyer, Part III: Japanese and Chinese Art*, American Art Association, Anderson Galleries, New York, April 14-19. On the subject of the Havemeyers' collection of Japanese lacquerware, see Barbara Ford's essay on this subject in MMA 1993, pp. 162-63.

22. There are two carved ivory *inro* in the Havemeyer collection at the Metropolitan Museum, (MMA 29.100.819 and 29.100.821). See Julia Meech, "The Other Havemeyer Passion: Collecting Asian Art," in MMA 1993, pp. 146, 150, fn. 49.

23. For the Havemeyers 1901 visit to the Capilla de Santo Tomé, Toledo to see El Greco's *Burial of the Conde de Orgaz*, see p. 132, 138f.

24. This Lang-yao baluster shaped vase, distinguished by its fine red glaze, was included in the 1929 Havemeyer bequest to the Metropolitan Museum (MMA 29.100.317). See Julia Meech, "The Other Havemeyer Passion," in MMA 1993, pp. 147-48, pl. 142.

25. Among the Havemeyers' purchases from the sale of the *Collection Ch. Gillot, Objets d'Art et Peinture d'Extrême Orient*, Galerie Durand-Ruel, Paris, February 8-13, 1904, were two Japanese lacquer boxes and two Japanese vases. These objects are now in the Metropolitan Museum (the boxes, MMA 29.100.689, .690 or .691 and MMA 29.100.712, and the vases, MMA 29.100.622 and 29.100.616). See MMA 1993, pls. 140, 235.

26. On the subject of the two Rimpa school screens, the left-hand screen depicting autumn that was acquired by the Metropolitan Museum in 1915 (MMA 15.127) and the right-hand screen representing spring, formerly in the Havemeyer collection (MMA 49.35.2), see Julia Meech,

"The Other Havemeyer Passion," and entries by Barbara Ford in MMA 1993, pp. 142-44, 160-61.

CHAPTER III
THE LIBRARY

27. For photographs and a description of the decor and furnishings of the Havemeyers' library, also called the "Rembrandt room," see Alice Cooney Frelinghuysen, "The Havemeyer House," in MMA 1993, pp. 182-86.

28. The skylit gallery was added in 1903.

29. For the eight Rembrandts, see pp. 19-20.

30. Samuel Colman (1832-1920), American artist, who from the late 1870s became interested in Far Eastern art and eventually amassed a large and multi-faceted collection of Japanese objects. His interest in the decorative arts was also evident in his collaboration with Tiffany on the design of numerous interiors, most notably, the Havemeyers'.

31. H.O. Havemeyer probably met Samuel Colman in December 1875. The Philadelphia Centennial Exhibition was held from May 10-November 10, 1876.

32. On the ceiling, see Frelinghuysen in MMA 1993, p. 184.

33. The Boston dealer of Oriental objects is probably a reference to Matsuki (see note no. 115). For Sir William Van Horne, see note no. 120.

34. For the Havemeyers' collecting of Japanese tea jars and potteries see Chapter VII, p. 70f.

35. The present whereabouts of this panel is unknown.

36. The Havemeyers amassed a large group of Chinese bronzes, including a number of incense burners and vessels, seven of which came to the Metropolitan Museum in 1929 (MMA 29.100.545-51; see Havemeyer 1958, p. 81); an additional 82 lots were auctioned from the 1930 Havemeyer estate sale. On this subject, see Meech in MMA 1993, pp. 146-47, and pls. 160, 161.

37. The paintings listed in the second paragraph, p. 19, are respectively:

Rembrandt, *Herman Doomer* (MMA 29.100.1 [A 449]), formerly called *Portrait of the Gilder, Herman Doomer*, purchased by the Havemeyers from William Schaus, New York, on March 7, 1889 for reputedly between $70,000 and $100,000. See pp. 24, 142.

Formerly Rembrandt, now considered Style of Jacob Adriaensz. Backer, *Portrait of an Old Woman* (MMA 29.100.2 [A 11]), purchased by the Havemeyers from Durand-Ruel on February 3, 1891 for $50,000.

Pieter de Hooch, *The Visit* (MMA 29.100.7 [A 326]), acquired by the Havemeyers from the sale of the *Collection de M.E. Secrétan*, Galerie Charles Sedelmeyer, Paris, on July 2, 1889, lot no. 128, for 276,000 francs.

Formerly Rembrandt, now considered Style of Rembrandt, *Portrait of a Young Man in a Broad-Brimmed Hat* (SM 27.1.1-150 [A 459]). This portrait was acquired by the Havemeyers from the Princesse de Sagan, Paris, shortly after they purchased two other Rembrandts from her collection. See p. 20.

Formerly Rembrandt, now considered Style of Rembrandt, *Portrait of a Man— The Treasurer* (SM 27.1.1-151 [A 456]), bought by the Havemeyers from Durand-Ruel, New York, in November 1890; the picture had been in the collection of A.J. Boesch, Vienna (in 1889).

The two Rembrandt portraits, formerly thought to represent Christian Paul and Volkera van Beresteijn, are now called *Portrait of a Man* and *Portrait of a Woman* (MMA 29.100.3 [A 445] and MMA 29.100.4 [A 446]). The Havemeyers purchased the pair of portraits from Cottier and Co., New York, on December 8, 1888 for $60,000.

38. The paintings referred to in the first paragraph, p. 20, are respectively:

The two portraits from the collection of

the Princesse de Sagan, Paris, were bought by the Havemeyers from Durand-Ruel on September 7, 1892: Formerly Rembrandt, "Portrait of an Admiral" and "Portrait of the Admiral's Wife," now considered Style of Rembrandt, *Portrait of a Man with a Breastplate and Plumed Hat* and *Portrait of a Woman* (MMA 29.100.102 [A 457] and MMA 29.100.103 [A 458]). See also p. 287.

Bronzino, *Portrait of a Young Man* (MMA 29.100.16 [A 45]), bought by the Havemeyers from Durand-Ruel, New York, on May 14, 1898, for $40,000. See p. 111.

The portraits by Frans Hals, *Petrus Scriverius* and *Anna van der Aar* (MMA New York, 29.100.8 [A 320] and 29.100.9 [A 319]), were purchased for the Havemeyers, by Durand-Ruel, from the Secrétan sale, July 2, 1889, lot nos. 124, 125, for 45,500 francs each.

Formerly Holbein, now considered Jan Cornelisz. Vermeyen, *Jean de Carondelet (1469-1545)* (The Brooklyn Museum, Brooklyn, New York, 47.76 [A 502]), bought by the Havemeyers from the Duc and Duchesse de la Trémoïlle, Paris around 1896 for 110,000 francs. (also mentioned pp. 24, 292-93).

Lucas Cranach the Elder, *Portrait of a Man with a Rosary* (MMA 29.100.24 [A 168]). According to Department of European Paintings archives, this portrait was a later acquisition; it was purchased from Cottier and Co., New York, by Louisine Havemeyer in January 1914.

Formerly Antonello da Messina, now considered Hugo van der Goes, *Portrait of a Man* (MMA 29.100.15 [A 290]), acquired by the Havemeyers from the sale, *La Collection Mame*, Galerie Georges Petit, Paris, April 26, 1904, lot no. 1, for 50,000 francs.

39. The bronze is listed as *Statuette* under Greek Bronzes in Havemeyer 1931, p. 457, where it is described as a standing draped figure of Venus, with right arm raised, measuring 20 in. in height, Collection of Horace Havemeyer.

40. Félix-Bienaimé Feuardent (1819-1907),

distinguished French archaeologist and
numismatist, and dealer of medals in Paris;
his son, Gaston-Louis Feuardent (1841-
1893), was also a numismatist.

41. For a sense of the Havemeyer coin collection see Havemeyer 1931, pp. 458-59
(listed as Collection of Horace Havemeyer). Yet this must represent only a portion
of their collection of coins, since Louisine
claims to have given the vast majority of
the coins to her grandchildren (see Havemeyer "Notes" [1974], pp. 26, 36).

42. An important Corinthian Bronze *Hel-
met* was included in the 1929 Havemeyer
Bequest to the Metropolitan Museum
(MMA 29.100. 488; see MMA 1993, pl.
107); the other, is listed as Collection of
Horace Havemeyer, in Havemeyer 1931,
p. 457, *Helmet with Pendant Ear-Pieces*,
Corinthian type, 7th cen. B.C.

43. Leading figures in the Beaux-Arts
movement in America in the late 19th century: the sculptor, Augustus Saint-Gaudens (1848-1907), and architect, Charles
Follum McKim (1847-1909), partner in the
architectural firm of McKim, Mead and
White, founded in 1879. Through his
affiliation with the firm, Saint-Gaudens
received numerous commissions for decorative and monumental sculpture. See also
p. 33

44. James J. Hill (1839-1916), founder and
head of the Great Northern Railway and
the Northern Securities Company. By the
time of his death, May 29, 1916, the
"Empire Builder" had filled his massive
stone house, at 240 Summit Avenue, in St.
Paul, Minnesota, with an impressive collection of paintings, largely of the Barbizon school. See pp. 35-38.

45. Oliver H. Payne, the Havemeyers' close
friend and neighbor, bequeathed to the
Metropolitan Museum, in 1917, a late
Gothic tapestry, *The Fall and Redemption
of Man* (MMA 17.189). Regarding Payne,
see pp. 32-34.

46. Anders Zorn (1860-1920), Swedish
painter, etcher and sculptor, who was
schooled in Stockholm (1875-81), worked

in London (1882-85) and Paris (1888-96),
and traveled widely; he made six trips to
the United States.

47. Isabella Stewart Gardner (1840-1924),
American collector who, under the guid-
ance of Bernard Berenson amassed an
impressive collection of paintings that, to
this day, is housed in her Venetian-style
villa, Fenway Court, in Boston; in 1924,
she bequeathed her house and its contents
to the city as a public museum. The visit
took place on January 17, 1903.

48. For the "Gilder" (A 449), see note no.
37; for "Holbein" portrait (A 502), see note
no. 38. Horace, who was given the portrait
of *Jean de Carondelet* (now considered to be
by Vermeyen) on his 21st birthday, March
19, 1907, donated it to the Brooklyn Museum in 1947.

49. Edith Thomas (1854-1925), American
poet, who moved to New York City in
1887 where her work was introduced by
Century magazine; between 1890-1909, she
enjoyed considerable popularity: more than
300 of her poems were published in leading literary magazines and she was
embraced by New York society and its
literati.

50. The Havemeyers' eldest daughter,
Adaline (later, Mrs. Peter H.B. Frel-
inghuysen, 1884-1963) graduated from
Bryn Mawr in June 1905.

CHAPTER IV
VISITORS I

51. Cornelius Vanderbilt (1794-1877), who
had earned the designation "Commodore"
for the extensive carrying trade he developed along the Northeastern seaboard,
sold his fleet of steamships in 1857-62, and
turned his attention to railways. At the
time of his death, he controlled the New
York Central and Hudson River, the Lake
Shore and Michigan Southern, the Harlem,
and the Canada Southern railways, and had
holdings in many others. His eldest son,
William Henry Vanderbilt (1821-1885),
inherited his father's financial empire,
which in turn, passed to his four sons,

though the eldest, named for his grandfather, Cornelius (1843-1899), presided over the family interests from 1885.

52. Standard Oil, a company established by the Rockefellers in 1870 was organized as a trust in 1882. The second trust, the Sugar Refineries Co., was formed, in December 1887, by the merger of seventeen refineries in Boston, New York, Philadelphia and New Orleans.

53. Grover Cleveland (1837-1908), 22nd and 24th president of the United States; a democrat who served two terms of office, 1885-89, and 1893-97.

54. The first telephone switchboards for commercial service were placed in operation in 1878, two years after Bell patented his invention; telephone communication along the eastern seaboard became possible by the mid-late 1880s, with long distance lines reaching Chicago in 1892, and San Francisco in 1915. See also p. 41.

55. John G. Carlisle (1835-1910), American politician, noted for his sound money policy, served as U.S. Secretary of the Treasury under Cleveland's second term in office (1893-97).

56. On June 14, 1899 H.O. Havemeyer appeared before the Industrial Commission in Washington, D.C. in connection with its investigation of trusts; his "testimony related almost wholly to the sugar industry, and he opened with a vigorous attack upon the custom's tariff." (See *New York Times*, June 15, 1899, p. 1, col. 2, under the headlines: "Mr. Havemeyer on Trusts. Tells the Industrial Commission the Tariff is Responsible. Discriminates Against Sugar. He Asserts that the Day of the Individual is Past and Business Combinations Are Necessary.")

57. John Davison Rockefeller (1839-1937), American oil magnate and philanthropist, who founded Standard Oil in 1870 and presided over the company until his retirement in 1911. He moved to Cleveland, Ohio in 1853 and married Laura Spelman (d. 1915) in 1864; they had three daughters and a son, John Davison, Jr. (1874-

1960), who was also associated with the oil industry and with the philanthropic foundations for education and medical research established by his father.

58. William Rockefeller (1841-1922), was associated with his brother in the development of the oil business from 1865 until 1911, and later served as director of numerous railroad and utility companies. He married Geraldine Goodsell (d. 1920) in 1864; they lived in New York and had two children, William Goodsell (1870-1922) and Percy Avery (1878-1934).

59. The Havemeyers' Connecticut home, Hilltop, was located on the highest point of Palmer Hill on a 90-acre site (subsequently expanded) in Greenwich. Colman, who was assisted by Tiffany, was placed in charge of the decor of the house, which was ready for occupancy in June 1890.

60. The reference is to one of John D. Rockefeller's three daughters: Bessie (Mrs. Charles A. Strong), Alta (Mrs. E. Parmalee Prentice), or Edith (Mrs. Harold Fowler McCormick).

61. Andrew Carnegie (1835-1919), American industrialist, humanitarian and philanthropist, who from 1873, concentrated on the steel industry, consolidated his holdings into Carnegie Steel Co. in 1889, and merged this company with U.S. Steel Corporation in 1901. After the merger, Carnegie retired and devoted himself to philanthropy and the promotion of peace; his benefactions included large contributions for public libraries, public education and international peace, in accordance with the views he expressed in his 1889 article, "Wealth," in the *North American Review.*

62. Louisine Waldron Elder and Henry Osborne Havemeyer were married in Greenwich, Connecticut on August 22, 1883.

63. Louisine's older sister, Anne Elder Munn (1853-1917).

64. Henry Phipps (1839-1930), who grew up next door to the Carnegie family in Allegheny City, Pa., was a manufacturer in the iron, and later steel, industry; he formed the Union Iron Mills Co. in 1867 with

Andrew Carnegie, and they remained business associates until they both retired in 1901. Like his boyhood friend, Phipps devoted his retirement to philanthropies for humanitarian purposes, in particular, toward the establishment of foundations for combating tuberculosis and mental disease.

65. Henry Clay Frick (1849-1919), American industrialist, art collector and philanthropist was associated with Carnegie from 1882, became chairman of Carnegie Steel from 1889-1900, and played an important part in consolidation forming U.S. Steel Corp. in 1901, of which he was later director. In 1919, he bequeathed his home in New York City, with its magnificent art collection and large endowment, to the public as a museum.

66. Oliver H. Payne (1839-1917), served bravely in the Union army from 1861-64, rising in the ranks from lieutenant to colonel; he resigned, after the arduous Atlanta Campaign in 1864, and returned to Cleveland, rapidly gaining a place in the iron and oil refining industries, and eventually aligning himself with Standard Oil. He moved to New York City in 1884 where he gradually divested himself of his oil holdings and invested in other fields, becoming a director in various banking firms and industrial corporations, a dominant figure in the American Tobacco Co. and its subsidiaries, and influential in the affairs of the Tennessee Coal and Iron Co., at the time of its absorption by U.S. Steel. A bachelor and avid yachtsman, his most notable philanthropy was a $500,000 gift to found Cornell Medical University to which he made further gifts totalling over $8,000,000.

67. Beginning in 1896, Harry Havemeyer took an active role in extending Payne's art collection by recommending works for acquisition, engaging the services of the Durand-Ruels and other art agents, and later, by making purchases on his behalf. Louisine Havemeyer assumed a similar role after Harry's death. See p. 178.

68. The references are to the following works in Payne's collection: Degas's *The*

Dance Class (MMA 1987.47.1) purchased by Payne from Durand-Ruel, New York, on April 4, 1898 for $25,000 (125,000 francs); Turner's *Juliet and her Nurse* (private collection [Butlin and Joll 1984, no. 365]), acquired by Payne by 1901; Corot's *The Golden Age* (Robaut 1905, no. 1976) and *Woman and Cupid* (Robaut 1905, no. 1998) secured by H.O. Havemeyer for Payne from Durand-Ruel, on January 9, 1897, along with Corot's *Portrait of Mlle de Foudras* (Robaut 1905, no. 2133), which he decided not to keep, for a total of 125,000 francs ($25,000). See also pp. 263-64.

69. Saint-Gaudens's *General Sherman Monument*, Fifth Avenue and 59th Street entrance to Central Park, was unveiled in 1903. The artist (see note no. 43) was favored with numerous commissions for public monuments relating to the Civil War and its military leaders.

70. Union army commanders and decorated Civil War heroes, William T. Sherman (1820-1891) and George Henry Thomas (1816-1870).

71. The famous Renaissance statue of Bartolomeo Colleoni, begun by Verocchio in 1481 and completed after his death by Leopardi (Venice, Campo Santi Giovanni), also noted, p. 103.

72. American railroad-builders and financiers, Sidney Dillon (1812-1892) and John Insley Blair (1802-1899), who were instrumental in the construction of the Union Pacific Railroad and responsible for implementing thousands of miles of track throughout the United States. In 1869, transcontinental rail travel became possible.

73. James J. Hill (see note no. 44), began collecting Barbizon pictures in 1883, purchasing his first of many Corots in 1884, and his first Courbet in 1890. See J. Hancock, S. Ffolliot, T. O'Sullivan, *Homecoming: The Art Collection of James J. Hill*, St. Paul, 1991.

74. The events recalled probably took place in the summer of 1910. That year, Louisine went to Chicago in June, and she returned in early September to attend to

the birth of Electra and J. Watson Webb's first child, her granddaughter, Electra, born on November 3. (Hill regularly and frequently travelled to Chicago). The ex-president discussed — given his aggressive policies in curbing trusts and regulating business — was undoubtedly Theodore Roosevelt, who completed his term in office in 1909. For Roosevelt, see pp. 54f.

75. Jekyll Island Club, a haven for American millionaires off the Georgia coast, of which Hill was a member from 1888-1916; he purchased an apartment at the club in 1904. (In addition to his primary residence in St. Paul, Hill also owned, from 1906, a house in New York City, at 8 East 65th Street — a block away from the Havemeyers.)

76. Theodore N. Vail (1845-1920), American communications executive, was general manager of Bell Telephone Co. between 1878-87, and in 1885 incorporated AT&T to unify the telephone industry and provide a long-distance system. He was president of AT&T, from 1885-89, and from 1907-19. Between 1894 and 1907, he superintended the construction of transportation and communication systems in Argentina. Vail, whom Mrs. Havemeyer met during his second tenure as president of AT&T — probably in late 1913 or early 1914 — had a farm in Lyndonville, Vermont.

Louisine Havemeyer presumably met the Vails through Cassatt. Having just seen "Mrs. Theodore Vail (telephone)" in Paris, Cassatt on September 4, [1913], wrote to Louisine: "I promised I would write to you, and introduce her, & that I was sure you would show her your house, so here is my introduction." (MMA/Havemeyer correspondence)

77. Nathan Corning Kingsbury (1866-1920), American lawyer and corporate executive, who from 1906 was associated with the telephone business, heading the Michigan State Telephone Co. (1906-1910), before he came to New York City, in January 1911, to become Vice-President of AT&T, an office he held throughout

Vail's presidency. He married Lillian B. Prescott in 1893.

78. Orville (1871-1948) and Wilbur (1867-1912) Wright achieved their first successful flight at Kitty Hawk, North Carolina, on December 17, 1903. Their "flying machine," pursuant to successful demonstrations on July 27 and 30, 1909, at Fort Meyer, Virginia secured acceptance by the U.S. Government. For the history of the telephone, see note no. 54.

79. The *Panama-Pacific International Exhibition* was held at the Fine Arts Palace in San Francisco from February 20–December 4, 1915, the same year that transcontinental telephone communication was developed. The first telephone conversation between Alexander Graham Bell in New York and Thomas Watson in San Franciso took place on January 25, 1915; commercial service was inaugurated on April 7, 1915.

80. Lila Vanderbilt Webb was Electra's mother-in-law. Electra (1888-1960), the Havemeyers' youngest daughter married James Watson Webb (1884-1960) on February 8, 1910.

81. Her daughter-in-law, Doris Anna Dick Havemeyer (1890-1982), married to Horace (1886-1956), her son, on February 28, 1911.

82. John Joseph Carty (1861-1932), American electrical engineer who made numerous contributions to the techniques of telephone construction and operation, achieving in 1915, both transcontinental and transatlantic voice connection; he became chief engineer of AT&T in 1907.

83. Alexander Graham Bell (1847-1922), American educator and inventor, who in 1871 came to the United States from Scotland as a teacher of speech for the deaf, patented the telephone in 1876, and in 1877, formed Bell Telephone Co., under the direction of lawyer, Gardiner G. Hubbard, whose daughter he married the same year. Among the many honors conferred upon Bell in his lifetime, he was awarded the Edison Medal in 1914.

CHAPTER V
VISITORS II

84. Komura Jutaro (1855-1911), Japanese foreign minister who figured significantly in such major diplomatic issues of the latter part of the Meiji period (1868-1912) as the Anglo-Japanese Alliance (1902), the Russo-Japanese war (1904–05), and the annexation of Korea (1910). Komura, a vigorous proponent of Japan's continental expansion, attended Harvard Law school from 1875-78.

The memoirs of Russian statesman, Sergei Yulievich Witte (1849-1915), were first published in English in 1921: *Memoirs of Count Witte* ed. A. Garmolinsky, London and New York, 1921. (This is among the handful of references that date after 1917).

At the peace conference convoked by Theodore Roosevelt in Portsmouth, New Hampshire in August 1905, Japanese delegate Komura and Russian delegate Witte were responsible for negotiating the treaty ending the Russo-Japanese War.

85. British soldier and statesman, Horatio Herbert Kitchener (1850-1916), First Earl Kitchener of Khartoum and of Broome, who served in the Middle East from 1874, including Wolseley's expedition for the relief of General Gordon (1884-85). In 1898 he invaded Sudan, annihilated al-Mahdi's army at Omdurman and reoccupied Khartoum. He was successively, commander in chief in South Africa (1899-1902), organizing forces to combat gorilla warfare of the Boers, and in India (1902-09); he later served as Proconsul of Egypt (1911-14). From 1914-16 Kitchener, as field marshal, engaged in organizing British forces for war. He was lost with the H.M.S. *Hampshire* on June 5, 1916.

86. The Havemeyers were in Egypt in February 1906.

87. British soldier, Charles George Gordon (1833-1885), who took part in the capture of Peking and the destruction of the Summer Palace in 1860 and was commander of the Chinese force, "Ever Victorious

Army," that suppressed the Taiping rebellion, 1863-64. He subsequently served in posts identical to those later held by Kitchener in Egypt, Africa and Sudan. Gordon failed to evacuate Khartoum before it came under siege by forces of the Mahdi in February 1884, and was killed, June 1885, in the fall of Khartoum, becoming in popular view a hero and a martyr.

88. Paul Dana (1852-1930), American journalist, who, in 1897, succeeded his father as editor-in-chief of the New York *Sun*.

89. The Havemeyers owned a total of thirty-six Imperial ware peachbloom glazes. In addition to several vases (MMA 29.100.325-33), the 1929 Havemeyer bequest to the Metropolitan Museum, also included "peachblow" water vessels and bowls or brush washers for the writing table (29.100.334-355). See Havemeyer 1958, pp. 106-108, and Meech in MMA 1993, p. 147, pls. 141, 142. These pieces are quite small and delicate in proportion. The slender vases measure 4-8 in. in height, and from 2-3 1/2 in. in diameter; the size of the writing table vessels and bowls are "tiny," with the largest, measuring, no more than 3 inches in height and 5 inches in diameter. See Louisine's description (p. 47) of the "peachblow ink bottles, the tiny salve cups and the slender vases."

90. El Greco, *Portrait of a Cardinal, Probably Cardinal Don Fernando Niño de Guevara (1541-1609)* (MMA 29.100.5 [A 304]), acquired from the Conde de Paredes de Nava, Madrid, by Paul Durand-Ruel on June 1, 1904, and sold to the Havemeyers on this date for 225,000 francs. See pp. 132, 138f, 152-59, 177-79.

91. Presumably the Ch'ing dynasty *Water Coupe* now in the Metropolitan Museum (MMA 29.100.331).

92. Johann Kaspar Lavater (1741-1801), Swiss poet, mystic, theologian and world renown "physiognomist" who taught that character and temperament could be read from outward appearances such as facial features, body type, handwriting and the like.

93. The Havemeyers' son, Horace, inherited his parents' large collection of Persian ceramics, as well as their interest in Islamic pottery. (He had an impressive collection, particularly rich in Raqqa ware, in his own right.) Thanks to Horace's generosity, a selection of bowls, jugs and plates were added to the 1929 Havemeyer bequest to the Metropolitan Museum (MMA 29.160.1-18), and a number of other pieces were donated to the collection over the next thirty years, indeed a total of 109 examples. See Havemeyer 1958, pp. 51-54. On this subject, see Alice Cooney Frelinghuysen, "The Forgotten Legacy: The Havemeyers' Collection of Decorative Arts," and Marilyn Jenkins' essay on Islamic pottery in MMA 1993, pp. 108-10 and pp. 119-21.

94. The date of Lord Kitchener's visit to the Metropolitan Museum is not recorded in the Museum's archives.

CHAPTER VI
VISITORS III

95. The French actor, Benoît-Constant, known as Coquelin (1841-1909), was with the Comédie-Française from 1860-92, and later, actor-manager of the Porte-Saint-Martin theater where, in 1897, he created his most successful role, Cyrano in *Cyrano de Bergerac.* Coquelin debuted in New York in 1888. During the 1893-94 winter season, Coquelin and Irving—the later performing in *The Lyons Mail*—both had engagements in New York at Abbey's Theater.

96. Sir Henry Irving (1838-1905), English actor, who was professionally associated with Ellen Terry from 1878-1902. During the same period he was manager of the Lyceum Theater, London, where the sumptuous, meticulously detailed productions for which he was noted, contributed to his eventual bankruptcy. The first actor to be knighted (1895), Irving made eight American tours, the first in 1883-84, the last 1903-04.

97. Sir John Hare (1844-1921), English actor and theater manager, who was con-

sidered one of the finest character actors of his day.

98. Edwin Austin Abbey (1852-1911), American painter and illustrator, whose work was represented in the Havemeyer collection by six pen and ink drawings (MMA 29.100.923-928 [A 1-6]).

99. Dame Ellen Terry (Alice Ellen Terry, 1847-1928), English actress who played Katherine to Irving's Petruchio in 1867, and went on to be his leading lady in Shakespearean roles and in plays by Wils, Tennyson, Reade, and Sardou between 1878-1902.

100. Edith Kermit Carow Roosevelt (1861-1948), second wife of Theodore Roosevelt, a childhood friend whom he married in 1886, mother of their five children, and first lady from 1901-09.

101. William McKinley (1843-1901), 25th president of the United States, a republican whose term of office, 1897-1901, was cut short by his assassination on September 6, 1901. Upon his death eight days later, Vice-President Theodore Roosevelt (1858-1919), succeeded to the presidency; he was elected to a second term in 1904, and remained in office until 1909. Louisine Havemeyer's less-than-favorable description of Roosevelt accords with sentiments expressed on pp. 36-37.

102. Mrs. John Milburn (née Mary Patty Stocking), wife of prominent lawyer, John George Milburn (1851-1930), to whose home McKinley was brought, and subsequently died, after being fatally shot at the Pan American exposition in Buffalo in 1901 (Milburn had been president of that event, and practicing in Buffalo at the time). The Milburns moved to New York City in 1904, where he became a distinguished member of the New York bar and participated in many cases of nationwide interest, among them, as counsel for Standard Oil in the government's anti-trust suit.

103. Helen Keller (1880-1968), American lecturer and author, who triumphed over being blind, deaf and mute.

104. Anne Mansfield Sullivan (later, Mrs.

John A. Macy, 1866-1936), her teacher and companion from 1887-1936.

105. For Adaline, see note no. 50.

106. Louisine Havemeyer's sister, Adaline Mapes Elder (Mrs. Samuel Peters, 1857-1943).

107. Helen Keller entered Radcliffe in 1900, and graduated cum laude in 1904.

108. William Shakespeare (1849-1931), English tenor, singing teacher and composer in the style of Mendelssohn.

109. The Havemeyer collection included three marbles of this subject attributed to Italian Renaissance artists. Two were included in the 1929 bequest to the Metropolitan Museum: Mino da Fiesole's *Virgin and Child* (MMA 29.100.25) and Master of the Marble Madonnas, *Virgin and Child* (MMA 29.100.26). The other is listed as by Bastianini (collection of Electra Havemeyer Webb) in Havemeyer 1931, p. 456.

110. For the Venus de Milo statuette and the Greek Helmets, see note nos. 39, 42.

111. Louisine Havemeyer became concerned with woman suffrage beginning in 1910, and actively campaigned for the cause up until 1920, when the nineteenth amendment was made part of the constitution. On this subject, see Weitzenhoffer 1986, pp. 204-07, 212, 220-23, 227-29, 232-36, 238, 242, 246, and Stein chronology in MMA 1993, pp. 256, 263-64, 267-70, 272-78.

CHAPTER VII
A GREAT ACTRESS OF JAPAN

112. Sadayakko (1872-1946) was a popular Tokyo *geisha* before her marriage to actor Kawakami in 1891; despite her lack of both formal training and previous acting experience, she became after 1900 one of the leading actresses of the time. See note nos. 116, 117.

113. Matthew Calbraith Perry (1794-1858), American naval officer, who under Millard Fillmore's administration, was sent in 1852-

53 in command of a squadron to negotiate a treaty with Japan that would open up the isolationist country to commerce. This was achieved in March 1854, when he secured a signed treaty granting the U.S. trading rights at two Japanese ports of call.

114. Ernest Francisco Fenollosa (1853-1908), among the first serious scholars of Asian art and culture in America, played a large part in the revival of the Japanese school of painting and in the movement to preserve ancient shrines, temples and art treasures. Fenollosa, a zealous collector of Japanese decorative arts, was Curator of the Department of Oriental Art, at the Museum of Fine Arts, Boston from 1890-97 and a professor at Columbia University in 1900, having earlier held museum and teaching positions in Tokyo. His first lectures were at the Metropolitan Museum in 1896.

115. Matsuki Bunkio (1867-1912), an art dealer in Boston who ran a gallery on Boylston Street, and after 1898 arranged auctions of Japanese art in Boston, New York and Philadelphia. Popular American writer, Bret Harte (1836-1902).

116. Kawakami Otojiro (1864-1911), Japanese actor, playwright, theatrical entrepreneur and reformer, who founded Shimpa drama, and wrote the first Japanese plays based on Western models. He introduced to Japan productions of Shakespeare, Maeterlinck, and Sardou.

Kawakami, his wife Sadayakko, and a small troupe of actors made three tours of America and Europe between 1899-1903 with a repertoire composed principally of kabuki adaptations. The death of the troupe's two female impersonators in Boston, in the winter of 1899–1900, launched Sadayakko's acting career: she took over all the female leads in the subsequent performances of the first and two later tours of the Kawakami company.

117. Louisine Havemeyer's date of 1889 is erroneous. The performance she attended presumably dates to 1900, the tour corresponding to the date of the Exposition Universelle in Paris of 1900, as opposed to the world's fair of 1889.

CHAPTER VIII
TEA JARS AND POTTERIES

118. On the subject of the Havemeyers' collecting and display of Japanese and Chinese art, including an appraisal of the pieces acquired and the context in which their collection was formed, see the excellent essay by Julia Meech, "The Other Havemeyer Passion: Collecting Asian Art," in MMA 1993, pp. 129-50. Her text has been consulted with great profit in compiling the annotations related to this aspect of their collection.

119. For the anecdote about the library ceiling, see p. 17. None of the Havemeyer tea jars now in the Metropolitan Museum still have their covers or original boxes.

120. Sir William van Horne (1843-1915), Canadian railroad executive, who was founder and head of the Canadian Pacific Railway and also implemented railroads in Cuba.

121. Daijiro Ushikubo, manager of New York branch of the international art firm of Yamanaka and Co., founded by Yamanaka Sadajiro (1866-1936).

122. A quantity of Japanese tea jars were included in the 1929 Havemeyer bequest to the Metropolitan Museum (MMA 29.100.644-667); see Havemeyer 1958, pp. 113-16. Some pieces of Japanese pottery were inherited by her children (see Havemeyer 1931, p. 484) but a far larger group, including a significant number of tea jars, were sold at auction in 1930 (see Havemeyer 1931, p. 524, and *The Estate of Mrs. H.O. Havemeyer, Part III: Japanese and Chinese Art*, American Art Association, Anderson Galleries, New York, April 14-19, 1930). On the subject of Japanese and Chinese tea ceramics, see Barbara Ford's essay on this subject in MMA 1993, pp. 151-53.

123. Reference to the porcelains produced during the Ming dynasty (1368-1644), and the reign of Ch'ing Emperor Ch'ien Lung (1726-95).

124. Kaolin, or China clay, the essential ingredient in hard-paste porcelain, known in China since the 7th or 8th century.

125. Noted Japanese artists, all of whom worked in diverse media: Hon'ami Koetsu (1558-1637), who is best known for his *raku* tea bowls, which were highly esteemed and often imitated; Ogata Shinsei, called Kenzan (1663-1743), one of the most famous Japanese potters, whose style was initially influenced by his elder brother, Korin (1658-1716), a celebrated painter, with whom he sometimes collaborated in decorative pottery; and Ogawa Haritsu, called Ritsuo (1663-1747), the versatile painter and lacquerer, who was perceived by Western collectors as also a potter and sculptor.

126. Representative examples of Oribe and Seto tea ceremony wares (from the province of Owari), Takori (from the province of Chikuzen) and Ohi ware (from the province of Kaga), among others, were included in the 1929 Havemeyer bequest to the Metropolitan Museum; see Havemeyer 1958, pp. 109-116. The bequest also included a square bowl with the imprint of Ninsei (MMA 29.100.668).

127. Nonomura Seibi, called Ninsei, a 17th century potter and pottery decorator, who is regarded as one of the greatest Japanese ceramicists and whose works were extensively copied, often fraudulently.

128. Edward Sylvester Morse (1838-1925), an American zoologist who, while a professor at the Imperial University of Tokyo (1877-80), immersed himself in the study and systematic collecting of Japanese pottery, becoming an authority on the subject. From 1880-1916, Morse was Director of the Peabody Museum, Salem, Mass., and from 1892 until his death, Curator of Japanese ceramics at the Museum of Fine Arts, Boston. He authored the catalogue on the collection he sold to the Museum, *Catalogue of the Morse Collection of Japanese Pottery* (Cambridge, 1901), in which 1545 potters' marks are identified in the text.

129. Thomas E. Kirby (1846-1924), New York art dealer who was the founder and principal auctioneer for the American Art Association from 1885.

130. Charles Lang Freer (1856-1919),

Detroit businessman in the railroad and car industries, patron of Whistler, and celebrated collector of Asian art. His vast collection and funds for the building of a museum in his name, the Freer Gallery of Art, were donated to the Smithsonian Institution, Washington, D.C. Mrs. Havemeyer later wrote a tribute to her friend Charles Freer, describing him as "an intrepid discover, a sagacious collector, and a munificent donor," in "The Freer Museum of Oriental Art, with Personal Recollections of the Donor," in *Scribner's Magazine*, Vol. 73 (May 1923), pp. 529–40.

131. The American Art Association sale of *Eastern Ceramics and other Objects of Art belonging to the Estate of the Late Charles A. Dana*, was held at the American Art Galleries, New York, February 24–26, 1898; Kirby was auctioneer for the 556 lots sold.

132. George Eumorfopoulous (1863–1939), whose collection of Chinese ceramics was featured in an *Exhibition of Early Chinese pottery and porcelains* at the Burlington Fine Arts Club, London in 1910.

133. Her brother-in-law, Samuel Twyfford Peters (1854–1921), a collector of jades and Chinese porcelains; husband of her sister, Adaline.

134. Twenty-one *temmoku* or Chien-An ware tea bowls were included in the 1929 Havemeyer bequest to the Metropolitan Museum (MMA 29.100.220–240). See Havemeyer 1958, pp. 95–97.

135. These two *temmoku* tea bowls—one with a leaf design in golden brown, and the other with plum blossoms outlined in black—are now considered late nineteenth century Japanese copies (MMA 29.100.220 and 29.100.221). See Meech in MMA 1993, pp. 129, 149, fn. 7.

CHAPTER IX
VISIT TO ITALY, 1901

136. The Havemeyers, in the company of Louisine's older sister, Anne Munn, departed for Italy on January 30, 1901 (see p. 85). Cassatt joined them in Genoa in mid-February. The party toured Italy until late March; they were in Spain from late-March through mid-April 1901.

137. "La Bella Librera" by Goya is a reference to the artist's *Young Lady Wearing a Mantilla and a Basquiña* (NGA 1963.4.2 [A 293]), a painting the Havemeyers purchased from Durand-Ruel, Paris, on May 4, 1906 for 90,000 francs. See also, pp. 153f, 158f, 292.

138. The "infanta's godson," is a reference to Joseph Wicht (d. 1902), also called "W." See p. 152f.

139. Louisine Havemeyer consistently refers to their *Majas on a Balcony*, which is now Attributed to Goya (MMA 29.100.10 [A 296]) as the more important or finer of the artist's two versions, an evaluation that is incorrect. On this subject, see Gary Tinterow, "The Havemeyer Pictures," in MMA 1993, pp. 15–17, 52–53, fn 3. See also pp. 138, 144, 153–58.

140. Louisine's mother, Mathilda Adelaide Waldron Elder (1834–1907).

141. The "black Rameses" is a reference to the large black diorite statue of Rameses II, in the Egyptian museum of the Palazzo dell'Accademia della Scienze, Turin.

142. Eventually the Havemeyers acquired two Egyptian statues: a limestone *Face of a Pharaoh* and a basalt *Statuette of Khnumhotep* (MMA 29.100.150 and 29.100.151; see MMA 1993, pls. 102,103).

143. Regarding Henry Irving and Ellen Terry, see note nos. 96, 99.

144. A copy of Titian's *Danäe and Cupid* (Gallerie Nazionali, Capodimonte, Naples) was offered to the Havemeyers by A.E. Harnisch in January 1903, who noted that it was available from a private collection in Florence for 120,000 lire. Correspondence pertaining to this offer and confirming the reason why the copy (possibly Wethey 1975, III, no. 5, under copies no. 12) was rejected by the Havemeyers is preserved in a series of letters on deposit at the Metropolitan Museum (Havemeyer correspondence). See Stein chronology in MMA 1993, p. 233.

145. For the independent art dealer, A.E.

Harnisch, whom Louisine Havemeyer refers to as "H.," see pp. 107-109.

146. The Havemeyers traveled to Greece in March 1906.

147. *La Grande-Grèce, paysages et histoire* (Paris, 1881, 3 vol.) by noted French Assyriologist and numismatist, François Lenormant (1837-1883). The first edition of *By the Ionian Sea, notes of a ramble in southern Italy*, by the English novelist, George Gissing (1857-1903), was published in London in 1901. Cassatt was the source for both books. In a letter to Mrs. Havemeyer of September 6, [1912], she wrote: "I sent you Gissing's "Ionian Sea" & it was reading it that made me get the *Gde Grece* which I sent to you...It is out of print I could not get a copy for Mrs. Sears." (MMA/Havemeyer correspondence). See also pp. 289-90.

148. The "one picture" that the Havemeyers bought from the English dealer Thomas Agnew is unknown. Agnew bid unsuccessfully for H.O. Havemeyer on Gainsborough's *Portrait of Lady Mulgrave* when it was auctioned at the estate sale of *James Price, Esq.*, Christie's, London, June 15, 1895 (lot no. 70); angered by his loss, the collector avoided further dealings with Agnew's firm after that date.

149. *The Rulers of the South; Sicily, Calabria, Malta*, by American novelist, Francis Marion Crawford (1854-1909) was published in New York and London, 1900. See also p. 290.

150. The Boer War, 1899-1902, in South Africa between the British and the Dutch was going on at the time (1901).

151. Of the four pictures once thought to be by Veronese in the Havemeyer collection, only one, *Boy with a Greyhound* (MMA 29.100.105 [A 503]) is authentic. For this picture, see pp. 103 f., 123-28. The others are *Portrait of a Woman*, now considered Style of Veronese (location unknown [A 504]); *Portrait of a Lady*, now Attributed to Fasolo (Art Institute of Chicago, 1946.382 [A 278]), and *Portrait of a Woman*, now considered Montemezzano (MMA 29.100.104 [A 417]). The

latter is discussed pp. 110-113, 293-294.

152. Velázquez's *Pope Innocent X*, in the Galleria Doria-Pamphili, Rome. The portrait of "his Negro slave" is a reference to Velázquez's *Juan de Pareja* (MMA 1971. 86), acquired by the second earl of Radnor, Longford Castle, Salisbury (Wiltshire) by 1811, and included in an 1893 exhibition of old master paintings at the Royal Academy, London, where it was again exhibited in 1904 and 1921.

153. El Greco's *Portrait of a Cardinal* (MMA 29.100.5 [A 304]). See note no. 90.

154. Of the numerous publications and treatises by English art critic, John Ruskin (1819-1900), it is likely that the Havemeyers consulted Ruskin's more popular, and exceedingly less weighty, travel guides—such as his *Traveller's Edition* of The Stones of Venice (1879-81), *St. Marks Rest. The History of Venice. Written for the help of the few travellers who still care for monuments* (1877-84) and *Guide to the Principal Pictures in the Academy at Venice* (1877), the latter directing them to Carpaccio's paintings, including the one noted, *Two Venetian Ladies*, Museo Correr, Venice.

155. The equestrian statue of Colleoni, see note no. 71.

156. The glass-mosaic-faced staircase in the Havemeyers' entrance hall is discussed and illustrated in Frelinghuysen, "The Havemeyer House," in MMA 1993, pp. 177, 180.

157. The Veronese portrait, *Boy with a Greyhound* (MMA 29.100.105 [A 503]) was acquired from the Martinengo family, Brescia, through A. E. Harnisch about 1904. See also pp. 123-28.

158. Under the rule of the Gonzaga family from 1328, Mantua flourished as a brilliant center of art and civilization ("Mantova la Gloriosa"), especially under the reigns of Ludovico II (1444-78) and moreover, Francesco II (1484-1519), husband of the great Renaissance patron, Isabella de Este (d. 1539).

159. A.E. Harnisch (b. 1843) referred to as "H.," a Philadelphian sculptor who exhib-

ited at the Pennsylvania Academy from 1859-69, before establishing himself in Italy, first in Rome, and from at least 1901, in Florence. Harnisch, who became the Havemeyers' art agent in Italy from 1901, continued to bring art works to Mrs. Havemeyer's attention until 1913. Over sixty letters between Harnisch and the Havemeyers are on deposit at the Metropolitan Museum (Havemeyer correspondence); in the last letter, dated September 20, 1913, he notified Mrs. Havemeyer that his wife had died that morning.

160. "La Signora," refers to Donna Rosalia Velluti-Zati, Countess Fossi, Florence, from whom the Havemeyers bought their supposed Veronese *Portrait of a Woman*, now considered Montemezzano (MMA 29.100.104 [A 417]). The picture, formerly thought to represent the artist's wife, was secured for them by A.E. Harnisch in July 1901, but seems not to have shipped until July 1905. As noted on p. 112, the portrait was referred to as "Venice" or "Venetia" in the correspondence between Harnisch, Cassatt and the Havemeyers dating from 1901-05 (MMA/Havemeyer correspondence). See Stein chronology in MMA 1993, p. 231.

161. The Havemeyers had purchased their Bronzino, *Portrait of a Young Man* (MMA 29.100.16 [A 45]), from Durand-Ruel on May 14, 1898, for $40,000.

162. The pictures formerly thought to be by Lippi, Del Sarto and Raphael were all acquired through Harnisch between 1901 and 1903, and are now considered respectively: Follower of Lippi, *Madonna and Child with Two Angels* (MMA 29.100.117 [A 340]); Attributed to Del Sarto, *Madonna and Child with Saint John* (location unknown [A 474]); and Copy after Raphael, *Bindo Altoviti* (location unknown [A 443]). See pages 115, 128f.

163. Both marbles depicting the *Virgin and Child* were included in the 1929 bequest to the Metropolitan: the version acquired through Harnisch from the Bombici collection, Florence, is now considered to be by the Master of the Marble Madonnas

(MMA 29.100.26); the other, by Mino da Fiesole (MMA 29.100.25) was purchased by H.O. Havemeyer, through Paul Durand-Ruel, from the Parisian collector Emile Gavet on July 31, 1895 for 120,000 francs. See also note no. 109.

164. The collection noted is that of the Martelli family, Florence. Mrs. Havemeyer, who again visited the collection in Harnisch's company in 1909, later pursued through him the acquisition of the marble bust of *Young Saint John the Baptist* (NGA, Widener Collection, 1942.9.142, by Rossellino). Her attempts to buy the marble in 1912 proved unsuccessful, and it was acquired four years later by Joseph Widener, along with a statue of *David*, for 1,300,000 lire. See Stein chronology in MMA 1993, p. 259.

165. The present whereabouts of this stucco are unknown. It is presumably one of the pieces of sculpture that were wrongly ascribed to Renaissance masters at the time of Mrs. Havemeyer's 1929 bequest to the Metropolitan Museum and that, as a result, were not accessioned. Among the spurious works named in the first codicil to her will, dated July 24, 1919, were: a "Madonna and Child. By Donatello—Stucco," and a "Bas relief: Madonna (and child) with Angels. By Desiderio da Settignano."

166. None of the letters nor documents cited are preserved in the correspondence on deposit at the Metropolitan Museum (Havemeyer correspondence).

167. The Havemeyers' second visit to Florence was in March 1903. See note no. 162 for the three works, previously noted, by Raphael (A 443), Del Sarto (A 474) and Lippi (A 340).

168. Mrs. Havemeyer's narrative of their expedition to see the Madonna by Lippi (A 340) very closely approximates an account that Harnisch gave of his own journey in a letter written to Mary Cassatt on March 23, 1901 (MMA/Havemeyer correspondence). In his letter Harnisch reported: "We have just come back from a long trip up in the mountains beyond Cortona, a carriage drive of several hours & and a climb

on foot of an hour. I had heard that here existed a very fine Lippi. We travelled as artists with paint box[es]....The farmer finding we were artists showed us an exquisite Madonna let into the wall of a little chapel....On getting back to Florence I looked the matter up and found we had been most fortunate to see the picture as orders had been given to the contrary. The price asked is—115,000 [lire]." The picture seems to have been secured for the Havemeyers by July 1903.

169. For the Veronese portrait (A 503), see note no. 157.

170. French critic and collector, Roger Marx (1859-1913), who held the post of general inspector of French museums.

171. Other works acquired through Harnisch are as follows:

Formerly Sienese school, *Madonna and Child with Saint John*, now considered Pseudo Pier Francesco Fiorentino (location unknown [A 436]) purchased through Harnisch by Louisine Havemeyer in spring 1911 for 15,750 lire.

Formerly Del Sarto, *Madonna and Child with Saint John*, now Attributed to Del Sarto (location unknown [A 474]) a picture that Harnisch secured for the Havemeyers in August 1901 with a down payment of 1,000 lire against the purchase price of 75,000 lire.

The pair of portraits, which in the 1931 Havemeyer catalogue are listed as School of Cologne, 16th century (p. 496), were thought to be by Holbein when the Havemeyers bought the pair for 18,000 lire through Harnisch in the fall 1901. They are now considered Unknown sixteenth century German painter, *Portrait of a Lady* (NGA 1942.16.3 [A 286]) and *Portrait of a Man* (location unknown [A 287]). Also mentioned pp. 292-93.

The Fra Diamanti is possibly *Madonna and Child in a Rose Garden*, now considered unknown fifteenth century Italian painter (location unknown [A 334]).

172. The "Raphael portrait" in the Havemeyer collection (A 443) is considered a Copy after Raphael's portrait of *Bindo Altoviti* in the Kress Collection, National Gallery of Art, Washington, D.C. Both the identification of the sitter as well as the painter, as noted, have been the subject of considerable debate. The picture now in the Kress collection had been in the Alte Pinakothek in Munich since the early nineteenth century, where it was originally listed as a self-portrait by Raphael. When Mrs. Havemeyer saw the picture in Munich in 1914 it was catalogued as "Brustbild Eines Jungen Mannes" by Giulio Romano (no. 1052).

173. The memoirs of French artist, Elisabeth Louise Vigée Le Brun (1755-1842), *Souvenirs de Madame Louise-Elisabeth Vigée le Brun*, were originally published in Paris, 1835/37, 3 vols. An abridged edition of the text in English, published as *Memoirs of Madame Vigée Lebrun* (New York, 1903), includes references to her copies after Raphael, but not to the Florentine portrait specifically. The picture (location unknown) is, however, listed in the appendix—the artist's catalogue of works—as "Copy of portrait of Raphael at Florence" under those "Done at Turin and other places," pp. 9, 22, 81, 223.

CHAPTER X
VISIT TO SPAIN

174. In late March 1901, the Havemeyers deposited Anne Munn at Cassatt's apartment, 10 rue Marignan, and proceeded to Spain. They returned to Paris by mid-April.

175. The "small Greco" is now considered a Copy after El Greco, *Christ Carrying the Cross* (location unknown [A 305]). See pp. 134f, 137f, 179.

176. The Hispano-Moresque plates are described on p. 179.

177. For the El Greco portraits that the Havemeyers would have seen in the Museo del Prado in 1901, see Wethey 1962, II,

nos. 133, 138, 142, 143, 144, 145, 149, X-197.

178. Namely, El Greco's *Purification in the Temple* or *St. Jerome as Cardinal* in the National Gallery, London, and *St. Louis of France* in the Louvre.

179. El Greco's *Portrait of a Cardinal* (A 304). See note no. 90.

180. El Greco's *View of Toledo* (MMA 29.100.6 [A 303]), purchased by Louisine Havemeyer from Durand-Ruel, Paris on April 29, 1909 for 70,000 francs.

181. Mrs. Havemeyer in a letter to A. de Beruete y Moret of August 15, 1915, enclosed a "list of all [her] canvases by Goya." The list included thirteen works, a number of which are no longer considered to be by Goya (A 277, 291-97, 299, 300-02; the seventh work on this list is the *Portrait of a Little Girl*, which her daughter Electra bought in 1909 (private collection). (MMA/Havemeyer correspondence.) Regarding the Havemeyers' collection of Goyas, See Gary Tinterow, "The Havemeyer Pictures," in MMA 1993, pp. 13-17.

182. The frontispiece to Manuel B. Cossío's monograph, *El Greco*, Madrid, 1908, is indeed the Havemeyers' *Portrait of a Cardinal* (A 304).

183. The visit described was to the home of Adelaida Gil y Zárate, Madrid, owner of Goya's portraits of *Antonio Zárate*; the larger, three-quarter length portrait showing her seated and wearing a black mantilla was acquired by an Irishman, Sir Alfred Beit, Blessington; the smaller, bust-length portrait, which Mrs. Havemeyer could have seen with the dealer Gimpel et Wildenstein, Paris, was later acquired by the Comtesse de Flers, Paris. (See Gassier and Wilson 1971, nos. 892 and 893 respectively.)

184. The Havemeyers' El Greco (A 305) is a copy after one of El Greco's compositions of *Christ Carrying the Cross*; it is erroneously suggested as a study for El Greco's *Espolio*, an undisputed masterpiece, in the Cathedral, Sacristy, Toledo.

185. Prior to World War I, the value of French francs, Spanish pesetas and Italian lire were equivalent, at an exchange rate of roughly one-fifth or twenty percent of a dollar. In 1901 a peseta (as well as franc and lira) was worth 19.3 cents.

186. The picture purchased by Electra Havemeyer in the spring 1909, *Saint Peter in Tears* (Oscar B. Cinta Foundation, Havana) is considered "a much repainted and somewhat saccharine replica," given to the School of El Greco (see Wethey 1962, II, no. X-440).

187. "Mr. F." refers to Henry Clay Frick, see note no. 65.

188. On April 24, 1910, Ricardo de Madrazo offered Louisine Havemeyer the opportunity to buy the half-length version of Goya's *La Tirana* (Gassier and Wilson 1971, no. 340) from the Condesa Villagonzalo at an asking price of 200,000 pesetas. (She considered the acquisition but, as Madrazo suspected, the price was too high). He had, however, asked if she were not interested to advise Henry Clay Frick of the picture since he was looking for an important Goya when he was in Madrid in 1909. In June 1910 Madrazo hoped to secure *La Tirana* for Frick for 200,000 pesetas; however, by November, the owner wanted 250,000 pesetas, and by March 1912, she would decide not to sell it for less than 400,000 pesetas, if at all. The picture was still available, for what Madrazo would deem a "fantastic price" in June 1914. (MMA/Havemeyer correspondence)

The full-length portrait of *La Tirana* (Gassier and Wilson 1971, no. 684) in the Real Academia de Bellas Artes de San Fernando, Madrid (since 1819).

189. Frick purchased Velázquez's *King Philip IV of Spain* (The Frick Collection, New York, 11.1.123) in 1911.

190. The Havemeyers acquired Goya's *The Duke of Wellington* (now considered Workshop of Goya, NGA 1963.4.1 [A 302]), through Joseph Wicht and Mary Cassatt in August 1901 for 17,975 francs. Their first Goyas, *Bartolomé Sureda y Miserol* and

Thérèse Louise de Sureda (NGA 1941.10.1 and 1942.3.1, [A 291, A 292]), were purchased from Galerie Durand-Ruel, Paris, on September 28, 1897.

191. This is a reference to the Conde de Pie de Concha, Madrid, former owner of Goya's *Marquesa de Santa Cruz* (Gassier and Wilson 1971, no. 828). Writing to Mrs. Havemeyer on March 22, 1912, Ricardo de Madrazo noted that the Conde de Pie had been offered 700,000 francs for the "portrait of his grandmother recumbent," and "he didn't want to sell!!! you see how soon they will offer *one million* and who knows then!" (MMA/Havemeyer correspondence). This letter discusses the escalation in prices for Spanish school pictures, and makes particular reference to *La Tirana* and "the beautiful Velázquez which Mr. Frick bought." It was no doubt consulted as she was writing pp. 136-37 of her memoirs. Mrs. Havemeyer saw the picture in 1909, see p. 171.

192. In 1914, Frick acquired three pictures by Goya, *Doña María Martínez de Puga*, *An Officer*, and *The Forge*; now in The Frick Collection, New York (14.1.63-.65). He purchased his first El Grecos *St. Jerome* and *Purification of the Temple*, in 1905 and 1909 respectively, and in 1913, *Vincenzo Anastragi*; now in The Frick Collection (05.1.67; 09.1.66; 13.1.68).

193. El Greco (A 305), earlier mentioned pp. 130, 134f.

194. Holy week commenced with Easter Sunday, April 7, 1901.

195. El Greco's *Portrait of a Cardinal* (A 304). See note no. 90.

196. Goya's *Majas on a Balcony* (now Attributed to Goya, MMA 29.100. 10 [A 296]), secured for the Havemeyers by Paul Durand-Ruel from the heirs of the 1st Duke of Marchena, Madrid, on October 9, 1904 and sold to the collectors on November 9, 1904. See pp. 144, 153-58.

197. El Greco's *View of Toledo* (A 303), see note no. 180.

198. The Marquis de la Vega Inclan, while

in New York in mid-January 1913, paid a visit to Louisine Havemeyer; four years earlier, she had purchased from his collection, Goya's *Doña Maria Teresa de Borbón y Vallabriga, condesa de Chinchón (The Princesa de la Paz)*, now Attributed to Goya, SM 27.1.1-153 [A 295]).

199. For El Greco's *Cardinal* (A 304), see note no. 90; for Velázquez's "Pope," see note no. 152.

200. William Schaus, a prominent New York art dealer from whom the Havemeyers purchased their "Gilder," namely, Rembrandt's *Herman Doomer* (A 449); see note no. 37.

201. A reference to her trip to Spain with Electra in 1909.

202. The "other version" of Goya's *Majas on a Balcony* (Gassier and Wilson 1971, no. 959), formerly owned by the duc de Montpensier, Seville, was sold by Durand-Ruel to the Rothschilds by 1911. The Havemeyers acquired their *Majas* (A 296) in 1904 (see note nos. 139, 196).

203. The "Infanta's godson" is a reference to Joseph Wicht (d. 1902); also referred to as "W."

204. El Greco's *Portrait of a Cardinal* (A 304), see note no. 90.

205. El Greco's *View of Toledo* (A 303), see note no. 180.

206. Goya's *Majas on a Balcony* (A 296), see note no. 196.

207. El Greco's *Assumption of the Virgin*, formerly high altar, Santo Domingo el Antiguo, Toledo, was at the time in the collection of the 1st Duke of Marchena, Madrid; it was purchased from the duke's heirs by Paul Durand-Ruel in late October 1904, and acquired by the Art Institute of Chicago in 1906, with funds provided by Nancy Atwood Sprague in memory of [her husband] Albert Arnold Sprague (Art Institute of Chicago, 1906.99). See pp. 154-56.

208. Goya's *The Duke of Wellington* (A 302); see note no. 190.

209. Goya's "La Bella Librera" (A 293),

see note no. 137, and p. 158f.

210. More than a dozen portraits by Goya were formerly in the collection of the Palace of Boadilla del Monte, including Goya's *Family of the Infante Don Luis* (Gassier and Wilson 1971, no. 208) and two full-length portraits of the *Condesa de Chinchón*, one as a little girl standing, and another, seated where her coiffure is adorned by sprigs of wheat—a symbol of fertility—possibly the "feathers" described by Mrs. Havemeyer— (Gassier and Wilson 1971, nos. 210, 793 respectively). The large Borbón family portrait was taken to Italy in 1904 when the Infante's last granddaughter married Prince Ruspoli; the Havemeyers could have seen it in the Ruspoli palace, Florence when they visited Italy in 1907. Since copies are known to have existed of Goya's Chinchón portraits one cannot be certain as to the portrait they were later offered but declined.

211. Paul Durand-Ruel made several trips to Madrid, beginning in February 1903, to negotiate Spanish pictures of interest to the Havemeyers. By the summer of 1904, when H.O. Havemeyer offered to advance the dealer 100,000 francs toward his acquisition of El Greco's *Assumption*—the collectors had already determined that the size of the altarpiece, measuring thirteen feet in height, was "an insurmountable obstacle" for them. On this subject, see Weitzenhoffer 1986, pp. 156-57, and Stein chronology in MMA 1993, pp. 233, 238.

212. El Greco's *Adoration of the Shepherds* was acquired by the Metropolitan Museum in 1905 (MMA 05.42).

213. On the subject of El Greco's *Fray Félix Hortensio Paravicino* (Museum of Fine Arts, Boston, 04.234) which was offered to the Havemeyers in December 1903 and acquired in early 1904 by Edward Robinson for the Museum of Fine Arts, Boston, see Stein chronology in MMA 1993, pp. 236-37.

214. Ricardo de Madrazo y Garreta (1852-1917), Spanish genre painter and art agent, who both as Durand-Ruel's representative in Madrid and as an independent dealer, arranged for the sale to the Havemeyers of

a number of pictures by Goya. Over sixty letters between Mrs. Havemeyer and Madrazo, dating from 1909-17 are on deposit at the Metropolitan Museum (Havemeyer correspondence).

On the subject of the protracted negotiations for these pictures, see Weitzenhoffer 1986, pp. 153-56, and Stein chronology in MMA 1993, entries 1903-04, pp. 233-38.

215. The *Majas on a Balcony* (A 296), after relining, was delivered to Galerie Durand-Ruel, Paris on December 23, 1904 and shipped to the Havemeyers six days later. El Greco's *Cardinal* (A 304) arrived at the gallery on May 30, 1904 and was shipped to the Havemeyers in October; the owner had insisted, as a condition of sale, that the painting had to be copied prior to its release. For Marx's comments, see also p. 292.

216. The Havemeyers must have seen a copy of the original painting, since by 1901, Goya's *Lady Wearing a Mantilla and a Basquiña* (A 293) had been for some time in Paris, having been sold by Benito Garriga, Madrid, in 1890. See note no. 137.

217. Raimundo de Madrazo y Garreta (1841-1920), Spanish portrait and genre painter of the family of artists that included court painters, José and Federigo, his grandfather and father, as well as his less-talented brother, Ricardo.

218. The so-called Velázquez is now considered Unknown seventeenth-century Spanish (Castilian) painter, *Head of a Man* (MMA 29.100.607 [A 481]). Mary Cassatt's high estimation of this work in Velázquez's oeuvre is recorded in a letter to Mrs. Havemeyer of January 26, 1903 in which she noted the very same qualities: "the head you have, so simple so full of style the wonderful painting of the mouth the way the eyes are 'enchasse'." (MMA/Havemeyer correspondence)

219. Aureliano de Beruete y Moret, art historian and director of the Prado, died on June 10, 1921.

220. In 1905 the Prado received a pair of full-length portraits by Velázquez that were formerly in the collection of the Duchess of Villahermosa, *Don Diego del*

Corral y Arellano and *Doña Antonia de Ipeñarrieta y Galdós, with one of her sons* (Museo del Prado, Madrid, nos. 1195, 1196).

For the two Velázquez portraits that Louisine and Electra Havemeyer saw at the Duchess of Villahermosa's villa in 1909, see López-Rey 1963, nos. 236 and 506. Benjamin Altman's acquisition of both portraits in 1912 generated great, albeit undesirable, publicity in the newspapers that April. One of the portraits, *Conde Duque de Olivares* (Museu de Arte, São Paulo), he returned to Duveen, and it was resold through Agnew's in 1919 to Lord Cowdray, London; the other, now considered Workshop of Velázquez, *Philip IV (1605-1665), King of Spain*, was bequeathed by Altman to the Metropolitan Museum in 1913 (MMA 14.30.639).

The receipt for the two portraits, signed by Velázquez and dated December 4, 1624 is preserved in the autograph letter collection, Watson Library, MMA.

221. Formerly Patinir, now considered Unknown early sixteenth-century Flemish painter, *The Rest on the Flight into Egypt* (MMA 29.100.599 [A 279]).

222. Regarding the exchange rate for pesetas in 1901, see note no. 185.

223. Goya's *Duchess of Alba* (Hispanic Society of America, New York, Gassier and Wilson 1971, no. 355), an indisputable masterpiece, unlike the portrait purchased by the Havemeyers from Durand-Ruel in 1906, now considered Agustin Esteve, *Portrait of a Lady with a Guitar* (The John and Mable Ringling Museum of Art, Sarasota, Florida [A 277]). See also p. 177.

224. Formerly Goya, now considered Copy after Goya, *Maria Luisa of Parma (1751-1819), Queen of Spain* (MMA 29.100.11 [A 299]).

225. Théodore Duret (1838-1927), French politician, journalist, art critic and collector, who was among the earliest defenders of Manet and the Impressionists and later, devoted himself to promoting modern French painting—both through his

publications and as an independent art dealer in Paris. Over thirty letters between Théodore Duret and Mrs. Havemeyer, dating from 1911-1922 are on deposit at the Metropolitan Museum (Havemeyer correspondence).

226. Regarding Mr. and Mrs. Dean Sage, see note no. 2.

227. Henriette Lucie (Dillon) La Tour du Pin Gouvernet, *Journal d'une femme de cinquante ans, 1778-1815*, Paris, 1907 (abbreviated version, 2 vol., Paris, 1913). Mrs. Havemeyer purchased the book while she was in France in 1914, but Cassatt who "was not very fond of memoirs, & took no interest in it" did not read it until six years later, when she borrowed it from a friend. In a letter to Mrs. Havemeyer of March 28, 1920, she noted the previous night's reading, about "the Empress Josephine's lending the Queen a yellow satin dress...and remembered the circumstances & your thinking that the portrait of the Queen by Goya which you have she might have been wearing that dress!" (MMA/Havemeyer correspondence)

228. Stephen Van Rensselaer (1764-1839), American army officer and politician, inherited the great Van Rensselaer estate in New York in 1769.

229. Louisine and Electra were in Spain from late March-April 1909, and at Cassatt's behest they went to see El Greco's *Saint Ildefonso* (Wethey 1962, no. 23) in Illescas. Mrs. Havemeyer did try to acquire this painting through Madrazo, but it proved impossible at the time. See Stein chronology in MMA 1993, p. 250.

230. On the subject of the two pictures by El Greco from the Capilla de San José in Toledo, *Madonna and Child with St. Agnes and St. Martin* and *St. Martin and the Beggar* (NGA, Widener Collection), see Stein chronology in MMA 1993, pp. 244, 248.

231. Regarding the Chinchón portrait formerly in the Boadilla Palace see p. 154; for the Havemeyer portrait see pp. 173-74.

232. Goya's *Marquesa de la Solana* (Gassier and Wilson 1971, no. 341, Musée du Lou-

vre, Paris), then in the collection of the Marqués de Socorro, was purchased for 600,000 francs by the Parisian collector Carlos de Beistegui in January 1913. Mrs. Havemeyer probably saw it in Paris in the spring 1914.

233. In the spring 1904, H.O. Havemeyer was interested in acquiring Goya's *Marquesa de Pontejos* (Gassier and Wilson 1971, no. 221, NGA) and had sent Paul Durand-Ruel to Madrid to negotiate the purchase with its owner, the Marquesa de Martorell.

234. Goya's *Condesa de Haro* (Gassier and Wilson 1971, no. 805, private collection, Switzerland), formerly the Marquis de Santa Cruz, Madrid.

235. For Goya's portraits of the Condesa and Conde de Fernán Nuñez, see Gassier and Wilson 1971, nos. 807, 808.

236. Regarding Goya's *Marquesa de Santa Cruz*, see note no. 191.

237. Formerly Goya, now Attributed to Goya, *Portrait of a Little Girl* (private collection), purchased by Electra Havemeyer through Ricardo de Madrazo on April 20, 1909 for 70,000 pesetas. See MMA 1993, fig. 84.

238. Formerly Goya, now Attributed to Goya, *Portrait of a Boy, Manuel Cantin y Lucientes* (private collection [A 297]), purchased by Mrs. Havemeyer from the collection of Don Francisco Cantin Gamboa, Zaragoza, through Ricardo de Madrazo in June 1910 for 27,500 pesetas.

239. Formerly Goya, now Attributed to Goya, *Doña Maria Teresa de Borbón y Vallabriga, condesa de Chinchón (The Princess de la Paz)* (SM 27.1.1-153 [A 295]), purchased by Mrs. Havemeyer from the collection of the Marquis de la Vega Inclan, through Ricardo de Madrazo, in April 1909. Regarding the owner, see p. 141.

240. Roland F. Knoedler (1856-1932), American art dealer, who during the 1880s succeeded his father, Michel Knoedler, as director of the M. Knoedler galleries, an international firm, with branches in London, Paris, and New York.

Between 1877-87, H.O. Havemeyer purchased a number of works from M. Knoedler and Co., New York, but after this date, the collectors bought the vast majority of their pictures through Durand-Ruel.

241. Ricardo de Madrazo noted in a letter to Mrs. Havemeyer on April 22, 1910: "Mr. H.C. Frick saw the portrait of the Princess de la Paz, which you bought from the Marquis de la Vega, he liked it, very much, it seems." (MMA/Havemeyer correspondence) While in Madrid in 1909, Frick had been looking for an important work by Goya; he acquired three works by the artist in 1914 (see note no. 192).

242. The exhibition, *Paintings by El Greco and Goya*, a small benefit exhibition in support of woman suffrage was held at M. Knoedler and Co., New York from April 2-20, 1912. Except for two paintings lent by Electra, all the works were drawn from Louisine Havemeyer's collection. She was involved in the design of the poster and in the hanging of the show. The works noted are: El Greco's *Cardinal* (A 304), the supposed "Duchess of Alba" (A 277), the "Countess of Goicoechea" (A 294), and "the princess" (A 295); they were shown as nos. 1, 6, 11, and 8 respectively.

243. Goya's *Doña Narcisa Barañana de Goicoechea* (MMA 29.100.180, [A 294]) purchased from Don Felipe Modet, Madrid by Paul Durand-Ruel on April 4, 1903, and sold to the Havemeyers on April 30, 1903.

244. Louisine Havemeyer, between December 1909 and February 1910, arranged for the sale to Payne of Goya's portraits of *Don Ignacio Garcini y Queralt, Brigadier of Engineers* and *Doña Josefa Castilla Portugal de Garcini* (MMA 55.145.1-.2). Ricardo de Madrazo, who had first offered the pair of portraits to Mrs. Havemeyer, secured them from Vincente Garcini, a descendant of the sitters, and sold them to Payne for 165,000 francs.

CHAPTER XI
COURBET

Gustave Courbet (1819-1877)

245. Namely, Velázquez's *Las Hilanderas* in the Prado (see note no. 7), Rembrandt's *The Night Watch* in the Rijksmuseum, Amsterdam, and Courbet's *L'Enterrement à Ornans* and *Le Combat de Cerfs*, acquired by the Louvre in 1881, now, Musée d'Orsay, Paris (R.F. 325, 326). For the Courbets, see Fernier 1977-78, nos. 91, 279.

246. Courbet's *L'Homme Blessé*, acquired by the Louvre in 1881, now, Musée d'Orsay, Paris (R.F. 338).

247. Regarding Courbet's imprisonment, exile and death, see note no. 14.

248. Regarding Théodore Duret, through whom the Havemeyers acquired over a dozen pictures by Courbet, including some fakes, see note no. 225.

249. Louis Adolphe Thiers (1797-1877), French journalist and historian who later became one of the leading statesmen of France; his enthusiastic review of Delacroix's first Salon entry, *The Bark of Dante* in 1822, launched the young artist's career.

250. Courbet's *Le Retour de la Conférence* (location unknown; Fernier 1977-78, no. 338).

251. Courbet's *L'Atelier* (Fernier 1977-78, no. 165) was offered for sale twice during the Havemeyers' marriage (1883-1907): in 1897, when it was acquired by Victor Desfossés at the Haro sale (April 2, 1897, lot no. 108), and in 1899, when it was bought back by his widow, Mme Desfossés, at the posthumous sale of her husband's collection (April 26, 1899, lot no. 20). It was used as a backdrop in the amateur theater at the Desfossés home, 6 rue Galilée, Paris, and in 1919, was sold by her to the dealer Barbazanges. It entered the Louvre, February 13, 1920 (Musée d'Orsay, Paris, R.F. 2257). For an in-depth discussion of this picture, including its contemporary, historical and allegorical references, see Hélène Toussaint, "The dossier on 'The Studio' by

Courbet," in *Gustave Courbet, 1819-1877*, Arts Council of Great Britain, 1978.

252. Velázquez's *The Surrender of Breda* in the Prado (since 1819).

253. The nude described is Courbet's *Woman with a Parrot* (MMA 29.100.57 [A 145]) purchased by the Havemeyers from Durand-Ruel, New York, on April 30, 1898 for $12,000. See pp. 195-97.

254. The "charming picture of a nude" is Courbet's *The Source* (MMA 29.100.58 [A 135]) purchased by Louisine Havemeyer from Durand-Ruel, New York, on March 11, 1916 for 50,000 francs. See also p. 191.

255. Courbet seascapes in the Havemeyer collection in order of mention: *The Wave* (The Brooklyn Museum, New York, 41.1256 [A 150]), purchased for Mrs. Havemeyer from the Dollfus sale, Galerie Georges Petit, Paris, March 2, 1912 (lot no. 24) for 16,000 francs; *Marine: The Waterspout* (MMA 29.160.35 [A 152]) acquired by Mrs. Havemeyer through Duret in December 1912 for 16,000 francs; *The Calm Sea* (MMA 29.100.566 [A 151]) acquired by Mrs. Havemeyer through Duret in the fall 1911.

256. Writing to Mrs. Havemeyer on January 9, 1913, Théodore Duret compared Courbet's *Marine: The Waterspout*, which she had just bought through him, to this seascape in the Louvre (Musée d'Orsay, R.F. 747, Fernier 1977-78, no. 747); he noted "*La mer orageuse* in the Louvre and the one in the National Gallery of Berlin which is thought to be first, approach in vigor your painting, but are less dramatic." (MMA/Havemeyer correspondence)

257. Regarding Courbet and Whistler, see note no. 260.

258. Both seascapes were acquired at the end of 1911, but not on the same day. Courbet's *The Lone Rock* (The Brooklyn Museum, New York, 41.1258 [A 136]) was purchased by Mrs. Havemeyer in November 1911, through Duret, who felt that it would "make an excellent pendant to the marine [*The Calm Sea* (A 151)] [she] recently received." (Théodore Duret to

Louisine Havemeyer, November 16, 1911, MMA/Havemeyer correspondence)

259. Subjects represented in the Havemeyer collection by: Courbet's *The Source of the Loue* (MMA 29.100.122 [A 140]), purchased by the Havemeyers from Durand-Ruel on August 21, 1889 for 15,000 francs, and *La Point de Vallières* (location unknown [A 160]) bought by Mrs. Havemeyer through Duret in February 1916 for 15,000 francs.

260. In the fall 1865, Whistler joined Joanna Heffernan and Courbet at Trouville; Whistler painted several seascapes (see Young et al. 1980, nos. 64–70) and Courbet his *Portrait of Jo (La Belle Irlandaise)* (MMA 29.100.63 [A 147]). The Courbet was purchased by the Havemeyers from Durand-Ruel, New York, on December 31, 1898 for $2,800.

Joanna Heffernan, a red-haired Irish woman who was Whistler's mistress and principal model in the early 1860s and subsequently, Courbet's mistress (according to Riat their liaison lasted five years and a son was born).

261. Courbet's *Madame de Brayer* (MMA 29.100.118 [A 129]), was acquired by the Havemeyers through Duret in late April 1907 and shipped to them by Durand-Ruel (as "Portrait de femme") on May 11. Until 1907, the portrait had remained in the family of the sitter in Brussels.

262. Formerly considered a portrait of Louise Colet, now called *Woman in a Riding Habit* (MMA 29.100.59 [A 127]), purchased by the Havemeyers from Duret in the spring 1906 for 15,000 francs. See pp. 201–203.

263. Whistler's *Arrangement in Flesh Colour and Black: Portrait of Théodore Duret*, was acquired from Duret (who had posed for the portrait in 1883) by the Metropolitan Museum in 1913 (MMA 13.20).

264. In 1874 Louisine Elder—then nearly nineteen years old—stayed at the fashionable boarding house of Mme del Sarte, 88 boulevard de Courcelles, Paris; the "lady" she met that June was Mary Cassatt.

265. The exhibition opened on June 4, 1881. The Havemeyers' painting, *Torso of a Woman*, formerly called, "Nude—La Branche de Cerisier" (MMA 29.100.60 [A 137]) was not included in this show. No doubt when Mrs. Havemeyer consulted Ph. Burty's introduction to *Catalogue de Trente-Trois Tableaux et études par Gustave Courbet et dépendant de sa succession* (Paris, 1881) and noted among the works listed, one titled, *Branche de cerisier anglais* (no. 19), she assumed this was her picture and that she must therefore have seen it as a young woman. For the picture exhibited in 1881, a still-life, see Fernier 1977-78, no. 368.

266. Courbet's *Torso of a Woman* (A 137) was purchased by the Havemeyers from Durand-Ruel, New York, on October 19, 1892 for $1,800. It was their first nude by the artist, but the fourth Courbet acquired. See also pp. 192, 196.

267. Courbet's *Landscape with Deer* was acquired by the Louvre from the *Collection de M.E. Secrétan*, Galerie Charles Sedelmeyer, Paris, July 1-7, 1889, lot no. 6, for 76,000 francs (Musée d'Orsay, Paris, R.F. 583).

268. Pieter de Hooch's *The Visit* (MMA 29.100.7 [A 326]), was one of a dozen pictures purchased by the Havemeyers from the Secrétan sale (lot no. 128, for 276,000 francs). For the other works, see Stein chronology in MMA 1993, pp. 208-09.

269. The Havemeyers purchased their first Courbet: *Landscape with Cattle* (location unknown [A 130]) from Durand-Ruel, Paris, on August 17, 1889 for 20,000 francs.

270. Regarding the history of ownership of Courbet's *The Stonebreakers*, see note no. 11. The Havemeyers, who visited the *Centennale de l'Art Français (1789-1889)* at the Paris World's Fair of 1889—as opposed to 1900—would have seen the definitive version of *The Stonebreakers* (Fernier 1977-78, no. 101); it was lent to this exhibition by M. Binant, no. 201. Mrs. Havemeyer saw the picture at the Gemäldegalerie zu Dresden in the spring 1914.

271. Courbet's *The Knife Grinders* (Columbus Museum of Art, Columbus, Ohio, 54.5 [A 123]) was purchased by Mrs. Havemeyer in the summer 1916 for 20,000 francs through Théodore Duret, who felt it would add a "new note" to her collection. (Théodore Duret to Mrs. Havemeyer, May 19, 1916, MMA/Havemeyer correspondence)

272. The chronology on the first acquisitions is askew:

"Les Chiens de Chasse," Courbet's *Hunting Dogs* (MMA 33.77 [A 128]) was purchased by the Havemeyers from Durand-Ruel in the summer 1892, three years after they purchased their second work by the artist, *The Source of the Loue* (A 140, see note no. 259). "Le Puits Noir," Courbet's *The Stream* (NGA 1943.15.2 [A 126]) was purchased from Durand-Ruel on October 19, 1897 for 66,950 francs.

Comparisons are made to Courbet's *La Curée* (Museum of Fine Arts, Boston, since 1918) and *Le ruisseau du Puits Noir*, formerly in the Louvre (now, Musée d'Orsay, Paris, R.F. 275). (Fernier 1977-78, nos. 188, 462)

273. The "two large hunting scenes," namely, *La Curée* in Boston, and Courbet's *After the Hunt* (MMA 29.100.61 [A 131]), a later acquisition, which seems to have been purchased by Mrs. Havemeyer from Cottier and Co., New York, around September 1910.

274. Mrs. Havemeyer continued to buy both genuine and spurious Courbets after 1917, the date of this chapter. At present, the Havemeyers are known to have owned a total of forty-three paintings by Courbet, and a handful of fakes (see A 123-167).

Mary Cassatt played a seminal role in shaping the Havemeyer collection, as acknowledged in Mrs. Havemeyer's chapter XV, and documented, in some detail, in Weitzenhoffer 1986 and in MMA 1993.

275. In order of mention, the "minor Courbets" include the following: snow scenes, *The Deer* (MMA 29.160.34 [A 144]), *Hunter in the Snow* (private collec-

tion, Japan [A 155]), *Hunter on Horseback* (Yale University Art Gallery, New Haven, Ct., 1942.301 [A 138]); two seascapes already mentioned, *The Wave* (A 150) and *Marine: The Waterspout* (A 152); *The Russet Wood* (Richard Shelton, San Francisco [A 161]); *Woman with a Cat* (Worcester Art Museum, Worcester, Mass., 1940.300 [A 142]). The still lifes include, *Spring Flowers* (now considered Copy after Courbet, MMA 29.100.121 [A 164]) and *Hydrangeas* (location unknown [A 159]), two of *Apples* (one, private collection [A 156]; the other, now considered Style of Courbet (MMA 29.100.123 [A 165]), and *Fruit and Vegetables* (location unknown, [A 158]).

276. On the subject of "Les Pivoines," see Stein chronology in MMA 1993, p. 252. The picture, which Mrs. Havemeyer "lost" in 1909, is either the still life in the Kunsthalle Hamburg or the one in the Kunsthalle Bremen; see Fernier 1977-78, no. 182 and 361, respectively.

277. Mrs. Havemeyer, who had lost Courbet's *Still Life—Fruit* (SM 27.1.3-23 [A 154]) to Paul Rosenberg at an auction in December 1912 and had declined to buy it after the sale at a premium above the 28,300 franc purchase price, managed to "salvage" the picture eight years later, when in February 1921, she bought it from Rosenberg for 205,000 francs. On this subject, see Stein chronology in MMA 1993, pp. 261, 278.

278. Courbet's *The Source* (A 135) and *Woman with a Parrot* (A 145), see note nos. 254, 253.

279. Courbet's *Torso of a Woman* (A 137) and *Woman with a Parrot* (A 145), see note nos. 266, 253.

280. Courbet's *Woman in the Waves* (MMA 29.100.62 [A 148]), the Havemeyers' second Courbet nude, was purchased from Durand-Ruel on January 30, 1893 for $5,000.

281. Courbet's *Woman with a Dog* (Musée d'Orsay, Paris, R.F. 1979-56 [A 149]), possibly the nude offered to Mrs. Havemeyer by Duret in September 1911.

282. For Mrs. Havemeyer's interest in *La Source*, the magnificent nude acquired by the Louvre in 1919 (Musée d'Orsay, Paris, R.F. 2240), see Stein chronology in MMA 1993, p. 269. For the picture she purchased in 1916, *The Source* (A 135) see note no. 254.

283. Courbet's *Les Cribleuses de Blé* (Musée des Beaux-Arts, Nantes, since 1861); *Young Ladies from the Village*, formerly owned by Oliver Payne (MMA 40.175); and two other masterpieces earlier cited (see note no. 245).

284. For the portraits named, see Fernier 1977-78, nos. 93, 39, 51 and 74, respectively.

285. Courbet's *Alphonse Promayet (1822-1872)*, purchased by Mrs. Havemeyer from Paul Rosenberg, Paris, in May 1914 and *Monsieur Suisse*, an acquisition that may be dated to about 1895-96 (MMA 29.100.132 [A124] and MMA 29.100.120 [A 132]).

286. *Mme Auguste Cuoq (Mathilde Desportes, 1828-1910)* (MMA 29.100.130 [A 133]), acquired by Mrs. Havemeyer from the sale of the collection of *Mme de V*. [Madame de Vermuelen de Villiers], Galerie Georges Petit, Paris, May 6, 1909, lot no. 38, for 50,000 francs.

287. Though the Havemeyers saw and purchased Courbet's *Woman with a Riding Habit* (A 127) in the spring 1906 (see note no. 262), it was not shipped until a later date, possibly not until 1916.

288. Louisine's sister-in-law, Emilie de Loosey Havemeyer (1840-1914), wife of Harry's brother, Theodore (1839-97).

CHAPTER XII
WHISTLER

289. James McNeill Whistler (1834-1903), was in fact, born in Lowell, Massachusetts, and, except for a short period (1842-49) when his father's job as railroad engineer occasioned a move to St. Petersburg, Russia, spent his youth in New England, where he attended school in Connecticut (1849-51), at West Point (1851-54) and worked for the Coast Survey in Washington, D.C. (1854-

55). He lived in Paris for three years (1855-58), before his move to London in 1859.

290. H.O. Havemeyer purchased Whistler's *First Venice Set* (NGA), from H. Wunderlich and Co., New York, shortly after March 1889, when he bought from the same gallery three watercolors, *Grey and Green, Grey and Silver, Marine* (private collections [A 513, 514, 515]) and one pastel, *The Greek Slave Girl* (SM 27.3.1-40 [A 512]) shown in the exhibition, "Notes—Harmonies—Nocturnes." In addition to the five pastels that Louisine Elder bought as a young woman (see pp. 208f), the Havemeyers owned two other works by Whistler, a watercolor *Winter Landscape* (private collection [A 521]) and a pastel, *White and Pink (The Palace)* (private collection [A 518]).

291. By the time Louisine Elder met Whistler in the summer of 1881, she already owned three Impressionist works (see also pp. 206f, 249-51). Her first acquisition was Degas's *Ballet Rehearsal* (The Nelson-Atkins Museum of Art, Kansas City, F 73-30 [A 215]), purchased for 500 francs probably from Julien Tanguy, Paris in 1877; her purchase of Monet's *The Drawbridge* (SM 27.1.2-109 [A 395]), may also date to 1877; it was probably in 1879 that she bought Pissarro's *The Cabbage Gatherers* (private collection [A 427]).

292. Whistler's *Portrait of Cicely Alexander* (Tate Gallery, London) was the only work by the artist shown in the *V. Summer Exhibition* at the Grosvenor, Gallery, London, from May 2-July 31, 1881, hence it is not surprising that she did not recall other "portraits or 'Nocturnes'" on view.

293. Actually, they visited Whistler's Tite Street Studio, which the artist had leased on March 22, 1881, but had not moved into until two months later. His recent occupancy of the studio would explain the lack of furnishings noted.

294. The Peacock Room or *Harmony in Blue and Gold* (Freer Gallery of Art, Smithsonian Institution, Washington, D.C.) was the dining room Whistler decorated for his patron, Frederick R. Leyland, in 1876-77.

295. Regarding the Degas, Monet and Pissarro, see note no. 291, and pp. 249–51.

296. Charles L. Freer, who met Whistler in March 1890, would become one of his principal American patrons. Regarding Freer, see note no. 130.

297. Harry Quilter, English art critic (1851–1907), bought Whistler's White House in 1879 after the artist's property was seized by his creditors. Quilter died four years after Whistler.

298. The five pastels: *Campo S. Marta: Winter Evening, Nocturne: San Giorgio, The Steps, Sunset in Red and Brown,* and *Winter Evening* (Freer Gallery of Art, Smithsonian Institution, Washington, D.C., 17.4–8 [A 511, 516, 517, 519, 520])—formed part of the unsold surplus from the artist's exhibition of 53 Venice pastels which opened at the Fine Art Society, London, on January 29, 1881. Mrs. Havemeyer gave the pastels to Freer in January 1917 for his intended museum; they were accessioned by the Freer Gallery of Art in 1919.

299. Oscar Wilde (1854–1900), Irish dramatist, poet, essayist, novelist, and wit, who published his first volume of poetry, *Patience,* in 1881 and the next year began his lecture tour of the United States, of which he would boast to Whistler "I have already civilized America."

300. By 1873 Maud Franklin succeeded Jo as Whistler's mistress and principal model, posing for several portraits in 1876. He abruptly abandoned her, when in August 1888 he married Beatrice Godwin, widow of E.D. Godwin (d. 1886) the architect with whom Whistler had collaborated on the decor of the White House. She died of cancer in 1896, after several years of illness.

301. In July 1902 while on holiday with Freer, Whistler became seriously ill; he stayed at the Hôtel des Indes, The Hague, during his convalescence.

302. Whistler died July 17, 1903 and was buried on July 23 at Chiswick Cemetery. Freer and Duret were among the six pallbearers.

303. Joanna Heffernan first posed for Whistler in 1860; they parted on friendly terms in 1866. Previously mentioned in the context of Courbet's *Portrait of Jo (La Belle Irlandaise)* (MMA 29.100.63 [A 147]). See p. 187 and note no. 260.

304. Whistler's *Arrangement in Brown and Black: Portrait of Miss Rosa Corder,* acquired by Henry Clay Frick in 1914 (The Frick Collection, New York, 14.1.134).

305. After the death of his wife in 1896, Whistler adopted his sister-in-law, Rosalind Birnie Philip, as his ward and made her his executrix.

CHAPTER XIII
MANET

Edouard Manet (1832–1883)

306. Henri Fantin-Latour's 1867 portrait of *Edouard Manet* (Art Institute of Chicago, 05.207, since 1905), also mentioned, p. 220.

307. Manet's famous, albeit then infamous, *Le déjeuner sur l'herbe* exhibited in the Salon des Refusés in 1863 (Musée d'Orsay, Paris, R.F. 1668).

308. The reference is to Titian's *Concert champêtre,* formerly attributed to Giorgione, in the Louvre, which according to Antonin Proust (1897) was the source of inspiration for Manet's *Le déjeuner*—"a modern Giorgione."

309. Manet's *Olympia,* formerly Louvre (Musée d'Orsay, Paris, R.F. 644), see note no. 344.

310. Cassatt and her family spent the summer 1880 at Marly-le-Roy. However, the following summer they rented a house, "Couer Volant," in Louveciennes, not far from the house Berthe Morisot and her family had taken for the summer at 4, rue de La Princesse, in Bougival, near Versailles, where Manet, his health failing, was spending his vacation at 20, avenue de Villeneuve-l'Etang. The visit presumably dates to 1881.

311. The Impressionist artist and Manet's sister-in-law, Berthe Morisot (1841–1896); she married Eugène

Manet, Edouard's brother, in 1874.

312. In the Salon of 1881, Manet exhibited *Portrait of M. Henri Rochefort* (Kunsthalle Hamburg) and *Portrait of M. Pertuiset, the Lion Hunter* (Museu de Arte, São Paulo); shown as nos. 1516, 1517 respectively.

313. Manet's *Ball at the Opera* (NGA 1982.75.1 [A 357]), was purchased by the Havemeyers from Durand-Ruel on January 16, 1894 for $8,000. Five years later, in January 1899, Parisian collector Comte Isaac de Camondo (1851-1911) bought Degas's *The Pedicure* (Musée d'Orsay, Paris, R.F. 1986), a transaction that caused considerable friction between the Havemeyers, who wanted the work, and the dealer, Paul Durand-Ruel, who sold it to him. On this subject, see Weitzenhoffer 1986, pp. 133-34. *The Pedicure* entered the Musée du Louvre in 1908 with the splendid Camondo bequest, which was finalized in 1911 and exhibited in 1914.

314. The Fantin-Latour portrait previously mentioned, see note no. 306.

315. Manet's still life, namely *The Salmon* (SM 27.1.3-24 [A 350]) was purchased by H.O. Havemeyer in the spring 1886 for 15,000 francs from the exhibition organized by Durand-Ruel, *Works in Oil and Pastel by the Impressionists of Paris*, which was held in New York at the American Art Galleries (from April 10) and at the National Academy of Design (from May 25). Manet's *Boy with a Sword* was lent to the exhibition by Erwin Davis, who gave it to the Metropolitan Museum three years later (MMA 89.21.2).

316. Manet's *Gare Saint-Lazare* (NGA 1956. 10.1 [A 356]), purchased by the Havemeyers from Durand-Ruel, New York, on December 31, 1898 for $15,000. See pp. 237-40. Manet's *The Dead Christ, with Angels* (MMA 29.100.51 [A 346]) purchased by the Havemeyers from Durand-Ruel, New York, on February 7, 1903 for $17,000. See pp. 236-37.

317. Namely, Manet's *Family at Home in Arcachon* (Sterling and Francine Clark Art

Institute, Williamstown, Mass., no. 552 [A 352]).

318. Manet's *In the Garden* (SM 27.1.1-200 [A 351]) acquired by the Havemeyers from the sale of the Gustave Goupy collection, *Collection de M.G.G...*, Hôtel Drouot, Paris, March 30, 1898, lot no. 21, for 22,000 francs.

319. Manet's *Roses in a Crystal Vase* (private collection, Japan [A 366]).

320. Mrs. Havemeyer confused *The Kearsarge at Boulogne*, formerly called "L'Alabama au large de Cherbourg," (private collection [A 347]) which they acquired from the Goupy sale on March 30, 1898, lot no. 20, for 4,000 francs with the seascape purchased in Cassatt's company: namely, *The Port of Calais* (private collection [A 353]), bought from Durand-Ruel, New York, on January 20, 1898 for $3,500. The latter picture had been in the collection of Harris Whittemore, Naugatuck, Ct., from 1893 until 1896, when he sold it back to the gallery.

321. Manet's *A Matador* (MMA 29.100.52 [A 348]) was purchased by the Havemeyers from Durand-Ruel, New York, on December 31, 1898—some six months after Cassatt had returned to France—for $8,000.

322. Manet's *Young Man in the Costume of a Majo* (MMA 29.100.54 [A 345]) was purchased by the Havemeyers from Durand-Ruel, New York, on February 24, 1899 for $10,000.

323. Actually, the Havemeyers purchased *Mlle V... in the Costume of an Espada* (MMA 29.100.53 [A 344]), on the same day as their "Bullfighter" (*A Matador* [A 344]): December 31, 1898, from Durand-Ruel, New York, for $15,000.

324. Manet's *Luncheon in the Studio* (Neue Pinakothek, Munich, no. 8638 [A 349]) was owned for only six months by the Havemeyers: they purchased it from Durand-Ruel on April 8, 1895 for $7,000, and returned it to the same gallery on October 28, 1895 for 35,000 francs.

325. The Havemeyers' "Marine," Manet's *Boating* (MMA 29.100.115 [A 358]), purchased from Durand-Ruel on September 19, 1895 for 55,000 francs is compared to *Argenteuil* (Musée des Beaux-Arts, Tournai, Belgium), which was acquired by the Belgian collector and painter Henri van Cutsem in 1889.

326. Manet's *The Grand Canal, Venice (Blue Venice)* (SM 27.1.5-30 [A 359]) was purchased by the Havemeyers from Durand-Ruel, New York, on April 8, 1895 for $12,000.

327. For Manet's *Ball at the Opera* (A 357), see note no. 313.

328. Georges Clemenceau (1841-1929), French political journalist and noted statesman, who later became Premier of France (1906-09; 1917-20), spent the years 1865-68 in New England, where he was a post-Civil War correspondent for the Paris *Temps*, and taught French at a girls' school at Stamford, Connecticut. His dislike of the portrait Manet painted of him in 1879-80 is well-documented. It was purchased by the Havemeyers in the fall 1896, and presented by Mrs. Havemeyer to the Louvre on July 4, 1927 (Musée d'Orsay, Paris, R.F. 2641 [A 363]).

329. Out of the turmoil of the Dreyfus affair (see note no. 414) emerged a sharper alignment of political and social forces in the third Republic, leading to such drastic anticlerical measures as the separation of church and state in 1905, a law carried out by Clemenceau.

330. For the original state of the larger canvas, see the Lochard photograph reproduced in MMA 1983, p. 446, fig. a. These turned-back sections (representing 20 cm. at bottom, and 10 cm., at the sides) are now gone; they were cut off at an unknown date.

331. For the portrait of *Jean de Carondelet*, formerly Holbein, now considered Vermeyen (A 502), see note nos. 38, 48.

332. The portrait described is Manet's *Portrait of Marguerite de Conflans* (Smith College Museum of Art, Northampton, Mass., 1945.6 [A 355]), but the acquisition information is erroneous. It was purchased from Paul Rosenberg, Paris, in April 1903 for 28,000 francs and shipped to the Havemeyers in early May. Perhaps the woman's portrait acquired from Clemenceau in the fall 1896 is *Young Woman with Loosened Hair* (private collection [A 354]).

333. Namely, Manet's *Springtime* (Rouart and Wildenstein 1975, I, no. 372), which was offered to the Havemeyers in March 1905 along with other paintings from the Faure collection (for Faure, see note no. 10; for the offer, see note nos. 477-78); unable to negotiate a lower price with Durand-Ruel, the Havemeyers reject the group of pictures. *Springtime* was acquired by Oliver Payne in 1909 (private collection).

334. Manet's portrait of *Constantin Guys (1802-1892)* (SM 27.3.1-35 [A 365]), purchased by the Havemeyers from Paul Rosenberg, Paris, in April 1903 for 22,000 francs and shipped to them in early May.

335. The Havemeyers are known to have owned thirteen drawings and watercolors by Guys, most of which were acquired by Mrs. Havemeyer after 1913 (MMA 29.100.567-572, 600-606 [A 306-318]).

336. Manet's *Mademoiselle Isabelle Lemonnier* (MMA 29.100.56 [A362]), purchased by the Havemeyers from Durand-Ruel on April 22, 1901.

337. Manet's *Mademoiselle Lucie Delabigne (1859-1910), called Valtesse de la Bigne* (MMA 29.100.561 [A 361]) was kept by the sitter until 1902, when it was included in a sale of her collection (Haro and Bloche, Paris, June 2-7, 1902, lot no. 78); it was acquired about this time by the Havemeyers.

338. Manet's *Mademoiselle Suzette Lemaire* (SM 27.3.1-36 [A 364]), purchased by the Havemeyers from Durand-Ruel on May 8, 1906 for 15,000 francs.

339. Manet's *George Moore (1852-1933)* (MMA 29.100.55 [A 360]), purchased by the Havemeyers from a private collection, Paris, through Alphonse Portier, around 1896 (see pp. 234-36).

340. Alphonse Portier (1841-1902), an art

dealer at 54, rue Lepic, Paris. The Have-meyers' purchases through Portier date to the period around 1896.

341. Regarding the early history of ownership of Courbet's *The Stonebreakers*, see note no. 11.

342. For the Degas acquired from the collection of Parisian dentist, Georges Viau, namely Degas's *Two Dancers* (SM 27.3.131 [A 227]), see also p. 259.

343. Before the Havemeyers acquired Manet's *The Dead Christ, with Angels* (MMA 29.100.51 [A 346]) in 1903 (see note no. 316) it had been with Durand-Ruel for over twenty years; it was transferred to the New York gallery in 1895, having been exhibited in the United States as early as 1883 in Boston.

344. Late in 1888, Monet learned from John Singer Sargent that Suzanne Manet, in need of money, was on the verge of selling *Olympia* to an American (possibly the Havemeyers?). Monet therefore initiated a public subscription to purchase it for the Louvre which raised nearly the 20,000 franc asking price. The picture was accepted for the Luxembourg in 1890, but not accessioned by the Louvre until January 6, 1907.

345. For Manet's *Boy with a Sword* (MMA 89.21.2), see note no. 315.

346. For Manet's *Gare Saint-Lazare* (A 356), see note no. 316.

CHAPTER XIV
EDGAR DEGAS

Edgar Degas (1834–1917)

347. Mrs. Havemeyer refers to the first and last literary works of Victorian novelist, Samuel Butler (1835-1902), his anonymous *Erewhon* (1872), and *The Way of All Flesh* (1903).

348. Degas's "Le Café Chantant" may refer to a specific work in the Havemeyer collection, namely, *The Song of the Dog* (private collection, U.S.A. [A 217], see note no. 356), or simply be a catch-all, like the "The Ballet Dancers" for the subjects

by which the artist is best-known.

349. The brilliant Scottish essayist and historian, Thomas Carlyle (1795-1881).

350. Noted American preacher and long-time rector of Trinity Church in Boston, Phillips Brooks (1835-1893), was born in Boston, educated at Harvard, and consecrated bishop of Massachusetts in 1891.

351. Degas's father, Auguste De Gas, a banker, was born in Naples in 1807; his mother, Célestine Musson, was born in New Orleans in 1815; they married in Paris in 1832. The artist was the eldest of their six children. He had four brothers, two of whom died in infancy: George (1835-37) and Edouard (born and died, 1839), as well as Achille (b. 1838) and René (b. 1845), who was the youngest and Edgar's favorite, though as noted, somewhat of a "bad egg." His two sisters were Thérèse (b. 1840) and Marguerite (b. 1842) who married Henri Fevre, an architect, in 1865. On the subject of Degas's family, see Riccardo Raimondi, *Degas a la sua famiglia in Napoli 1793-1917*, Naples, 1958 and more recently, the excellent biographical study by Henri Loyrette, *Degas*, Paris 1991.

352. Degas probably met the French painter, Gustave Moreau (1826-1898) in Rome in 1858; their friendship lasted until about 1864.

353. As documented elsewhere, this accurately reflects Degas's estimation of American artist John Singer Sargent (1846-1925); see William Rothenstein, *Men and Memories, Recollection 1872-1938*, London, pp. 54, 56.

354. Paul Durand-Ruel (1831-1922), the pioneering dealer of Impressionist works, who was director of the Durand-Ruel galleries in Paris at 16, rue Laffitte and 11, rue Le Peletier, and in 1887, opened a branch of the family firm in New York. His long commercial association with Degas dates from 1872 on.

355. Cassatt's "Boy before the Mirror," namely, *Mother and Child* (MMA 29.100.47 [A 58]), which Degas must have seen at the Galerie Durand-Ruel, Paris, between April 21, 1899, when it was purchased from

the artist, and July 8, 1899, when it was shipped to the New York branch; it was sold to the Havemeyers on July 25, 1899 for $2,000. Degas's "opinion of the picture," is recorded in a letter from Paul Durand-Ruel to H.O. Havemeyer of July 7, 1899, in which the dealer wrote: "he considers it the finest work that Mary Cassatt ever did, he says it contains all her qualities and is particularly characteristic of her talent." See Weitzenhoffer 1986, p. 136.

356. Degas's *Song of the Dog* (private collection, U.S.A. [A 217]) was acquired by Mrs. Havemeyer from the Rouart estate sale, *Dessins et Pastels anciens et modernes... composant la collection de feu M. Henri Rouart*, Galerie Manzi-Joyant, Paris, on December 16, 1912, lot no. 71, for 55,100 francs.

357. References to prima ballerina, Rosita Mauri, who made her debut at the Opéra in Gounod's *Polyeucte* in 1878, and to ballet master, Ernest Pluque, who was formerly misidentified as the *maître* represented by Degas, Jules Perrot.

358. The pictures noted, *The Mante Family* (Lemoisne 1946, nos. 971 and 972) and *Waiting: Dancer and Woman with Umbrella on a Bench (L'Attente)* (A 237). See note nos. 378, 383.

359. From 1890–1912, Degas occupied a three-story apartment/studio on 37, rue Victor-Massé (the former rue de Laval, renamed in 1887 in honor of the late composer). Since the building was slated for demolition, he was forced to move to a new apartment—his last address—at 6, boulevard de Clichy; at the time of this move, on February 22, 1913, he left his *Family Portrait*, also called *The Bellelli Family*, 1858-67, (Lemoisne 1946, no. 79) on deposit with Durand-Ruel; it was purportedly "covered with an ancient coat of dust that has not been disturbed for years." The picture received considerable attention in 1918 when it was acquired from the artist's heirs by the Musée du Luxembourg (Musée d'Orsay, Paris, R.F. 2210). On this subject, see Boggs et al. 1988, no. 20, pp. 77f.

360. Possibly a reference to the pastel of this subject in her collection: Degas's *Race-*

horses in Training (Thyssen-Bornemisza collection [A 255]), purchased by the Havemeyers from Durand-Ruel on March 30, 1895.

361. Degas's revival of pastel in the late 19th century, was seen by his earliest critics as aligning him with the great tradition of the French portraitist, Maurice Quentin de la Tour (1704-1788) who worked almost exclusively in this medium. Regarding Degas's visits to see La Tour's pastels in the Musée Lécuyer in Saint-Quentin, see p. 256. The influence of, and Degas's long-standing admiration for, Jean Auguste Dominique Ingres (1780-1867) is well-documented. Degas owned over fifty paintings and drawings by Ingres, whom he met in 1855.

362. Unlike the earlier comparison to Butler (see p. 241), Degas's artistic contribution, no less than his approach, find a fitting analogy in the literary genius of French novelist, Honoré de Balzac (1799-1850) and to his writing of *Le Lis dans la vallée* (1835). Balzac's contemporaries, Amandine-Aurore-Lucile Dupin Dudevant, who wrote *Consuelo* (1842-43) and other novels under the pen name, George Sand (1804-1876), and composer Frédéric Chopin (1810-1849).

363. Mrs. Havemeyer had last seen Cassatt in Paris in the spring 1914; Degas died on September 27, 1917.

364. Louisine Elder was in her late teens when she met Cassatt, and in her early twenties when she purchased her first Degas, *Ballet Rehearsal* (A 215); see note nos. 264, 291.

365. For the Monet (A 395) and Pissarro (A 427), see note no. 291.

366. She lent her Degas pastel (A 215), under the name G.N. Elder to the *Eleventh Annual Exhibition of the American Water Color Society*, held at the National Academy of Design, New York, February 3-March 3, 1878. It was shown as no. 233, "A Ballet." This was the first Degas exhibited in North America.

367. In December 1883, Erwin Davis lent his Degas, "A Ballet," (Hill-Stead

Museum, Farmington, Ct.) to the *Pedestal Fund Art Loan Exhibition* at the National Academy of Design, New York (no. 169), however, twenty-three works by the artist were exhibited in New York in the 1886 exhibition of *Works in Oil and Pastel by the Impressionists of Paris* (see note no. 315).

368. This etching by Degas, *Self-Portrait* (MMA 29.107.53) was acquired by Mrs. Havemeyer immediately after the sale, *Estampes Modernes Composant la Collection Roger Marx*, held at the Hôtel Drouot, Paris, April 28, 1914, lot no. 389.

369. Guy's pen and ink portrait of Degas was shown in the exhibition that Mrs. Havemeyer organized for woman suffrage, *Masterpieces by Old and Modern Painters*, held at M. Knoedler and Co., New York, April 6-24, 1915. The exhibition included over 24 works by Degas, at least 19 by Cassatt, and 18 old masters. The Guys, though not listed among the works lent, is visible in an installation photograph of the show. See Rebecca A. Rabinow, "The Suffrage Exhibition of 1915," MMA 1993, pp. 93-95, fig. 13.

370. The three Degas drawings on pink paper, now in the Metropolitan Museum, are, respectively: *Little Girl Practicing at the Bar* (MMA 29.100.943 [A 221]); *Dancer Adjusting her Slipper* (MMA 29.100.941 [A 206]) and *Seated Dancer* (MMA 29.100.942 [A 208]).

371. This visit to Degas's studio and their purchase of his *The Collector of Prints* (MMA 29. 100.44 [A 197]) probably dates to April 1891. However, Degas did not release the picture to them until the end of 1894; Cassatt intervened with the artist toward this end in October, and on December 13, 1894, it was finally shipped to Havemeyers. See also p. 288.

372. Degas's *Dancers Practicing at the Bar* (MMA 29.100.34 [A 216]) was purchased by Mrs. Havemeyer from the Rouart estate sale, *Tableaux Anciens...et des Tableaux Modernes... composant la collection de feu M. Henri Rouart*, December 10, 1912, lot no. 177, for 478,500 francs (inclusive), a record

price for a work by a living artist and perhaps the costliest acquisition ever made by the Havemeyers. The picture had been given by the artist to Henri Rouart as a replacement for an earlier work, now lost, which Degas wished to alter and destroyed in the process. On this subject, see Boggs et al. 1988, p. 257, and no. 165, p. 278.

373. The Havemeyers owned a different version of this subject, Degas's *Woman Ironing* (MMA 29.100.46 [A 205]), which they purchased from Durand-Ruel on December 18, 1894 for 2,500 francs.

374. This visit to Degas's studio took place in April 1903; she describes the original wax sculpture of *The Little Fourteen-Year Old Dancer*, 1879-81, (collection of Mr. and Mrs. Paul Mellon, Upperville, Va.) which Degas had exhibited in the sixth Impressionist exhibition in Paris in 1881. Regarding Mrs. Havemeyer's efforts to purchase this piece from the artist in 1903, and from his heirs in 1918-19, see Boggs et al. 1988, pp. 344-45, 350-352. She obtained a bronze cast of the statue in 1922 (MMA 29.100.370).

375. Regarding Maurice Quentin de la Tour, see note no. 361.

376. Of the sixty-five pictures that the Havemeyers are known to have owned by Degas (A 196-260), one was returned immediately after its purchase (A 248) and eight (A 196, 198, 223, 231, 232, 239, 240, 244) were acquired by Mrs. Havemeyer after the date of the "last" acquisitions described (see p. 264f). During the period 1917-23, she also purchased another Degas print (MMA 29.107.52)—one of six in the collection (MMA 29.107. 51-57)—as well as a set of Degas bronzes (MMA 29.100.370-438). For the bronzes, see pp. 296-97.

377. The first Degas described is *Dancers at Rest* (private collection [A 209]), purchased by the Havemeyers from Durand-Ruel on February 20, 1899 for $7,000.

378. There is no record of the Havemeyers having owned either version of Degas's *La famille Mante* (Lemoisne 1946, nos. 971 and

972); however, both pastels would have been well-known to Mrs. Havemeyer, since they were owned by collector-friends, Mrs. Montgomery Sears of Boston and Mrs. Potter Palmer of Chicago, respectively. Louisine Havemeyer, in fact, borrowed the former from Mrs. Sears for her 1915 suffrage exhibition at Knoedler's. (The "daughter dressed and waiting to be called for her turn," in the Mante family pastel, is shown standing at the bar in a pastel that Mrs. Havemeyer would purchase in 1921, *Dancer at the Bar* (SM 27.3.1-34, [A 244]). It is also possible, since the description provided for "La Famille Mante," loosely accords with a work in the Havemeyer collection, that she is referring to Degas's *Dance Examination* (Denver Art Museum, 1941.6 [A 228]), which was purchased from Durand-Ruel, New York, between December 31, 1898 and January 3, 1899.

379. The two versions of "Danseuses à la Barre:" namely, *Dancers Practicing at the Bar* (MMA 29.100.34 [A 216], which the artist had given Henri Rouart, from whose estate sale it was acquired by Mrs. Havemeyer in 1912 (see note no. 372), and *Dancers at the Bar* (private collection [A 218]), possibly the "Etude de danseuse (pastel)" purchased by the Havemeyers in Paris in the spring 1907.

380. The two "Horses and Jockeys" are the oil, *Jockeys* (Yale University Art Gallery, New Haven, Ct., 1942.302 [A 234]) and the pastel, *Racehorses in Training* (A 255), see note no. 360.

381. Degas's *At the Milliner's* (MMA 29.100.38 [A 236]), purchased by the Havemeyers from Durand-Ruel on January 24, 1899. Regarding Cassatt as model for another work in the "modiste" series, see p. 275.

382. Degas's *Little Milliners* (The Nelson-Atkins Museum of Art, Kansas City, Missouri, F 79-34 [A 235]), acquired by Mrs. Havemeyer from the sale of the *Collection de Feu M. Alexis Rouart*, Hôtel Drouot, Paris, May 9, 1911, lot no. 214, for 51,000 francs.

383. On September 19, 1895, the Have-

meyers acquired from Durand-Ruel's private collection, Paris: Degas's *Waiting: Dancer and Woman with Umbrella on a Bench (L'Attente)* (jointly owned by the J. Paul Getty Museum, Malibu, 83.GG.219, and the Norton Simon Art Foundation, Pasadena, M.1983.1.P [A 237]) for 15,000 francs, and two other pastels, *Dancer in Green* (A 230) for 5,500 francs and *Dancer in Yellow* (A 219) for 3,500 francs (SM 27.3.1-33, and 27.3.1-32).

384. The Havemeyers acquired Degas's *Two Dancers* (A 227) from Georges Viau, Paris, probably around 1896, as previously mentioned (see note no. 342), and from Cottier and Co., New York, Degas's *Dancers in White* (private collection [A 220]).

385. Degas's *Dancers in the Rehearsal Room, with a Double Bass* (MMA 29.100.127 [A 238]) was acquired by the Havemeyers from the American Art Association sale of *Mr. E.F. Milliken's private collection of Valuable Paintings*, New York, February 14, 1902, lot no. 11, for $6,100. There does not seem to be a "pastel of the same subject," though there is a variant in oil, a closely related oil sketch and several preparatory drawings. See Lemoisne 1946, nos. 900, 902, and Boggs et al. 1988, no. 239, pp. 405-06.

386. The Havemeyers owned Degas's *Dancers in Blue* (private collection [A 259]) and a pastel and an oil *Dancers, Pink and Green* (private collection, Tokyo [A 256] and MMA 29.100.42 [A 252], respectively).

387. The two "Répétitions" by Degas: *The Rehearsal on the Stage* (A 211), pastel over brush-and-ink drawing, and *The Rehearsal of the Ballet on Stage* (A 212), oil colors freely mixed with turpentine, with traces of watercolor and pastel over pen-and-ink drawing (MMA 29.100.39 and 29.160.26, respectively). The former (A 211) was one of two pictures that had been bought in at the Ernest May sale in 1890, that the Havemeyers purchased from Durand-Ruel on February 17, 1899; the other "done in egg," is Degas's *Rehearsal in the Studio* (SM 27.3.1-35A [A 210]). The "other Répétition" (A 212), formerly owned by Walter Sickert, was purchased by the Havemey-

ers from Boussod, Valadon et Cie, Paris, on February 7, 1902 for 82,845 francs.

388. Namely, Degas's *The Artist's Cousin, probably Mrs. William Bell (Mathilde Musson, 1841-1878)* (MMA 29.100.40 [A 204]), purchased by the Havemeyers from Edmond Taigny, Paris, through Alphonse Portier, probably in 1896.

389. It was probably in the summer 1889 that Cassatt presented Louisine Havemeyer with a monotype by Degas of a nude putting on her stocking (MMA 29.107.54; see MMA 1993, pl. 80). The Havemeyers purchased their first nude by Degas, *The Bath* (MMA 29.100.186 [A 260]), from Durand-Ruel, Paris, on September 19, 1895, and their second, *Woman with a Towel* (MMA 29.100.37 [A 257]), from the same gallery on April 22, 1901. Between 1910-19, Mrs. Havemeyer would purchase five more bathers (A 239, 241, 242, 243, 253). Those specifically noted are: *Bather Stepping into a Tub* (MMA 29.100.190 [A 253]), acquired by Mrs. Havemeyer from the sale of the *Collection of the Late Tadama Hayashi*, American Art Association, New York, January 8, 1913, lot no. 85, for $3,100, and *Woman Drying Her Arm* (MMA 29.100.553 [A 243]), from the posthumous sale of *The James S. Inglis Collection*—the former president of Cottier and Co.—American Art Association, New York, March 10, 1910, lot no. 63 for $2,500.

390. Degas's *Woman Having Her Hair Combed* (MMA 29.100.35 [A 242]), acquired by Mrs. Havemeyer from the sale, *Tableaux, Pastels, Dessins, Aquarelles... Faisant partie de la collection Roger Marx*, Galerie Manzi-Joyant, Paris, on May 12, 1914, lot no. 125, for 101,000 francs.

391. Mrs. Havemeyer visited these cities in Germany during the last week of April and the first week of May 1914; however, by May 7, she went to Montreux, Switzerland, to attend to the death of her sister-in-law, Emilie Havemeyer. Presumably she departed Montreux, by car, on Sunday, May 10, in order to be present at the Roger Marx sale on the 12th. On this subject, see

Stein chronology in MMA 1993, p. 265.

392. Degas's *Joseph-Henri Altes (1862-1895)* (MMA 29.100.181 [A 199]), purchased from Durand-Ruel on March 4, 1903.

393. The Havemeyers owned three portraits that had been variously attributed to either Clouet or Corneille de Lyon. They purchased a *Portrait of a Woman* by Clouet from the *Collection Mame* sale in Paris in April 1904, which is now Attributed to Corneille de Lyon, *Anne de Pisseleu (1508-1576), Duchesse d'Estampes* (MMA 29.100.197 [A 96]); from Durand-Ruel in 1889 they bought Corneille de Lyon's *Portrait of a Man* (MMA 29.100.22 [A 97]), which is now Attributed to Corneille de Lyon, but had at one time been attributed to Clouet; and they also owned another *Portrait of a Man*, Attributed to Clouet (location unknown, [A 84]).

394. The two Degas oils representing the most famous scene from Meyerbeer's opera are: *The Ballet from "Robert le Diable"* (MMA 29.100.552 [A 202]), purchased by the Havemeyers from Durand-Ruel, New York, on February 14, 1898 for $4,000, and the version, now in the Victoria and Albert Museum, London (Lemoisne 1946, no. 341), that was purchased from Durand-Ruel by Constantine Alexander Ionides, London on June 7, 1881 and bequeathed by him to the museum in 1900. On this subject, see Boggs et al. 1988, nos. 103, 159.

395. The Degas "relinquished" to Payne is *The Dance Class* (MMA 1987.47.1); for this work and for the Turner and Corots, see note no. 68.

396. Degas's portrait of *Madame Théodore Gobillard (Yves Morisot, 1838-1893)* (MMA 29.100.45 [A 200]), representing the eldest of the three Morisot sisters (Yves, Edma and Berthe) is compared to Degas's 1867 portrait of *Madame Gaujelin*, also depicting a woman in black seated against a light background, which was acquired by Mrs. Gardner through Berenson in 1904 (Isabella Stewart Gardner Museum, Boston).

397. The other painting that Cassatt secured for Mrs. Havemeyer through

Charlotte Manzi in 1916 is Degas's *The Dancing Class* (MMA 29.100.184 [A 203]), and the sketch on pink paper, the artist's *Woman on a Sofa* (MMA 29.100.185 [A 213]). The transaction was completed on December 5, 1916 and the three works were shipped to Louisine Havemeyer in April 1917. Some of the correspondence regarding these acquisitions is preserved in letters on deposit at the Metropolitan Museum (Havemeyer correspondence).

398. The letter, albeit unknown, presumably dates to the summer of 1917, just prior to the artist's death on September 27. The quote, "Poor Degas is always the same," bears comparison with what Cassatt had written to Mrs. Havemeyer on October 2, 1917, concerning Degas's death: "Oh my dear Louie humanity is always the same." (MMA/Havemeyer correspondence)

CHAPTER XV
MARY CASSATT

Mary Cassatt (1844-1926)

399. For the Havemeyers' 1901 trip to Italy and Spain with Cassatt, see chapters IX and X, p. 83f.

400. The Havemeyers' 1889 trip to Europe was of great immediate and long-term importance to their collection. During this trip they saw, at the *Exposition Centennale des Beaux-Arts* of the Paris world's fair, Courbet's *Woman with a Parrot* (A 145) and Manet's *Boating* (A 358), two works they would later acquire. They purchased a dozen pictures from the Secrétan sale and an additional fifteen works, including their first paintings by Courbet, through Paul Durand-Ruel who, from this date on, would become their principal dealer. Regarding Mr. Havemeyer's first meeting with Cassatt, in late August, see pp. 280-81. For the Havemeyers' activities and acquisitions during their 1889 trip to Europe, see Stein chronology in MMA 1993, pp. 208-10.

401. This cable, offering condolences on H.O. Havemeyer's death, is not preserved in the correspondence on deposit at the Metropolitan Museum (Havemeyer correspondence).

402. In June 1874, Louisine Elder met Cassatt at Mme Del Sarte's *pensionnat* through Emily Sartain, a fellow boarder and art student from Philadelphia with whom Cassatt had worked in Parma in the winter of 1871-72. As previously noted, Louisine Elder was nearly nineteen years old at the time (see note no. 264).

403. Alexander Johnston Cassatt (1839-1906), the artist's brother, an American railroad executive, who worked his way up from rodman in 1860 to become President of the Pennsylvania Railroad from 1899, until his death in 1906.

404. Regarding the Easter fêtes in Madrid in April 1901, see also p. 138.

405. Mary Cassatt was born on May 22, 1844 in Allegheny City, Pennsylvania (now a part of Pittsburgh), where her grandfather, Dennis Cassat (1776-1807) had been a banker, as was her father. The family moved to Philadelphia in 1849.

406. Her parents, Katherine Kelso Johnston (1816-1895) and Robert Simpson Cassatt (1806-1891), and her eldest sister, Lydia Simpson Cassatt (1837-1882) moved to Paris in 1877. The period 1878-1886 was a particularly difficult one for the artist: Lydia, who had been a semi-invalid for several years, died of Bright's disease in 1882 and by 1884, her mother was fighting off a nearly fatal illness. Cassatt would take charge of the family affairs, caring for nieces and nephews and nursing her sister and her parents through 1895.

407. Cassatt's homes: the Château de Beaufresne at Mesnil-Théribus, some thirty miles northwest of Paris, which she purchased in the spring 1894, and which remained her country home until her death; her residence in Paris, at 10, rue Marignan, from 1887 on; and the Villa Angeletto in Grasse, where she spent most of the war years.

408. For Cassatt's portraits of Lydia shown seated in a garden, see Breeskin 1970, nos. 94, 95, 96, 98.

409. For Clemenceau, see note no. 328.

410. Reference to the famous eighteenth-century English stage actor, David Garrick (1717-1779).

411. Cassatt's gouache *Self-Portrait* (MMA 1975.319.1 [A 49]) was probably acquired by Louisine Elder in 1879, and loaned to an exhibition in New York in 1880.

412. Namely, Degas's *At the Milliner's* (Lemoisne 1946, no. 693, The Museum of Modern Art, New York). See also p. 258.

413. Cassatt and Degas were most friendly in the late 1870s and 1880s.

414. The trial and conviction of Jewish officer Alfred Dreyfus (1859-1935) for treason in 1894 was a case that polarized France for the next twelve years, with lines sharply drawn between defenders of Dreyfus and the Third Republic, and opponents, whose ranks were swelled by antisemitic support. Dreyfus, whose innocence was proclaimed in Zola's *J'accuse* letter (January 13, 1898), was eventually pardoned by President Emile Loubet, and in 1906 was cleared of all charges and decorated with the Legion of Honor.

415. Because of his staunch Anti-Dreyfusard stance, Degas became increasingly estranged from his old friends, Louise and Ludovic Halévy (1834-1908), the French writer and successful librettist, between November and December 1897. On December 23, 1897 he dined at the Halévys for the last time. On this subject, see Linda Nochlin, "Degas and the Dreyfus Affair: A Portrait of the artist as an Anti-Semite," in *The Dreyfus Affair: Art, Truth and Justice*, Berkeley, Los Angeles and London, 1987, p. 96f, and Boggs et al. 1988, p. 493.

416. Mathilde Valet, Cassatt's Alsacean maid and housekeeper from about 1884 on.

417. General Auguste Mercier (1833-1921), French officer responsible for Dreyfus's arrest in 1894, who continued to abet his accusations, maintaining at the Zola trial of 1898, that he had firm proof of Dreyfus's guilt.

418. Durand-Ruel père, namely, Paul Durand-Ruel, who began handling Cassatt's works in 1881. Regarding him, see note no. 354.

419. The group of ten nudes that Degas exhibited as "Suite des nus de femmes se baignant, se lavant, se séchant, s'essuyant, se peignant ou se faisant peigner," in the last Impressionist exhibition of 1886 created quite a sensation and, indeed, elicited a good deal of harsh criticism.

420. It is true that Cassatt was among the earliest admirers of Degas's bathers; after the close of the 1886 exhibition she gave Degas her *Girl Arranging Her Hair* (NGA, Chester Dale Collection, 1963.10.97 [A 51]) in exchange for one of his nudes, *Woman Bathing in a Shallow Tub* (MMA 29.100.41 [A 239]). Mrs. Havemeyer acquired the former from the artist's estate sale in 1918, and the latter from Cassatt in 1917.

Paul Durand-Ruel seems not to have bought any of Degas's bathers until the early 1890s, and then, as indicated by the gallery's few transactions, seemingly only for immediate re-sale to interested clients.

421. There is some difference of opinion as to which Cassatt was called the "Florentine Madonna." It is either the artist's *Mother and Child* (destroyed in a fire [A 52]), purchased by the Havemeyers from Durand-Ruel on April 8, 1895 for $2,000 or the *Mother and Child* (MMA 29.100.47 [A 58]), previously mentioned, see note no. 355. For the two proposals, see, respectively, Weitzenhoffer 1986, p. 104, and Spassky et al. 1985, pp. 646-48.

422. This letter of August 2, 1914 is not preserved in the correspondence on deposit at the Metropolitan Museum (Havemeyer correspondence), but the sentiments expressed are reflected in a number of letters dating to the same period, including one written a couple of weeks later. On August 13, [1914], Cassatt also remarked on the "great drama going on so near us," and added "Oh Louie dear women must be up and doing let them league themselves to put down the war...women must fight in a body against war."

423. Kneippism, named for the Bavarian priest, Sebastian Kneipp (1821-97), who advocated the treatment of disease by hydrotherapy in various forms, albeit especially, walking barefoot through dewy grass. His "water-cure" was highly touted in the early 1890s for its therapeutic benefits and was seen as a treatment that would revolutionize the present state of medicine.

424. Cassatt seems to have adopted a vegetarian diet around the same time as their 1901 trip to Italy (see chapter IX), and more or less adhered to it—save indulgences on the holidays—until at least 1906. She wrote to Mrs. Havemeyer on December 25, [1902] that "Vegetables & water seem to agree with me very well," though four years later, she confessed on December 27, to "breaking through my vegetarian rule, with no ill effects." (MMA/Havemeyer correspondence)

For Cassatt's interest in other "cures" as well as spiritual and psychical phenomenon see Weitzenhoffer 1986, pp. 183, 186.

425. Cassatt's riding accident took place in early August 1889, and their meeting took place at the end of the month, after they had acquired their first landscapes by Courbet: namely, *Landscape with Cattle* (A 130) on August 17, and *The Source of the Loue* (A 140) on August 21. For these paintings, see note nos. 269, 259.

426. François Vincent Raspail (1794-1878), French chemist and political activist, who brought to light the therapeutic benefits of camphor treatments in two popular treatises, *Le Médecin des familles* (1843) and *Le Manuel de la santé* (1846), that earned him considerable renown in the mid-late nineteenth century.

427. Regarding the Vêndome affair, see note no. 14; for the 1881 Courbet exhibition, see p. 190.

428. In the spring 1887, Cassatt moved with her parents into the apartment at 10, rue de Marignan (one block from the Champs-Elysées) that she kept for the rest of her life. Ten years earlier, in the fall 1877, her parents and sister had come to live with

her in Paris at 13, avenue Trudaine; they lived at 14, rue Charron from 1884-87.

429. Several works by Degas that had been in Cassatt's collection were acquired by Mrs. Havemeyer, including the three by Degas that Cassatt sold to her for $20,000 in December 1917, *Woman Bathing in a Shallow Tub* (A 239), *Portrait of a Young Woman* (A 240) and *Fan Mount: Ballet Girls* (A 223), and an etching, acquired in 1920, *Head of a Young Woman in Profile* (MMA 29.100.41, 29.100.183, 29.100.555, and 29.107.52, respectively).

430. The "fine Courbet" may be Courbet's *Woman with a Cat* (Worcester Art Museum, Worcester, Mass. 1940.300 [A 142]) which Cassatt acquired after 1900, and was later owned by Mrs. Havemeyer.

431. For Degas's visits to Lille and Saint-Quentin, see p. 256; for Berthe Morisot, see note no. 311.

432. Cassatt had followed this artistic route herself: early on, in the late 1860s–early 1870s, she had spent time in Courances and Ecouen, small art colonies near Paris, to study with Edouard Frère and Paul Soyer, and she also settled in Villiers-le-Bell to work with Thomas Couture.

433. Cassatt and Emily Sartain (1841-1927) spent eight months in Parma in the winter of 1871-72; in the fall 1872, Cassatt went to Madrid and then to Seville, where she had a studio at the Casa de Pilatos.

434. Cassatt, who experimented with etching and drypoint in 1889, became interested in 1890—under the impact of the exhibition of Japanese art at the Ecole des Beaux-Arts—in producing color prints. Over the next year she energetically devoted herself to printmaking, and in April 1891, a set of ten color prints were featured in her first solo show, *Exposition de tableaux, pastels, et gravures par Mlle Mary Cassatt* at Galerie Durand-Ruel, Paris. The Havemeyers purchased a complete set of prints (Breeskin 1948, nos. 143-52) in August.

435. From 1891-97, Cassatt executed nine more color prints, including *The Banjo Lesson* (Breeskin 1948, no. 156)—which was one of two specially made for her second exhi-

bition in 1893 at Durand-Ruel. Despite the dealer's small profit margin, the prints were well received by critics and also sold well.

436. On the subject of Cassatt's prints, see Nancy Mowll Mathews and Barbara Stern Shapiro, *Mary Cassatt: The Color Prints*, New York, 1988.

437. Cassatt, who had kept the portrait of *Adaline Havemeyer in a White Hat* (MMA 1992.235; see MMA 1993, fig. 8) for over twelve years, sent it to Adaline for her daughter Frederica's nursery around January 1912.

438. The artist's brother, J. Gardner Cassatt fell deathly ill while they were traveling in Egypt in February-March 1911, and died on April 5, 1911. Sir William Osler (1849-1919), Canadian physician and professor of medicine, had been aboard the boat that transported her brother from Egypt to Paris, and had written a "most kind note" to Cassatt "telling [her] he was very ill...& saying to get him home as soon as possible." Cassatt and Mrs. Havemeyer corresponded in the summer 1913 about her "great desire to do something for Sir William Osler" as a token of gratitude, but as of December she had "not yet" sent "Dr. Osler a pastel," though hoped that in Grasse she "may do something suitable." (Mary Cassatt to Louisine Havemeyer, March 31, [1911], July 16, [1913], and December 4, [1913], MMA/Havemeyer correspondence.) The excerpt quoted is from Mary Cassatt's letter to Mrs. Havemeyer of July 16, [1913], which reads: "I was able to show Joseph [Durand-Ruel] a pastel nearly finished, he wanted it but my great desire [is] to do something for Sir William Osler (Dr Osler) in recognition of his kindness to Gard[.] I know he likes my work. Until I have done that I don't want to give up a pastel."

439. Four works by Cassatt—two pastels, a drawing, and an oil—were included in Roger Marx's estate sale, *Tableaux, Pastels, Dessins, Aquarelles...de la Collection Roger Marx*, Galerie Manzi-Joyant, Paris, May 11-12, 1914; lot nos. 101, 103 (pastels); lot no. 102 (drawing). The painting, *Mother and Child* (NGA, Chester Dale Collection, 1963.10.98 [A 60]) was acquired by Mrs. Havemeyer for 15,500 francs (lot no. 15).

440. Cassatt was decorated with the Legion of Honor on December 31, 1904.

441. In 1893 Cassatt received the first of several requests from the French government for an example of her work for the official collection of modern art in the Palais du Luxembourg; she donated a pastel mother and child in 1897 (Musée d'Orsay). According to her correspondence with Louisine Havemeyer, Cassatt was approached by the "Director of the Petit Palais Museum...for a drawing or a pastel" in 1906, and in 1915, she had "more than half-promised...to the Petit Palais" her *Lady at the Tea Table* (a painting that eight years later, she gave to the Metropolitan Museum, MMA 23.101). Cassatt did, donate an oil to the Petit Palais in 1922, a *Portrait of Lydia Cassatt* (Breeskin 1970, no. 96). (Mary Cassatt to Louisine Havemeyer, December 21 [1906], February 4, [1915], MMA/Havemeyer correspondence)

442. Over two-hundred letters written from Mary Cassatt to Louisine Havemeyer, dating from the period 1900-1920, are on deposit at the Metropolitan Museum (Havemeyer correspondence).

443. This letter, which must date to the fall 1892, is not preserved in the correspondence on deposit at the Metropolitan Museum (Havemeyer correspondence). The reference is to a pair of portraits, now considered Style of Rembrandt (A 457 and A 458, see note no. 38), that Charles Durand-Ruel secured for the Havemeyers from the Princesse de Sagan in June 1892, and which Cassatt saw at the gallery that July before they were shipped to New York and purchased by the Havemeyers in September.

444. The Havemeyers owned four landscapes by French artist Constant Troyon (1810-1865), of which at least two were acquired in the early 1890s (see A 491-94).

445. For Duret, see note no. 225.

446. Courbet's *Torso of a Woman* (A 137),

the Havemeyers' first nude by the artist, acquired in October 1892, see note no. 266; her husband's opinion, as previously mentioned, see p. 193.

447. This letter, which must date to late May 1892, is not preserved among the correspondence now on deposit at the Metropolitan Museum (Havemeyer correspondence). On June 17, 1892 Cassatt wrote to Pissarro: "I have begun a great decoration for one of the buildings in Chicago (for the Worlds Fair)—You ought to hear Degas on the subject of a woman's undertaking to do such a thing, he has handed me over to distruction [sic]." (Cited in Mathews 1984, p. 229)

448. Cassatt, who had been commissioned by Chicago collector Mrs. Potter Palmer to paint a mural for the south tympanum of the Women's Building at the World's Columbian Exposition, executed the large canvas, *Modern Women* (now lost, see Breeskin 1970, no. 213) from June–December 1892 in a specially built studio at Bachivillers. The exhibition took place in Chicago from May 1–October 30, 1893. For correspondence on the mural, see Mathews 1984, pp. 229f.

449. Albert Bartholomé (1848-1928), French sculptor and Degas's close friend from the 1880s on.

450. The picture Degas was finishing for the Havemeyers is presumably *The Collector of Prints* (A 197), regarding which, see note no. 371.

451. Henri Eugène Philippe Louis d'Orleans, Duc d'Aumale (1822-1897), French military officer, zealous art collector and bibliophile, to whom Chantilly was left by the last of the Condé family, and who devoted himself to reestablishing its former splendor, first by financing the restoration of the Grande Château, and after by donating to the Institut of France his enormous and varied art treasures. His collection forms the basis of the present-day Musée Condé housed in the Petit and Grande Châteaux of Chantilly, and includes Fillipino Lippi's *Esther and Ahasuerus*, which the Duc d'Aumale acquired at the sale of the collection of Maurice Le-clanché, Galerie Georges

Petit, Paris, on May 25, 1892 (lot no. 21).

452. The second exhibition of the Société National des Beaux-Arts, Champs de Mars, Paris, opened on May 7, 1892; Sargent's *La Carmencita*, was shown as no. 926 and acquired that year for the Luxembourg (now, Musée d'Orsay, Paris); Whistler exhibited five Nocturnes as well as *Harmony in Pink and Grey: Portrait of Lady Meux*, shown as no. 1066 (The Frick Collection, New York, 16.1.133).

453. For works by Whistler in the Havemeyer collection, see note no. 290.

454. Jehan Georges Vibert (1840-1902), French artist who is best-known for his satirical genre scenes of the clergy; in a letter to Mrs. Havemeyer of December 25, [1912], Cassatt noted: "I have told you of Degas['s] fine answer to Vibert, when the latter said to him, 'after all pictures are luxuries,' 'Yours are,' said Degas, 'ours are first necessities.'" Cassatt also cited the Degas quote in a 1904 letter to Carroll Tyson (see Mathews 1984, p. 293).

455. The first exhibition of the Société d'aquarellistes française took place in 1879.

456. The unknown letter presumably dates to after April 1898, when Payne acquired Degas's *The Dance Class* (MMA 1987.47.1). See note no. 68. For Degas's *Dancers Practicing at the Bar* (A 216), see note no. 372.

457. This unrecorded letter, which dates to late 1901 or 1902, was written shortly after the Havemeyers' 1901 trip to Italy and Spain with Cassatt, during which the Boer War (1899-1902) was discussed; see p. 96.

458. Professor S. is presumably a reference to James Stillman (1850-1918), an American banker who settled in Paris in 1909. He was a patron of Cassatt's and also a collector whom she advised.

459. Regarding the Dreyfus affair, see note no. 414.

460. Georges Picquart (1854-1914), French general who played a significant role in the defense of Dreyfus; in 1896, he came forward with a document that established Dreyfus's innocence and Esterhazy's guilt.

461. For these publications by Lenormant and Crawford, see note nos. 147, 149.

462. Two letters concerning *The Duke of Wellington*, now considered Workshop of Goya (A 302; see note nos. 15, 190) are preserved at the Metropolitan Museum: a letter from Joseph Wicht to Mary Cassatt, July 8, [1901], enclosing a larger and better photograph of the portrait, which was forwarded to the Havemeyers; and an undated letter, written between August 5-9, 1901, from Cassatt to H.O. Havemeyer in which she announced: "Wellington is yours at 17,975 frcs. As you left it to my discretion I bought it on the principal I have always seen you follow of getting a fine thing when it came in your way...I send you the history of the picture which I told Wicht to get." (MMA/Havemeyer correspondence)

463. The excerpt is from Cassatt's letter of June 16, [1901] to Louisine ("Louie") Havemeyer (MMA/Havemeyer correspondence), which reads: "Your telegram, or rather cable came yesterday; and I must explain why I said I thought it would be better to see about the pictures before September. All the pictures Wicht spoke about were in private collections where they had been probably for generations, & the suggestion was made either by Wicht or some one for him that the owners should sell, now *he* thinks that any time will do, my opinion is in the contrary that if you shake the tree you ought to be around when the fruit falls to pick it up; in other words now that the idea of selling has been put in their heads, if some one else offers to buy they will let the things go."

464. For El Greco's *Portrait of a Cardinal* (A 304) and *Landscape of Toledo* (A 303), and Goya's *Majas on a Balcony* (A 296), see note nos. 90, 180, 196.

465. For El Greco's *The Assumption of the Virgin* (Art Institute of Chicago), see pp. 153-56 and note nos. 207, 211.

466. J. Pierpont Morgan (1837-1913), American banker and financier who in November 1904 became president of the Metropolitan Museum's Board of Trustees.

467. This excerpt is from Mary Cassatt's letter of October 17, [1906] to Louisine Havemeyer (MMA/Havemeyer correspondence).

468. This letter must also date to the end of 1906. On December 11, 1906, Cassatt wrote to Mrs. Havemeyer about "the Greco Assumption, The Art Institute has sent for it, and funds are not subscribed, Mr. Hutchinson and Mr. Ryerson will pay for it between them." (MMA/Havemeyer correspondence.) Charles Lawrence Hutchinson (1854-1926) and Martin Antoine Ryerson (1856-1932), who, at the time, were, respectively, President and Vice-President of the Art Institute of Chicago.

469. For Roger Marx, see note no. 170. A number of letters written around 1903-06 record the opinions that Cassatt had solicited from Roger Marx on pictures the Havemeyers were considering as acquisitions. The letter from which she quotes is unknown. However, another dated December 27, [1906], reveals that Marx saw the *Majas on the Balcony* (A 296), after it was relined and felt "it was not well done."

470. The letter must date prior to May 1906, when the Havemeyers' acquired "La Librera," namely, Goya's *Young Lady Wearing a Mantilla and a Basquiña* (A 293) (see note no. 137). It is compared to Manet's *Lola de Valence* (Musée d'Orsay, Paris), a picture reminiscent of Goya's full-length portraits, especially, his *Duchess of Alba* (Hispanic Society of America, New York).

471. For the four Veroneses (A 503, 504, 278, 417) see note no. 151.

472. For the two "Holbeins" (A 286, A 287) see note no. 171. For the portrait of *Jean de Carondelet* (A 502) formerly Holbein, now considered Vermeyen, see note no. 38.

473. This letter presumably dates to after August 1896, when the Havemeyers had been in touch with Sara Hallowell about the portrait of *Jean de Carondelet* (A 502) owned by the Duc and Duchesse de la Trémoïlle, at 4 avenue Gabriel, Paris. Correspondence concerning the "two Holbeins" (A 286, A 287) dates to the summer

through fall 1901. From the extant correspondence, it is clear that Cassatt was consulted on and endorsed the latter acquisitions; she felt "it would be a pity to miss two Holbein portraits at 18,000 lira." (Mary Cassatt to Louisine Havemeyer, August 9, [1901], MMA/Havemeyer correspondence)

474. The reference is to Hans Holbein the Younger's portrait of King Henri VIII's astronomer, *Nicolas Kratzer* (Musée du Louvre, Paris, no. 1343).

475. For the so-called Veronese portrait of the painter's wife, now considered Montemezzano, *Portrait of a Woman* (A 417), see note no. 151, and pp. 110-13.

476. This letter is previously cited, see pp. 286-87.

477. These excerpts from Cassatt's letters have been dated to July and to September 1905, respectively. The latter refers to Cassatt's purchase for the Havemeyers of Courbet's *Portrait of a Man* (MMA 29.100.201 [A 143]), a work that Ambroise Vollard acquired at auction in late March 1905. On the subject of the Manets offered and declined from the Faure collection, and relevant correspondence, see Weitzenhoffer 1986, pp. 159-61.

478. Between March and November 1905, the Havemeyers failed to come to terms with Durand-Ruel for three Manet pictures from the Faure collection: *Le Bon Bock, The Virgin with the Rabbit*, and *Springtime* (Rouart and Wildenstein 1975, I, nos. 186, 5, 372 respectively). For Faure, see note no. 10.

479. With the outbreak of fighting in northern France during World War I, Cassatt fled Mesnil-Théribus in November 1914; she spent most of the war years in Grasse.

480. Owing to her failing eyesight, in 1915 Cassatt underwent the first of several operations for cataracts on both eyes.

481. This letter, though unknown, echoes the ideas in a number of letters written from Cassatt to Mrs. Havemeyer during the war;

it can, for example, be compared to one of June 26, [1916], which reads, "After the war is over, Heaven knows when that will be, there will be a great revival; and surely a new view of things. It is then that the women ought to be prepared for their new duties, taking part in governing the world." (MMA/Havemeyer correspondence)

482. This letter is not preserved among those on deposit at the Metropolitan Museum (Havemeyer correspondence). Mary Cassatt was responsible for Mrs. Havemeyer's later acquisitions of several Gothic sculptures, some of which are now considered fakes (see Stein chronology in MMA 1993, entries 1909-1918, pp. 252, 255, 258, 266, 274). Cassatt also arranged for the sale to Mrs. Havemeyer of two pictures by Rubens, both now considered Workshop of Rubens: *Saint Cecila* (MMA 29.100.14 [A 471]), purchased from Trotti et Cie, Paris on April 26, 1909, and *Ladislas Sigismund IV (1595-1648), King of Poland* (MMA 29.100.13 [A 472]), bought through Trotti in May 1914. The reference is to the latter acquisition.

483. In early 1912 Renoir moved into an apartment in Nice because his rheumatism prevented him from using his studio at Les Collettes. From 1913, until the artist's death in 1919, Cassatt—in nearby Grasse —saw "Poor Renoir" on several occasions. The comment on Degas may date to around the time of his death, on September 27, 1917.

484. While in Paris, in August 1921, Louisine Havemeyer purchased a set of Degas bronzes (series A) that had been cast posthumously at the foundry of Adrien A. Hébrard (MMA 29.100.371-438). On this subject see Clare Vincent, "The Havemeyers and the Degas Bronzes," MMA 1993, pp. 77-80.

485. Mrs. Havemeyer anonymously lent her set of bronzes, as well as seventeen Degas drawings and pastels, two fan mounts, and four prints to the exhibition, *Prints, Drawings and Bronzes by Degas*, held at the Grolier Club, New York, from January-March 1922.

486. Cassatt's admiration for Degas's sculptures, though not relative to his merits as a painter or etcher, is well-documented in her extant correspondence with Louisine Havemeyer. One comparison to "Egyptian sculpture" is made in a letter to Mrs. Havemeyer of June 25, 1918; and on January 16, 1920, she remarked that Degas was "known only to a *very* few people as a sculptor," but the casting of the bronzes would certainly establish "his reputation as a sculptor." (MMA/Havemeyer correspondence)

PUBLICATIONS CITED IN THE NOTES

Boggs et al. 1988
Boggs, Jean Sutherland, et al. *Degas.* Exh. cat., MMA,. New York. 1988.

Breeskin 1948
Breeskin, Adelyn Dohme. *The Graphic Work of Mary Cassatt, A Catalogue Raisonné.* New York, 1948.

Breeskin 1970
Breeskin, Adelyn Dohme. *Mary Cassatt: A Catalogue Raisonné of the Oils, Pastels, Watercolors, and Drawings.* Washington, D.C., 1970.

Butlin and Joll 1984
Butlin, Martin, and Evelyn Joll. *The Paintings of J.M.W. Turner.* New Haven and London, 1984.

Fernier 1977–78
Fernier, Robert. *La Vie et l'oeuvre de Gustave Courbet: Catalogue Raisonné.* 2 vols. Lausanne and Paris, 1977–78.

Gassier and Wilson 1971
Gassier, Pierre, and Juliet Wilson. *The Life and Complete Work of Francisco Goya, with a Catalogue Raisonné of the Paintings, Drawings, and Engravings.* Rev. ed. New York, 1971.

Havemeyer 1931
H.O. Havemeyer Collection: Catalogue of Paintings, Prints, Sculpture and Objects of Art. Portland, Me., 1931.

Havemeyer 1958
The H.O. Havemeyer Collection: The Metropolitan Museum of Art. 2nd ed. New York, 1958.

Havemeyer Correspondence
Letters to the Havemeyers on deposit in the Department of European Paintings, Archives, The Metropolitan Museum of Art, New York.

Havemeyer "Notes" [1974]
Havemeyer, Louisine. "Notes to Her Children." Typescript [1974]. Archives, The Metropolitan Museum of Art, New York.

Lemoisne 1946
Lemoisne, P.A. *Degas et son oeuvre.* 4 vols. Paris, 1946.

López-Rey 1963
López-Rey, José. *Velázquez: A Catalogue Raisonné of His Oeuvre.* London, 1963.

Mathews 1984
Mathews, Nancy Mowll, ed. *Cassatt and Her Circle: Selected Letters.* New York, 1984.

MMA 1983
The Metropolitan Museum of Art. *Manet: 1932–1883.* Exh. cat. New York, 1983.

MMA 1993
The Metropolitan Museum of Art. *Splendid Legacy: The Havemeyer Collection.* Exh. cat. New York, 1993.

Rouart and Wildenstein 1975
Rouart, Denis, and Daniel Wildenstein. *Edouard Manet: Catalogue raisonné.* 2 vols. Lausanne and Paris, 1975.

Spassky et al. 1985
Spassky, Natalie, et al. *American Paintings in The Metropolitan Museum of Art.* Vol. 2. New York, 1985.

Young et al. 1980
Young, Andrew McLaren, et al. *The Paintings of James McNeill Whistler.* New Haven, 1980.

- *shibley* - P V Nehra

- N.Y.C -
   P212 - 749 - 1675 (PL)
      7 18 - 935 - 9060 (PL).

   fax: 212 - 319 - 4526.
      AH
         c/o Paltawshal.

- Aseel Rais
      010 - 331 - 45 - 41 - 47 - 19.

   [305] - Peter: